We were on the backside of the Temple of Heaven in Beijing in July 2006 when I was approached by a boy of perhaps ten or eleven years old. In pretty good English he asked "Where are you from?" I promptly replied: "New York City." I reciprocated appropriately by asking "And where are you from?" He responded without hesitation: "China."

JAZZ in CHINA

From Dance Hall Music to Individual Freedom of Expression

Eugene Marlow

UNIVERSITY PRESS OF MISSISSIPPI • JACKSON

www.upress.state.ms.us

The University Press of Mississippi is a member of the Association
of American University Presses.

First printing 2018

∞

Chapter 2 includes material copyright © 2004 by Frank Sanello and
W. Travis Hanes III PhD. Reprinted from the book *The Opium Wars:
The Addiction of One Empire and the Corruption of Another* with
permission of its publisher, Sourcebooks.

Material from *Buck Clayton's Jazz World* © Buck Clayton, 1995,
Bloomsbury Continuum, an imprint of Bloomsbury Publishing Plc.
Reprinted with permission.

Library of Congress Cataloging-in-Publication Data

Names: Marlow, Eugene, author.
Title: Jazz in China : from dance hall music to individual freedom of
 expression / Eugene Marlow.
Description: Jackson : University Press of Mississippi, [2018] | Includes
 bibliographical references and index. |
Identifiers: LCCN 2017060741 (print) | LCCN 2018005449 (ebook) | ISBN
 9781496818003 (epub single) | ISBN 9781496818010 (epub institutional) |
 ISBN 9781496818027 (pdf single) | ISBN 9781496818034 (pdf institutional)
 | ISBN 9781496817990 (hardcover : alk. paper) | ISBN 9781496818553 (pbk. :
 alk. paper)
Subjects: LCSH: Jazz—China—History and criticism. | Jazz musicians—China.
 | Music—China—Western influences. | China—social life and customs.
Classification: LCC ML3509.C59 (ebook) | LCC ML3509.C59 M37 2018 (print) |
 DDC 781.650951—dc23
LC record available at https://lccn.loc.gov/2017060741

British Library Cataloging-in-Publication Data available

CONTENTS

Preface   VII
Acknowledgments   XX

PART I: BEFORE MAO

CHAPTER 1
China: East Is East . . .   3
CHAPTER 2
The Opium Wars   14
CHAPTER 3
The Influence of Early Twentieth-Century Technology   21
CHAPTER 4
Shanghai in the 1920s–1930s: The Joint Was Jumpin'   32
CHAPTER 5
International Jazz Musicians Flock to Shanghai: 1920s–1930s   39
CHAPTER 6
The Formation of All-Chinese Jazz Bands   57
CHAPTER 7
The Japanese Invasion   67

PART II: DURING AND AFTER MAO

CHAPTER 8
Jazz and Individual Freedom of Expression   81
CHAPTER 9
The Influence of Mid-Twentieth-Century Technologies on the
Expansion of Jazz in China   91
CHAPTER 10
First a Trickle, Then a Flood: Jazz Musicians Perform in China
from All Over   102

CHAPTER 11

Martin Fleischer, Godfather of Jazz, and Liu Yuan, So-Called Father
of Jazz in Early Post-Mao Beijing   118

CHAPTER 12:

Liu Sola: China's Musically Eclectic Composer   126

CHAPTER 13

The Beijing Jazz Scene   136

CHAPTER 14

Beijing's Leading Indigenous and Expat Jazz Musicians   155

CHAPTER 15

Shanghai's Jazz Venues   179

CHAPTER 16

Shanghai's Leading Indigenous & Expat Jazz Musicians   187

CHAPTER 17

Jazz Education in China   210

CHAPTER 18

Jazz in China in the Twenty-First Century   224

APPENDIX I

Reported American Jazz Musicians Who Performed in China
1981–2016   240

APPENDIX II

Reported International Jazz Musicians Who Performed in China
1992–2016   247

Notes   251
Bibliography   271
Index   281

PREFACE

Jazz in China is a happy accident from which I have grown personally and professionally. From research precipitated by a chance invitation to teach at the University of Shanghai School of Film and Television in 2000, I have learned that the story of jazz in China is not just about jazz in China. The subject has much larger meaning. It is about the impact and unintended consequences of war and political upheaval on a culture. It is about the evolutionary fusion of local culture with outside influences, whether desired or not. It is about the impact of information, communications, and transportation technologies in the twentieth century on the spread of content and with it implicit new ideas and values from one part of the world to another and vice versa.

The story of jazz in China is also about the break between the Victorian/Confucian culture of China in the nineteenth century versus the march of individualism, democracy, and globalism in the second half of the twentieth century. It is about the initial embracing of Western economic and cultural values in such non-Western cultures as China, and the subsequent rejection of these values as some in the culture benefited and many others did not. It is about the clash between the conservatism of the old generation versus the inherent drive of the younger generation for new forms of political and social expression. It is about the inexorable evolution, subtle and otherwise, of culture on the planet despite efforts by some to maintain the status quo.

In most of the first half of the twentieth century, jazz *was* the music of Shanghai (and by implication, China) because of the strong presence of Western culture there. In the last quarter of the twentieth century and going into the twenty-first century, the re-emergence of jazz in Shanghai and Beijing and other China cities is emblematic of China's shift to Western-style entrepreneurialism and by implication "individual freedom of expression." In effect, the evolution of jazz in China—from the 1920s in Shanghai to now—parallels China's social, economic, and political evolution in the twentieth century and into the twenty-first century. In turn, China's evolution over this period of time serves as an example of larger, more macrocosmic events. The story of jazz in China is exemplary of inexorable social and economic change on a global scale.

I have made two trips to China: one in May–June 2000, the other in July–August of 2006. The first trip was an eye-opening, emotionally and intellectually profound experience squeezed into two weeks. The second trip took several years to prepare for—research-wise as well as logistically. This latter trip lasted thirty days. The second trip was both too long and too short. While the first visit was a cultural splash of cold water in the face, the latter trip was laced with magical occurrences. It was as if there was an angel on my shoulder providing whatever was needed to move the research forward. In both instances, the experience went beyond a search for Western jazz in an Eastern culture—the trips also became springboards for personal reflection and professional growth.

FIRST CONTACT: SHANGHAI UNIVERSITY

My first visit to China was in late May and early June of 2000. I had been invited there by Professor Peter Hitchcock, a colleague in the Department of English at Baruch College (City University of New York), to lecture at the University of Shanghai School of Film and Television on the status of "media" in the United States—i.e., newspapers, magazines, radio, broadcast and cable television, and the Internet. Hitchcock, who spoke Mandarin well, himself had visited coastal and inland China numerous times and had been asked to arrange an exchange program between the City University of New York and the University of Shanghai School of Film and Television. He also invited another English Department colleague, Professor Thalia Schenkel (since retired) whose expertise was in film criticism. The ostensible reason for my participation was my multi-decade, eclectic, hands-on background in print and electronic media, my recently acquired full professor status (2000), together with a PhD in media studies from New York University (1988). My classical and jazz music background would come into play after I arrived in Shanghai.

When Peter first approached me I was hesitant. I knew virtually nothing about China, let alone the language. I also do not travel well as a rule, and an eighteen-hour plane journey was not exactly my idea of a quick, relaxing trip. Previously, I had traveled to and from Europe, the Middle East, Brazil, and Guam in the South Pacific—all long trips. But China was different. I had no clue what to expect in terms of accommodations and protocol in a country with a long history of hostility toward the West and suppression of its own population. In effect, the prospect of a journey to a foreign land with perceptually vastly different customs and attitudes raised my anxiety level more than a little. My next immediate feeling was I would be a fool not to accept this invitation to a country halfway around the world that I would never voluntarily decide to visit. Besides, the trip would be financially supported by the City University of New York and I was told the University of Shanghai would proffer some "walk-around money," as Hitchcock put it. Despite some moments of hesitation and projected trepidation, I signed on for the two-week visit.

FIRST LECTURE

That first afternoon (two days after leaving New York) I was sitting in front of a group of perhaps thirty to thirty-five undergraduate students. I was scheduled to give three lectures: one to these undergraduate students, a second to graduate students on Thursday, and a third to about forty members of the radio and television news industry in China on Friday.

It was my very good fortune that the translator assigned to me for most of the two weeks was one Chen Xihe. He had earned bachelor and master degrees from the graduate college of the China Film Art Research Center. As a research fellow of the China Film Art Research Center, he was, at the time, completing a PhD at Ohio State University. He was an editor of *Film in Contemporary China* (Praeger, 1993). Not only did he speak excellent English, he also had a background in what I was expected to lecture on. It made the initial lecture content much easier to communicate. I was also reminded from my previous film and television production experience (when I occasionally had to produce foreign-language tracks for extant short programs) that Chinese takes twice as long to translate from English. Regardless, the eighteen-hour journey, lack of sleep, and lack of familiar food in the early going was taking its toll. I arrived at the classroom with prepared talk and videotapes in hand, but my body was telling me otherwise. Fortunately, with Chen Xihe's warm demeanor and excellent translation skills and my weeks of preparation to fall back on, I was able to launch into a presentation that lasted well over two hours.

The first thing I noticed while I was talking was the heightened formality. My translator and I sat at a longish, elevated desk. The students sat in what seemed like communist-style benches—ten to twelve in a row. If you were in the middle of the row and had to leave for any reason, you were out of luck. I recall there being three sections to the room, each with these rows of benches. The sense of "group" as opposed to "individual" was palpable. The sense of "teacher authority" as opposed to "learning experience" was also prevalent.

Frankly, while some of the content I had to present was of interest to the students, I came away with the impression these students were more interested in me as a Westerner than my academic presentation. If I had given a quiz at the conclusion of my remarks, I'm certain most if not all the students would have failed. The content I was showing was just as foreign to these students as the entire cultural environment was to me. I also began to observe a significant cultural difference. When it came time for questions, there was much hesitation among the students. I got the strong feeling that the expectation was for me to make a "doctrinaire" presentation, as if what I had to say was "law" or "the final word." After much prompting, a few students did ask questions. I do not remember the questions or what I answered, but I got the strong sense that these students, at least, were more interested in making contact rather than gaining any greater depth of knowledge from my expertise. I finally began to answer the questions with a diplomatic tone. My answers, as I recall, were more about "outreach" and "cultural commonalities" than specific facts that would have had no meaning to these students anyway. At the end of the session there was the traditional group photo. Many students gave me their email addresses with promises to stay in touch.

SECOND AND THIRD LECTURES

The next day (in the afternoon fortunately) I had a roundtable discussion with twelve to fourteen graduate students. This session also lasted about two hours. There were many more questions. The students seemed a lot more serious than the undergraduate students. They were less interested in personal contact and more interested in the content of my expertise, even though I don't recall showing any videotapes. It was all talk and repartee. Our conversations were punctuated by occasional power outages (the lights would go out), apparently a routine occurrence in this part of Shanghai at the time.

The most stimulating and exhilarating lecture of the three was the last one: a talk in front of thirty to forty radio and television news professionals from various parts of China who had gathered in Shanghai for a conference. For this talk I had to be driven into downtown Shanghai to a hotel along the

Huangpu River on the Bund in downtown Shanghai. It was now Thursday evening and I was somewhat recovered from the trans-Pacific journey but still feeling the stress of the shift in time zones, culture, food, etc.

In China, radio and television programming is controlled by the government, which is to say the Chinese Communist Party. Journalism as we know it in the West is quite a different animal in China (when I returned in 2006 much had changed, but more on that later).

The room was outfitted with a VHS deck and two television monitors. This enabled me to present some of the video material I had brought with me. I condensed my presentation, partly to abbreviate the lecture, partly to engage in interaction with these professionals sooner than later. I expected some benign questions and we would be out of there. Instead, I was asked some highly penetrating questions regarding the relationship between the government, sponsoring corporations, and the media. I never had the feeling I was being attacked or criticized. But the questions were of such a nature that I had to take on the role of "representative." All of a sudden I found myself making statements and taking positions as if I were representing the United States. I never felt defensive, but some of the questions pushed me to deal with the contradictions inherent in a democracy, to talk about the veracity of the government, and the values inherent in a media and journalistic system in continual consolidation. I was no longer acting in the role of Baruch College professor. I was talking to these folks as a spokesperson for a media-oriented culture with which I had some argument. The session lasted two hours. The conversation was so stimulating I could have gone on for hours more, but my translator, Chen, saw the exhaustion on my face and took the initiative to end the session.

MEDIA CONFERENCE

Toward the end of the two-week trip I had the honor of participating in a conference hosted by the University of Shanghai with more than forty professors, students, and film and television professionals from the United States and China in attendance as part of a two-day salon on "Film and TV in the Millennium." The conference was held in a large conference room in the on-campus hotel where we were housed. The shape of the conference setting itself was quite interesting: It was rectangular. Not just the room, but the setting of the chairs. While all the chairs were very comfortable, they were arranged around the room; there were no rows of chairs in the middle of the room. In retrospect, if one looked at the room from the vantage point of the ceiling, it was remindful of the outside edges of a Chinese scroll, or the doorframe of an entrance to many of China's ancient monuments. The organizational shape of the room was a reflection of China's hierarchical view of itself and the world.

During the two days of presentations and side meetings, two themes emerged: first, the film industry in China was declining at the time in terms of audience (a decade later it was a very different story; see chapter 3). The question arose: "What can be done about this?" Second, there was great concern about the influx of new technology, particularly the Internet. The question was: "What do we do about the challenge of the Internet?" There was concern about the influence of the Internet and American film and television programs on the Chinese aesthetic and culture. As I have come to learn, these technology issues have a direct bearing on the advent of jazz in China, not only now, but also in the early 1920s.

At one point in the proceedings, a member of the Party was given the floor to talk to the attendees. I was sitting in the middle of the room with my translator behind me. The party member began to talk about these issues, moving quickly to a tone and voice level that can only be described as a rant. I conjectured, "Was this what it was like during the Cultural Revolution?" After about ten minutes I finally told my translator to stop. This man's highly agitated content was less important than the almost psychotic tone of his presentation. It belied a fear of newfangled technologies and the inherent change they would bring. If this was the daily reality of communism under Mao, especially during the Cultural Revolution (which in terms of violence was much, much worse), then China must have been a horrific place to live. He practically yelled at the attendees with fists pounding the side table next to him for about an hour.

Here I would like to add an observation I understood only academically before visiting China but that became real once I was there. From my brief initial stay in Shanghai it was clear that one of the significant differences between China (as an Asian country) and the United States (as a Western country) is the meaning of "community" versus the "individual." In Western culture the individual is the cultural, political, and economic centerpiece, brought about from a centuries-old tradition of writing. In China, it was my impression that what counts is the community—the country, the immediate community, the family. The individual is secondary. To a large degree, the country *is* one's family. As John King Fairbank and Merle Goldman articulate in their book *China: A New History*, "Until very recently the

Chinese family has been a microcosm, the state in miniature. The family, not the individual, was the social unit and the responsible element in the political life of its locality. The filial piety and obedience inculcated in family life were the training ground for loyalty to the ruler and obedience to the constituted authority in the state."[1]

In Western culture it is the reverse. One can see this in the postal system. In Western countries you address a letter or package in the following order: name (or names) of the person, their address, city, zip code, country. In China, it is the complete reverse. The first thing you write is "China." The person to whom the letter or package is sent appears on the last line if at all.

I observed the contrast and transition from "community" to "individualism" at the old and new campuses of the University of Shanghai. To recap, in the building that served the Film and Television School at the University's old campus I lectured to undergraduate students in a room where the chairs were made for ten to twelve people at a time. If someone in the middle of the row had to leave for whatever reason, they would have to disturb several people in order to do so. Besides, there was no travel room anyway. At the new campus, however, I could see a transition. In the new classrooms chairs were built for two people at a time—a lot less than ten to twelve. However, in the computer rooms of one building (where there were at least a thousand units, row after row) each computer hosted a chair for a single person! My guess is that as China accelerates its adoption of computer technology and the Internet, so, too, will it elevate the importance of the individual.

The issue of community vs. individualism in China, I have learned since beginning research on the subject of jazz in China, is not new. Stella Dong, author of the detailed historical account of the city of Shanghai, refers to Lu Hsun, an acknowledged giant of Chinese letters in the 1920s. She writes: "Lu Hsun became the leader of a loose association of China's most prominent writers. . . . Known as the Creationists, the members of this clique modeled themselves after the Western romantics and wrote about such themes as romantic love, breaking away from the restrictions of family, and the need for personal freedom."[2] Another leading creationist was Hsu Chi-mo, a poet, according to Dong, whose "lyrical, if overly emotional, verse about love and despair won him a large following among young people." Against his family's wishes, Hsu gave up banking and economics for poetry. Hsun once wrote, "To my mind, democracy is only individualism universalized. The spirit of real democracy lies in an individual's self-awareness and self-improvement."[3]

An academic, Chen Tu-hsui, former dean of the literature department at Peking (now Beijing) University, was among those leading massive protests in Shanghai in 1919 following the news that the Versailles Treaty at the conclusion of World War I called for the handing over of Germany's former leased territories in China to Japan. Chen spent three months in jail for helping students distribute anti-Japanese literature. Dong recounts: "Chen called for the abandonment of the 'old, rotten, and useless' values of China's past, which were to be replaced by 'fresh' and 'vital' ideas from the west: freedom of speech, of choice, and of political opinion; the right to be an individual independent of one's family; equal rights for women; and an end to Confucianism."[4] I have the feeling that over time, given China's current and potentially enormous economic and, therefore, political impact on the world in the next twenty-five to fifty years, there will be a "trade of values" of sorts: in China people will increasingly learn more about the benefits of individualism from Westerners, and Westerners will learn more about the benefits of community from China.

THE MEANING OF JAZZ IN CHINA

Of more immediate moment, however, the relevance of the community vs. the individualism issue to jazz in China is several. At the center of the parallel, of course, is the meaning of jazz as an expression of individuality within the context and collectivity of a group. There is the aspect of improvisation in jazz as an expression of individuality versus the "apparent" lack of improvisation in classical Chinese music as well as Western classical music. Granted, there is much aleatoric composition in Western music, especially in twentieth-century classical music, but classical music largely requires interpretation, not individual invention.

The word for improvisation in Mandarin is *jixing*. Improvisation in Chinese music was especially applied in folk music that harkens back a couple of thousand years. However, the Chinese language (consisting of sixty thousand characters—there is no alphabet) is about stability and adherence to the past. The English language (based on the twenty-six-letter alphabet), which comprises a million-plus words, is highly verb-oriented. Verbs imply action, action that may reflect activities that differ from the past. In contrast, Chinese culture has placed a high value on that which does not change. Many dialects feature a predominance of nouns rather than verbs.

Nouns represent people, places, and things that will last, while verbs (actions) will be here today and gone tomorrow. Improvisation, the creation of something new on the spot, therefore, is not something inherent in traditional Chinese music.

IS THERE JAZZ IN SHANGHAI?

In between my initial three lectures and the two-day salon at the University of Shanghai at the end of the trip, I asked what was for me a natural question: "Is there jazz in Shanghai?" As a jazz and classical composer and occasional player, I was curious about the jazz scene in Shanghai. The answer from my English-speaking hosts was "Of course." A couple of nights later I was taken to the Peace Hotel in downtown Shanghai, near the Bund virtually on the bank of the Huangpu River.

We arrived early to listen to the Peace Hotel Jazz Band at about 8 p.m. I could hardly wait. I ordered some sandwiches. The room was fairly empty. At last, six gentlemen in their seventies walked onto the stage. I thought to myself, "Oh, good, some Chinese-style Dixieland." No sooner had they started to play than the room started to fill up with mostly non-Chinese patrons: Australians, Germans, some British, I think.

The music? The music was something like jazz, but it was more like the musicians' "impression" of 1940s jazz they had heard on the radio or from phonograph records. Many of the chords and chord progressions were wrong. Improvisation was tepid at best. I was perplexed. The rest of the crowd, however, was oblivious. They had no clue. They didn't care. The dance floor was packed. Everyone was having a wonderful time. They thought the band was terrific!

Before the band's first break, I coaxed my English-speaking graduate student host to arrange for me to speak to the bandleader. A few minutes into their first break I was sitting in the lobby of the Peace Hotel just outside the club with Zhou Wanrong, former principal trumpeter with the Shanghai Symphony Orchestra, now leader of the Peace Hotel Jazz Band. He greeted me with a big smile and a handshake. I started to ask him questions through my interpreter about his background, what music he had listened to, his training. The interview lasted, perhaps, four minutes. The most I could get out of him was that his group had played every night at the Peace Hotel since 1980 or so without a break. No vacations. Illness was not an option.

Apparently, my basic questions were too invasive or perhaps were remindful of a time gone by when questions of a quasi-personal nature elicited uncomfortable feelings.

I left the Peace Hotel inwardly disappointed from this encounter. I could not explain to my host how less than professional the playing was. It occurred to me on the way back to the university campus in the cab that there had to be more to jazz in Shanghai than what I had just heard. This brief encounter and the questions it raised in me, of course, was the genesis of my research into jazz in China, the result of which is this volume.

While I had wanted to find more examples of jazz in Shanghai, the days between the first three lectures and the two-day conference were filled with several "organized" day trips: one to a contemporary painter who had a studio in the Pudong; another to Suzhou, the so-called "silk capital of China," about 80 km west from Shanghai. We also visited the Shanghai Museum and Shanghai's newly constructed television news and entertainment studios. This visit was in itself a telling experience. We were shown with great pride the offices where reporters sat, the control room, the satellite dishes on the roof, and a sound stage that could accommodate a thousand-person audience and several football fields. It was enormous. But during our visit, at least, there were no reporters to be found, no technicians, no one to speak to other than the heads of the television station, accompanied, of course, by a representative of the Chinese Communist Party (CCP), who sat quietly but authoritatively in a chair to one side in the executive office where we met.

The two-week visit came to an end and I had to return to New York City in order to begin teaching a summer session course at Baruch College. The return to the Shanghai International Airport was in itself an adventure. "Stone," my English-speaking graduate student host, had arranged for a taxi to get me there. He would accompany me to the airport. We had not been on the road for more than ten minutes when the taxi broke down. We waited for some time for another taxi to arrive to get me to the airport on time. An hour later, I arrived at the airport. Stone helped me get into the building. At the customs gate I decided to give him a Western-style hug. I'm certain he was taken aback. But he (as well as Chen, my translator) had provided me with much assistance. I was grateful.

It was daytime so there were more people in the airport than when I arrived two weeks earlier, but there were still only three or four planes parked at gates. On my second trip, six years later, it would be quite different! The plane on the return flight was not full, fortunately. As I sat in my seat I reflected on the two-week experience I had just gone through. I was both glad to be returning home and sad the trip had been so short. I had learned more about myself as well as a culture I had only known superficially through books, television, and films. It brought a few tears to my eyes. As I looked out the plane's window while we were taking off, I said to myself: "I'll be back."

A SECOND PLANNED TRIP INTERRUPTED

Shortly after I returned to the United States in the summer of 2000 I started to plan a revisit to Shanghai. I learned of the Beijing International Jazz Festival that was to take place in October 2001. It was too late for me to plan a return trip in 2000, but 2001 was doable. By the summer of 2001 I had a hotel reservation, plane tickets, and some contacts. Then 9/11 happened. The Chinese government cancelled the festival. I was encouraged to come over anyway; I was told I would be introduced to everyone. I reluctantly demurred in favor of staying close to family. In retrospect it was a good decision.

PLANNING A SECOND TRIP—AGAIN

While I was initially disappointed in my decision to cancel the October 2001 flight to Beijing, in retrospect I realized what a favor I had done for myself. First, I needed more time to research the subject. I needed to know more about the history of jazz in China, especially before Mao. Second, I needed to more fully identify the indigenous jazz musicians in Beijing and Shanghai. Third, I needed to plan the trip very well to maximize my time there. If I had learned anything at all from the 2000 visit, it was that going to China for a few days, even a couple of weeks, was not doing it right. I estimated a thirty-day trip: two musician interviews a day (if I was lucky) and I would come back with forty to fifty interviews. I wound up with thirty-two, but they were all golden. In fact, I came back with much more than I expected, the interviews notwithstanding. Last, but not least, I needed to raise money to finance the thirty-day marathon.

Little did I realize when I started to Google "jazz in China" what would confront me. The simple question "Is there jazz in China?" turned into a multi-century history lesson that encompasses numerous continents, let alone countries, hundreds of articles, dozens of books (including several autobiographies), DVDs and CDs, and interviews with many musicians, club owners, academics, music promoters, even diplomats, both Western and Eastern.

Without reviewing the content of what appears elsewhere in this volume, the core purpose of the second trip to China—this time to Beijing *and* Shanghai—was to interview indigenous Chinese jazz musicians. I uncovered all sorts of material dealing with visits of non-Chinese jazz musicians who had performed in China, including Willie Ruff (late of the Yale School of Music) and about eighty other musicians and groups. But when I started my research there was little to be found dealing with indigenous Chinese jazz musicians. It was clear early on there was sufficient material, but equally clear that any book on the subject had to include commentary from Chinese jazz musicians. Lacking these voices and perspectives would undermine the book's credibility.

A first task, of course, was to identify working jazz musicians in Beijing and Shanghai. How do you identify these musicians, let alone make initial contact with them, from eight thousand miles away? My instinct was to Google the topic of "jazz in China" as thoroughly as I could. It took a couple of months of tedious research, but it was worth the trip. From the several hundred articles I had gathered I created two lists: one of musicians who had traveled to China from every corner of the globe (starting in 1981, as it turned out); a second of indigenous Chinese jazz musicians. This latter list was frustrating. While several musicians' names and the venues where they performed were mentioned often enough, there was nothing to indicate if they were still performing or if the places where they performed were still open.

By pure luck sometime in 2004 I happened to glance through an issue of *Jazz Educators Journal*, the publication of the now defunct International Association for Jazz Education (IAJE). I serendipitously looked at the list of new members. Lo and behold, there was the name of one Peter Zanello, a new member from China. I couldn't believe it. Next question: was it Taiwan or mainland China? There is a saying: "When the student is ready, the teacher appears." I called the IAJE office to double-check his contact information. It was correct. I sent Zanello an email, explaining the project I was working on. Could he help me? Could he help me indeed! This contact initiated many, many emails back and forth, together with several phone calls. It took about two years of periodic contact for Peter to begin to trust the commitment I had made to this project. Zanello has spent many years in China (he has a Chinese wife) developing an export-import business throughout Asia. Though not a musician himself, his love for the music enabled him to befriend virtually all of the jazz musicians in Beijing. After repeated requests, Peter was generous enough to send me a list of names, the instruments they played, and phone numbers I could call once I got to Beijing. This list came none too soon: about three months before a flight to Beijing.

But my plans also called for a trip to Shanghai. Since I had already been to Shanghai (which has a more compact geography, somewhat like Manhattan), I arbitrarily chose to spend more time in Beijing. The thirty-day trip evolved into eighteen in Beijing, twelve in Shanghai. Obviously, I also needed a list of contact names in Shanghai. Even though I had already visited there, my research up to this point showed several clubs, including the already visited Peace Hotel. By luck I hooked up with musician and composer Phil Morrison. According to several articles, he and his musical partner had spent time performing in Shanghai. He knew where everyone was. After several phone calls back and forth, he generously sent me a list of musicians, their instruments, where they usually played, and numerous email addresses and phone numbers. As it turned out, both lists became starting points for the research once back in China.

I am deeply grateful to both entrepreneur Peter Zanello and musician Phil Morrison. Without their willingness to open up their Chinese rolodex, the return trip to Shanghai and first visit to Beijing in 2006 would have been for naught and in large part the second half of this volume would not have been written.

EM
2017

ACKNOWLEDGMENTS

With my trip to Shanghai in 2000 as the "accidental" genesis of this book, it took several years to plan a return trip to not only Shanghai, but also Beijing. A major piece of the organizing puzzle was the money. I applied to the Professional Staff Congress (PSC) of the City University of New York (CUNY) for a grant to help fund the trip through CUNY's Research Foundation. It was a long shot. The Asian Cultural Council (an arm of the Rockefeller Foundation) had already turned me down. To my surprise, I received notice I had been given a PSC grant to help fund the trip. Then I was informed that Myrna Chase, then dean of the Weissman School of Arts and Sciences at Baruch College (where I have been teaching for the last thirty years as of this writing) had provided an additional grant for the trip. Without these initial funds the 2006, thirty-day research trip to China would have been for naught.

Upon my return in late August 2006, I again applied for PSC funding for transcription and editorial purposes. In spring 2007 I was informed the PSC had given me yet another grant for these aspects of the project. And, again, Dean Chase proffered funding.

All told I was provided with financial support for the research and writing that appear in the following pages. In 2012 Jeffrey Peck, former Dean of the Weissman School of Arts and Sciences (Baruch College), provided funds in support of graphics research for each book chapter. The PSC additionally provided funds to digitally transfer the video footage we had shot while in Beijing/Shanghai in anticipation of developing a DVD documentary based on the book.

A SMALL ARMY OF INFLUENCERS AND ASSISTANTS

This volume has evolved over a period of sixteen years and, like all work worth doing, it could not have eventuated without the input of others, as follows:

- Professor Peter Hitchcock, Department of English/Graduate Center, City University of New York. His invitation for me to speak on American media at the University of Shanghai in May–June 2000 was the beginning of a compelling adventure.

- Andrew F. Jones, Professor and Louis B. Agassiz Chair in Chinese, University of California, Berkeley, California. His book *Yellow Music* and article "Black Internationale: Notes on the Chinese Jazz Age" in *Jazz Planet* (E. Taylor Atkins, editor) are seminal to the current volume.

- Peter Zanello, entrepreneur, Beijing, China. Peter's commentaries on jazz in China and many contacts in the Beijing jazz community were pivotal in garnering interviews with extant jazz musicians there. Likewise, musician Phil Morrison, who generously offered detailed insights into the Shanghai jazz community.

- David Moser, Academic Director, CET Chinese Studies & Internship in Beijing, Capital Normal University, also a jazz pianist, for his various commentaries on the Beijing jazz scene.

- Baruch College colleague Professor Eva Chou (Baruch College), current chair of the Department of English, for her many hours translating material provided by Da Ren Zheng, former bass player with the Jimmy King Band of the 1940s in Shanghai.

- Former student Scarlett Shao and her father, Zhi Fang Shao, who squired us around Shanghai for almost two weeks in August 2006 with unrelenting energy, and for Scarlett's role as translator on many occasions in Shanghai, where they speak a special Mandarin dialect known as "Shanghaiese."

- Graduate assistant Ed Sandler and undergraduate student Raqshinda Khan for their collective research follow-up work on the material dealing with non-Chinese jazz musicians who traveled to China after 1980.

- Former Baruch College journalism student Andrea Kayda for her deft editorial work on numerous chapters throughout the book. Also Ellie Eckert for her editing of several chapters in the latter half of this book, Elisha Fieldstadt and Aaron Ferrer for researching and organizing material dealing with non-Chinese jazz musicians who performed in China, 1981–present, and Jiayu Li for her work compiling the initial bibliography of this volume.

- The following individuals granted permission for me to quote from their various publications: David Moser, Dan Ouellete, Desmond Power, Dennis Rea, Willie Ruff, and Peter Zanello. Thank you.

- Also, the many members of the Baruch College Library Reference Desk, especially Rita Ormsby, for their collective, effective, and efficient work finding numerous documents in support of my research.

- To Richard Scheiwe, CUNY doctoral student, for working with me on correctly formatting the end notes and bibliography.
- To Craig W. Gill, Director, University Press of Mississippi, and his able assistant Emily Bandy, for their collective patience and guidance as I worked through the several drafts of this volume.
- Last, but not least, life partner (and wife) Janice Sileo for her never-ending support, encouragement, incisive critiques, and organizational and logistical wizardry.

And to the dozens of jazz musicians, club owners, promoters, journalists, and diplomats in Beijing and Shanghai who welcomed us so generously. Their frank and open conversations provided a real view of the jazz world in China and a perspective on China itself that you cannot gain just from reading books, articles, and surfing websites.

EM
2017

PART I

BEFORE MAO

CHAPTER 1

China: East Is East . . .

Jazz is a highly democratic form of music. In performance—through the characteristic of improvisation—soloists enjoy a freedom of individual expression, while participating with the support of the larger ensemble.

China has a long history over thousands of years of adherence to a central authority—whether the emperor, the dictator, or the one-party rule. This mindset pervades Chinese society from the highest levels of government to the family unit, in the urban centers and the countryside. While in the West the individual is paramount, in China the central authority is paramount.

Jazz has been a presence in China since the late 1910s, especially in Shanghai, and since Mao's demise in 1976, this musical genre has returned to China, first in Shanghai, then in Beijing. And since the early 1990s, jazz performance by indigenous musicians and jazz players from all over the world has expanded to many of China's cities. This return of a Western style of music appears to have the blessing of the Chinese government, more for economic reasons, however, than aesthetic motivation.

The question is this: given that jazz is a democratic form of music that enhances individual freedom of expression enjoyed not only by indigenous and international musicians, but also by a growing number of Chinese audiences in many urban centers, and given that China has become the world's second largest economy, has fostered an inexorable entrepreneurial drive, and has brought hundreds of millions of Chinese out of poverty into the middle class, how can China maintain a one-party rule that appears to be increasingly rigid in this kind of social environment?

CHINA'S LONG HISTORY

China is a country with a very long history—thousands of years in fact—longer than the Hebrews, Arabs, Greeks, and Romans. The authors of *China: A New History*, for example, trace China's population beginnings to at least 400,000 years ago with the discovery of so-called "Peking Man" (Homo erectus) in China. The beginnings of agriculture in China can be traced to five to eight thousand years ago. Yangshao painted pottery goes back three to five thousand years.[1]

This is a country steeped in traditions that trace back thousands of years and that persist to this day, particularly the mindset that country and leader come first, followed by community, then family. The individual is not even secondary. The individual is last in line, and if you're female, your status, generally, is even lower.

In the first quarter of the twentieth century these hierarchical traditions of country, community, family, and individual were, for a time, turned upside down. In 1911 China turned away from the rule of the emperor and became a republic. This later gave way to an intense nationalistic fervor in response to the colonial powers that owned China, ultimately settling into a communist state of mind and body under the dictatorial leadership of Mao Zedong in 1949. However, when Mao died in 1976 China began to evolve once more, and as the 1980s dawned, China began to open up to the West— not politically but economically. And for the last thirty years or so, China's Communist Party (CCP) leadership has walked a fine line between a desire for continued political control and the encouragement of individual economic entrepreneurship. Clearly, the twentieth century and the early part of the twenty-first century has seen China move through several political and economic upheavals—dramatic revolutions that have witnessed the extermination of millions of Chinese (by the Japanese in mid-1930s and during Mao's "Cultural Revolution"), on the one hand, and the rise of hundreds of millions of Chinese out of poverty into China's burgeoning new middle class in the last 20 years, on the other.

Throughout all the political and social dynamics of China's history in the twentieth century and into the twenty-first century, jazz—a musical genre born in the West, namely the United States, whose underlying characteristic is individual freedom of expression—has been a presence in China, particularly its urban centers, such as Shanghai and Beijing. The evolution of jazz in China parallels China's own political, social, and economic evolution. It is a story of cultural juxtaposition and cultural clash.

EAST IS EAST, AND WEST IS WEST[2]

Chinese culture is strongly rooted in past traditions, one of which is a deep respect for dragons. Respect for dragons in China, in Asia, for that matter, is exemplary of the cultural divide between East and West.

There are no dragons in China, of course, or anywhere else in the world. Nonetheless, the very presence of dragon imagery in sculpture, architecture, clothing, plate`ware, symbols of the monarchy, lore, myth, and celebrations are indicative of the benign and beneficent characteristics given to dragons in China and, in fact, many parts of Asia. Westerners are probably most familiar with the Chinese dragon as a recurring element of the Chinese New Year.

The importance of the dragon in Chinese culture is described in the *Shuōwén Jiězì* dictionary of 200 CE: "of the 369 species of scaly reptiles, such as fishes, snakes, and lizards, the dragon is the chief; it wields the power of transformation, and the gift of rendering itself visible or invisible at pleasure."[3] The Chinese sign for the dragon first appeared on turtle shields as a tribal totem during the Yin and Shang dynasties, and was eventually emblazed on the national flag during the Qing Dynasty [1644–1911 CE]. Chinese mythology is rich with the artwork, tales, and depictions of dragons. Dragons are thought to give life, hence their breath is called "sheng chi" or divine energy. They are essentially benevolent and associated with abundance and blessing. They are helpful, wise, and generous with their gifts when people encounter them. Known as the sons of heaven and the governors of rainfall, they symbolize royalty, nobility, and good fortune. Some possess great powers that allow them to make rain and control floods, hence the dragon is a symbol of the natural world as well.[4]

The beneficent dragon's deep roots in Chinese culture is exemplary of the cultural differences between East and West. In Western culture, for example, with its long history of writing since the invention of the Greek alphabet circa 700 BCE, contracts are based on what is written down and signed. In Eastern cultures one's word is one's bond. In Western cultures *what* you know is paramount. In Eastern cultures it is *who* you know that counts, especially if it's family or extended family. In Western cultures meals are an occasion for discussing business. In Eastern cultures a meal is for camaraderie, expressions of character, and adherence to traditional culture. In Western culture the individual is paramount. In Eastern culture the family, qua nation, is foremost. The Eastern dragon is beneficent. The Western dragon of heraldry and mediaeval mythology is "ferocious."[5] This difference alone has contributed to the notion that "East is East and West is West and never the twain shall meet." Of course, East and West have met over the centuries with various results—some mutually beneficial, some disastrous.

As the following chapters will attest to, the pendulum between East and West contact and beneficial and disastrous results is clear when it comes to the interaction between Western nations and China. The cultural differences are evident in its folk music and classical Chinese music—a repertoire that in some ways parallels American folk music and European classical music, and in other ways is 180 degrees from the inherent drive and improvisational nature of jazz, an art form "grounded in the rhythms of the real world."[6]

CHINESE FOLK AND CLASSICAL MUSIC: CHINESE MUSIC CENTRISM

Jazz is a style of music that inherently combines structure, i.e., a defined melody and chord progressions, with improvisation. The advent of jazz in Chinese culture, therefore, both pre-Mao and post-Mao, needs to be understood in the long tradition context of Chinese folk and classical music.

China's approach to many things, even in the last few decades, including music, reflects a certain centrism and anti-Western attitude. By "music" is meant Chinese classical music, including to a large degree its folk music.

One leading contemporary advocate of Chinese classical music is Sin Yan Shen, author of *Chinese Music and Orchestration: A Primer on Principles and Practice* (Chinese Music Society of North America, 2005).[7] It is clear from the book's narrative throughout that the author takes great pride in Chinese classical music to the extent that he pits it against Western music wherever possible, expressing an attitude of mostly subtle, sometimes blatant superiority.

For example, in his introduction Shen states: "Chinese music, however, is unique in its uninterrupted history of more than 8,000 years and very early development of theoretical systematic, acoustical and material science and orchestral practice."[8] This upfront competitiveness with Western music finds further expression in his discussion of "The Acoustic Space of the Chinese Orchestra":

> The European symphony is a more recent product of mankind. Its orchestral spectrum is quite a bit simpler than that of the Chinese orchestra and

is therefore better understood. It utilizes a basic tonal spectrum of the violin family. All other instrumental spectra present are not fundamental to the orchestra's orchestration and are supplementary. These other spectra are used for special color and function in contrast with the fundamental spectrum of the violin family. The sound of the symphony orchestra when it comes through our perception is that of the violin group.

The Chinese orchestra also has both types of spectra, fundamental versus supplementary. But because of the extraordinarily extensive period of practice, the Chinese orchestra possesses an extraordinary range of resonators and acoustical materials. Its fundamental tone thus can have several possibilities. Broadly speaking, the Chinese orchestra has two groups of fundamental tones, and the Western symphony has one.[9]

His statement is all the more puzzling because earlier in his narrative he describes the instrumental makeup of the Chinese orchestra as divided among plucked strings, bowed strings, percussions, and winds, a description not unlike the European orchestra of the twentieth century. All that is missing is the brass section. One wonders, though, if the absence of trumpets, trombones, and tubas in the traditional Chinese orchestra is not just of musicological significance, but also has cultural meaning.

These queries are answered in part by Hongwan Liu, who writes:

The Chinese orchestra is not a traditional concept, but rather is an artificial creation of the 20th century. Although music has been played in groups since ancient times, large orchestras playing harmonic or polyphonic music (as compared to a single melodic line shared by every instrument) is a distinctly western concept. In the early 20th century, during a time [pre-Mao] when modernization was equated with westernization, Chinese musicians formed Chinese orchestras based on western symphony orchestras. . . . As a result, music theory in Chinese classical music is essentially identical to music theory in western music.[10]

However,

There are apparently several traditional brass instruments in Chinese culture, but somehow none of them has been successfully incorporated [into the Chinese orchestra]. The main wind instruments in the Chinese orchestra (sheng, dizi, suona, and guan) are traditionally too individual and too piercing to reproduce the same effect as a brass chorale or fanfare.

All of these instruments now come in many different sizes and pitches in the Chinese orchestra to overcome these difficulties. The resulting sound is brighter, braver and more energetic than a symphony orchestra's wind and brass sections, but doesn't have the solidity and solemnity.[11]

The lack of a brass section aside, the singleness of melodic line in the traditional Chinese classical orchestra is yet another example of the centrality of Chinese thinking. In other words, there is only one way of playing; harmony—different instruments playing different lines—is an expression of individuality, something anathema to prior Chinese social and therefore political values.

CHINESE MUSIC/CHINESE CULTURE

Shen's abovementioned volume is instructive not only about Chinese folk and classical music, but also about Chinese culture. For one, he affirms the importance of music to Chinese culture: "The Chinese people have, since remote days, considered musical expression a very high form of human interaction."[12] Further on he states: "Ultimately, music is a culture-independent human creation. True music lovers, who by default always have more experience in one cultural system than others, will appreciate the artistic value and the virtuosity of a top notch musical performance, no matter what the cultural background of the performer may be. This phenomenon however represents a very high level of human communication, and does not take place on an everyday basis."[13]

With this it is hard to disagree. He then comes to the conclusion that "the preference of musical tonality of a culture, to a fairly large extent, implicitly defines the concept of harmoniousness of the culture."[14] The "concept of harmoniousness" is very Eastern, one that you will also find expressed in Japan and India. But it is also an ideal left wanting, especially if you review China's history—a history fraught with extreme violence, autocracy, fratricide, patricide, extermination, and revolution.

Shen also puts Chinese composers on a pedestal. After describing Chinese musicians as "a most sensitive breed," he waxes philosophical about Chinese composers: "Philosophically, the [Chinese] composers treasured the feelings of joy and friendship which occurred in certain periods of their life, and viewed such feelings as eternal joy and encouragements. . . . its implication in the area of entertainment is very low. In contrast, Western

classical music in all categories, was written with more entertainment purposes in mind. It was a result of a work-for-hire system."[15]

THE BLUES NOTE

Earlier in his narrative, however, Shen makes this definitive claim: "Do you
know the earliest musical interval documented in human history? The very
same interval which is 7000 years old now still exists today. This interval
is contained on a *xun* [pronounced shun], globular flute, unearthed in this
century. It is a minor third!"[16] This is an astounding statement for a scholar
steeped in and a champion of classical Chinese music. In the context of this
volume, a minor third is a "blues" interval found throughout early jazz and
contemporary jazz. Was prehistoric European man a progenitor of jazz?

All in all, it is possible to conjecture that while Shun's attitude is shaped
by a strong nationalist feeling (one he is certainly entitled to), it is also a
possibility that his attitude is shaped by politics. During Mao's tenure as
China's head of state, all things Western—including Western classical and
jazz music—were severely repressed.

But how things change with time! According to an April 2007 *New York
Times* article:

> One of the clearest signs that [Western] classical music has official ap-
> proval in China came from Li Lanquing, a retired member of the ruling
> Politburo Standing Committee and former minister of education. Mr. Li
> wrote a lengthy, loving tribute to 50 Western composers in which he ar-
> gued that you cannot be a true intellectual if you don't understand West-
> ern classical music.
>
> In a surprisingly bold statement he said that Chinese composers
> should "borrow theory and technique from European classical music to
> reform Chinese music."[17]

FAMILY AND NATURE: CONSISTENT MUSICAL THEMES

Shen does point us in the right direction with respect to Chinese culture
and music when he articulates the titles of many classical Chinese works
for orchestra, namely, "Galloping on the Prairie," "Fishing Song of the East
China Sea," "The Season Melody," "Going to the Fair," "Dadu River," "My

Brother Comes Home," "The Flower Does Not Bloom Before the Hero Ar-rives," "Purple Bamboo Melody," "Wedding Processional," "Trip to Suzhou," "Mile After Mile of Green Mountain,"[18] "Flower Riddles,"[19] "The Little Cow-herd,"[20] and "Rain Falls on the Plaintains."[21]

Quite obviously these are all titles dealing with nature, agriculture, and family life. These orchestral pieces are not unlike the titles of many tradi-tional Chinese melodies, including folk melodies, such as "The Moon Mir-rored in the Pool," "The Moon on High," "Dance of the Yao People," "Spring on the Pamir Plateau," "Dancing in the Moonlight," "Spring on a Moonlit River," "Song of the Herdsman,"[22] "Winter Crows Skimming over the Water," Combating Typhoon," "Autumnal Moon over Han Dynasty," "Lofty Moun-tain and Bubbling Streams," "A Sea Eagle Snatching a Swan,"[23] "Fish Playing with Water," "Sunny Spring and White Snow," "Snow Flakes Embellishing the Green," "Spring in the Tianshan Mountains,"[24] "Song of the Fisherman," "Beautiful Evening," "Spring Water Reflects the Moon," "Bumper Harvest," and "Flowing Water from the High Mountain."[25]

These melodies are all well-known throughout China and reflect the his-torically dominant demographic of the Chinese people: farmers. For mil-lennia China has been a nation of farmers, a nation that until very recently delayed its entry into the industrial revolution and the information age. Certainly, China is a country not just playing catch-up, but also moving forward at the beginning of the twenty-first century. But its classical music and the nationalistic description of it reflects a culture previously mired in a hierarchical mode of thinking, where people did not move up the scale of economic mobility, but rather were restricted by intervals of class, mostly positioned in a peasant, farming class. At the same time China's ruling elite projected and believed that its way was *the* way, an attitude that helped nineteenth-century Europeans, Russians, and Americans defeat the Chinese in two mid-nineteenth-century Opium Wars, which early in the twentieth century ultimately opened the door to the introduction of Chinese society to jazz—especially in Shanghai.

JAZZ IN THE MIDDLE KINGDOM

In the first half of the twentieth century China evolved politically from a rejection of the monarchy, to a republic, to a nationalistic fervor, and ulti-mately a communist regime. At the same time the world experienced two world wars, a depression, and an explosion of new technologies. In this same period the world began to hear music that broke from the traditional classical and Romantic trends of the nineteenth century. This was as true of classical music as it was of a new music style called jazz. The late renowned composer, conductor, and musical scholar Gunther Schuller—in his seminal work *Early Jazz: Its Roots and Musical Development*—articulates this development as follows:

> During the second decade of the [twentieth] century, while the world was engaged in its first "global" war, and European music was being thoroughly revitalized by the innovations of Arnold Schoenberg and Igor Stravinsky and the radical experiments of the musical "futurists" and "dadaists," America was quietly, almost surreptitiously, developing a distinctly separate musical language it had just christened with a decidedly unmusical name: jazz. . . . This new music developed from a multi-colored variety of musical traditions brought to the new world in part from Africa, in part from Europe. It seems in retrospect almost inevitable that America, the great ethnic melting pot, would procreate a music compounded of African rhythmic, formal, sonoric, and expressive elements and European rhythmic and harmonic practices.[26]

Schuller later concludes: "It is thus evident that many more aspects of jazz derive directly from African musical-social traditions than has been assumed. . . . The analytical study . . . shows that every musical element— rhythm, harmony, melody, timbre, and the basic forms of jazz—is essentially African in background and derivation."[27]

While Chinese dance hall owners, Chinese society elite, and European/ American/Russian expatriates did not stop to analyze the roots of the music they adopted (especially in Shanghai), the record shows a strong demand, in the main, for "black" jazz musicians in the 1920s and 1930s—performers like pianist Teddy Weatherford, trumpeter Valaida Snow, and band leader/ trumpeter Buck Clayton. These performers and many others—including Filipinos, Russians, Japanese, and ultimately indigenous Chinese—brought jazz to China. It was a new music befitting a new century, new ways of thinking, and new ways of being. It was a break from the Victorian/emperor past. Ironically, it presaged the beginning of the end of colonialism and the dawn of the globalism that characterizes the second half of the twentieth century and the beginning of the twenty-first century.

Jazz is a style of music that incorporates agreed-upon melodies and chords combined with individual improvisation. Jazz is both a collective and individual musical art. It requires study, practice, and, in the context of performance, a great deal of listening and cooperation. As the following narrative will show, jazz has been present at every stage of China's development in the twentieth and early twenty-first centuries. It is present in Shanghai, particularly, when the political and economic influence of the various colonial powers are at their height. It is there in Shanghai when the Communist Party begins to form with Mao as one of the founders. It is even there when the Japanese invade in 1937 and the colonial powers pull out. It is absent during Mao's tenure, but almost immediately begins to trickle back to China after he dies in 1976. And today, jazz—as well as contemporary rock, pop, and classical Western music—is very much in evidence in Shanghai, Beijing, and other Chinese cities.

Moreover, jazz is not only a part of China's cultural landscape because of globalization brought on by leaps in information, communications, and transportation technological development in the twentieth century. Jazz also has metaphorical meaning. The inherent characteristics of jazz—of playing together and individuality of expression—express the economic-political context of China today: a country on the rise globally because of individual entrepreneurship in the context of a country where country (the group, the ensemble) usually comes first.

Jazz, too, has evolved through various iterations, or styles, from its African roots, to New Orleans jazz, Dixieland, blues-boogie, ragtime and stride, to swing, bebop, cool jazz, hard bop, progressive jazz, funky jazz, post-bop, and neo-gospel, abstract jazz, modal jazz, electronic jazz, and fusion.[28] Today, jazz has a global presence, not unlike China, but in a different sense, of course. How China and jazz in China will further evolve is an open question.

There is much to learn and appreciate from observing the relationship between China's evolution and that of jazz in the last hundred years. But if there is any single lesson to be learned from observing this relationship, it is this: political and social change occur not so much because of pure ideology projected by a charismatic figure, but from economic pressures and necessity. Economics usually leads the way. The Soviet Union was created—and later collapsed—because economic goals projected as political idealism and vision were not compatible with realistic factors of supply and demand and the nature of human behavior. What may have worked for smaller, prehistoric tribes in terms of "communal needs" did not work on a much larger scale, especially when the populace is more literate. The basic relationship between supply and demand—the fundamentals of economics—is the ruling principle. It is what makes the world go around. It drives everything. When suppressed for too long, the result—ultimately—is revolution.

In the context of China's more recent history—relative to its long history—jazz came to China because non-Chinese people, motivated by economics (and, in various ways, greed) brought their culture with them in the mid-nineteenth century following the Opium Wars—the musical culture was classical European music, and in the first quarter of the twentieth century it was jazz. Nothing much has changed in a hundred years. Now that China has opened up even more to Western-style economics and trade, especially since 1980, there is even more Western-style music present in China; this includes jazz, rock, and pop. The westerners inevitably brought with them their musical culture, among other behaviors. Moreover, jazz, in particular, is not just a style of music. It is also a carrier of a way of thinking and behaving: where the group *and* individuality of expression are paramount, the antithesis of thousands of years of Chinese cultural history.

Jazz in China is the story of jazz's thread-like presence in China in the last hundred years. It is also the story of China's evolution as seen through the prism of the United States' indigenous, classical music: jazz.

CHAPTER 2

The Opium Wars

In the late 1910s, 1920s, and even into the 1930s "jazz" is the music of the age in the Republic of China, especially and primarily in Shanghai on China's east coast. It is enjoyed equally by sophisticated Chinese gentry and upper-class people in the many dance halls dotting various parts of Shanghai and by the many Europeans, Russians, and Americans living and working in the so-called "Paris of the East."

These same Europeans, Russians, and Americans also own pieces of Shanghai, literally. As Lynn Pan describes it in her book *Shanghai: A Century of Change in Photographs*, "Shanghai became not just one city but three—the Chinese City, the International Settlement, and the French Concession, each with its own administrative, legal and police systems."[1] These same foreigners have access to several key ports on China's eastern coast—a result of "agreements" with previous Chinese emperors in the nineteenth century.

How did this come to pass? How did several foreign nations come to own sections of Shanghai, and have unrestricted access to numerous key ports throughout China's eastern coast? The answer to these questions can be found in a conflict initially between the British (and ultimately the French, Russians, and Americans) and the Chinese in the mid-nineteenth century: the Opium Wars, two wars that had roots in late eighteenth-century China.

THE ROOTS OF THE OPIUM WARS

The two Opium Wars (1839–42 and 1856–60) pitted the British and later the French empires (with some help from Russians and Americans during the Second Opium War) against the Chinese Qing Empire. According to authors Hanes and Sanello, the roots of the conflict lay in three interlocking problems:

> First, China's conviction, sustained by nearly four thousand years of historical memory, that it represented the pinnacle of civilization on the

planet and that all other nations were barbarians, to be dealt with not as equals but as "tribute bearers." Second, China's monopoly of the production of tea ..., combined with its insistence on being paid for such goods only with silver bullion [the international currency of the time]. Third, the emergence of Britain as the premier industrial power of the world, with an equally overweening conviction of its own Christian civilization's moral, ethical, and material superiority, and a determination to be treated by other peoples and nationals not as a subordinate, but as an equal (if not a superior)—even if this meant supplying millions of fellow human beings with a devastating drug. . . . Opium entered China on the back of a camel, one historian wrote, and it ended up breaking the back of an entire nation.[2]

China and Britain's self-images at the time were equally self-centered. This was never so apparent than in August 1793, when Viscount Lord George Macartney landed in China with a simple brief from King George III: "establish a British embassy in the capital [Peking] and get permission for British ships to dock at ports besides Canton, the only harbor then open to foreigners." The problem was this: trade with China was booming and lucrative, but it had become bottlenecked in overcrowded Canton, the only port open to foreigners. The British were so eager to open China, Macartney had instructions to offer an end to the importation of opium there from British-controlled India, which was officially illegal in China but difficult to stop both because of enthusiastic customers of the drug and the riches that the trade generated."[3]

Macartney brought with him over six hundred gifts for the emperor, but the Chinese perceived that with disdain. China had become the richest nation in the world (an economic feat it might be in the process of duplicating in the twenty-first century). During Emperor Qianlong's reign that began in 1736, "China had become the richest and most populous country in the world. . . . the empire doubled in size and area as its armies conquered huge swaths of Central Asia, Outer Mongolia, and parts of Russia."[4] China, at least from the perspective of the emperor's court, was the superior empire, requiring foreigners to bow, or "kowtow" in the Mandarin dialect.

Therein lay the problem. Despite the wagonloads of gifts, the ritual of bowing to the emperor, a "custom accepted by every other nation doing business with the huge market that was China," was refused that fateful day, September 14, 1793, at the Summer Palace. The British plenipotentiary did not bow to the emperor, and the emperor did not bow to the painting of

George III Macartney had brought with him as a surrogate for the "real" king. The mission was a failure.

And then there was the opium problem. The East India Company, at the time a monopolistic entity, not only imported various goods from England, it also permitted its ships to carry opium. The fact was it was just too profitable. In all fairness, it should be mentioned the British were not the first to import opium to China: during the Middle Ages opium had been imported to China through what is now modern Turkey. It was used primarily for medicinal purposes as an analgesic. In the seventeenth century the French and Dutch picked up the trade. In 1659 the Dutch began export of opium from its base in Bengal, India.

The importation of opium into China was officially condemned by the Dragon Throne government. The East India Company, as well as many British officials, likewise "officially" condemned the drug. But it was lip service. In the early part of the nineteenth century, opium addiction grew slowly. In radical contrast, by the end of the century opium addiction reached all the way to the emperor's court, including his empress of the Western Palace: Cixi, a former concubine. Cixi ruled China after the death of the Emperor Xianfeng and the subsequent death of the empress of the Eastern Palace, Xianfeng's first wife. Cixi died in 1908. It took Mao and the Communist Revolution in 1949 to eradicate the drug for non-medicinal purposes. He summarily executed all drug dealers.

For a time, there was an economic balance between the exportation of Chinese tea—a growing habit on the part of the British populace—and the importation of opium. The two powers remained as equal, with both assuming superiority over the other. Then a technological innovation in Britain upset this equilibrium: "The invention of the steam engine in the previous century had resulted in the mechanical production of cotton by factories in the north of England."[5] Over a period of a few decades since Lord Macartney's failed mission, the relationship between both governments became increasingly strained. Britain was now the world's superpower. It had defeated Napoleon, but it had also lost the American colonies, twice, the last time in the War of 1812. It wanted not only ostensible equanimity with China, it wanted a lot more. The link between tea, opium, and other exports and empire building was inexorable.

In 1833 a reform-minded British Parliament abolished the East India Company's monopoly in China. The amount of tea imported into Britain quadrupled. The trade in opium to pay for all this tea also dramatically increased. One Chinese courtier estimated that four million Chinese were habituated. A British doctor in Canton suspected the figure was three times that. Hanes and Sanello write: "The [Chinese] economy, government services, and standard of living all declined because of substance abuse."[6] Meanwhile, the opium trade replenished Britain's treasury. Increasingly, the Chinese government pressed its case. The situation came to a head with the First Opium War, 1839–42.

Apart from atrocities, strategic and tactical blunders, and omnipresent arrogance on both sides, the tipping-point difference between the Europeans and the Chinese was technology. Despite their long history of technological innovation—such as a printing press centuries before Gutenberg and the invention of gunpowder—the Chinese army was still medieval, not only in terms of tactics, but, more importantly, in terms of weaponry. On the other hand, the British, and later the French, had industrial-age weaponry, partly based on the steam engine, i.e., steam-driven ships that the Chinese had never seen. Their tactics were also more modern. It was Chinese bows, arrows, and spears versus British steam and modern cannon.

The end of the First Opium War resulted in the Treaty of Nanking. It gave the British everything they wanted, except the legalization of opium. The British demanded and the Chinese acquiesced to pay an "extortionate $21 million, half of all of China's yearly tax revenues. . . . which would be paid on the installment plan."[7] The British also gained access to and the right of permanent residence at the ports of Canton, Amoy, Fuzhou, Ningbo, and Shanghai. Each port would house a British consular official. The irritating pretense that the British were tribute bearers inferior to China's superior civilization now melted away in the face of superior British military might, as the treaty now codified the equal status of both nations. Hong Kong was declared a permanent British colony.[8] It was a major humiliation for the Chinese and a major victory for the British. And while military hostilities ceased, the treaty and the continuation of the opium trade remained a source of seething anger among the Chinese. It also created a schism among British government officials. The power of the opium merchants remained intact, however, and provided the impetus for the Second Opium War.

As Hanes and Sanello put it: "Tragically, the Treaty of Nanking represented only a truce, not an end to hostilities between China and Britain. . . . Officially, the narcotic [opium] remained illegal to use and import. Unofficially, it continued to be big business and provided the tinder for the

Second Opium War of 1856."[9] In other words, the Treaty of Nanking caused more problems than it solved. Again Britain's superior technology—with additional military assistance from the French, Russians, and some Americans—resulted in another win for the British and the further weakening of the Chinese emperor.

To add deep cultural insult to deep military injury, at the conclusion of the Second Opium War in 1860 a Scottish earl—Britain's plenipotentiary to China—burned down the Yuan Ming Yuan, the Summer Palace of the Xianfeng Emperor outside Peking (now Beijing).

This person was James Bruce, the eighth Earl of Elgin, a direct descendent of Robert the Bruce and son of the seventh Earl of Elgin, who earlier had sent Greece's Parthenon friezes to Britain to reside in London's British Museum. The son, who, for the most part, was a man of gentle conscience but prone to depression, decided to extract from the Chinese in the mid-nineteenth century a price for their several decades of obstinacy and arrogance toward westerners (particularly the British) and the horrific treatment and death of allied troops toward the end of the Second Opium War. The looting (initially by the French) followed by the burning to the ground of the Summer Palace outside Peking, a highly prized work of architecture, was exacted as a punishment. This act, the endgame of a series of acts begun in the late eighteenth century, would have consequences to this day.

THE AFTERMATH: EARLY COLONIALISM IN CHINA

The Opium Wars concluded, the Europeans had solidified their trade foothold in China. The Chinese were reduced to a secondary power. The presence of opium continued well beyond the demise of the empire:

> Opium cultivation and use thrived in Ch'iang Kai-shek's China during the 1920s and 1930s. Ch'iang used the revenue from opium taxes to bankroll his regime and army. By the time of the Japanese invasion of China in 1937, forty million Chinese, 10 percent of the population, were addicted to the drug. British-controlled Hong Kong had an even bigger problem, with an estimated 30 percent of the colony's population dependent on opium. The Japanese occupiers encouraged opium consumption for political rather than fiscal reasons: an intoxicated population was also a docile [one].[10]

In the sixty-seven years from 1793 to 1860 the British, primarily, secured their place on the Chinese mainland. The French did as well, with designs on other parts of Asia, leading to the Vietnam War in the twentieth century. The Germans, Russians, and Americans, and eventually the Japanese, also lay claim to China in various ways: some as émigrés, some as invaders. Fifty-one years after the end of the Second Opium War, in 1911 the Chinese empire fell, giving rise to the Chinese Republic and, ultimately, the People's Republic of China (PRC) in 1949. While the Europeans certainly had impressed their culture on the Chinese in the latter half of the nineteenth century, it was American culture that came to the fore in China in the first quarter of the twentieth century, especially in the form of popular music and jazz.

The timing of the fall of the last Chinese emperor, Emperor Xuan Tong (also known as Pu Yi) of the Qing dynasty in 1911—which followed the end of the Victorian era, and closely preceded World War I, the Russian Revolution, the distribution of sheet music, piano rolls, the birth of film and radio as news and entertainment, the gramophone, trans-Pacific steamships, and early commercial flight and global telecommunications—coincided with the birth of jazz in the United States, specifically in the horns of Buddy Bolden and Louis Armstrong, the fingers of Jelly Roll Morton, and the nascent big band sounds of King Oliver and Kid Ory. In very short order, perhaps ten years or less, this new style of music—a youthful music that is a radical departure from the staid constrictions of the Victorian era—found its way not only to Europe and other parts of the world from the United States, but also to China, particularly Shanghai, where it was embraced by expatriates and Chinese alike in the many dance halls there.

In turn, this cultural migration from the West, together with the colonial imposition of several non-Chinese powers, fostered a heightened "anti-Yellow music" nationalism in China, leading ultimately to the rise and "victory" of communism in the late 1940s. This sequence of events is of significant historical moment not only for China, but also for the West. In this instance, history shows us that the United States' leading cultural gift to the world—jazz—did not find its way to China by accident. It was a sociocultural consequence born out of two drug wars that occurred decades before jazz as we understand it historically was even invented! Economic and profit incentives were driving forces. Military and transportation technologies of the nineteenth century had a strong hand in this development. Later, early twentieth-century entertainment technologies played a role. The sequence of events shows how history is connected, sometimes by small matters made large, sometimes by larger although not so obvious occurrences.

In no small measure, jazz was not only the music of social interaction in the Shanghai dance halls, such as the famed Paramount, it also mirrored the tempo of the times. Between 1919–21 the Chinese Communist Party, of which a young Mao Zedong was a founding member, was also formulating a new sound—a battle cry for political and social reform in China. One such early meeting took place in July 1921 . . . in Shanghai![11] Meanwhile, several technologies—namely, the aforementioned steamship, plus the gramophone, the locomotive, and early film—permeated Chinese society. Their collective impact was palpable, leading first to a larger embrace of Western culture, then a growing rejection, followed by complete suppression by Mao and the Communists.

CHAPTER 3

The Influence of Early Twentieth-Century Technology

Without question, the superior war-making technology of the Western colonial powers—the steam-driven warship and cannon—made the difference between China prevailing and its defeat during the Opium Wars. It resulted in the colonial powers controlling Shanghai, tantamount to controlling China. In turn, the colonial powers brought their culture with them to Shanghai, and in the first quarter of the twentieth century that included jazz. Jazz—at that time still relatively new on the American cultural landscape—was, within a couple of decades, not only the music of Shanghai, it was global. How did it get halfway around the world to China (and in the other direction, to Europe) so quickly? And how did the non-American musicians in Shanghai (Russians, Filipinos, and Chinese) learn to play the music for dance hall purposes?

Transportation and communications technologies of the early twentieth century—the steamship, the locomotive, the gramophone, and early film—also were major influences in bringing jazz to China's shores.

THE STEAMSHIP

In the first quarter of the twentieth century, the steamship was a key technology bringing jazz to China, not only in the transport of sheet music, gramophone and phonograph records, early Hollywood films, and non-Chinese musicians, but also by facilitating the influx of Europeans, Russians, and Americans who constituted a dominating presence in China, especially in Shanghai.

Moreover, just as there is a strong connection between the military victory of the Europeans due to technological superiority over the Chinese during the Opium Wars in the nineteenth century, on the one hand, and the Europeans dominance of China in the first half of the twentieth century, on the other, there is also a strong connection between another technological feat in the second half of the nineteenth century and the dominance of the steamship as a mode of transportation in the first quarter of the twentieth century. That technological feat was the building of the Suez Canal.

As Malcolm Falkus, author of *The Blue Funnel Legend: A History of the Ocean Steam Ship Company, 1865–1973*, points out: "Within a few years the new Suez Canal, opened in [November] 1869, had made the Cape route to Asia largely obsolete for steamships. China was suddenly more than 3000 miles closer to Europe, and steamships flocked to the new route."[1]

The early dominant player in the steamship trade routes to China was the Blue Funnel Line, established in 1865, a mere four years before the advent of the Suez Canal. Falkus describes the very beginnings on the steamship line that was to become one of Britain's leading shipping lines:

> On 19 April 1866, the 2300 ton steamer *Agamemnon*, set out from Liverpool on a historic voyage. Agamemnon was a square-rigged barque, powered by high pressure compound engines, and she carried cargo for Penang, Hong Kong, and Shanghai. Within a few months two sister ships, *Ajax* and *Achilles*, had set out on similar journeys. The trio were owned by the Ocean Steam Ship Company, a new enterprise set up in 1865 by the brothers Alfred and Philip Holt. . . .
>
> *Agamemnon*'s voyage opened a new chapter in shipping history. Her journey marked the first attempt to run a line of steamers directly from the United Kingdom to China; it was the first time a steamship had ever attempted a non-stop journey so great (Liverpool to Mauritius via the Cape); and it marked the start of the Blue Funnel Line, long known on Merseyside as the China Company, and destined to become one of the great names in British merchant shipping.[2]

The combination of the successful opening of the Suez Canal in 1869, the construction and launching of cargo-carrying and ultimately people-carrying trans-Pacific steamships, and a colonial mind-set on the part of several European nations—underscored by the one-sided agreements forced upon the Chinese by their loss in the two Opium Wars—resulted in a growing and profitable trade with China in the second half of the nineteenth century and into the early part of the twentieth century.

THE LOCOMOTIVE

The locomotive was also a major influence on Chinese jazz and popular music of the 1920s. We should not be surprised. On both sides of the Pacific, the locomotive was a central theme, both literally and metaphorically, of popular music. In the United States, over a period of several decades many popular songs and jazz works reference the locomotive, the train, or the railway.

The first railroad in China was the Woosung Railway in 1876, a fifteen-mile railway from Shanghai to Woosung. It was, however, demolished by the Qing government a year later. Neglected by China, railroad building was promoted by the imperialist powers in their spheres of influence after 1898.[3]

As a result, by 1911 there were around 9,000 km of tracks in mainland China. During the Republic of China era, however, from 1912 until 1949, the development of the railway network in China slowed due to repeated civil wars and the invasion of Japan in the Second Sino-Japanese War. But during the reign of the Fengtian warlord from 1912 until 1931, several railway lines were built, particularly in Manchuria. The invading Japanese later accelerated the process, and after the establishment of the People's Republic of China under Mao in 1949, railroading grew even more. All in all, the railroad is an ever-present fact of social and economic life in China and has been for over 125 years.

Two jazz pieces from 1928 and 1933—one Chinese, the other American, respectively—are exemplary of the train's presence as an international reference point. The first is "Express Train." I came by this recording courtesy of Andrew F. Jones, a professor in the department of East Asian languages and cultures at the University of California at Berkeley, and the author of *Yellow Music*, a definitive book on media, culture, and colonial modernity in the so-called Chinese Jazz Age. Jones writes that he discovered the track in 2001, on a "dusty gramophone record in a Beijing antique stall." "Express Train," written in 1928 by Li Jinhui, a pioneering composer who is often called the father of Chinese popular music, the tune is performed on the recording by Zhou Xuan, the most famous chanteuse of the era. In the song, the train symbolizes rapid social change and satirizes the breathless pace of modern courtship by way of the story of a couple who are engaged, marry, and have two children—all within five minutes of having first met. Li Jinhui's music—influenced by his relationship with trumpeter Buck Clayton, who performed in Shanghai in the early 1930s—was immensely popular, so much so that he was persecuted and died during the Cultural Revolution.

Strikingly similar to Li's "Express Train" is Duke Ellington's "Daybreak Express," which has a 1933 copyright date. Ellington never traveled to China, Li never to the United States. Yet both cuts reflect the speeded-up pace of life that got started back in 1844, when the commercial introduction of the telegraph inaugurated the era in which information could move around the planet at the speed of light. As Jones puts it, "both composers were participating in a globalized musical idiom for which the speed of modern transport (trains and ocean-going vessels) and modern communications (gramophones, radio, and cinema) were a fundamental condition of possibility."

THE GRAMOPHONE

The abovementioned similarity between Li Jinhui's "Express Train" and Duke Ellington's "Daybreak Express" is not only of value with respect to the influence of the locomotive; it gives further credence to the enormous impact of the gramophone and flat disc records in the first half of the twentieth century to the spread of jazz to China and the rest of the world.[4]

In 1888 the German American Emile Berliner (1851–1929) demonstrated a new type of talking machine. While the American Thomas Alva Edison had conceived of recording on discs, the novelty of Berliner's invention was that the movements of the cutting stylus in sympathy with the diaphragm were lateral but flat, rather than vertical, or "hill and sale," as on the earlier Phonograph. This was just one of several features and benefits to the improvement on Edison's design. It could also be made more cheaply than a Phonograph.[5] However, consumers could not record their own gramophone records, as was possible with a phonograph. That feature would have to wait well into the twentieth century with the gramophone's technological progeny.

By the 1920s the gramophone was a highly popular means of listening to music and the human voice in the United States and China. With respect to the latter country, Frank Dikötter[6] reports, "One of the first households in China to enjoy [a gramophone] was that of Yang Renshan, who purchased his equipment during official tours to Europe in the 1880s. In 1904 he bought a His Master's Voice machine with a horn, and the family would often gather and listen to music while stories were being told."[7] Further, Gramophones "could be obtained in Shanghai during the First World

War, the class model being the Victor Victrola player. Easily transportable, the Victrola promised invariable quality and countless hours of entertainment."[8] Dikötter points out that this technological marvel was not restricted to major urban areas, such as Shanghai and Peking: "In faraway Chengdu gramophones were on sale even before the collapse of the empire in 1912. A few years later a newly installed gramophone became a major attraction in Chengdu's annual flower fair, as the crowds listened to it playing traditional music and opera in respectful silence. Dozens of farmers in remotest Gansu province would gather around a phonograph in 1925."[9]

An early example of jazz in China using the nascent sound recording technologies is "Nighttime in Old Shanghai," a piece recorded in that city circa 1928 by the Whitey Smith Majestic Hotel Orchestra. The opening section is imitative of Chinese folksong, but the music eventually morphs into a dance hall piece typical of the day: an instrumental section, followed by a vocal, and then a section hinting at swing, with the emphasis on beats one and three. This piece is, to my knowledge, one of very few extant jazz recordings done in the Far East during that era. Smith, born into a family of Danish immigrants, was a drummer and bandleader who came to China from San Francisco on August 24, 1922, via the *SS Nile*, a steamship of the China Mail Line. He helped popularize American music in Shanghai with his Westernized arrangements of Chinese folksongs, and in 1956 published an autobiography, *I Didn't Make a Million*. His story is related in a later chapter.

The timing of these technological events with respect to recorded music and the early growth spurt of radio broadcasting converged with the omnipresent nature of race relations in the United States at the time and the dominance of steamships as *the* mode of transoceanic transportation. The result: both "white" jazz of the major labels in the United States and "black" jazz of Black Swan, founded by William C. Handy and Harry Pace in 1921,[10] found its way around the world in short order, and to China, especially Shanghai, almost within a blink.

While jazz rapidly found its way east to Europe and west to the Orient from the United States, another technological connection was emerging between the United States and Germany—despite the fact that the United States twice went to war with Germany in the first half of the twentieth century.

It is probably no historical accident that a relationship—technological and musical—would exist between the Germans and Americans. While the American Edison first evolved the concept and first practical phonographs, it was a German—Emile Berliner—who took the recording technology the necessary step further by developing a successful flat disc approach that became popular with the general consuming public. The Germans were also at work developing a different kind of recording device—sound not on a hard disc, but on magnetic tape. In 1928, Dr. Fritz Pfleumer received German patents covering the application of magnetic powders to paper or plastic backing media. In that same year AEG and BASF, both German companies, worked on developing this concept. AEG carried out a project resulting in a product to be known as the "Magnetophon." In 1934 the world's first magnetic tapes were manufactured in Germany, fifty in all, each 1,000 meters long. In 1938 the German Reichs-Rundfunk-Gessellschaft adopted the Magnetophone and magnetic tape as the future standard for radio broadcast recording in Germany.

Another German-American link is the clear presence of Germans in Shanghai following the two Opium Wars and into the 1920s. Following the demise of Mao in 1976, three other Germans—jazz bassist (and diplomat) Martin Fleischer in Beijing (see chapter 11), jazz festival entrepreneur Udo Hoffman (also in Beijing; see chapter 13), and tenor saxophonist Rolf Becker in Shanghai (see chapter 16)—would exert prime influence on indigenous and emerging jazz musicians in the 1980s, 1990s, and the early twenty-first century with respect to spreading the American jazz tradition in China.

EARLY FILM

The development of the motion picture industry in the late 1800s was an outgrowth of developments in still photography. For example, on October 19, 1878, *Scientific American* published a series of pictures depicting a horse in full gallop, along with instructions to view them through the zoetrope. The photos were taken by an English photographer, Edward Muybridge, to settle a bet between California businessman Leland Stanford and his colleagues. Stanford contended that at some point in a horse's stride, all four hooves were off the ground. He enlisted Muybridge to take photographs of the positions of a horse's hooves in rapid succession. Muybridge's twelve pictures showed that Stanford had won the bet.[11]

Meanwhile, in Paris, noted physiologist Etienne-Jules Marey was doing similar work:

> His studies of animals in motion drove him to experiment with photography, and he fashioned a camera that could take 12 pictures per second

of a moving object. The technique, called chronophotography, along with Muybridge's work, were the founding concepts for motion picture cameras and projectors. In 1888 in New York City, inventor Thomas Edison and his British assistant William Dickson set out to create a device that could record moving pictures. In 1890 Dickson unveiled the Kinetograph, a primitive motion picture camera. In 1892 he announced the invention of the Kinetoscope, a machine that could project the moving images onto a screen. In 1894, Edison initiated public film screenings in recently-opened "Kinetograph Parlors." Again, the French were working towards the same end. In 1895, Auguste and Louis Lumière introduced the Cinématographe, a projector that could show 16 frames per second. In their public cinema, audiences were spellbound by the films of simple movement and action: images of a baby eating, a hose squirting water, and the workers pouring out of the Lumière factory.[12]

From these early beginnings grew a fledgling motion picture industry that today is a global, multi-billion-dollar business. It is interesting to note that throughout the nineteenth century technological developments in the area of communication and information were evolving at an accelerating rate—beginning with the development of the commercially viable telegraph in 1838, then still photography, followed by the phonograph that could record the human voice, then, almost simultaneously, early developments in motion pictures (without sound), and Marconi's early experiments with radio. Taken together, these developments reflected a period during which technologies in their early forms were capable of reproducing and reflecting the human condition either visually or aurally. It would take other technological developments in the early twentieth century for sight and sound to merge, but by the end of the nineteenth century there are the beginnings of ways for human beings to see and hear a mirror of themselves that heretofore was not accessible.

This mirroring of human behavior is described with insight by Marshall McLuhan in his 1964 book *Understanding Media: The Extensions of Man*. Besides his prophetic coining of the phrase "the global village," McLuhan posits that much of man's technologies are essentially extensions of man's physical, mental, and sensory being. The consequences—intentional and unintentional—of communications media developments in the nineteenth century are very much with us in the early twenty-first century. Among them are that externalizing how we sound and look—quite apart from portrait paintings—must and does have a profound impact on our perceptions of ourselves and the world around us. This last is nowhere more true than in China in the late nineteenth century.

A usual mantra when it comes to the influence of mass media, such as film, is that it helps spread the positive and negative values inherent in a medium's content. With respect to China, early film was greeted with awe, then highly politicized criticism. The more American films were shown in China in the first half of the twentieth century, the more American, and therefore, Western values were devalued. In no small part, the end result was a Chinese civil war between Nationalists and Communists, with the latter the ultimate victor, at least for a few decades.

Chaoguang Wang, writing on "American Films in Chinese Reviews," summarizes the impact of early American films this way:

> The Chinese audience was stricken with the novelty of the film when they first saw it. . . . In the 1920s, [however], the Chinese people's response to the U.S. film began to switch from a sense of novelty to criticism, and gradually to a pan-politicized criticism at that. . . . The Chinese criticism of the American films arose first of all from the ethical conflicts. It dealt with three questions: evil, pornography and humiliating China.[13]

For example, in some instances, Wang recounts, the Chinese learned how to conduct a robbery by watching American detective movies.[14] Wang elaborates:

> This criticism of the American detective films showed the Chinese people's moral reflection on the onrush of Western culture. In a country of loyalty, piety, rites and righteousness, where ethics have always been held in high esteem, the chain reactions set off by the American detective films would, as a matter of course, cause great pains among its nationals and made them think that these films were an evil, even saying that China now has robbers of the foreign fashion that it never had known before and has foreign style robberies that it had never known.[15]

Over a century since the introduction of film to China, criticism and rejection of American/Western values has evolved into adoption of American/Western filmmaking techniques and commercialism.

Today, China's film industry is one of the largest in the world and competes now with films produced by Hollywood (the United States) and Bollywood (India). In fact, a recent article out of Britain—"China Film Market

Set to Take Over Hollywood: The film industry is thriving despite the limitations of censorship, and here are predictions it may overtake Hollywood"—attests to this trend, predicting that "China has become the world's second largest film market and is predicted to be the largest, overtaking Hollywood, by the end of the decade"—this despite the fact that foreign films make up 60 percent of the Chinese box office market.[16]

To reiterate, in between these time frames, the influence of "Western" films, particularly in the 1920–40s with their jazz and pop music soundtracks, contributed to the several political upheavals China experienced. The result was the communist revolution of 1949, in no small measure a violent overthrow of Western colonialism that reaches back to the mid-nineteenth century.

Professor Andrew Jones, in his seminal book *Yellow Music*, puts it this way:

> The arrival in China of media technologies such as the cinema and the gramophone did, of course, result in a fundamental dislocation of certain indigenous forms of cultural production and cultural authority, particularly for the landed Confucian literati whose dominance had been culturally constituted through command of the classical literary tradition. . . .
>
> This sense of threat was compounded in China by the exploitative economic arrangements and imperialist violence (both real and symbolic) that often accompanied the diffusion of media technologies.[17]

In other words, we should not be surprised. Technological developments—wherein the new technology provides some effective and/or efficient characteristic that outshines the earlier technology or that allows people to do something they could not do before—causes "dislocations" in a culture. These dislocations are sometimes silent and invisible, sometimes "in your face."

THE CONSEQUENCES OF CULTURAL DISLOCATION

In the case of cinema and the gramophone, the influx and dominance of Western culture and values into China, in tandem with the arrival of people from the West via steamships was clearly more than a novelty for a time. The music of the United States and Europe in the first half of the twentieth century—jazz—was part and parcel of this cultural dislocation. Westerners already in places like Shanghai embraced jazz with open arms. Indigenous urban Chinese, desirous of breaking with the Confucian past and wanting to bring themselves out of the oppressive Chinese way of adhering to a central authority, i.e., the vestige characteristics of the emperor's court, also took to the music and its inherent values. This conclusion squares with Frank Dikötter's overall observation of indigenous Chinese with respect to modern China from the middle of the nineteenth century to the advent of communism in 1949. He writes:

> far from being self-contained, the everyday was already inextricably linked to global trends by the last decades of the nineteenth century, from the yarn of clothes, the iron of tools and the oil in lamps among ordinary farmers to electric fans and imported phonographs among wealthy elites . . . Just as early modern Europe was spellbound by the technical wizardry and fine skills behind Oriental commodities, late imperial China praised the intricate craftsmanship and exotic appearance of "foreign goods." . . . things local were increasingly rejected as signifiers of backwardness, while imported goods were welcomed instead as prestige symbols: modernity had to be brought home in order to propel the country into the universe of "civilized" nations and join a universal march towards progress.[18]

This "march towards progress" was not universally accepted. Some forces viewed this perspective as a "cultural dislocation." By the 1940s, given Japan's blatant and violent invasion of China in 1937 and the Communists' growing numbers (with such leaders as Mao Zedong), the "cultural dislocation" boiled over into a conflict between Nationalists and Communists and ultimately the wholesale rejection of Western values and thought and jazz by the early 1950s.

To reiterate, China's relationship with jazz parallels the country's political and social evolution during the twentieth century. The music arrived shortly after the fall of the Qing Dynasty in 1911, as the imperial period gave way to a republic under Sun Yat-sen. The rest of the century was turbulent: the republic was followed by a warlord period, occupation by Japan, Chiang Kai-shek's Nationalist movement, and the 1949 Communist Revolution that established the People's Republic of China of today.

These political outcomes notwithstanding, the convergence of the abovementioned technologies at the beginning of the twentieth century coincides with the emergence of early jazz in the United States, namely in

New Orleans. While it is a probable historical coincidence that these early twentieth-century technologies emerged at the same time that jazz came to the forefront as a new style of music and an icon that defined the 1920s (as in the phrase "the Jazz Age" and the film *The Jazz Singer*), it can also be argued that jazz—with its inherent improvisational and individual freedom of expression within the structure of a group characteristics—was a cultural expression of the aforementioned technologies that ushered in new modes of traveling, new ways of perceiving and expressing, and new ways of socializing and governing. All together, they bade farewell to the Victorian era and ushered in the "globalness" of the twentieth century.

CHAPTER 4

Shanghai in the 1920s–1930s: The Joint Was Jumpin'

Our Western perspective of mainland China as a country dominated by a harsh, paranoid, and obsessive-compulsive leadership has not been without some merit. Movies and television programs have tended to perpetuate a somewhat distorted, one-sided view of China as a culture devoid of "fun." Certainly, the people of mainland China under Mao Zedong and his followers experienced decades of cultural squalor. But prior to Mao's ascent to power in 1949 there is clear evidence that China, especially in coastal cities such as Shanghai and Peking (now Beijing), were "jumpin'" with music, especially jazz.

JUESHI YINYUE=JAZZ

As longtime American expat living in Beijing, jazz musician, and Chinese studies expert David Moser has written:

> Before the communist takeover in 1949, Shanghai was filled with hip nightclubs where Westernized young people danced to the music of Glenn Miller and Benny Goodman, played by indigenous musicians who had free access to the latest records from overseas. Though it didn't catch on with the general population (80% of whom were and are peasants in the countryside), there was among the urban population a small but devoted following of this frenetic American noise called jueshi yinyue, "knight music" (jueshi "knight" being a phonetic rendering of "jazz").[1]

The Ugly Daughter Rises

In Shanghai's prime, no city in the Orient, or the world for that matter, could compare with it. At the peak of its spectacular career the swamp-ridden metropolis surely ranked as the most pleasure-mad, rapacious, corrupt, strife-ridden, licentious, squalid, and decadent city in the world. It was the most pleasure-mad because nowhere else did the population pursue amusement, from feasting to whoring, dancing to powder-taking, with such abandoned zeal. It was rapacious because greed was its driving force; strife ridden because calamity was always at the door; licentious because it catered to every depravity known to man; squalid because misery stared one brazenly in the face; and decadent because morality, as every Shanghai resident knew, was irrelevant. . . . as a popular Chinese saying aptly observed, "Shanghai is like the emperor's ugly daughter; she never has to worry about finding suitors."[2]

So begins Stella Dong's detailed and highly descriptive "biography" of Shanghai between 1842 and 1949, from the "invasion" of Westerners, starting with the British and the Opium Wars, to the takeover of China by the Communists in 1949. Reflecting the description of the Opium Wars in chapter 2, Dong writes, "Western gunboats and firepower were the instruments by which Britain defeated the five-thousand-year-old Flowery Kingdom, but opium paved the way." Dong adds: "Opium, the addictive drug that Britain was so bent on selling to the Chinese that it waged a war against them for the privilege, built modern Shanghai. Without the opium poppy, the most evil and profligate of flowers, the 'Whore of Asia' would never have been created."[3]

Further, Dong writes: "Within decades, she had become Asia's greatest metropolis, a brash sprawling juggernaut of a city that dominated the rest of the country with its power, sophistication, and, most of all, money."[4] Dong also points out, "However high the . . . port might rank on the list of the world's most corrupt and decadent spots, its reputation did nothing to prevent it from becoming the destination of so many Chinese that its population doubled in the fifteen years between 1895 and 1910 and nearly tripled in the next twenty, to three million. So well traversed were the footpaths, canals, rail routes and riverways that led to this Asian mecca that by 1885, only one out of every ten Chinese living in Shanghai could claim to be a native son or daughter."[5] By the 1920s and 1930s—almost eighty years after the Opium Wars—Shanghai would become the nexus between the Chinese mainland and jazz. It was no accident.

JAZZ ARRIVES AROUND THE GLOBE

The apparent arrival of jazz in China (or at least in the Pacific Rim) in the early 1920s coincides, according to renowned American composer Aaron Copland, with the arrival of jazz in Europe. He writes: "the first arrival in Europe, around 1918, of American jazz was followed by a wave of interest in chamber orchestra and chamber opera, with emphasis on new tonal experiments. Stravinsky's *Histoire du Soldat* was such a work and so was Milhaud's *La Création du Monde*. Manuel de Falla's Harpsichord Concerto dates from the same period, and in its modest contrast of two strings and three woodwinds against the newly revived harpsichord tone, we get an offshoot of the new sonorous vitality and a new tonal landscape."[6]

It is of some interest, and not merely an aside, that Copland specifies the names of Stravinsky, Milhaud, and Manuel de Falla, but fails to mention the name of African American Lt. James Reese Europe, the renowned leader of the 369th United States Infantry Band during World War I. Perhaps it was Copland's greater interest in modern classical music. Nonetheless, it should be mentioned that Europe's all-black marching band, part of the 2,000-strong all-black 15th Regiment as it was first designated, was the first African American combat unit to set foot on French soil on New Year's Day 1918.[7] Lt. Europe brought jazz to France. It ultimately spread to many parts of Europe. Lt. Europe was also the first African American officer to lead troops into combat in the so-called Great War.[8] In 1919 upon returning to New York City, his "Hell Fighters Band" recorded twenty-four of his compositions and arrangements. Tragically, on May 9, 1919, during the intermission of a concert, his twenty-four-year-old drummer, Herbert Wright, knifed him in anger, and Europe subsequently died.[9]

As early as 1922, journalist Burnet Hershey, writing in the *New York Times Book Review and Magazine*,[10] traced jazz around the globe from its meridian in Tin Pan Alley to such places as the Barbary Coast in San Francisco to the Hawaiian Islands, Japan, the Philippines, Siam and India, Egypt and Palestine, Monte Carlo and the French Riviera, and China.

Hershey points out that "Jazz follows the flag. [Steam]Ships freighted with jazz—'Made in America'—form the newest product of export to the Orient. Cargoes of jazz are laden on all vessels passing through the Golden Gate. To the Orient they sail, carrying the jazziest song hits, the latest dance steps and the phonograph records."[11] With particular reference to China, Hershey observes:

Jazz is the new idol in China, the new joss, especially the cymbal and cow-bell part, so similar to their tinny music. The Temple of Temples where his Pagan Highness King Jazz is worshiped in the Orient is Shanghai—"Paris of the East." There is the exotic atmosphere of the gay and cosmopolitan, in that city which is a mixture of the familiar and the strange, jazz has come to mean Shanghai. Shanghai without jazz, without its night clubs, without its ballrooms crowded with diplomats, business men, tourists and that ever picturesque rabble of European fortune hunters, adventurers and derelicts cluttering the gay cities of the East, would not be Shanghai. Jazz is the very essence of its existence. An American post office, an American Tribunal of Justice, American banks and shops, a real soda fountain and a place where they serve honest-to-goodness griddle cakes—and jazz. With it all the fascination of Chinatown and a good measure of Paris, and do you wonder why no one is homesick in Shanghai?[12]

Hershey adds, "The sale of American jazz records in the Far East is enor-mous,"[13] and "Jazz has now supplanted a number of peculiarly Chinese vices. It is 'all the rage.' If you've heard the crash of Chinese cymbals and tintin-nabulation of their gongs, you will understand the popularity of jazz."[14]

SHANGHAI'S DANCE HALLS: WHERE DECADENT MUSIC WAS PLAYED

Hershey's description of jazz as an integral element of life in Shanghai in the 1920s is echoed by Stella Dong's "biography" *Shanghai, 1842–1949*. Ac-cording to Dong, "There were all kinds of nightclubs. Some were posh and expensive, like the ornately decorated Majestic Cafe with its high chande-liers, polished dance floor, and 'American' orchestra as opposed to the Rus-sian or Filipino musicians who performed elsewhere. . . . At the Canidrome, right across from the dog-racing track, patrons could dance and watch greyhounds at the same time."[15]

It was at the Canidrome that American trumpeter Buck Clayton and his fourteen Gentlemen of Harlem performed from 1934 to 1936. The band split up there; Clayton stayed on until he earned enough money to return to the States, where he joined Count Basie's band. Another American, Va-laida Snow, the most widely traveled jazz woman of the prewar years, trav-eled from Sweden to Shanghai and hit a lot of stops in between. When her fellow trumpeter Buck Clayton spent two years in Shanghai in the mid-thirties—at the instigation of pianist Teddy Weatherford, who had been bouncing around Asia for years, and would spend his final years playing in India—he found that Snow had taught some Shanghai chefs how to cook soul food. All three African American jazz musicians are covered in the next chapter.

In 1923 a number of foreign- and Chinese-owned radio stations in the city began to broadcast jazz for their listeners, and the bouncy music was being played in the foreign clubs and cafés. Western social dance parties were being held among Shanghai's foreign residents as early as the 1850s, but they did not catch on among the Chinese until the prosperous 1930s, largely pushed by Chinese students who attended Western schools. Clearly, from its beginnings in New Orleans, in the 1920s jazz swept across the world like wildfire, including China.

The Chinese/American jazz relationship had a reverse flow. There is evidence that not only China, but also the entire Orient had some influence in the United States in the early part of the twentieth century on the naming of jazz songs, for example, "Shanghai Shuffle," which Louis Armstrong performed and recorded with the Fletcher Henderson band in 1924. Hershey refers to this as Tin Pan Alley exoticism and Orientalism, pointing to such songs as "The Sheik of Araby" (1921), "Hindustan" (1918), "The Japanese Sandman" (1920), "In a Persian Market" (1920), "China Boy" (1922), and R. H. Bauer's "China Lullaby" (1919).

JAZZ AND THE DANCE HALLS: FROM THE CHINESE PERSPECTIVE

All the above descriptions of early jazz in Shanghai, of course, have a strong "Western" influenced perspective. By strong contrast, Da Ren Zheng, double bass player in the Jimmy King Band—one of the all-Chinese jazz bands to form in Shanghai in the 1940s (see chapter 6)—has written about the evolution of jazz in Shanghai in the 1920s–30s. His "on the ground," firsthand recollections of the jazz scene in Shanghai in the first half of the twentieth century are clearly from a unique Chinese perspective.[16]

For example, his description of the emergence of jazz in New Orleans in the early part of the twentieth century is informed, if somewhat stereotypical, i.e., blacks have rhythm, they can "swing"; whites don't. He writes:

Jazz is the folk music of the U.S., originating from the early African American slaves. Jazz was born in the early twentieth century at the river mouth of the Mississippi River in New Orleans where brass bands flourished. At the very beginning, there were only bands organized by migrating European white men, and later afterwards some blacks who won their freedom from the civil war, organized their own bands, who performed for their black siblings. However, beyond expectations, these black bands brought a fantastic feeling of swing that the white bands lacked. The music performed by these black bands had a very strong rhythm so that people who were listening to the music could not control themselves in dancing with joy. And then some white American musicians learnt and utilized the features of this black music and they combined these features with traditional European harmony and musical forms (these whites all received formal musical training). Therefore, this unique American jazz music occurred. Shortly, this new style of jazz became fashionable in the U.S. and even all over the world. In the 30s, it reached the foreign concessions of Shanghai in our country.[17]

Da Ren Zheng then describes in detail the emergence of jazz in Shanghai. His account goes beyond the generalized overviews provided by Dong and Hershey. His recollections are an in-the-trenches account from an indigenous musician:

In the 1930s, in the old concessions of Shanghai, the commercial market was already very prosperous, where merchants at home and abroad gathered and the market was extremely bustling, especially in the area of Waitan (Shanghai Bund on the Huangpu River). Many business ships came and went frequently from every country. Also, warships, which were used to invade China, of foreign imperialists were often seen in the Huangpu River; and many foreign crew members and warship sailors drank and amused themselves when they came on land. Hence, this brought about the growth of bars along the Waitan which were used to satisfy the recreation activities of these foreign seamen ashore.

Zhu Baosan Road was a small road closest to the shore in the early years. It was between the Yan'an East Road and the Jinling East Road of today. It was no longer than 100 or 200 meters (today's Henan South Road). In actuality, "Zhu, Baosan" was the name of a fake wealthy merchant in the French Concession—in fact he was the head of the local criminal syndicate. This road used his name. On this short and small road, every landlord, large and small, in order to gain the seamen's money, set up a great many bars, selling wines and running pornographic business. Most of these bars had music. No matter if it was records or piano solo or band ensemble, they invariably played the popular American jazz of the time. This was the beginning of the inroads of jazz into Shanghai. In those days, the bars along Zhu Baosan Road all employed bar girls to dance with the foreign seamen, so that the accompanying music had to be bu-lu-si or jitterbug ("Jitterbug was called the seaman's dance" came from this). It was inevitable that jazz prevailed in the bars of Zhu Baosan Road.

The earliest musicians of jazz music playing in the bars of Zhu Baosan Road were gypsies or Jews, and some Westerners. All of them came to Shanghai—which was called an "adventurer's playground" in the early twentieth century—to make a living. They were wandering artists and their skill level was very average. The bars were quite small; no more than one or two rooms. The bands were no more than three or four persons. What they played was early black jazz, which only depended on the main melody of a song and each person performed it freely—there was no music score. Everyone played extemporaneously. During the thriving period of the bars in Zhu Baosan Road, the noise lasted all through the night and people sang and danced rapturously. Moreover, due to the rustic and coarse behavior of the seamen, they often went insane after getting drunk and became violent in order to fight for the Bar Girls' favor. Zhu Baosan Road became an ugly symbol of the darkest and dirtiest of colonized Shanghai. It was a place where no decent Shanghai citizen would consider going for a moment.

Later, comparatively larger size jazz bands and cafes grew up along Sichuan North Road and Nanjing Road, which needed larger bands of jazz. The band members of Zhu Baosan Road bars sought jobs in these larger bands. The bars of Zhu Baosan Road began to decline and in the end were eclipsed.

The growing popularity of jazz in Shanghai, beyond the Zhu Baosan Road bars and the concomitant "bar girls," was also to be found in the more elite dance halls in the city. This demand gave rise to a supply of jazz musicians—not only from the United States, but also from many parts of Asia and Europe. It also fostered a demand for "black jazz musicians" lured by the prospect of steady work and the absence of racism.

CHAPTER 5

International Jazz Musicians Flock to Shanghai: 1920s–1930s

Bassist Da Ren Zheng describes the rise of the dance halls that in turn result in the prominence of a large number of foreign, i.e., Western, jazz musicians. For example:

> Soon after the bars of Zhu Baosan Road were founded, dance halls and cafes, like mushrooms after the rain, arose to a great number in the foreign concessions. The several earliest dance halls were established, including "Yipin Xiang" which was along Yuqiaqing Road (today's Tibet Road) and close to Nanjing Road, "Juelu" dance halls, "Moon Palace (yue gong)" on Sichuan North Road, and "Great China (da hua)" dance halls; and then there were dance halls as an attached institution of big companies or big hotels, for example, the "Dadong Dance Hall" inside the Yong'an Company (today's Hualian commercial building), and the "Yangtze Dance Hall" inside the Yangtze Hotel. Shortly, a group of dance halls of grand scale and resplendent décor arose in the vicinity of Jing'an Temple Road (today's Nanjing West Road). Four of famous dance halls included the "Baile men," "Xian yue," "Li du," and "Da du hui." Of lesser importance was the "Da Hu," "Xin Xian lin," "Gao shi man," "Wei an si [Venus]," "Mi gao mei," and "Wei ye na [Vienna]."[1]

According to Da Ren, there were around fifty to sixty establishments in total. All these dance halls needed to hire jazz bands to accompany social dances (dance of social intercourse), but at that time in Shanghai there were almost no Chinese jazz musicians, so a great number of foreign jazz musicians were contracted to play in Shanghai. The large-scale dance hall jazz bands were made up of around ten to fifteen people, and even small-size dance halls had five or six members. In a few years, more than five hundred foreign musicians had surged into the Shanghai concessions. This huge contingent played jazz music day and night so that the entertainment life of Shanghai people was influenced unconsciously. "People began to understand the subtleties of the music," Da Ren recounted.

THE FILIPINO BANDS DOMINATE

The Paramount in Shanghai, the largest dance hall in the Far East, and Ciros, then owned by Victor Sassoon, hosted these jazz bands. The music of choice was American jazz. There were many Gypsy, Austrian, Jewish, and Russian jazz bands, but the most popular bands were the Filipino bands. The demand was for either American bands, particularly "black" bands, or Filipino bands. The Philippines, of course, was close to China geographically. Moreover, the 1898 Treaty of Paris between Spain and the United States following a war between these two countries, negotiated on terms favorable to the United States, allowed it temporary control of Cuba, and ceded ownership of Puerto Rico, Guam, and the Philippine islands. Consequently, Filipinos learned not only English, but also about jazz from American soldiers before and during World War II.

According to the Filipino Music Collection of FHL,

Jazz music came to the Philippines in 1921, with the help of a Cebuano named Luis Borromeo. Upon returning from a trip to the United States and Canada, he renamed himself Borromeo Lou, formed a jazz band, and brought the "American-style stage entertainment" of "Classic-Jazz Music" to the country. He became known as the Philippine "King of Jazz." Meanwhile, the 1920s was known as the "golden age" of jazz. It was then that American military troops introduced jazz music to the Philippines. They brought with them phonographs with 78-rpm discs of the blues and early jazz music. During this decade, vaudeville and jazz shows became popular forms of entertainment in the country.

In the 1930s, Filipinos danced to swing music performed by jazz dance bands in dance halls around the country. Jazz was played during social events and fiestas, and was widely heard on local radio. Popular bands during this period included the Shanghai Swing Masters, Pete Aristorenas Orchestra, Cesar Velasco Band, Tirso Cruz Orchestra, Mabuhay Band, and Mesio Regalado Orchestra.[2]

According to Filipino author Richie C. Quirino, son of Carlos Quirino, noted Filipino writer and historian, "One of the most notable musicians to ply the Shanghai route in the early thirties was trumpeter Apolo Dila. Born in Sta. Cruz, Laguna, Apolo, the eldest of the boys, belonged to a fairly large family that consisted of seven girls and six boys. . . . Apolo was the first to play jazz and the first to travel overseas for a couple years in Shanghai where Filipino musicians were much in demand. . . . According to [fellow musician] Angel Peña, Apolo was the best jazz trumpet player in the late 1930s [in Shanghai]. Angel had the opportunity to play by his side which Apolo managed, called the Shanghai Swing Masters [mentioned above]. . . . Apolo passed away after World War II."[3]

The Philippines was not far from Shanghai. Musicians could easily "jump ship" through Hong Kong. Large numbers of them surged into Shanghai, so that they were able to make the Shanghai dance halls their territory.

According to Da Ren, among these many Filipino bands,

The Tang qiao si Band of Li du Garden Dance Hall, the Luo ping Band of Xian Yue Dance Hall, and the Kang tuo cai la si Band of Mi gao mei Dance Hall were the best known (jazz dance bands were customarily named after the bandleader). The Tang qiao si Band at "Li du Dance Hall" was broadcast live every night on the private "Ya-mei" Telephone Company and citizens could easily listen to the jazz performed by the Tang qiao si Band via their radios at home. The Tang qiao si's performance was very famous in the entertainment industry of Shanghai because Luo ping himself was an excellent guitar player and singer, whose singing and playing were very well received. "Xian Yue" hired Yao Li, the popular singer of the time as well. The Luo ping Band of Xian yue Dance Hall came to enjoy a very high reputation in the entertainment world of Shanghai. Regarding the Kang tuo cai la si Band of "Mi gao mei" Dance Hall, Kang himself was a high-level musician of heiguan, a "black pipe" (jazz clarinet). The 12-member jazz band led by him was mostly composed of young musicians of high-level skills who could perform many extremely difficult American jazz melodies, and thus they found a good reception among customers. Also this band had a very good Filipino singer, called An-pei-la. This female singer was of a high level, her range encompassed three octaves, from the coloratura soprano of the famous "The Garden that was Kissed" dance melody, "The Blue Duo-ni River (Blue Danube)" to many American popular jazz tunes. She could sing them all without effort (with ease), and her presence on the stage was good. The Kang tu cai la si Band became the best known (most famous) in the popular music world (circles) of Shanghai.[4]

OTHER NATIONALITIES POUR IN

According to Da Ren, among professional musicians in Shanghai, aside from Filipinos, the others were Jews, gypsies, and a few Europeans like Hungarians and Czechs. There were also White Russians (Russians who fled from Soviet Union after the Russian Revolution in 1917). Two require mention: Oleg Lundstrem and Sergei Ermolaeff.

Oleg Leonidovich Lundstrem (also spelled Lundstroem, Lundström, April 2, 1916, Chita—October 14, 2005, near Moscow) was a Soviet and Russian jazz composer and conductor of the Oleg Lundstrem Orchestra, one of the earliest officially recognized jazz bands in the Soviet Union (full official name: The State Oleg Lundstrem Chamber Orchestra of Jazz Music, Russian):

> Lundstrem was born to a family of musicians in Chita (Siberia). His family moved to Harbin, China when he was five. In 1935, inspired by Duke Ellington's "Dear Old Southland" record which he occasionally purchased in Harbin for a private party, Lundstrem joined forces with eight other young Russian amateur musicians and formed the Oleg Lundstrem Orchestra. In 1936, the band moved to Shanghai, where they immediately became popular among the public. Until 1947, the band was an important part of the Shanghai jazz scene, along with the Buck Clayton Orchestra.
>
> After World War II, in 1947, Lundstrem returned to the Soviet Union and settled in Kazan, where he worked as a violinist in the opera and ballet theatre, while keeping his jazz orchestra as a side act. In 1956, the Oleg Lundstrem Orchestra moved to Moscow; Lundstrem was appointed by the Soviet cultural authorities as the orchestra's art director and conductor. In 1994, the Guinness Book of Records recognized the Lundstrem band as the oldest continuously existing jazz band in the world. In 1998, he was awarded the Russian Federation State Award. He died at the age of 89 from natural causes at his home in the village of Valentinovka, Moscow suburbs, and was buried at the cemetery of the Obraztsovo village, Moscow suburbs.[5]

Sergei Ermolaeff was a Manchurian-born, Russian jazz orchestra leader. In China, Sergei worked as a drummer/musician, building a reputation as one of Shanghai's more notable orchestra leaders during the 1930s and 1940s. While experiencing the onset of the Communist Revolution in China, Sergei and his wife Xenia (a singer/dancer) and son Serge Jr. won passage on the Chan Sha ship migrating to Australia in 1951.[6] Ermolaeff had performed at the Paramount Ballroom and played at the wedding of Generalissimo Chiang Kai-shek at the Majestic Hotel in 1927 with his friend, drummer and band leader Whitey Smith.[7]

THE AMERICAN JAZZ MUSICIANS

Whitey Smith (Sven Eric Heinrich Schmidt) was reportedly the earliest American to play in Shanghai; he arrived in 1922. A drummer of Danish heritage, he wrote a book, *I Didn't Make a Million*, of his exploits in Shanghai and his internment by the Japanese in the Philippines. Other Americans jazz musicians traveled to China, especially Shanghai. These African American musicians were motivated to perform in the diaspora because of rampant racism in their own country. Among them were pianist Teddy Weatherford, trumpeter Valaida Snow, and trumpeter Buck Clayton.

DRUMMER WHITEY SMITH: "I DIDN'T MAKE A MILLION"[8]

The story of drummer Whitey Smith in the context of jazz in China is significant if for no other reason than it spans several decades: from 1922 when he arrived in Shanghai, to his incarceration by the Japanese after he and his wife fled to the Philippines during World War II. But his story has other importance: he was one of the first Western jazz musicians, let alone an American, who brought jazz and Western-style dance music to China, specifically Shanghai. He provided the house band for the wedding of Generalissimo Chiang Kai-shek and the American-educated daughter of a Chinese-Methodist minister, Miss Soong Mei Ling. The two were married on December 1, 1927, with the second half of the wedding held Chinese-style in the Majestic Hotel. Thirteen hundred guests were invited and thousands of people crowded the streets in hopes of seeing the proceedings. Smith played "Here Comes the Bride," "I'll Be Loving You Always," and "A Love Nest for Two," among other tunes.[9] His descriptions of life in Shanghai also provide a panorama of the social milieu of the time. His story is one of ambition, tenacity, and survival against the backdrop of historical events in China and the Philippines before, during, and after World War II.

Whitey Smith was born in Vejle, Denmark, on September 14, 1897. His father, a cabinetmaker, immigrated to San Francisco, and sent for his wife and three sons in 1906. After the great earthquake in San Francisco, the family moved to Oakland, California, where Smith was raised.

Smith's musical education began with piano lessons before his family realized his natural talent for drumming. His father took his "last sixty-five dollars over and above his beer money to buy me a set of drums,"[10] Smith recalled. He began taking jobs as a drummer around town right as "jazz was just beginning to get a toe hold" and Smith "got a head start on what was later to be popular." He left home to live on his own and was soon asked to play in bigger and better places, even with combos and small bands. "I drummed every night and began developing innovations in my style and learning new songs."[11] Another hobby of Smith's during childhood was fighting, which is how he received his nickname, Whitey Smith. His boxing career did not last long, though, and soon Smith was working as a bartender, waiter, bouncer, and drummer in a town close to Oakland.

In 1922 Smith was in San Francisco playing drums at both Tait's, across from the Orpheum Theatre, and its upstairs place, the Little Club. "The two jobs were a lot of fun but neither one was a sure thing because of prohibition [...] So when I got up each morning I was always wondering whether I would have one job, two jobs or no job at all at the end of that day,"[12] he said. Smith noticed a newcomer among the clientele during his act who later introduced himself as Louis Ladow, owner of the Old Carlton Café in Shanghai, China. "How would you like to come to Shanghai and work for me?" Ladow said to Smith. "Just like that. He proceeded to offer me a year's contract, complete with passage over and back. Just like that I said I'd take it."[13]

He and his first wife, Florence, boarded the SS *Nile* steamship and sailed westward through the Golden Gate on August 24, 1922. On September 14— Smith's birthday—Mr. and Mrs. Whitey Smith steamed up the Woosung River into Shanghai harbor and tied up at the Merchants Wharf.

Smith recalled that the first night in China made them feel like Hollywood celebrities. They were wined, dined, and treated as if they were the greatest thing that happened to Shanghai in years. Ladow's place, the Old Carlton, according to Smith was a ramshackle two-story building by day, but by night it had glamour. Because the Chinese hadn't learned to dance Western-style, the clientele was strictly foreign.[14]

When he arrived there were already six men in the band and Smith was later made the leader. He made many changes, including bringing in new musicians, mostly from San Francisco.

Ladow opened the New Carlton, located across the street from the Shanghai Race Track, in December 1922. "It was a mammoth thing, beautifully appointed and many years ahead of its time. Inside was a huge night club. Adjoining it on the Nanking Road side was a super-plush dining room. Adjoining that was the Carlton movie theatre,"[15] Smith said.

The band opened with a tremendous show but the crowd ultimately could not support the overhead and the New Carlton eventually closed, breaking Ladow financially.

Without the New Carlton, Smith did not have money to pay his first-class band. Soon, however, Hongkong & Shanghai Hotels, Limited—which controlled the top-level hotel business throughout China—offered Smith and his band a job playing in the Peacock Grill Room at the Astor House in Shanghai. They happily accepted.

Hongkong & Shanghai Hotels had big plans of turning the McBain mansion into a new hotel—called the Majestic Hotel—with a three-million-dollar ballroom big enough to accommodate eighteen hundred people. Smith worried that Hongkong & Shanghai Hotels were making the same mistake that Ladow made by opening an overly grandiose and excessively expensive ballroom:

> The ballroom was goldleaf and marble in the shape of a four-leaf clover with a huge fountain in the middle. There were two-inch Peking carpets covering the table area. Murals and ceilings were done by famous artists of Italy and France. [. . .] Who was going to support this big layout? The foreigners in Shanghai and the tourist trade certainly were not enough to pay off even the investment. I told Mr. Taggert [the managing director] that without a doubt he had built the world's most beautiful ballroom, but if China didn't learn to dance and begin to patronize us, he had just buried three million dollars. Mr. Taggert told me with a quick parry and thrust—that was my responsibility.[16]

Smith, unsure of what to do, settled for many things bizarre with plenty of novelties, including, for example, building a miniature train to run around the ballroom. As Smith stood out in front of the band swinging a red lantern calling out the names of Chinese stations, the musicians rendered choo-choo effects in the background.

He eventually received advice from a friend of his, General William in the Chinese Army. He told Smith that if he wanted to bring more Chinese, he was going to have to play music that the Chinese understood. "The Chinese ear," he said, "is educated only for melody. You must get that modern deep harmony out of your music and stay more with the melody."[17] Smith took his advice.

Although Smith described the new process as "monotonous torture," they stuck with it and eventually more Chinese came. The band, however, did not play only Chinese music; they alternated between Chinese music and their usual tunes—"The Charleston," "Singing in the Rain," "Stumbling All Around," "Somebody Loves Me," etc.—and "gradually got something of a dance beat into them." The Majestic Ballroom began to pack to capacity—1,800 people, with usually about 400 waiting outside to get in. Writer Pearl Buck, according to Smith, apparently remarked to some of her friends that Whitey Smith had brought more good will to China than many an ambassador. He had taught China to dance.[18]

In February 1929, Smith's wife Florence died. "I knew she hadn't been well since her brief recovery on our trip back to the States, but . . . well it kind of cut the ground out from under me."[19]

Smith's band provided some solace. The band's music was featured in a movie showing the Chinese dancing to the latest American music. Smith made a Victor record of it and sold thousands to the Chinese. The band also made records for local companies every now and then as well. Smith was doing well: "The stock market was crashing in the States, but I still had my band earning a good salary and only the death of my wife to cast a pall over my life. My heart wasn't in my work."[20]

Suddenly, however, the Majestic Hotel was scheduled for sale. "I had two months' notice, six months' pay, and first class transportation back to the United States," Smith said. Not wanting to return home to the States, Smith was offered a contract to play a Japanese chain of theatres. Smith believed that the band was going to go with him; however, he soon learned that most of his bandmates had contracted with the new owners of the Majestic Hotel to stay in Shanghai. When he learned of the double-crossing scheme, Smith fired his disloyal members.[21]

Little did anyone know, however, a war would soon develop. "In September came what the newspapers called the 'Manchurian Incident.' It was some incident. [. . .] My friend J. B. Powell always claimed that was the real beginning of World War Two. However that may be, it eventually ruined the Cinderella Club," Smith recalled. According to Smith, the US government ordered in the 31st Infantry from Manila to help protect the foreign settlement, and business just about had to shut up shop all over the city. A curfew was set at 9:00 p.m. lasting until dawn. When the curfew was lifted after about four months, "business was pretty well shot," Smith admitted. He handed over the club and Arthur's financial obligations to a Chinese caterer in town and walked out.

After a brief stint opening and abandoning another Shanghai nightclub, a short-lived gig in Tokyo, and a transitory flirtation with the prospect of getting rich from synthetic gasoline, Smith moved out into the French Concession and lived in an attic room of a boarding house. He could not pay his rent and was close to being evicted. That night Smith ran into Joe Grove, Smith's Burma oil friend. Joe, sensing Smith's burden, gave Smith $4,500. Smith moved into the best hotel in Shanghai with all the trimmings.

Smith's band was called to perform at the Edgewater Mansion Hotel, a summer resort that was opening in Tsingtao up the coast from Shanghai. However, this gig did not last long either. "The hotel was too modern and too big for a resort season of two months a year," Smith said.

Smith returned to Shanghai, released his band and went to work at the New Paramount nightclub as a master of ceremonies. It was there that Smith met his second wife, Helen.[22]

Smith then went to Chefoo, a US naval base, with a four-piece combo for a new venue called the St. George's, owned by Jimmy James. Helen eventually joined him and worked as a dancer at another venue. They travelled again to Shanghai, where Smith played with his band in another venue owned by James, also called the St. George's. "The Shanghai St. George's was a success because the band was pulling them in. We were on the air every night since Jimmy had his own radio station, RUOK."[23]

The Paramount Night Club in Shanghai asked Smith to move his band over to their place, and Smith accepted the offer. "We did well at the Paramount, but there was talk of war with Japan and everybody, including Whitey Smith, had the jitters," Smith said. Helen was offered to go with a show to Manila and Smith encouraged her to go. Smith himself opened up another club, the Little Club, at Chefoo. "Everything started out with a bang—and everybody told me that I was sure to make a million."[24]

Smith recollected one night that changed everything:

One night when the Little Club was really jumping a flash came over the air, "Shanghai Bombed Thousands killed." It was 1937, Bloody Saturday. Some scared Chinese pilot started out to drop bombs on the Japanese warships . . . lying in the Whangpoo River. [. . .] I held on for a couple of months. One day I received a letter from Helen. She told me, "Darling, come to Manila. Everybody here knows you and anyway it's better to be in Manila than Shanghai in case of war. The Americans are here."[25]

Unsure of how to get to Manila, Smith prayed for guidance. The next day, the American consul notified Smith that Americans would be evacuated— to either the United States or to Manila. He chose Manila and one week later, he left on the USS *Chaumont*.

After arriving in Manila and reuniting with Helen, the two had no choice but to turn themselves in at the Los Baños internment camp where they were mistakenly identified as missionaries by the Japanese, who by this time had conquered the Philippines. They boarded trucks and headed to Santo Tomas Internment Camp, where they spent the next three years as prisoners of the Japanese.

After his three-year sojourn in a Japanese camp during the war, Smith delved back into the club/restaurant business, operating a place called Town's Tavern—at 507 United Nations Avenue—at least into the early 1970s. He ultimately sold the restaurant. It was later converted into a bank. He also published another book, *Whitey of Shanghai*, in 1966.[26]

Whitey Smith died in the Philippines in 1972. He was seventy-five years old.[27] What happened to his wife Helen has not yet been determined, despite several attempts to ascertain this information through the American embassy in Manila.

AFRICAN AMERICANS IN THE DIASPORA, INCLUDING CHINA

White American jazz musicians were not the only ones lured to China during this time. In no small measure, racism in the United States was the push that motivated numerous African Americans to cross the Pacific to Asia and China, specifically. In the preface to Dr. Larry Ross's book *African American Jazz Musicians in the Diaspora*, Professor Kirk Anderson (English, Lincoln University) writes:

the first nationally recognized New Orleans jazz band, the so-called Original Dixieland Jazz Band, was oddly all-white. Fletcher Henderson, the Black composer who pioneered swing music, privately sold scores to Paul Whiteman, the popular [white] radio bandleader whose color made these hot new rhythms palatable to [white] audiences across America. The African American William Grant Still labored in anonymity while

George Gershwin built on his work to compose Broadway musicals. Gershwin could incorporate blues rhythms and Negro characters into his classic American opera *Porgy and Bess* while just a few years earlier Scott Joplin, the Black genius of ragtime, saw his own brilliant Negro folk opera *Treemonisha* languish for want of patronage.[28]

The list of African Americans who initially found rejection because of race in the United States but who found acceptance in Europe and Asia is extensive, not just in the early part of the twentieth century, but even after World War II. Among them are: James Reese Europe, Josephine Baker, Sidney Bechet, Dexter Gordon, Kenny Clark, Ed Thigpen, Lil Hardin Armstrong, Art Farmer, Albert Ayler, Dr. Nathan Davis, Benny Carter, Garvin Bushell, Doc Cheatham, Don Byas, GiGi Gryce, James Moody, Tadd Dameron, Roy Eldridge, Dickie Wells, Kenny Clarke, Donald Byrd, Bud Powell, Kenny Drew, Johnny Griffin, Donald Bailey, Teddy Weatherford, Valaida Snow, and Buck Clayton.[29]

While ultimately becoming the United States' popular music in the second quarter of the twentieth century through the end of World War II, with both all-white and all-black big bands in the forefront—such as those of the Dorsey Brothers, Benny Goodman, Glenn Miller, Artie Shaw, Woody Herman, Duke Ellington, Count Basie, Cab Calloway, Lionel Hampton, and many others—the fact remains that even though jazz was the music of the land, blacks could perform at Harlem's Cotton Club in New York City, but couldn't enter as patrons. Even well into the second half of the twentieth century, particularly in the South, African American jazz musicians still felt the sting of segregation, even though their skill and performance acumen were superior in many cases to white jazz musicians.

In the conclusion to *African American Jazz Musicians in the Diaspora*, author Ross states: "jazz will never again dominate America's musical culture; however, it will certainly survive in the diaspora as a highly respected genre, its creators becoming legends and role models for jazz praxis."[30]

Ross's perspective that racism in the United States in the first half of the twentieth century was a major factor in pushing African Americans out of their native land and into the diaspora—in the context of this volume, Asia and especially China—is nowhere more evident than in the travels of such African American jazz musicians as pianist Teddy Weatherford, female trumpeter Valaida Snow, and trumpeter Buck Clayton. Clayton, in particular, experienced racism firsthand in China—not at the hands of the Chinese, but at the violent hands of American marines in Shanghai.

PIANIST TEDDY WEATHERFORD[31]

Teddy Weatherford (11 October 1903–25 April 1945), jazz pianist and bandleader, was born Theodore Weatherford at Pocahontas, Tazewell County, Virginia, the son of Jack Weatherford, a miner, and Kate Weatherford. In 1907 his father was severely injured in an explosion at the Landsberry Mine, and Teddy spent much of his childhood in the family of his married sister, Lovey Poindexter, in Bluefield City, Mercer County, West Virginia. He studied music at Bluefield State College and worked for about two years with the local Harry Watkins band.

In 1922 Weatherford moved to Chicago and soon joined trumpeter Jimmy Wade's band. From 1923 to 1925 the band was resident at the Moulin Rouge in Chicago, and was billed as Wade's Moulin Rouge Orchestra on three recording sessions for the Paramount label in 1923–24, which represent Weatherford's recording debut. In 1925–26 Weatherford worked with Erskine Tate's orchestra at the Vendome Theater in Chicago, recording with trumpeter Louis Armstrong in May 1926.

In August 1926, after a brief period as a solo pianist at the Dreamland in Chicago, Weatherford departed as a member of the drummer Jack Carter's band for an engagement at the Plaza in Shanghai. The engagement was extended from ten weeks to a year. Then in 1927–28 the band filled engagements in Surabaja and Batavia (now Djakarta) in the Dutch East Indies (now Indonesia) and in Singapore before returning to Shanghai. Weatherford stayed on in Shanghai, performing in a piano duo with the African American pianist Bill Hegamin before joining Balaleinikoff's Orchestra at the Carlton Palais de Danse. After playing with other dance bands, Weatherford took over a band formerly led by the California trumpeter Robert Hill for a residency at the Canidrome in Shanghai's French Settlement in 1929.

In late 1933 the management of the Canidrome sent Weatherford to the United States to recruit new talent. During his only return to his native country, Weatherford worked with Noble Sissle's band in Boston and recruited a band led by the trumpeter Buck Clayton to play at the Canidrome. Back in Shanghai, Weatherford played only as an intermission and concert pianist until August 1935, when he moved to the Raffles Hotel in Singapore.

The renowned "Harlem Renaissance" poet and novelist Langston Hughes visited Shanghai in 1934, and noted that while he never saw all there was to see in Shanghai—it was, of course, an "enormous city of almost four million people" (today it is closer to 24 million)—he did see "a great deal of it," including the Canidrome Gardens, where he met Weatherford, who was famously known as the head of the best American jazz band in the Orient:

> This group of Negro musicians at the Canidrome was known from Cal-cutta and Bombay through the Malay States to Manila, Hong Kong and Port Arthur. They were very popular in Shanghai, which seemed to have a weakness for American Negro performers. . . .
>
> Teddy could play some wonderful blues when he wanted to, but he had to be in the mood. He had played at the old Sunset in Chicago in the days when Louis Armstrong first came north from New Orleans, and he had played with Sidney Bechet, Noble Sissle and Eddie South, and had been all over Europe as well as Australia. But now the Far East was his personal stomping ground. Stiff-necked Britishers and Old China hands from Bombay to the Yellow Sea swore by his music. It was the best! A big, genial, dark man, something of a clown, Teddy could walk into almost any public place in the Orient and folks would break into applause.[32]

In October 1935 he joined the band of the expatriate African American trumpeter Crickett Smith for a season in Surabaja and returned with that band to its residency at the Taj Mahal Hotel in Bombay (now Mumbai). He appears on their only record, made in Bombay in late 1936.

In 1937 Weatherford visited France and Sweden. In September 1937 Weatherford returned to Bombay to become the leader of the band at the Taj Mahal, working also in Colombo, Ceylon (now Sri Lanka), and again at Surabaja in the summer of 1939. The band returned again to Colombo in 1940–41, but Weatherford left in September 1941 to move to Calcutta, India, where he performed at the Grand Hotel, first as a solo pianist but soon also as leader of the resident band. He was a fixture at the hotel until his death from cholera at the Presidency General Hospital in Calcutta, one of the first victims of an epidemic.

TRUMPETER VALAIDA SNOW[33]

Valaida Snow (2 June 1905–30 May 1956) was born in Chattanooga, Ten-nessee, into a large family of musicians. Her father was a performer, and her mother—who had trained at Howard University—taught Valaida and her three sisters, Layaida, Alvaida, and Hattie, and her brother, Arthur Bush, to play multiple instruments. Snow learned how to play cello, bass, violin, guitar, mandolin, harp, accordion, clarinet, saxophone, and trumpet, and was performing by the age of four. "It is easy to understand the reason for her later developing a sophisticated stage presence. She was an early pro," jazz historian Rosetta Reitz wrote.[34]

From 1930 to 1950, she toured and recorded frequently in the United States and Europe with her own bands and other bandleaders, including Count Basie, Willie Lewis, Fletcher Henderson, and Teddy Weatherford. Snow also regularly performed in the Far East with drummer Jack Carter's jazz octet, the Jack Carter Orchestra—Teddy Weatherford on piano—with her sister and singer Lavaida. Shanghai was a police state at the time—with Chiang Kai-shek, head of the military forces of China's ruling Kuomintang (KMT), massacring thousands of civilians suspected of Communist ties.[35]

According to Brendan I. Koerner's book *Piano Demon*, the band was protected by thousands of American and British troops and enjoyed lives of supreme comfort, "awash not in blood but in money generated by any number of shadowy schemes, notably the burgeoning opium trade." The Jack Carter Orchestra was among the many entertainments available to the foreign residents, or Shanghailanders. An account of their performance in *Piano Demon* reveals:

> Obsessed with hipness and style, the Shanghailanders fetishized black jazz musicians. The Jack Carter Orchestra thus commanded a handsome price for its show, which provided a slickly packaged taste of African American culture—or, more accurately, what foreigners expected African American culture to be. The show's star attraction was Valaida Snow, a 22-year old Tennessean trumpeter and singer who was widely considered the female Louis Armstrong. After belting out a version of "Ol' Man River," she would be joined onstage by a comedian named Bo Diddley, who would sling jokes before dueting with Snow on a song called "Black Bottom." Snow would then cap the evening with an early version of crowd surfing: at the end of a manic tap-dancing number, she would leap onto the dance floor, fall to her knees, and wriggle her way through the stunned audience. The routine rarely failed to bring down the house.[36]

After headlining at the Apollo Theatre in New York, Snow returned to Europe and the Far East to perform around the outbreak of World War II. She was arrested by the Germans for theft and misuse of drugs, and from 1940 to 1942 was held for eighteen months at the Nazi concentration camp Wester-Faengle. Although Snow resumed performing—and even married her second husband, producer Earl Edwards—after her release as an exchange prisoner in unstable health, the imprisonment greatly affected her physical and psychological health and led to her untimely death in New York City in 1956 of a cerebral hemorrhage.

TRUMPETER BUCK CLAYTON[37]

> I still say today that the two years I spent in China were the happiest two years of my life. My life seemed to begin in Shanghai.
> —BUCK CLAYTON, *BUCK CLAYTON'S JAZZ WORLD*

Wilbur "Buck" Clayton (12 November 1911–8 December 1991), trumpeter, composer, arranger, and bandleader, was born in Parsons, Kansas. He studied piano with his father at the age of six, and took up the trumpet at the age of seventeen. After playing in his church's orchestra and later moving to the West Coast to play in various bands, Clayton assembled a band of his own, and in 1934 brought the band to Shanghai to perform.[38] The band included Clayton (trumpets), Teddy Buckner, Jack Bratton, Happy Johnson, Duke Upshaw (trombones), Arcima Taylor, Caughey Roberts, Hubert Myers (saxophones), Eddie Beal (piano), Baby Lewis (drums), Frank Pasley (guitar), Reginald Jones (bass), and Joe McCutchin (violin). In Shanghai the band lived in an international settlement where most people were English, French, Russian, or American, and were introduced to many American musicians who showed them all the hot spots in Shanghai. Clayton's band was to play at the Canidrome Ballroom.

Clayton compared the first rehearsal to "being in a different world." He and the band met the other entertainers, including Teddy Weatherford, who would perform only one number with the band because Teddy Weatherford played at four different nightclubs each night. Weatherford's specialty with the band was *Rhapsody in Blue* and marked Clayton's first time directing a number. The band typically played classical music from 9:00–9:30 p.m. and then it was "back to Harlem."

Clayton recalled the band's first performance at the Canidrome as "fantastic" and said it was the first time the band was recognized and treated with a great deal of respect, even earning raves in all the Shanghai papers. However, after about a month of working in Shanghai, Clayton ran into American southern prejudice:

I happened to be walking down the street and they seemed to be looking for somebody. I wondered who they were looking for as nobody even mentioned that they were looking for someone. I just assumed that they were looking for some girls as they kept telling me to go home to Derb. I said, "No, whatever you guys are looking for I want to be in on it too." So I kept on with them. [. . .] I stayed with them until we turned a corner and I see about four rickshaws coming down the street with some white American marines in them. The next thing I heard was the white guys saying, "There they are. Niggers, niggers, niggers!" And before long one of them threw a brick that they had piled up in the rickshaws. [. . .] They jumped out of their rickshaws and soon fists were flying everywhere.

Fortunately, the incident did not affect the band's business at the Canidrome and they continued to perform.

The band was soon informed that a new act from Los Angeles was coming to Shanghai to perform with them at the Canidrome. They were glad to hear the news; however, when Clayton and the band members finally got a chance to see the new act, they were not impressed. "They were the raggedest bunch of guys we ever saw. One of them didn't even have a seat in his trousers," Clayton said. The new act was called the Chocolateers and consisted of three men, two of which Clayton knew: Esmond Mosby, who was related to the bandleader of the Curtis Mosby Blue Blowers, and a twelve-year-old boy named Gyp, who had a travelling show called Gibson's Hot Chocolate Box Revue. "The guys were so poor and raggedy that we had to lend them some of our costumes so they could make the first show. They had absolutely nothing and I don't know how they got booked over there in such bad condition," Clayton said.

The Five Hot Shots were the next group to join the band and were "really a first-class act," according to Clayton. Originating in New York, the Five Hot Shots had played in the major European cities—Paris, Vienna, and Cannes—and had worked with Louis Armstrong and Fats Waller. "I'll never forget the first time when I went to meet them at the club where they were working, the Paramount I believe. As I walked down the hall to their rooms all I could hear was trumpets and when they met me it wasn't long before we became real friends. Even today when there is only one of them left we are the greatest friends," Clayton remembered.

The band continued to be successful at the Canidrome but, to the band's surprise, they soon became "victims of one of the biggest frame-ups in theatrical history." The Hollywood Blondes, twelve blonde California girls were booked to play the Canidrome. They were quite talented and proved to be extremely popular, with most of Shanghai turning out to see them, including the French, English, Japanese, and Russians. The trouble began about a week after the opening of the Hollywood Blondes: "There were two little Russian girls in the audience and one asked me for my autograph. I signed my name on a piece of paper and gave it to her and then she jerked a monogrammed handkerchief out of my coat pocket that had my initials, B.C., on it along with an embroidered trumpet that I had made by a special seamstress." However, the next night:

> As the show was about to begin, I noticed these same two girls who had been there the night before and had taken my handkerchief, only this time they came in with a big guy. All three of them were showed to a table and the two girls sat down. The big guy didn't sit down but just stared at me. [. . .] He was looking at me with such hostility, no longer staring but now glaring. He was still standing and just as the Mistress of Ceremonies finished her introduction he crossed his arms and yelled out at me, "Turn your eyes the other way, you black son of a bitch." I was so surprised. The guy had said it in such a loud voice, such language in such an elegant club like this, and in front of so many respectable people. I could see he was a hoodlum. [. . .] I decided to go over to this cat's table and ask him what was wrong or ask him to go outdoors. Before I could get to his table he took a Sunday punch on me and hit me right between the eyes.

Soon the whole band had jumped off the stand and started fighting the man—named Jack Riley—and eventually Clayton was sitting on top of him and "trying to do as much bodily harm to him as I could." The next day, Clayton received a telegram saying that if he came to work that night he would be met with a hail of machine-gun bullets, and the band was eventually let go from the Canidrome. But Clayton and the band members could not return home right away because they had not saved their return fare and were therefore stranded in Shanghai. "I had paid some dues in my short life in show business but I had never paid those kinds of dues. Stranded half way around the world. Those were really some dues," Clayton said. While a few of the members were able to make it back to the United States with help from their families, Clayton and the remaining members were asked to open at another nightclub in Shanghai, the Casa Nova Ballroom—"not quite as elegant as the Canidrome but at least a job where we could prove ourselves."

Clayton and the remaining band members eventually saved their fare back home. "My biggest concern then was the Japanese Army. They were becoming more and more open in their contempt for the Chinese government and I saw many things that disturbed me," Clayton observed. He told his band members that they should all begin making preparations to return home because "Shanghai was going to explode and soon." Clayton booked passage home on a Japanese boat and less than two weeks after he left, the Japanese "sailed a warship right down the middle of Shanghai and bombarded the city on both sides."

The Japanese invasion of China—its unilateral earlier annexation of Manchuria notwithstanding—starting with Shanghai impacted white and African American jazz musicians alike, as chapter 7 attests to.

CHAPTER 6

The Formation of All-Chinese Jazz Bands

As chapter 3 mentions, "Express Train," written in 1928 by Li Jinhui, a pioneering composer often called the father of Chinese popular music, is performed on a recording by Zhou Xuan, the most famous chanteuse of the era. In the song, the train symbolizes rapid social change and satirizes the breathless pace of modern courtship by way of the story of a couple who are engaged, marry, and have two children—all within five minutes of having first met. Li Jinhui's music—influenced by his relationship with trumpeter Buck Clayton, who performed in Shanghai in the early to mid-1930s—was immensely popular. He composed hundreds of tunes.

His name resurfaces in the context of the current chapter. As author of *Yellow Music* Professor Andrew Jones reports:

> In 1935, Li was asked to organize a band for the dance hall at the Yangtze River Hotel by the notorious gangster (and erstwhile civic leader) Du Yuesheng. Du requested, and Li agreed, that the band be composed entirely of Chinese musicians—an unprecedented move when most bands were either imported from the United States (such as Buck Clayton's Harlem Gentlemen), or the Philippines, or were made up of White Russian émigrés. . . . The group, which Li called the "Clear Wind Dance Band" (Quingfeng wuyue dui), had a repertoire consisting of jazz versions of Chinese folk songs combined with the latest dance tunes and screen songs from the United States.[1]

The formation of the Clear Wind Dance Band is, therefore, reportedly the first instance of the formation of an all-Chinese-member jazz band. But this "history" is subject to some debate.

Shanghai-based double-bass player Da Ren Zheng—now in his nineties, an original member of the so-called Jimmy King band that successfully performed at the Paramount Ballroom in the 1940s, *the* dance hall in Shanghai—published a recollection of the jazz scene in Shanghai before and right after World War II and during Mao Zedong's era. It is one of very few firsthand accounts of that era with respect to jazz. In his account he recalls the formation of an all-Chinese-member jazz band, also in 1935.

What follows is his description of the evolutionary formation of all-Chinese jazz bands in this period. The detail provided by his narration is not only informative, but also highly credible if for no other reason than all other descriptions of this period with respect to jazz and the dance halls are told by non-indigenous Chinese writers, such as Andrew F. Jones in *Yellow Music*, Andrew David Field in *Shanghai's Dancing World*, even Stella Dong in *Shanghai*. All three volumes provide an excellent and highly detailed picture of this period and there is plenty of corroboration. On the other hand, Da Ren Zheng, while not an academic, provides detailed descriptions that have the strong ring of authenticity. He was in his late twenties and early thirties when these events took place. He was there observing these events unfold. His narration is first person, not based on secondary or tertiary sources.[2]

THE EARLY CHINESE JAZZ MUSICIANS

Da Ren Zheng writes:

> When jazz bands began to flourish in the dance halls (ballrooms) of Shanghai in the 1930s, the band members were mostly Filipinos, and there were almost no Chinese. Several years later, a few Chinese tried to have these foreign musicians to be their teachers from which they could learn the skills, because they realized the income and interests of the band musicians were very high. In this way, shortly, several Chinese musicians appeared in the dance hall bands, such as: the drummer Liang Min (he was invited to join the Shanghai Symphony in 1948, where he worked until the early '90s when he was retired and died); the trumpeters He Da and Zheng Guangwei (who later enrolled in National Music Academy); and saxophonists Zheng Rongchu and Qiu Zongliang, etc. After that, these Chinese musicians had their own disciples and developed into a second generation; and in this manner there were more and more Chinese jazz musicians.

YU YUEZHANG ORGANIZES THE FIRST ALL-CHINESE JAZZ BAND

According to Da Ren, Yu Yuezhang, who had studied in Japan, was the first person in Shanghai to organize a jazz band that only consisted of Chinese musicians. The original household of Yu was in Xiamen City, Fujian Province. He graduated from the Japan Tokyo Music College in 1926 and was employed by Xiamen University as a music professor.

A few years later, he came to Shanghai and became the chairman of the music department at Shanghai Arts Academy. There were so few students learning piano that his income was not enough to support his family. The career of musicians in dance halls of Shanghai-tan (the beach of Shanghai) was already quite prosperous. He found a teacher to learn about jazz piano, and thus made a living in the ballrooms playing jazz. In 1935 Yu Yuezhang gathered a group of Chinese musicians and organized the Yu Yuezhang Band, which performed at the Lao da hua Dance Hall, a third-rate ballroom run by a Japanese boss in Hongkou area. This was the earliest all-Chinese band in Shanghai-tan. There were nine musicians in the band: three saxophonists, two trumpeters, one trombonist, one pianist, a drummer, and bassist. Yu was both leader and pianist. Because the lower performing level of this Chinese band compared to the Filipino bands and the thoughts of worshiping everything foreign, the owners looked down upon Chinese musicians. That's why they could only work at the third-rate small dance halls, and did not have the opportunity to break into the first-class big dance halls. After the establishment of Yu Yuezhang's band, several other Chinese bands appeared. However, Chinese jazz bands were only a small proportion among the jazz bands in Shanghai in those years.

THE CANTONESE JAZZ BANDS EMERGE

Almost at the same time as the establishment of Chinese jazz bands, it suddenly became popular that some of the mid- and small-sized dance halls hired the "Cantonese music" bands. Da Ren adds:

These Cantonese music bands originated from the amateur Cantonese music communities. The members of these Cantonese music communities were mostly employees at foreign firms or small businessmen. They liked Cantonese music, so in their spare time from work they got together and organized the Cantonese music community in certain residences to entertain themselves. These were amateur organizations rather than professional groups. Around 1936 or so, in the area of Hongkou, there was a "Sanyu Cantonese Music Society" on Sichuan North Road. The scale of this community was bigger and the membership was larger, and its level of playing Cantonese music was higher too. Across the street from this society was the mid-level dance hall—"Yue gong Dance Hall (Moon Palace)." Coincidentally, "Sanyu Society" sent a Cantonese band, which was composed of several members, to perform in "Yue Gong Dance Hall" because the melodies of Cantonese music were graceful and the rhythm was light and quick. Their playing was perfect for the tastes of the Chinese dance customers. Compared with American Jazz, it was easier for dance customers to accept. Since then, this kind of Cantonese-music bands flourished among the small- and mid-sized dance halls of Shanghai-tan. In the dance halls, these Cantonese bands not only played "Canton Qing-music," such as "Every step higher" (bu bu gao), "Yuyue shengping" and "Wang Zhaojun," they also played the popular songs of the day such as "When will he come again?" "The Song Girl at the World's Edge," and "My Beloved Brother." They also hired singers to accompany the bands. Since then, popular Chinese songs of the 1930s and 1940s came to occupy a certain place in these dance halls, and the cooperation of these two trends became rooted in the entertainment world of Shanghai.

In 1942, among the many Cantonese band leaders there was one leader called Chen. He came up with the idea to establish a "new band." This "new band" was reorganized on the basis of the Cantonese music band. It abandoned the Canton instruments, like the erhu and dulcimer, and was changed to use the violin, accordion, guitar, banjo, harmonica, piano, drum, bass, and other instruments. It played the popular Chinese songs of the day to accompany dancing, mostly performing the extremely popular songs "The Moon Is Round, the Flowers Pretty," "Rose, Rose, I Love You," and "Picking Binlang." Many famous singers took their turns singing in this band. With these changes Chen's band was very well received, and became wildly popular at the large-scale Migaomei Dance Hall. Soon all of the other Cantonese bands met the demand of the owners of dance halls that they change themselves into the "New Style Band." A great many singers developed accordingly in the dance halls, and due to their singing, the popular songs which were performed by Zhou, Xuan, and Yao Li and other singers became more popular in society.

A TRANSITION AFTER WORLD WAR II

Da Ren recounts that when World War II ended in 1945, the economy of Shanghai was in overdevelopment:

> The marketers became unprecedentedly prosperous. Accordingly, the business of dance halls was more booming than before. At this time, American products were dumped into our country so that all of a sudden, Coca-cola, Hollywood movies, and jazz music were plentiful in Shanghai's markets. There were lots of scenes of the performance of the American jazz bands especially in the musical films shown in the Shanghai movie theaters. The movie interlude songs and American pop music arrived continuously. The dance hall bands in Shanghai performed the new-arrival pop music against each other, which made the Chinese of these "New Bands" feel that they were at the end of their rope and failed to secure a prominent place. However, these so-called "New Bands," the same as the Cantonese bands that were assembled on the spot, lacked a strict system and were mostly melodies played in unison that was simple and monotonous, compared to the jazz bands where the tunes were completely arranged. They lacked competitiveness, so their existence was threatened.

At this time, some "New Band" Chinese musicians who desired to do better began to seek teachers to learn about jazz band instruments. They learned about the five-line music staff and worked very hard, according to Da Ren. They changed from the Chinese "New Band" to properly trained jazz bands. A great number of Chinese jazz musicians were born from this change.

JIN HUAIZU, A.K.A. JIEMEI JIN, A.K.A. JIMMY KING'S BAND AT THE PARAMOUNT

Among these Chinese jazz musicians, there were three ensembles that were of better quality. The first was the Jiemei Jin Band, which played at Bai le men Dance Hall (also known as the famous Paramount dance hall). He was a college student in the science and engineering department at Shanghai Guanghua University. After graduation he was an officer in the bufang [=(old) a police station] of the foreign concessions. Because he loved music, he sought out Lo Ping, Filipino leader of the Xian Le Dance Hall, to learn about guitar and to sing popular songs. After that he joined the Lo Ping band as the guitarist and sang Hawaiian folk songs. The Bai Le Men owner admired him and hired Jin Jiemei to organize a Chinese band that played at his dance hall. In a short time, Jin gathered together a group of the best and relatively young Chinese musicians to form the Jiemei Jin Band, starting playing at the Bai Le Men, and played jazz in 1947. It also accompanied vocalists who sang popular songs at this dance hall. The performance of the Jiemei Jin Band at Bai Lo Men was very well received by customers and was an overnight success for the band. They became known as a Chinese band that could compete with Filipino bands in the Shanghai musical world. Besides the five years they played at Bai Le Men, they once played in other famous ballrooms, such as Da Du Hui, Xin Xian Bei, and Yi Yuan Hotel. The band was dismissed when the ballroom was closed in 1952, three years after Mao and the Chinese Communist takeover in 1949.

Joshua Shi, writing for the *Shanghai Star*,[3] provides another of the few accounts of Jimmy King, leader of one of the first all-Chinese jazz bands in China:

> After the war, jazz was all the rage along with flooding American goods. Most of the foreign jazz bands returned to their home countries—it was time for the Chinese to take up the horns. Jimmy King, or Jin Huaizu, a graduate of St. Johns University (Shanghai), was the most famous Chinese jazz player of his time. Born into a rich family, King was a young, handsome gentleman who spoke good English. He had learned his craft playing in Filipino bands and in 1947 he led the first Chinese jazz band to play at the Paramount. Most fans at that time were university students from St. Johns and University of Shanghai, and the Universite L'Aurora. Many were ardent fans of Jimmy King.

Da Ren Zheng, double bass player in the Jimmy King Band, recalls playing at the Paramount[4] with the legendary King: "The Paramount was the best dance hall in Shanghai, very high class. There were dancing girls, and all the businessmen and big bosses went there. Ordinarily, we weren't allowed in, but then we became band members. The boss and customers liked us, and our wages were very high. We played three hours a night. We were very happy."[5]

Zheng began playing violin and trumpet when he was in middle school, around 1941. With his father outside of the country at the time, Zheng was the man of the household and had to provide for himself, his mother and four younger siblings. During the day, Zheng took classes at the renowned Shanghai Conservatory of Music, later graduating in 1946: "At the Conservatory of Music, only one out of four musicians were Chinese. Everybody was from Russia, from Italy, from Europe, because this was a very famous conservatory. And everybody came from outside to learn music."

At night, Zheng played violin for money at the Paramount, the most popular dance hall in Shanghai at the time. It was at the Paramount that the Filipino Jazz Band—a band that played popular Chinese music at the venue—introduced Zheng to jazz music. Using American sheet music brought to Shanghai during World War II, Zheng and the Philippine Jazz Band would take turns listening to each other play. The Paramount marked Zheng's first real encounter with jazz music, other than from the movies and from 78 RPM recordings. A few years later, in 1947, the owner of the Paramount introduced Zheng to King, and the two men started to perform jazz together.

Zheng liked jazz because it was not easy to play: "Classical music and jazz you need a high expertise to play it well." He believes that his classical training helped his transition into jazz music: "The fundamentals are the same," he said. "Everything else is different, but the fundamentals are there."

The Jimmy King Band played from 8:00 p.m. to 11:00 p.m., and performed for two to three hundred people a night. They also played continuously, with no breaks. "Because there's many instruments and even a person singing," the members would alternate, Zheng said. Each member of the band made 300 yuan a month, which was considered very high—the most basic jobs at the time averaged about 100 renminbi.[6] They played popular American tunes: "Whatever people listened to," Zheng said.

The band performed for audiences that included "two kinds of people," Zheng said. "Business owners, people with a lot of money. They would bring someone to accompany them and dance with them. And then there were professionals: doctors, teachers, and students." Zheng remembers his time playing with the Jimmy King band as "really enjoyable," although when the war started, Zheng recalled, "everything kind of got depressing. And music wasn't the same anymore."

Even though the Japanese captured Americans and Europeans in 1942 in Shanghai, Zheng did not recall much interference with the band playing Western and American jazz music at the Paramount: "There were a lot of American movies and music. It was very popular. And a lot of American music had a lot of jazz in it," he said. "And that was a lot about entertaining. And it was dance music. So it was allowed," he added.

However, in 1951, six years after Japan's defeat in World War II, two years following Mao's defeat of the Nationalist Chinese, who fled to what is now Taiwan, and the Communists' assumption of the country's leadership, all Western music was stopped in China; the United States was now considered the enemy. "There wasn't any jazz music. Everything was shut down," Zheng recounted.

Zheng refers to this time as the "gap": "There were no American musicians between that gap. Everything closed. No American musicians. Only Chinese musicians—200 to 300 Chinese musicians during that time in that gap. They all found jobs, you know, to get through life." During the gap, Zheng introduced King to the double bass so he could perform and make a living, and Zheng himself played contrabass in the Shanghai Symphony Orchestra.

As for Jimmy King:

> In 1952, all dance halls in Shanghai were ordered closed and after only five years of playing, Jimmy King's band was dismantled. Some members were recruited into orchestras and became leading musicians of new China.[7] But Jimmy King could only make a living by teaching students at his home in Shanghai. Eventually, he was prevented even from doing this. He played guitar in the Anhui Provincial Song and Dance Troupe for a time, but was later sent to the countryside to work.
>
> In 1985, the owners of Jinling Hotel in Nanjing, an overseas returned Chinese couple who were Jimmy King fans, invited him to perform at the hotel. He lived and played there for three years, until Alzheimer's disease brought his career to an end. He retired to a friend's home in Zhangjia-gang, a county in Jiangsu, where he died later that year. However, the surviving members of Jimmy King's bands—Zhou Wanrong, Chao Ziping, [and Da Ren Zheng]—are among the Peace Hotel's Old Jazz Band.

The Huang Feiran Band

Zheng recalled two other bands of good quality, the Huang Feiran Band and the Kaixuan Band:

> Another relatively good Chinese band, formed in 1947 at the same time as the Jiemei Jin Band, was the "Huang Feiran Band" that played at "Wei ye na Dance Hall" (Vienna Dance Hall). Huang Feiran graduated from

the prestigious University of Shanghai—"St. John's University." He also studied voice and cello at Shanghai National Music Academy. He was a young musician of a fairly high artistic level. Although at the time the "Huang Feiran Band" was not as well known as "Jiemei Jin band," it was nonetheless a first-class Chinese jazz band, especially Huang Feiran himself, who used meisheng (bel canto) to perform Chinese and foreign popular songs, which was extremely well received. In 1949, on the eve of Shanghai's liberation, Huang Feiran left Shanghai and arrived in Hong Kong, where he became a governor of Hong Kong government.

The Kaixuan Band

The "Kaixuan Band" was also a relatively excellent Chinese band of that period. It was entirely composed of young musicians who came to Shanghai from Wuhan to make a living. In Wuhan they studied at the "Juyuan Music School" where they were taught to play jazz by foreign instructors. Thus their foundation of jazz knowledge was pretty good, plus they were not only colleagues but also classmates and from the same province, so their cooperation was very close. This band had been performing in the "Yangzi Hotel" dance hall all the year round. It was a popular Chinese band as well.

POSTSCRIPT

Zheng concludes:

During the years from 1945 to 1954, Chinese jazz bands grew rapidly so that there were as much as three or four hundred indigenous Chinese performing jazz. In 1949 after the country was "liberated," all of the ballrooms stopped doing business in 1954 because they were not in keeping with the political situation at that time. Musicians had to find out another way of living. Among them, those musicians in Jeimei Jin Band who were of a higher skill level enrolled into "Shanghai Symphony" as national cadres of literature and art [i.e., a government job]. Some people of the other bands enrolled in "opera" orchestras, the "Shanghai movie Band/Orchestra," the "Shanghai wind orchestra Band" (Shanghai guanyue tuan), and other specialized units as performers. Many other musicians with lower level skills gradually joined the acrobatic troupe of Shanghai and other cities or provinces as band accompanists. A few people tested into the song and dance ensemble of the army. After the new China was founded, most of them contributed something useful for the socialism cultural undertakings.

Mao's Communist Party takeover of China in 1949 resulted in the shutting down of all of China's dance halls and the suppression of jazz and all things Western. Ironically, the Japanese invasion of China (starting with Manchuria in 1931), particularly the shelling of Shanghai and larger invasion of China thereafter in 1937, would ultimately enhance the appreciation and embracing of jazz by the Japanese—even during the war.

CHAPTER 7

The Japanese Invasion

THE JAPANESE CAMPS

During World War II the Japanese constructed prisoner of war camps in fifteen countries, including the Philippines, Malaya/Singapore, Formosa (now modern Taiwan), North Borneo, Sarawak, Manchuria, the Dutch East Indies (now modern Indonesia), Thailand/Burma, New Guinea, Korea, Hong Kong, Japan, and, of course, China.[1] These camps numbered approximately 240.

The Japanese—whose attack on Pearl Harbor in 1941 brought the United States into World War II—saw their global role as manifest destiny, particularly with respect to China. Militarist Japan's attempt to conquer China began by seizing Manchuria in 1931 and became a full-fledged invasion from 1937 [when they attacked Shanghai] to 1945. Japanese historians saw Japan following in the footsteps of the Manchu conquerors of 1644, while Tokyo's modernizers saw Japan shepherding the Chinese people into the modern world.[2]

Mass killings committed by the Japanese military have been summarized as follows:

R. J. Rummel, a professor of political science at the University of Hawaii, states that between 1937 and 1945, the Japanese military murdered from nearly 3,000,000 to over 10,000,000 people, most likely 6,000,000 Chinese, Indonesians, Koreans, Filipinos and Indochinese, among others, including Western prisoners of war. . . . According to Rummel, in China alone, during 1937–45, approximately 3.9 million Chinese were killed, mostly civilians, as a direct result of the Japanese operations and 10.2 million in the course of the war. The most infamous incident during this period was the Nanking Massacre of 1937–38, when, according to the findings of the International Military Tribunal for the Far East, the Japanese Army massacred as many as 300,000 civilians and prisoners of war, although the accepted figure is somewhere in the hundreds of thousands. . . . In Southeast Asia, the Manila massacre resulted in the death of 100,000 civilians in the Philippines. It is estimated that at least one out of every 20 Filipinos died at the hand of the Japanese during the occupation.[3]

American jazz musicians—all of whom were playing in Shanghai—were not immune to the Japanese invasion and occupation. Some landed in internment camps in China and the Philippines.

BUCK CLAYTON'S ACCOUNT

Trumpeter Buck Clayton—who had arrived in Shanghai in 1934—saw the larger Japanese-Chinese conflagration coming. He recalled these events in his autobiography *Buck Clayton's Jazz World* (1986):

> My biggest concern then [in 1936] was the Japanese Army. They were becoming more and more open in their contempt for the Chinese government and I saw many things that disturbed me. They would hold maneuvers early in the morning right in the middle of the main streets of Shanghai. . . . They were having real maneuvers in the city and I could see that before long the real thing was going to happen. I went to my guys and told them that they had better soon make preparations to go home because Shanghai was going to explode and soon. They all listened and soon we were making bookings to get back home—all except [Reginald] "Jonesy" [Jones], our bass player. He had either married a Filipino girl, or was living with her, and didn't want to go back home, so he stayed.
>
> . . . I booked passage on a Japanese boat that I believe was named the "Tayo Maru." . . . In less than two weeks after we left the Japanese sailed a warship right down the middle of Shanghai and bombarded the city on both sides. I thanked God that I had got out in time. That was only the beginning. I learned later that Jonesy had been put in a concentration camp and had suffered many physical torments. . . . [He] had lost weight and looked very bad.[4]

Clayton was misinformed.

"JONESY" AND EARL WHALEY AND HIS COLORED BOYS

Canadian Desmond Power[5] was interned in the same Japanese camp as Jonesy. Power was fourteen years old at the time (he was born on February 15, 1923).[6] When World War II broke out in Europe, "I did my duty by enlisting in the Volunteer Defence Corps." He had good reasons: "Being in the Corps . . . I could pass as a full blown adult and so gain entrance to the Little Club Ballroom, the night spot that was the talk of the town."[7]

His "cozy world," as he puts it, ended when on December 8, 1941, Japanese storm troops swarmed into the British concession in Tientsin. He further writes: "With the help of the Swiss Consul, the Masonic Hall on Race Course Road was converted into a mess where [Allied nationals] could get a free meal. When I showed up there, the man running the place asked if I would help out by serving as a waiter. My OK was the best decision I made for a long time. One of the first tables I served was occupied by several of 'Earl Whaley's Coloured Boys.'"[8] Among this troupe were a man named F. C. Stoffer (a pianist), clarinet man Wayne Adams, saxophonist Earl Whaley, and "the boisterous happy-go-lucky string bass player" Jonesy! Apparently, Jonesy did indeed leave his Filipino girlfriend and travel North from Shanghai to Tientsin. Power's initial relationship with the members of this swing group lasted a year.

Power had an opportunity to hop a prisoner exchange ship, the *Kamakura Maru*, in Shanghai (south of Tientsin) in August 1942. He leaped at the opportunity, but his berth was snapped up by British Taipans. He then found himself "in Pootung camp . . . one of the worst of all Japanese prison camps in China."[9]

Pootung Camp received the first internees in late January 1943. Originally a men-only camp, it held single men, men who had sent their families home before the war, and men married to non-interned third nationals or Asians. The buildings consisted of the condemned go-downs of the British American Tobacco Company and was located not far from Pootung Point, across the Whangpoo River[10] and Shanghai's Bund, which could be seen from the upper stories of the buildings. The compound was littered with junk and debris and included the bombed-out ruins of a Chinese village destroyed in the 1937 fighting. By manual labor alone, internees cleared this area to construct playing fields and garden plots; this area was christened the "Happy Garden." After the September 1943 repatriation of Americans and Canadians, many Pootung internees were transferred to other camps—including

Power and his African American jazz musician friends—to provide manual labor there, while many women were transferred to Pootung from other camps, including two of the Yangchow camps that the Japanese closed. 1,519 internees called Pootung home at one time or another.[11]

In effect, Power was in Shanghai from August 1942 until March 1943 where all US, British, Belgian, Dutch, Greek, and Norwegian men, women, and children were confined within the boundaries of the International Settlement and French Concession. He writes:

> We all had to wear red arm bands denoting that we were enemy subjects. We were forbidden to go to the movies, but we did, and we were forbidden to go to bars and night clubs but we did. I went twice to the Paramount, which was quite close to where I lived, but don't remember what band was playing. Then in March 1943 the Japanese consigned us to prison camps situated in and around Shanghai. There were no exceptions except for those who defected to them.[12]

The jazz "thread" followed Power to Pootung. He writes:

> Passing through the camp's crowded quadrangle one day I stopped to watch a dozen or so men, mostly Blacks, all with musical instruments seated on stools and chairs in two close rows. The sharp rap of a baton started off a beautifully stroked intro from a guitar that lifted saxophones, trombones, cornets into a buoyant rendition of that old standard *There'll Be Some Changes Made.* . . . A guitarist at heart, I stayed glued to the spot in seventh heaven. . . . What a godsend, that band, lifting the camp's morale as nothing else could! All top musicians they had played at Shanghai's best ballrooms and nightclubs. There was Jim Staley of Shanghai Little Club Fame, and Bob Hill of Venus Ballroom, and there was Tommy Missman, Charlie Jones, Lestor Vactor, Fred Haussman, Sonny Lewis, each a star in his own right. The U.S. and Japanese governments had agreed to an exchange of civilian prisoners, and when that big moment came in September 1943 the band gave a rousing send off to those hundred lucky ones exiting Pootung. And when one of their own, Freddie Haussman, went past waving good-bye they broke into a number right on the button—*San Francisco Here I Come.*[13]

Not many days later, Power was transferred to Lunghua camp at the opposite end of Shanghai. Located about eight miles southwest of the Bund on

Minghong Road, Lunghwa was the former Chinese Kiansu Middle School, which was heavily damaged during the 1937 fighting. It was about two miles from the Lunghwa airdrome. The camp was large, containing seven concrete buildings, three large wooden barracks (originally built as stables by the Japanese), and numerous outbuildings. There were fifty-nine dorms and 127 rooms for families. A number of ruins were on the grounds as well. Lunghwa held 1,988 internees during the war and saw a number of escapes, most of them successful. Nine internees eventually made their way to free China.[14]

In this camp Power was recruited into the camp dance band to play guitar. His sojourn there was relatively short-lived. Five months later he was again transferred to Weihsiein (also spelled Weihsien) camp in Shantung Province, 700 miles north of Shanghai.

Located two miles east of Weihsien, the American Presbyterian Compound in Weihsien was known by the Chinese name of "Courtyard of the Happy Way." Its Shadyside Hospital, constructed in 1924, was considered one of the best constructed mission hospitals in North China. However, by the time internees arrived, all useable equipment had been looted or carried off. Student dormitories, consisting of rows and rows of rooms, as well as large buildings originally used as classrooms and libraries, housed the internees. One of the largest camps in China, Weihsien housed, at one time or another, almost 2,250 internees. Two internees who escaped provided information on the camp to OSS operatives in Chungking, while remaining in the vicinity of the camp with Nationalist [GMD] guerrillas. At the end of the war, Weihsien was the scene of an exciting drama when a seven-member OSS team parachuted near the camp and were welcomed by the overjoyed internees. Afterwards, Chinese Communist guerrilla activity prevented the evacuation of the camp. After an initial group was removed by rail to Tsingtao, the railway line was blown up. Internees were finally airlifted out by Army Air Force planes.[15]

This was a fortuitous transfer for Power. Bass player Jonesy came back into his life. Power describes the reunion: "I was together again with my family and Tientsin school pals. Assigned to work as a stoker at Tientsin Kitchen where 900 internees were fed, I was astounded to find that my fellow stoker on our two-man shift was none other than Reginald Jones that marvelous bass man from Little Club. He didn't remember me at Tientsin's Masonic Hall. No wonder, it was 3:45 a.m., the single incandescent dangling from the ceiling giving off only a dim light, it was freezing cold, and no time to talk. The water in the giant cauldrons was supposed to be on boil before the cooks arrived on shift at 6:30, so we had to go hard at it, drawing clinkers and hustling life into the fires."[16] Power also recalls:

> We were alone in the kitchen from four till six when the cooks arrived, so plenty of time for talk. He told me a lot about himself, his upbringing in the States and the jazz bands he played for. One of his stories remains absolutely clear in my memory is that in the part of the U.S. in which he was brought up the bull frogs were huge and fierce, and that if you were bitten by one "you grew all funky and died." He made it plain that he did not come out to China with Earl Whaley's band but with Buck Clayton's. And this Earl Whaley himself confirmed. Because my memory is so vague of Jonesy telling me that he had played in Louis Armstrong's band that I did not use it in my [unpublished] article. However, a week or so back when doing some research on the Internet there it was plain as day that back in the late twenties the tuba player in Louis Armstrong's band was Reggie Jones. (As with most string bass players, Jonesy doubled on the tuba.)[17]

In his article Power adds this to Jonesy's résumé: "his father [was] a teacher at Michigan Conservatory, and a brother, Reunald, [was] number one trumpeter with Count Basie and Woody Herman. He himself was no slouch on the double bass, starring at Harlem's Cotton Club before joining Charlie Echol's renowned fourteen piece band. When trumpeter Buck Clayton joined that band he must have hit it off with Jonesy, for when in 1934 he formed his Harlem Gentlemen to go out to Shanghai to play at the Canidrome Ballroom, he took Jonesy with him."[18]

There are other details of Jonesy's background worth mentioning. Jones came from the same extended musical family whose most famous member was cousin Roy Eldridge, one of the great jazz trumpeters. The bassist, who also shows up credited as Reg Jones and Reggie Jones, had more musical brethren, including Reunald Jones Sr., yet another trumpeter, who begat a son, Reunald Jones Jr., who followed in his father's footsteps and also became a trumpeter. Another brother, Leopold Jones, was also a professional musician, although so little information exists about him that it is difficult to determine even what instrument he played.[19]

This is fortunately not the case for Reginald Jones, whose bass lines empowered cooking R&B sides by Joe Houston with provocative titles such as "Earthquake," "Cornbread and Cabbage," and "Goofin." Reginald Jones started out with the New Orleans jazz sound, playing both tuba and bass with Louis Armstrong in the '20s during one of that trumpeter's incursions north to Chicago.[20] Jones is also mentioned in *The Jazz Bass Book: Techniques and Traditions* by John Goldsby (2002) as one of the early great jazz tuba players.

Power continues:

> In Weihsien, not only did we spend all those hours together on shift, when off shift we took our meals alongside off duty cooks and stokers in a hut called Kitchen 2 Annex. There with his irrepressible sense of humor he kept us all in fits of laughter. I can still picture him very clearly, his heavy build, his impish grin and that's exactly how he appears in the prewar photos of him in my June article. I am certain that he lost little if any weight in camp and was in sound health when the war ended.[21]

Jonesy gave Power the news that Earl Whaley and Wayne Adams were in Weihsien, but not pianist F. C. Stoffer. His appendix had ruptured the day he arrived in camp when the hospital was still in shambles, and he died before they could get him to one in Tsingtao.[22]

In the building where Jonesy and Power were quartered he met up again with Earl Whaley and Wayne Adams: "I gave them the bad news I'd heard when in Lunghua that Tommy Missman had fallen from a skywalk and was lying with broken bones in Pootung's sick bay. As for the good news, all the other jazz players were fit and well. They kept their hand in by giving regular concerts that were eagerly attended not only by internees, but also the Japanese from the high and mighty Commandant down to the lowly guards who always grabbed the front seats."[23] This last recollection is telling. It connects with the perspective of the appreciation for jazz by the Japanese in between the two world wars, and thereafter.

Power adds: "Earl Whaley offered that they too kept in practice by playing at dances. He and the others had brought their instruments with them, but not Jonesy, though he fared well enough on the cello the good Anglican Bishop lent him. As for the Shanghai jazz men I named, he knew most of them when his Red Hot Syncopators played there at St. Anna's Ballroom."[24]

St. Anna's Ballroom (Sheng Aina) is one of the forty cabarets and ballrooms prominently mentioned in Andrew Field's deeply documented work, *Shanghai's Dancing World*. It was located on Love Lane (Xieqiao lu): "a street known for its brothels, [it] seemed to have served as a springboard for courtesans who wished to change their profession to dance hostesses."[25]

Health issues at Weihsien were ever-present. Power recalls: "Deep concern spread among us when in the spring of 1945 Earl Whaley was rushed to the camp hospital suffering from acute appendicitis. We who knew of Stoffer's tragic end kept our fingers crossed. Thank God, Earl survived the surgery. Soon as visitors were allowed, I went around to see him. He lay in much distress, his stomach bloated with gas. He asked me to call the nurse. When I did, that fierce matron of the Royal College of Nursing gave me hell and sent me packing. Back in his quarters, Earl's full recovery took weeks during which time he avoided getting involved in the sometimes noisy discussion with his roommates . . ."[26]

On August 17, 1945, a lone four-engine plane flew over the camp, circled it once, twice, and dropped a team of seven OSS parachuters within two hundred yards of the camp walls. The Japanese Commandant and the guards handed over control of the camp to US authority. Japan had surrendered unconditionally following the destruction of Hiroshima and Nagasaki by atomic bombs dropped by the United States.

One war over, another immediately exploded. Japan's defeat, in China, in particular, "caused the long brewing Chinese Civil War [between the CCP and the GMD] to burst into the open, bringing road and rail traffic to a standstill." This challenge notwithstanding, Power recalls "We'd apparently escaped starvation, disease, and bestiality of the guards . . . My family and friends had come through in reasonably good shape, the jazz musicians: Whaley, Adams, West, Jones . . . were all sound of life and limb."[27] Two trains finally made it through to Tsingtao (about three hours from the camp) taking a quarter of the camp population with them. Power's mother, half-brother, half-sister, and he were taken by C47 plane to Tientsin, his hometown before the war. Power's sojourn in Japanese internment camps had come to an end. From there he moved to England to New Zealand to West Vancouver, British Columbia, Canada, where he now resides.[28]

Power writes a postscript on Jonesy:

Sometime in the mid-sixties when I met up with schoolmate and Weih-sien roommate Douglas Finlay, I bemoaned the sad fact that every member of the camp band disappeared off the face of the earth the moment they departed by train to Tsingtao. He looked me in the eye and said not so. A few years back he had run smack into Jonesy. It happened he said on a Sunday morning when he and his wife Yvonne had walked past Hotel Vancouver on Georgia Street. Approaching them on the sidewalk was a hefty Black. In the instant that he and Jonesy recognized each other they embraced and exchanged shouts of joyous laughter. As it turned out, they were to have no opportunity of renewing their friendship, for Jonesy had just completed a gig at The Cave Supper Club and was heading back to the States.[29]

Attempts to discover Jonesy's whereabouts once he had returned to the United States, or when and where he died, so far have revealed nothing. Also, it is puzzling that Buck Clayton's autobiography published in 1986 makes no apparent attempt to rectify his perception that Jonesy had not fared well in China after the 1937 Japanese occupation of Shanghai. It also does not stand to reason, given the personal and professional interconnections in Buck Clayton's jazz world, that he would not have known about Jonesy's situation once the latter had returned to the United States.

THE JAPANESE JAZZ EXPERIENCE

It is an irony that despite Japan's apparent highly nationalistic, empire-building attitude in the first half (approximately) of the twentieth century—which also included a rejection of Western values—jazz was a style of Western music embraced by many Japanese, despite the political enmity between Japan and the United States and its allies. Today, of course, Japan is one of the major strongholds of jazz at least in Asia, if not on the entire planet.

Recall Desmond Power's observation about the jazz concerts in the Lunghua internment camp: "They [the jazz musicians] kept their hand in by giving regular concerts that were eagerly attended not only by internees, but also the Japanese from the high and mighty Commandant down to the lowly guards who always grabbed the front seats." In historical context, this anecdote apparently is not an isolated connection.

The strong prevalence of jazz in Japan can be traced to two historical periods. The first is the mid-nineteenth century expeditions by American Admiral Matthew Perry to Japan that resulted in the Treaty of Kanagawa with the Japanese Tokugawa Shogunate. These agreements effectively ended Japan's two hundred years of isolation. The Treaty of Kanagawa also sparked other Western nations' interest in Japan. Great Britain, Russia, France, and the Netherlands signed "unequal treaties" with Japan. These "unequal treaties" granted foreign nations more rights than Japan. This also helped overthrow the Shogun in 1867 and re-establish the authority of the emperor. It is reasonable to conclude that, with the continued presence of Western power in Japan into the first quarter of the twentieth century, when jazz traveled to

Japan and other ports west, especially via steamship, that the music would establish a foothold.

The second historical period is the 1920s–30s in Shanghai. E. Taylor Atkins frames the period with respect to the Japanese jazz experience in his evocative essay "Jammin' on the Jazz Frontier: The Japanese Jazz Community in Interwar Shanghai": "It is difficult to conceive of a better descriptive term than 'frontier' for portraying the Chinese port city of Shanghai in the early twentieth century. In the years between World Wars I and II, Shanghai was virtually everyone's frontier, the colonial playground for transients from over 20 nations."[30] Atkins describes the Japanese jazz community there:

> Among these "Shanghai sojourners" were a number of musicians, singers, stage and "taxi" dancers, and cabaret and dance hall proprietors of Japanese nationality who comprised a distinct "jazz community" within the Chinese city. Entrusted with entertaining the Japanese settlement in the Hongkew district (which boasted 20–30,000 residents in the mid-1930s), this community created a jazz frontier in Shanghai.[31]

The term "jazz frontier" is one Atkins coined "after a close reading of the imagery, language, and thematic content of the jazz community's oral accounts and folklore, which describe all the romance, danger, and personal transfiguration that are fundamental to frontier experiences. . . . But the jazz frontier is more idea than place, the product of the Japanese jazz community's collective imagination, and thus a frontier by virtue of its meaning as well as its location or inherent transformative power. For Japanese musicians, Shanghai represented a rite of authentication and initiation into the jazz culture, an alternative experience, and a stepping stone to fame and fortune in the homeland's entertainment industry.[32]

William Minor's encyclopedic homage to jazz in Japan, *Jazz Journeys to Japan: The Heart Within*,[33] also attests to the depth of the Japanese jazz experience.[34] Not only is *Jazz Journeys to Japan* a broad, historical discourse on the jazz scene in Japan over a seventy-five-year period, it also provides—in voluminous quotes, reminiscences, observations, and analysis—the backgrounds, struggles, and triumphs of the who's who of Japanese jazz composers, performers, promoters, and jazz journalists and their publishers.

Minor pinpoints the initiation of jazz in Japan: "Purportedly, jazz arrived in Japan as early as 1921, when a young man named Shigeya Kikuchi, serving as secretary to his father on a U.S. business trip, returned to his native country with a load of Dixieland 78s."[35] In a larger cultural context, therefore, *Jazz Journeys to Japan* is also about the influences that shape our cultural lives, let alone the lives of Japanese jazz musicians. It is about the relationship between masters (teachers) and students, colleagues and peers, learning communities, educational systems, and performance venues. It is also about information, communication, and transportation technologies: boats, planes, the phonograph, radio, film, television, and print mass media. In this regard, while *Jazz Journeys* is focused on jazz in Japan, the book clearly can be universalized to a more global context.

For example, in an early chapter dealing with the inaugural days of jazz in Japan, you are struck immediately with the parallel to the evolution of jazz in China. In both nations, jazz popped up in the early 1920s (in China it was primarily in Shanghai), then declined in the 1940s (in both countries anti-Americanism or anti-Westernism was a strong root), but then resurfaced after World War II in Japan and in the early 1980s in China (following Mao's death).

Further, while Minor spends a good 85 percent of his book lovingly telling the individual stories of Japan's jazz luminaries (both past and present, known and rising) chapter by chapter, he also touches on larger issues, for example, the manner in which many American jazz writers between the 1960s and 1990 demeaned Japanese players. Minor writes: "Early American (post-World War II) critical commentary on the Japanese attempt to play 'our music'—'America's classical music,' an indigenous art form—was frequently condescending, the tone mocking, belittling, if not laced with outright bigotry."

This appalling and provincial attitude is countered in no small part by the eminent Japanese jazz writer Yui Shoichi. As E. Taylor Atkins points out in his introduction to the anthology *Jazz Planet*: "According to [Yui's] theory (first articulated in the late 1960s), jazz, rather than sweeping away the diversity of global cultures, provides a mechanism for rediscovering indigenous traditions. Yui argued that as ethnic pride and liberation movements swept the globe in the postcolonial era, peoples of color drew on their respective heritages to create original music that was both part of a universal language called jazz and a singular expression of national or ethnic identity."[36] Minor's narrative is full of examples of how Japanese jazz musicians have drawn upon their own musical heritage to create new jazz works, "Haiku" among them.

The arc of the Japanese jazz experience continues to this day not only in Japan, but also in China. In Beijing one can find Japanese-born drummer

Izumi Koga who performs regularly with saxophonist Liu Yuan's ensemble (and other groups) at the East Shore Café. In the mid-2000s in Shanghai you could have visited Wine Red, a jazz club that catered primarily to Japanese businessmen, established and run by saxophonist Simon Wu. The former club in Beijing is thriving; the latter club in Shanghai has, unfortunately, closed.

PART II

DURING AND AFTER MAO

CHAPTER 8

Jazz and Individual Freedom of Expression

MAO'S TWENTY-SEVEN-YEAR TENURE

> Control of the people by government rulers and bureaucrats had been
> the usual basis for peace, order, prosperity, and power in the Chinese
> state. Under the Chinese Communist Party, efficient control would be by
> ideological indoctrination and by self-sustaining motivations of fear and
> hope among the people. Killing need be only enough to keep the motive
> of terror always in the background.[1]

So begins Fairbank and Goldman's chapter on "Establishing Control of
State and Countryside" in their encompassing volume dealing with China's
long history. Somewhat later in the chapter they write: "The state cult of
Mao was already beginning in order to meet the Chinese need for a single
authority."[2]

It is not the intent of this chapter or this volume to recount the complex
and long history of China's social and political history. Fairbank and Goldman handle that admirably. However, the outcomes—including the suppression of jazz and all forms of Western culture—of Mao's policies during
his twenty-seven-year tenure as master of China (he took over in 1949, and
died on September 9, 1976) provide a chilling backdrop and prelude for the
more productive changes China's successive leaders have promulgated since
his demise.

The reference to "Killing need be only enough to keep the motive of ter-
ror always in the background" cannot be taken too lightly. During Mao's
tenure millions of Chinese died in one way or another. In a chapter titled
"The Great Leap Forward 1958–1960" the abovementioned authors write:
"In 1958–1960 some 20 to 30 million people lost their lives through mal-
nutrition and famine because of the policies imposed upon them by the
Chinese Communist Party. Measured by the statistics showing an increase
in mortality, this was one of the greatest of human disasters." Later they

point out "All central orders, however, had to be applied by local authorities. Part of China's inheritance was that their state of morale, their loyalty to the center, would be a key determinant of the results achieved."[3]

The authors' perspective is corroborated in the extreme by an even more recent work, this by Yang Jisheng, a now retired journalist with the Chinese state news agency Xinhua who spent fifteen years piecing the real story together. In his book *Tombstone: The Great Chinese Famine, 1958–1962*,[4] Yang estimates the famine killed up to 45 million people! In an interview with the *Guardian* in early 2013, Yang describes the horrific ordeal:

> People died in the family and they didn't bury the person because they could still collect their food rations; they kept the bodies in bed and covered them up and the corpses were eaten by mice. People ate corpses and fought for the bodies. In Gansu they killed outsiders; people told me strangers passed through and they killed and ate them. And they ate their own children. Terrible. Too terrible.[5]

Yang's book underscores the emotional and intellectual resistance in the Communist Party to deal with the reality that the Great Leap Forward was a failure almost from the beginning. Mao knew his "economic" plan wasn't working early on, but in order to keep power he turned a deaf ear to those few who were advising him otherwise. Given China's long-embedded cultural ethos of obedience to central authority—described in chapter 1—from Mao's "court" in Beijing to local authorities in the hinterlands, the "vision" of the Great Leap Forward was kept intact even in the face of stark reality. As Yang reports: "When the head of a production brigade dares to state the obvious—that there is no food—a leader warns him: 'That's right-deviationist thinking. You're viewing the problem in an overly simplistic manner.'"[6]

The second (and last) horrific disaster in China's mid-twentieth-century history is the Cultural Revolution of 1966–76. This was Mao's last decade as China's leader. Estimates on how many people died in this "domestic political struggle that convulsed China"[7] vary widely—from a few million to 78 million. There is no official estimate to this day. Suffice it to say, Mao's political ideology—while successful in wresting control of China from the Nationalists and purging the country of all vestiges of Western dominance and culture—left the country in worse shape than before 1949. Fairbank and Goldman offer this image of the country's susceptibility to Mao's ideology:

imagine a society [of hundreds of millions of people, mostly peasants] that can be run by a Great Leader and a party dictatorship simply because the citizenry are passive in politics and obedient to authority. They have no human rights because they have been taught that the assertion of human rights (such as due process of law) would be selfish and antisocial and therefore ignoble. It would also be punished. The problem begins on the ground in the family life of the Chinese village, where the Confucian teaching of social order through dutiful self-subordination has left its mark even today.[8]

As earlier chapters have iterated, this last sentence references the wall that Western values and culture, including jazz and rock, have had to climb after Mao suppressed it during his tenure as leader of China. What emerged after his death in 1976 was a slow, yet inexorable movement toward Western entrepreneurialism and with it the reemergence of jazz, especially in Shanghai, and a nascent individual freedom of expression supported explicitly and implicitly by China's new leadership.

THE 3RD PLENARY SESSION OF THE 11TH CENTRAL COMMITTEE OF THE COMMUNIST PARTY OF CHINA

With Mao's death in September 1976, the new Communist leadership began to open the door to the West, and to permit an economy that today boasts high (some say too high) rates of growth. Today in Beijing and Shanghai, and even in other smaller Chinese cities, jazz performance—not only by local musicians, but also by expatriates and visiting jazz artists from all over the world—has reemerged in large venues and numerous jazz clubs.

The 3rd Plenary Session of the 11th Central Committee of the Communist Party of China was a pivotal meeting of the Central Committee of the Communist Party of China held in Beijing, China, from December 18 to December 22, 1978. The conference marked the beginning of the "Reform and Opening Up" policy, and is widely seen as the moment when Deng Xiaoping became paramount leader of China, replacing Hua Guofeng, who remained nominal chairman of the Communist Party of China until 1981. The meeting was a decisive turning point in post-1949 Chinese history, marking the beginning of the repudiation of Mao's Cultural Revolution policies, and set China on the course for nationwide economic reforms. The meeting took place at the Jingxi Hotel in Western Beijing.

The "Reform and Opening" policy of the late 1970s had its own roots in the death of Mao in 1976. Not more than a month later the so-called "Gang of Four," including Mao's wife, were arrested and ultimately jailed. Yet these deliberate acts on the part of reformist Chinese leaders, such as Deng Xiaoping, to repudiate Mao's disastrous policies—such as the Cultural Revolution—were reinforced by several other events that brought the outside world to China. While there is no extant "official" statement by either Deng Xiaoping or the Chinese Communist Party that expressly supports permissiveness with respect to Western-style culture—such as classical music and jazz—four events took place in the period between the 3rd Plenary Session and 1981 that give credence to China's emergent attitude toward the West.

The first is *From Mao to Mozart: Isaac Stern in China*, a 1980 documentary film [shot in 1979] about Western culture breaking into China produced and directed by Murray Lerner:

> It portrays the famous violinist and music teacher Isaac Stern as the first American musician to collaborate with the China Central Symphony Society (Now China National Symphony Orchestra). The film documented Mr. Stern's rehearsals and performances of Mozart and Brahms violin concertos with the famous Chinese conductor Li Delun, who also acted as his guide and translator on his trip. The film also included footage of Mr. Stern's visit to the Central Conservatory of Music and Shanghai Conservatory of Music where he lectured to the Chinese music students on violin playing and the art of musical expression. Most of those musicians were playing mechanically, especially the String section, prior to the human improvements, concerning the qualities of the orchestras. One conductor was imprisoned in a closet for playing Beethoven, during the great Proletarian Cultural Revolution of the 1960s, when Western music was prohibited under Mao. Among many others talented players, young cellist Jian Wang (at the time only ten years old) is featured briefly. Jian Wang has gone on to international stardom. The film won the 1980 Academy Award for Best Documentary Feature.[9]

A second example is the Boston Symphony Orchestra's (BSO) historic tour to China in 1979, which was put together in less than two months following an official invitation from the Chinese Ministry of Culture and marked the opening exchange in the then recently signed cultural pact between the United States and the People's Republic of China:

The BSO performed one concert in Shanghai on March 15 and three concerts in Beijing (called Peking at the time) on March 17, 18, and 19, the last of which was a joint performance with the Central Philharmonic Orchestra of Peking performed in the 18,000 seat Capital Stadium. During the tour BSO principal players held master classes at the Shanghai Conservatory, and Seiji Ozawa conducted a reading rehearsal with the Shanghai Symphony Orchestra. The BSO brought four complete sets of strings, brass mouthpieces, orchestra scores of music by Copland, Gershwin, Bartók, and Schuman [sic], and sets of recordings, as well as United States-China Flag pins, Boston Symphony T-shirts, and frisbees—all to be presented to the Chinese musicians.[10]

A third example—to be detailed in a later chapter dealing with Shanghai's indigenous and expat jazz musicians—is the reintroduction in 1980 of a jazz sextet at the Peace Hotel in downtown Shanghai. This occurrence was not so much an embrace of Western culture through jazz as it was motivated by economics: as China opened up to the West after the 3rd Plenum, more and more Westerners started to travel to China to do business in China, as well as explore China's culture as tourists. Shanghai was one of China's natural starting points. The Peace Hotel was probably the most famous (and popular) hotel in Shanghai.

A last example is the 1981 visit to Shanghai by French horn and bass player Willie Ruff. His adventure in China at the Shanghai Conservatory of Music is detailed in chapter 10.

THE EMERGENCE OF INDIVIDUAL FREEDOM OF EXPRESSION

Since 1978, therefore, when the post-Mao Chinese leadership began in earnest to open up China to the rest of the world, jazz—starting with French horn player Willie Ruff's sojourn in Shanghai in 1981—began to trickle back into China. Since then, a steady stream of touring jazz musicians from all over the world has flowed into China, primarily to perform in the major cities. This trend accelerated in the early 1990s with the founding of the Beijing Jazz Festival by German entrepreneur Udo Hoffman.

Rock music also invaded the Chinese mainland in the 1980s. A seminal, personal, and musical relationship emerged between trumpeter/songwriter Cui Jian, the so-called father of rock in China, and tenor saxophonist Liu Yuan, the country's so-called father of jazz. In their early years, they played together. Cui Jian became immensely popular in China because he used rock lyrics as protest against the government. Liu Yuan has been less politically assertive; he is now part owner of one of Beijing's leading jazz clubs. Similarly, bassist Ren Yuqing was also a member of this troupe in the 1980s. While Cui Jian is politically oriented, and Liu Yuan is strongly musically oriented, Ren Yuqing has an entrepreneurial streak. He is the founding owner of the JZ Club in Shanghai, and started a jazz school and a jazz festival. He has also opened other jazz clubs in other parts of Shanghai, and a club in Hangzhou.

Today, a growing cadre of indigenous jazz musicians can be found in Shanghai and Beijing. The styles they play range from blues to swing, bebop, and contemporary. The pianist Kong Hong Wei, for example, plays virtually every jazz club in Beijing, including the East Shore Club, partly owned by Liu Yuan, and the CD Café. His pianistic dexterity recalls that of virtuoso jazz pianist Oscar Peterson. An alto saxophonist—who goes by the English name "Kenny"—with American expat trombonist Matt Roberts's Ah Q Band, was born in Mongolia and is self-taught. Close your eyes and "Kenny" reminds you of bebop innovator Charlie Parker. In Shanghai, the major jazz venue is the JZ Club, founded by the abovementioned virtuoso electric bassist Ren Yuqing. The city also boasts the Cotton Club and the Peace Hotel Jazz Bar, among several others.

Most Chinese jazz artists have had no formal training in the jazz idiom. Most are either self-taught or started out being educated formally in classical music. But this, too, is changing. An interesting case is the Beijing-based "cool" pianist Xia Jia, who studied at the Eastman School of Music in Rochester. If you listen to Xia's music, you can hear not only the American influence, but also the multi-dimensionality and multiculturalism characteristic of today's Western jazz, as well as some forms of pop music.[11]

In effect, what has also evolved slowly at first and accelerated in the early 1990s is the reemergence of jazz as a music style of interest not only to Westerners coming to China's urban centers, such as Beijing and Shanghai, mostly for business reasons, but also to a growing number of indigenous Chinese who find in jazz that "individual freedom of expression" long suppressed under Mao. Further, it is not only jazz that has seeped back into China's urban culture; there is also rock and American pop. The three are linked, especially since the mid-1980s.

The other cultural mode of expression that lands on China's shores in the early 1980s is the concept of improvisation—a word that has no direct translation in Mandarin. It is also an individual mode of expression diametrically opposed to China's long history of adherence to well-established social norms and central authority.

JAZZ MUSICIANS RETURN TO CHINA

Jazz musicians from all parts of the world began to trickle back to China to perform starting in 1981 in response to the opening up of China by Premier Deng Xiaoping in the wake of Mao Zedong's death in 1976. The motivation for their travels to China was several. Some came to China for the same reason many jazz musicians left the United States for Europe earlier in the century—to find work and to escape racism. Others traveled to China merely to find work. While the standard of living in China is not the same as it is in the United States, there was enough work to make the trip worthwhile.

There are American expatriates in Shanghai, for instance, who play almost every day of the week. Rents are cheaper than in the United States and the dollar is relatively strong compared to the yuan, so they are making a living. Still others traveled to China because they were sponsored by a government agency and the opportunity to travel to a foreign, distant land was too compelling. More recently, jazz musicians travel to China because China has become one of the places to visit and discover.

The reports of these musicians (in books, articles, and one-on-one interviews) have value for various reasons. In the context of this volume, the primary reason is that, put in chronological sequence, their reflections on the Chinese people and culture serve as testimony to the evolution of China economically and socially over the period of the last quarter of the twentieth century and the opening of the twenty-first. Some were there almost at the reopening at the initiative of the Chinese government in the late 1970s, such as Willie Ruff, a professor emeritus at Yale University. Others include pop/jazz guitarist Dennis Rea who landed in the city of Chengdu in Sichuan Province early in 1989 just months before the "incident" at Tiananmen Square in Beijing later in the year. While he did not experience Tiananmen Square directly, his observations of parallel happenings in Chengdu at exactly the same time are telling.

As one moves from the early 1980s to more recent times, the pace of jazz musicians traveling to China from the United States and other parts of the world accelerates. This, too, is an indication and reflection of the accelerating pace of economic development in China, at least in the eastern major cities such as Beijing and Shanghai. Of course, it is not only jazz musicians who travel to China. Jazz musicians are a mere blip on the Chinese visa radar screen. The world began to travel to China, especially for the singular purpose of developing business relationships. In the late 1790s the British, for example, traveled to China to do just that: establish closer business ties with the Chinese emperor and open China up for the purposes of profitable trade (see chapter 2 on the "Opium Wars"). More than two centuries later the emperor is long gone, although the Chinese government remains a single-party establishment. The draw, so to speak, then as now, is China's huge population. When visiting Shanghai for the second time in August 2006 it was a surprise, for example, to find a Kentucky Fried Chicken franchise in the heart of the city. It was a further surprise to learn Kentucky Fried Chicken had established itself in Shanghai in the early 1980s. Business is always business.

For some of the former members of the Jimmy King Jazz Band of the 1940s who reemerged in 1980 as members of the Peace Hotel Jazz Band, the motivation was economic. Hotel owners, such as those who managed the famed Peace Hotel in downtown Shanghai, needed jazz music to entertain Westerners. For other indigenous Chinese musicians, exploring jazz was purposeful, in some instances accidental, but also liberating. One such example is Gao Ping.

GAO PING, PIANIST AND COMPOSER: FROM CLASSICAL TO JAZZ TO CLASSICAL[12]

A classically trained player, he "accidentally" became involved in an early attempt by another indigenous musician to record jazz. At the time the extant recording medium was tape, not CD. In Ping's case, the venture was short-lived and he returned to his classical roots. But his story of his involvement in this venture, albeit short-lived, is telling in terms of his own evolution as a pianist and composer. It is also telling with respect to the evolution of jazz in China, post-Mao.

> Born in Chengdu[13] (Sichuan Province) in 1970, Gao Ping's music has been performed in Europe, Asia, Russia, and across the Americas. In demand as a composer and pianist, he has received commissions from the Zurich-based Ensemble Pyramide, pianists Frederic Rzewski and Ursula Oppens, violinist Arnold Steindhart, the Starling Chamber Orchestra, Dutch flutist Eleonore Pameijer, the Taiwan National Chinese Orchestra,

Cincinnati Chinese Music Society, and the Shenzhen Dance Company. He was a composer-in-residence at the MacDowell Artist Colony.

His work for narrator and chamber orchestra, "The Emperor and Nightingale," was premiered at the Aspen Music Festival in 2002 and is now featured as an audio/visual display in the National Underground Railway Freedom Center in the U.S. "The Concertino for Violin and Strings" was premiered in Beijing and has subsequently met with critical acclaim throughout China and the United States. Other compositions have appeared at venues such as the Gaudeamus International Music Week in Amsterdam, the 2005 World Music Festival and Conference in Bangkok and the Beijing Modern- International Music Festival. Gao Ping's music has been heard on National Public Radio's "Performance Today," WNYC, as well as having been featured on Chinese broadcasts reaching millions of listeners.[14]

The aforementioned "tape," produced in Chengdu in 1988, wasn't something Ping had previously thought to do. "It certainly wasn't me," he notes. "It was a friend of a friend . . . I think he runs this [recording] studio . . ." With Ping on piano, vocalist Xiao Yi Buan singing on the tracks, and the man who ran the studio producing sounds on a "drum machine," the trio finished recording the tape within three days. "I was in high school or middle school, so [I] had to go there at night."

Dennis Rea (author of *Live at the Forbidden City*) describes the tape in the context of reemergent jazz in China as follows:

> The first evidence of a nascent jazz movement among younger Chinese was pianist Gao Ping's 1988 tape "Jazz in China," in all probability the first indigenous jazz recording made in the country since 1949. Released by the state-run China Record Company, "Jazz in China" was a curious mélange of mostly non-jazz material, ranging from Canton-pop melodies to the "Theme from Love Story," from bubbly synthesizers to sampled operatic tenors. While the recording did display jazz sensibilities, with a fair measure of improvisation and identifiable jazz harmonies, it was a far cry from what jazz partisans in the West would consider jazz. This was hardly surprising, considering the scarcity of authentic jazz recordings in China [at the time], official disapproval of this "degenerate" art-form, and above all a predisposition in modern China against the type of spontaneous expression embodied in jazz.[15]

Unlike modern-day music production, there were few (if any) arrangements made prior to recording. Mr. Ping recalls the days in the studio, when he first laid out piano tracks, and the rest (sounds produced on the drum machine, bass accents to correspond with the piano) followed shortly after. "One original composition at the very end of the tape was a little piano piece I wrote," Ping notes. "It's all improvised." Ping, who started taking piano lessons at the age of six, began to improvise his music at just eight years old. "I was asked by my piano teacher not to do it because it would have ruined my technique. But I just kept on improvising."

At just seventeen years old, Ping was already a classically trained pianist. He recalls hearing jazz only occasionally when tapes were sent over. "Sometimes people have something and you hear it, [but] sometimes even those are not labeled with the names of the musicians." At the time, there was no jazz music playing on the radio.

Ping wasn't the only one interested in this wave of music banned from China. He remembers classmates who were also intrigued with jazz. "It's certainly different from anything we listened to at the time," Ping notes, "Anything that's American seemed to be very welcome back then. I think it was more than just being music. I think it was a symbol of something else."

A common theme among the musicians interviewed for this volume is the use of jazz to communicate individual freedom of expression. According to Ping, "To improvise is liberating." That impulse encouraged Ping to improvise in his music then and now.

Those four words—"To improvise is liberating," expressed by Gao Ping—are thematic of the motivations of many, if not all indigenous Chinese jazz musicians interviewed for this volume. Interview after interview, when asked why they chose to study, perform, and compose jazz music, the overarching answer (expressed one way or another) was "individual freedom of expression." This is in stark contrast to the highly regimented and structured Chinese society of yesteryear and especially during Mao's tenure. In this context, the reemergence of jazz in Chinese urban society in the 1980s—at least in the major cities of Shanghai and Beijing—represents literally and metaphorically the beginning of a shift in the perception of the individual in China. While jazz was the music of Shanghai before Mao, after Mao's passing, and after the Chinese government began to open up again to the West in the late 1970s, jazz began to represent a new mode of expression—for Chinese society, that is: the importance of the individual as opposed to the central importance of the state.

The Influence of Mid-Twentieth-Century Technologies on the Expansion of Jazz in China

Gao Ping's "accidental" experience with jazz and Dennis Rea's reporting of it would not have happened were it not for two genres of technology: one, electronic, i.e., "audiotape," and one transportational, i.e., the plane. Generally speaking, in the second half of the twentieth century jazz traveled to China in one of two ways (or both): (1) electronically by several means, and (2) by air, that is, by plane. Plane travel has also provided the means for indigenous jazz musicians from various parts of China to travel to the United States and other parts of the globe to study jazz and perform.

In the second half of the twentieth century, all manner of electronic and filmic media—such as radio, television, movies, CDs, DVDs, satellites, teleconferencing, computers, and the Internet—and transcontinental modes of transportation such as the plane have supplanted the steamship, the locomotive, the gramophone, and early movies as technologies influencing the growth of jazz in China. The characteristics of the abovementioned communications, information, and transportation technologies cannot be underestimated in terms of their cultural impact, not only on the spread of jazz globally, but also on the spread of information and knowledge generally around the world. Both technology categories have at least one thing in common: faster speed—that is, information and people could now travel from one place to another faster than at any time in human history.

THE ELECTRONIC AGE[1]

The characteristics of even the earliest electronic media still apply today. Electronic media carry messages at the speed of light, a vastly superior speed to that of paper, which moves at the speed of bureaucrats and clerks. Second, with today's global telecommunications networks, messages can reach far beyond local or regional geography. Third, all manner of physical and perceived political, economic, and social boundaries are transcended by electronic media, including time of day or season. Last, as *Megatrends* author John Naisbitt has argued, electronic media foster increased personal contact, not less, as some pundits are fond of pronouncing. All this began with the introduction of the telegraph early in the nineteenth century.

In early 1838 Samuel Finley Breese Morse—artist, daguerrotypist, a so-called "American Leonardo"—gave a series of public demonstrations of the first practical electromagnetic telegraph. In 1844, after receiving a thirty-thousand-dollar grant to construct a telegraph line between Baltimore and Washington, DC, the year before, Morse opened the nation's first commercial telegraph line on May 24 with the now famous query "What hath God wrought?" On that day the electronic communications age was born.

Electronic technologies have acted true to Marshall McLuhan's 1964 contention that "Once a new technology comes into a social milieu it cannot cease to permeate that milieu until every institution is saturated."[2] The consistent message of electronic media over time is an evolution of media that can reach many people at one time (such as broadcast radio and television) to media that can reach a few people at any time (such as the CD-ROM and the World Wide Web). In effect, as the twentieth century has progressed into the twenty-first, electronic communications media have become more accessible to more people on a global scale. Geographic, physical, and political boundaries have been transcended. Time, similarly, has been transcended. A corollary to this is that over time electronic communications media have moved from linear (one-way communication) to interactive (two-way communication). News and information travel fast on a global scale. The global inter-telecommunications network has shrunk the planet to a "global village," to again quote Dr. McLuhan.

Electronic communications devices of several kinds, therefore, have had direct impact on the spread of Western culture, jazz notwithstanding, to the East, China in particular. China's "traditional electronic media," such as television and radio is exemplary:

> In 1978 . . . fewer than ten million Chinese had access to a television set. . . . in 2014 . . . roughly a billion Chinese (out of a 1.3 billion total population) have access to television. Further, sales volume of television sets in China in 2011 was 125.04 million. In 2015 it was 162.3 million![3]
>
> Similarly, in 1965 there were 12 television and 93 radio stations in China; today there are approximately 700 conventional television stations—plus about 3,000 cable channels and 1,000 radio stations.[4]

However,

Television broadcasting is controlled by Chinese Central Television (CCTV), the country's only national network. CCTV, which employs about 2,400 people, falls under the dual supervision of the Propaganda Department, responsible ultimately for media content, and the Ministry of Radio, Film, and Television, which oversees operations. A Vice Minister in the latter ministry serves as chairman of CCTV. The network's principal directors and other officers are appointed by the State. So are the top officials at local conventional television stations in China—nearly all of which are restricted to broadcasting within their own province or municipality—that receive CCTV broadcasts. CCTV produces its own news broadcasts three times a day and is the country's most powerful and prolific television program producer. It also has a monopoly on purchases of programming from overseas. All local stations are required to carry CCTV's 7 p.m. main news broadcast; an internal CCTV survey indicates that nearly 500 million people countrywide regularly watch this program.[5]

The Internet, however, is cutting into this monopoly: "There were 731,434,547 Internet users in China (representing approximately 52.7% of the population) as of December 2016. This represents a rise of 23% since 2012, even as communist authorities tightened controls on content."[6]

The fastest-growing segment is the urban consumers aged 51 and older—a sign the Internet is spreading through Chinese society. China's Internet population is massive. Though annual growth will ultimately taper to the single-digit range, China still has the largest online audience in the world, and it is only getting bigger.

VOICE OF AMERICA AND JAZZ PROGRAMMING

One of the electronic communications technologies that bridges the "Before Mao" and "After Mao" chronological divide with respect to jazz in China is radio, more specifically, Voice of America:

On December 27, 2011, Voice of America (VOA) celebrated the 70th anniversary of the first U.S. shortwave radio broadcasts to China, which began on the 28th of December 1941, just weeks after the Japanese attack on Pearl Harbor and the start of World War II. Voice of America was still months away from being officially established when the first Chinese language shortwave broadcasts were transmitted from studios in

San Francisco. U.S. government broadcasting operations to China were eventually moved to New York and then Washington under the Voice of America. VOA programs in Mandarin, Cantonese and Tibetan are delivered on radio, television, the Internet, mobile platforms, satellite, and by proxy servers designed to circumvent Chinese Internet blocking. VOA English language teaching programs, including the social media sensation, OMG! Meiyu, enjoy a large audience in China.[7]

Further,

Voice of America (VOA) is the official external broadcast institution of the United States federal government. It is one of five civilian U.S. international broadcasters working under the umbrella of the Broadcasting Board of Governors (BBG). VOA provides a wide range of programming for broadcast on radio and TV and the Internet outside of the U.S. in 43 languages. VOA produces about 1,500 hours of news and feature programming each week for an estimated global audience of 123 million people, "to promote freedom and democracy and to enhance understanding through multimedia communication of accurate, objective, and balanced news, information and other programming about America and the world to audiences overseas." Its day-to-day operations are supported by the International Broadcasting Bureau (IBB). VOA radio and television broadcasts are distributed by satellite, cable and on FM, AM, and shortwave radio frequencies. They are streamed on individual language service websites, social media sites and mobile platforms. VOA has more than 1,200 affiliate and contract agreements with radio and television stations and cable networks worldwide.[8]

Alan Heil, author of *Voice of America: A History*, writes: "Over the years, the music gurus of the Voice have attempted to offer a full range of American music and, in some regions, indigenous songs and ballads to an eager listening public around the world. The best-known VOA effort, clearly, has centered on jazz, that unique blend of ragtime and blues combining American with African and Caribbean musical traditions. It also became celebrated in much of the twentieth century as the 'music of freedom.'"[9]

Jazz programming has been a steady aspect of VOA's programming. The *Voice of America Jazz Hour* was broadcast beginning on January 6, 1955, through 2003; it was then folded into Voice of America Music Mix's program *Jazz America*. It began broadcasting in 1955, hosted by Willis Conover;

in its current form, it is hosted by Russ Davis. It began broadcasting over the initial objections of Congress. The program's theme song was Duke Ellington's "Take the A Train." At its height, the *Voice of America Jazz Hour* was listened to by up to thirty million people, almost none of them in the United States, as Voice of America was prohibited from broadcasting in the United States by the Smith-Mundt Act. As jazz was frequently banned in the Soviet Union and countries sympathetic to its views, Voice of America was often the only way people in those countries could listen to jazz, and Willis Conover's politics-free broadcasts are widely credited for keeping interest in jazz active in Soviet satellite states.[10]

Conover was a force to be reckoned with. Heil recounts: "If Conover has been a prophet unheard in his own land," *DownBeat* magazine said, "he has been a messiah 'round the globe, the best-known and best-loved ambassador for America's art form since Louis Armstrong and Dizzy Gillepsie."[11] Heil further writes: "Jazz touched the lives of professionals other than musicians. The music stirred souls in countries where it was officially considered 'decadent' and 'forbidden fruit.'"[12] This last observation is a probable reference to the former Soviet Union, and, by extension, Communist China under Mao.

Willis Conover was on the air during the administrations of eight US presidents, and he was the master of ceremonies at White House concerts for several of them. "Every emotion—love, anger, joy, sadness," he once said, "can be communicated with the vitality and spirit that characterizes jazz and our country at its best, which, of course, is the same freedom that people everywhere should enjoy." Conover died in 1996.[13]

However, the technological means of disseminating programming, jazz programming included, has changed with the times. The Mandarin Service stopped broadcasting all music programs to China by shortwave in 2012. Shortwave transmissions were cut from twelve hours a day to eight. VOA English still broadcasts jazz and other programs that are all available now via Internet streaming. VOA currently uses Russ Davis's weekly two-hour syndicated program *Jazz America.*[14]

There was a brief attempt by the Broadcasting Board of Governors to shut down the VOA China branch in 2011. Thanks to numerous protests in China (apparently people there have been listening) and in the United States and members of Congress from both sides of the aisle, it did not happen. Moreover, in 2012 Mainland China–born Dr. Sasha Gong (who spent a year in a Chinese jail for her anti-government views) became the first Asian American to become chief of the VOA China Branch.[15]

THE PLANE, THE PLANE!

While in the first half of the twentieth century the steamship, the locomotive, the gramophone, and early movies influenced the spread of jazz to China and much of the world, and electronic media in various forms accelerated this process, another technology added to the spread of cultural information, including jazz, to all parts of the world: the plane.

The plane is a transportation technology with a relatively short history in contemporary terms. The beginning occurs, of course, in 1903 when Orville Wright completes the world's first powered, sustained, and controlled flight in a heavier-than-air airplane.[16] This seminal event within a century leads to an industry involved in passenger air traffic, cargo transportation, a cornucopia of military aircraft, and the space industry.

A second pivotal event in the evolution of the aircraft industry is the development of the jet engine. Two people are credited with the development of the turbojet engine: Dr. Hans von Ohain, a German, and Sir Frank Whittle, of Britain. Each worked separately and knew nothing of the other's work. Hans von Ohain is considered the designer of the first operational turbojet engine. Whittle was the first to register a patent for the turbojet engine in 1930; von Ohain was granted a patent for his turbojet engine in 1936. However, von Ohain's jet was the first to fly in 1939. Frank Whittle's jet first flew in 1941.[17]

The inexorable influence of the plane in the second half of the twentieth century and the early part of the twenty-first century can be seen in a chart devised by Shaw Aviation Economics covering the years 1971–2010. Despite two oil crises (circa 1976 and 1980), reactions to the First Gulf War in early 1991, the Asian economic crisis of the late 1990s, the 9/11 attack on the United States in 2001, followed by the Iraq War and the SARS epidemic, and the Great Recession that started in 2008, the pattern of world air traffic growth reflects a steady upward climb that many observers peg at a 5 percent yearly growth rate.[18]

In 1971 world air traffic was at 0.5 trillion RPKs (Revenue Passenger Kilometers). By 2010 RPKs numbered just slightly lower than 4.5 trillion—a ninefold increase in traffic. This compares to world population growth in roughly the same time period: in 1970 world population stood at 3.7 billion; in 2011, 7 billion; in 2016, 7.3 billion.[19]

While the world's population doubled in this time period, world air traffic grew nine times. Part of the reason for the air traffic growth was the development in the second half of the twentieth century of faster, larger jet planes for international travel, and faster, smaller jet planes for regional travel—a definitive move away from prop and/or turboprop planes to jet travel with such companies as Airbus (Europe), Boeing (United States), Bombardier (Canada), Embraer (Brazil), and Tupoloev (Russia) leading the way.[20]

The growth of air traffic to and from China and within China shows a similar growth pattern. According to World Bank Data covering the period 1974–2010, air passengers from all over the world and air passengers traveling within China itself rose from 710,000 in 1974 to just under 268 million in 2010. The numbers clearly show a slight rise in the early 1980s, a stronger uptick in the early 1990s, and a very strong surge since the beginning of the twenty-first century.

A chart that tracks "Air Passenger from US Airports to China"—i.e., arriving from China and departing to China from 1990 to 2011—underscores the same pattern. In 1990 the number of passengers arriving from and departing to China numbered almost the same: slightly more than 600,000. By 2011 that number had risen by 62 percent: 971,480 air passengers arriving from China to US airports, 965,184 air passengers departing to China from US airports!

Today, dozens of airlines carry passengers and cargo to and from various parts of China to the world. The list of air carriers with flights directly from the United States includes United, Delta, American, China Eastern, China Southern, and Hainan. Other airlines flying to China from other parts of the world include: Cathay Pacific, Korean Air, ANA, Air France, British Airways, US Airways, Asiana, Air Canada, Japan Airlines, KLM, Swiss Airways, EVA Air, Emirates, Virgin Atlantic, China Airlines, Etihad Airlines, Aeroflot, Singapore Airlines, SAS, Aeroméxico, LOT, Philippine Airlines, Saudia Airlines, Transaero Airlines, EL AL Israel Airlines, and Brussels Airlines.[21]

Collectively, these airlines fly to fifty of China's cities, including Beijing, Shanghai, Jinan, Xining, Guiyang, Lhasa, Guangzhou, Harbin, Shantou, Chengdu, Taiyuan, Tengchong, Kunming, Changchun, Weihai, Shenzhen, Wenzhou, Dayong, Xi An, Sanya, Kashi, Hangzhou, Shijiazhuang, Yiwu, Chongqing, Nanning, Korla, Qingdao, Haikou, Wuyishan, Wuhan, Guilin, Dali City, Urumqi, Lanzhou, Tunxi, Changsha, Ningbo, Jinjiang, Xiamen, Hefei, Jiayuguan, Shenyang, Yantai, Dandong, Dalian, Fuzhou, Xiangfan, Zhengzhou, and Lijiang City.[22] The significant growth of passenger air traffic to China is reflected in the reverse direction. According to the International Trade Administration of the US Department of Commerce:

In the first 10 months of 2011, visits from mainland Chinese rose 36% year-over-year to 940,000 . . . Chinese visitors' spending in the U.S. shot up 39% in 2010 to $5 billion, a growth rate that outpaced visitors from all other countries who have been traditionally high spenders here. That spending put the Chinese in seventh place among foreign visitors, over-taking France. "U.S. travel and tourism exports to China have increased by at least 30% in six of the last seven years," the trade administration's 2010 report says. "U.S. travel and tourism exports account for 24% of all U.S. services exports to China."[23]

Air cargo traffic appears to follow a similar pattern. For example—in yet another instance of a German company influencing events beyond its bor-ders—in December 1986 the German company Deutsche Post DHL signed a 50/50 joint venture with Sinotrans in Beijing to become the first express company to operate to and from and within China.

Accordingly,

Founded in 1950, a year after Mao's successful takeover of mainland China, the China National Foreign Trade Transportation (Group) Cor-poration (SINOTRANS) operates under the direct administration of the State-owned Assets Supervision and Administration Commission of the State Council. Sinotrans is China's largest company specializing in in-ternational freight forwarding, air cargo and international express, the second largest shipping agency and the third largest shipping company.[24]

The aforementioned joint venture combined DHL's leading expertise in the global air express industry and Sinotrans's unrivalled local knowledge in the China foreign trade transport market. DHL-Sinotrans has since devel-oped a comprehensive service network covering 401 cities throughout Chi-na. In keeping with China's booming economy, DHL-Sinotrans's business performance has grown almost sixty-fold at an astonishing average rate of 40 percent in the past decade.[25]

Following suit, in 1988, two years after DHL's agreement with the Chinese, American company UPS established operations in the China market by also signing a cooperation agreement with Sinotrans Group. By 1994 the com-pany announced the opening of representative offices in China's three major gateways—Beijing, Guangzhou, and Shanghai.[26] FedEx (founded as Federal Express in 1971 in Little Rock, Arkansas) began service to China in 1995. It did so by acquiring air-route authority from Evergreen International.[27]

DEMOCRACY EXPANDS

Collectively, electronic media in various forms and the plane—a combination of information, communications, and transportation technologies—accelerated the dissemination of cultural content and values from many parts of the world *to* many parts of the world in the second half of the twentieth century. The wings of these technologies (pun intended) also carried the concept of democracy.

By several definitions, at the dawn of the twentieth century not one country on the planet could be considered democratic in the sense of a full-population electoral democracy. Not even in the United States did women have the vote until 1919. And it was not until the advent of the Civil Rights Movement in the 1960s and 1970s that African Americans began to have full access to the right to vote. In effect, in 1900 zero countries could be considered truly democratic.

However, in the last quarter of the twentieth century, it is observable that things were beginning to change. Larry Diamond of the Hoover Institution has written:

> If the twentieth century was the century of totalitarianism, total war, genocide, and brutality, it was also the century of democracy. As Freedom House notes in its latest annual survey of freedom in the world, there was not a single country in 1900 that would qualify by today's standards as a democracy. By 1950, only 22 of the 80 sovereign political systems in the world (28 percent) were democratic. When the third wave of global democratization began in 1974, there were 39 democracies, but the percentage of democracies in the world was about the same (27 percent). Yet by January 2000, Freedom House counted 120 democracies, the highest number and the greatest percentage (63%) in the history of the world.
>
> Since the fall of the Berlin Wall and the collapse of Soviet communism at the beginning of the 1990s, democracy has been the dominant form of government in the world. By the end of 1991, half the states in the world were at least electoral democracies, and by the mid-1990s that proportion rose to three-fifths, where it has held for several years. It is not difficult to infer from this dramatic expansion a nearly universal legitimacy for democracy, a global hegemony.[28]

The evidence shows that since the late 1980s the number of autocratic nations has declined and the number of democracies has increased, even though following World War II the reverse was true. What event took place at this time or right before this period that might have spawned a rise in democracy globally? The answer appears to be the World Wide Web, an invention of CERN's Tim Berners-Lee in 1989. What else happened in this year? Tiananmen was brought to the world's attention via numerous electronic means in 1989. 1989 was also the year of the fall of the Berlin Wall.

The Web, also called the Net, exploded into consumer consciousness within a few years following. And, if you leap forward to the present day, especially to places like China where electronic media and print media (i.e., newspapers) have grown exponentially, and Arab Spring countries like Tunisia, Egypt, Morocco, Libya, and Syria, where uprisings have led (or could lead) to regime change, you see the inexorable explosion of electronic devices and the apparent attendant desire for democracy. All these political and social events are on the social continuum inaugurated by the introduction of the telegraph in the second quarter of the nineteenth century!

What is also true is that countries that do not in reality practice a democratic form of government, even though there are superficial signs of a democratic process—such as North Korea, Syria, Turkey, Iran, Venezuela, Saudi Arabia, Russia, and China, among several others—have become more apparent because they are in the minority relative to other more democratic countries in the world. These same countries have dug in their autocratic, dictatorial heels in the face of the palpable and inexorable global democratic trend.

Jazz is inherently a form of aesthetic democracy. In this context, without any prompting, the vast majority of indigenous jazz musicians interviewed in China for this volume stated they were drawn to the art form because it offered an opportunity for *individual freedom of expression*, a very democratic ideal. In a country where this is a relatively new value, the appeal of jazz is understandable. Kabir Sehgal, in his 2008 book *Jazzocracy*, links jazz with democracy in two ways: "First, jazz is music of negotiation, conversation, reconciliation, and making.... The second reason ... is the invitational spirit of jazz."[29] Indeed, more than any other musical style, jazz invites artists not only to play with the group, but also to solo and to improvise with a group backing them up. This is the musician's chance to make an individual statement in the context of the group. Jazz is the musical epitome and exemplar of democracy.

China's inexorable economic expansion has also had a role in fostering jazz. Westerners traveling by plane to do business in China are often sophisticated travelers who bring with them an expectation of hearing "their" music—an echo of what happened a century and a half earlier after the Opium Wars. Further, as China's own middle class expands, more are listening to Western music and are beginning to appreciate the United States' unique contributions.

Today's Chinese jazz musicians benefit from listening to recordings and hearing the touring jazz artists who arrive by plane from all over the world. The Internet, of course, is also a major influence. China has one of the fastest Internet growth rates on the planet.

Nonetheless, jazz occupies much the same position in Chinese culture as it does in the United States: in visibility, it ranks below Western classical, rock, and popular music, including Chinese folk music. As in the West, jazz appeals to musically educated ears and an economically capable populace. It is likely that, as China's middle class expands, jazz will have an opportunity to reach a larger public. The economic entrepreneurial opportunities supported and encouraged by the current Chinese government offer a new context for economic individualism—and thus for jazz.

CHAPTER 10

First a Trickle, Then a Flood: Jazz Musicians Perform in China from All Over

Mao's demise in 1976—resulting a few years later in the reemergence of China as part of the world community in the last quarter of the twentieth century—together with the influence of electronic and transportation technologies in the second half of the twentieth century (described in the last chapter) had a direct impact on the rejuvenation of jazz in China, especially in Shanghai and Beijing. It provided opportunities for jazz musicians from all over the world to perform in China. Again, the locus of this activity, at least in the beginning, was Shanghai and the opportunity fell to African American bassist and horn player Willie Ruff.

VERY FIRST ARRIVAL POST-MAO: AFRICAN AMERICAN BASSIST AND HORN PLAYER WILLIE RUFF

A longtime professor and founder of the Duke Ellington Fellowship program at the Yale School of Music, Ruff is one half of the Mitchell-Ruff Duo with pianist and friend Dwike Mitchell. In 1959 the pair "introduced jazz to the Soviet Union, playing and teaching in Russian conservatories, and in 1981 they did the same in China."[1]

In his 1991 memoir, *A Call to Assembly*,[2] Ruff revealed his connection with Shanghai and how his interest began: "When Beijing and Shanghai natives began arriving in my classroom believing that the Stephen Foster they'd heard back home was jazz, I knew it was time to knock on the door of Yale's Chinese Department." The bass and French horn player immediately began studying Mandarin and soon Ruff was known as the "strange black music man in New Haven" that "wouldn't shut up in Chinese."[3] At the same time, Chinese interest in American music was flourishing. One day, Ruff received a call from Professor Tan Shu-chen, deputy director of the Shanghai Conservatory, wishing to see Yale and needing a host. Ruff accepted.

Professor Tan Shu-chen was born in Shanghai in 1907, learned European languages and music, and by 1930, was teaching in six Shanghai colleges. But from 1966 to 1976, Western music of all kinds had been silenced in China and Professor Tan, like all teachers in the People's Republic, was publicly humiliated and accused of being a "tool of decadent cultural influences from the West."[4] It is noteworthy that Professor Tan was a renowned violinist in China who eventually spawned an even larger music family. His daughter, Lucy Tan, became an accomplished pianist and taught at the Manhattan School of Music as a visiting professor from 1982 to 1984. A granddaughter, Wei Tan, earned bachelor and master of music degrees (violin) from the Manhattan School of Music. She made her New York debut at Weill Recital Hall of Carnegie Hall in 2002.[5]

Professor Tan Shu-chen was seventy-three years old when he visited Yale. Ruff compared his face to "a composite of all the good teachers"[6] he had ever known. He invited Professor Tan to attend a performance of he and Mitchell's for undergraduate Yale students. Afterward, Ruff detected Professor Tan's fascination with improvisation. When he left Yale, he insisted that Ruff and Mitchell visit his conservatory if they ever made it to Shanghai.

Ruff soon took Professor Tan up on his offer. He applied for a travel grant with Coca-Cola, received a check and, with Mitchell, travelled to Shanghai in 1981. Upon arriving, Professor Tan asked the duo to play a concert the next day and they happily agreed.

"There were about three hundred students and their teachers sitting in the informal concert space the next day," Ruff recalled of he and Mitchell's performance on June 2, 1981. Professor Tan introduced the duo and announced that Ruff would be addressing them in Chinese. "My first words were an apology and a plea for their patience with the poor Chinese of a foreigner who wanted passionately for them to know his people's music. Their friendly applause relaxed me, and I went to work."[7] Ruff explained the music created by black people in the United States and the importance of the drum in West African music, comparing the drum in West African society to the book in literate society. He told the story of when the Africans were brought to the United States as slaves and their drums were taken from them, because their slave owners feared its power. "While no instrument can replace the drum, we developed musical devices that can be thought of as drum substitutes,"[8] Ruff elucidated.

Professor Tan had asked Ruff and Mitchell to explore improvisation for the students, and with no exact Chinese translation to define the word, Ruff settled for, "something created during the process of performance,"⁹ and the rest was as follows:

> Mitchell whispered, "Let's make up one. You start on the horn." I didn't even tell the audience what was coming. I just played the first theme that popped into my head: nothing grand, no virtuoso flash or dazzle. Any student there could have thought up its simple four- or five-note design and played it on its own instrument. As I blew on, Mitchell played a countermelody to match the horn's. I caught it and turned it around, and we exchanged parts, supported one another and entered into the nip and tuck, the call and response, the pauses and the breaks, of the improviser's game.
>
> Improvising is interesting and exhilarating. It is art so thoroughly complex and difficult that it engages all your instincts and intelligence. Doing it before an audience always heightens the stakes; if you play to teach, the stakes automatically double. Putting forth a new musical thought means putting something personal on the line. It is the ultimate gamble; you stick your neck out, push the limits, pace yourself, and learn what to leave out. The overworked myth that improvising jazz means "going wild" and "letting it all hang out" is just that, myth. It's no cinch to make musical sense spontaneously. There is discipline, and there are rules. Sorry.
>
> When the number ended, I told the audience, "This is the newest music you have ever heard. I can be sure of that, because we just made it up right here, right now. We call it 'Shanghai Blues.'"
>
> Bedlam. Roaring applause, cheers, and approval.¹⁰

Professor Tan started taking questions at once: "When you created 'Shanghai Blues' just now, did you have a form for it, or logical place? Could two total strangers improvise together? Could a Chinese person improvise?"¹¹

Ruff invited students to play pieces of their own and he and Mitchell would try to make jazz out of it. A young man was called to the stage and, after some coaxing, went to the piano. As he played, Ruff observed the scene:

> I sensed Mitchell fastening his concentration on that flavor, his emotional radar homing in on the music's essence and telling him the secrets of its "Chineseness" and its spirit. And then, after about a dozen bars, the

perfectly constructed little piece came to its pleasant and unexpected conclusion.

The audience went berserk.

It was the moment I'd waited years for. If the game were golf, smart money would be on the kid from Dunedin. Mine was on a hole in one. I just stood there holding the bass, waiting. I saw Mitchell's eyes surveying the keyboard as he sat down. He took a moment to map his course. Nothing stirred on the stage, or anywhere in the hall.

Suddenly the Steinway rang out with the *exact* notes the students had played. No one-finger pick-out-the-tune. There, in full cry, were the composer's big two-fisted chords, complete with his melody and, more important, with all his original expression.

A youthful Chinese voice in the audience cried out, "That American is a human tape recorder!"[12]

A video of that historic performance can be found at http://www.willieruff.com/. After teaching at the Yale School of Music for forty-six years, Professor Ruff retired in 2017.[13]

POST–MITCHELL AND RUFF

While Willie Ruff is certainly the first "reported" jazz musician from outside China to perform in China following Mao's passing, the historical record shows that in both Shanghai and Beijing jazz is an "international" happening. Visit any major city in the world—such as New York, Chicago, London, Paris, Moscow—and you will find jazz musicians of various nationalities and ethnicities playing with each other. But in China this mixing of nationalities and ethnicities seems even more common. On a visit to the Cotton Club in Shanghai, for example, of the various musicians on the bandstand one was from the United States, one from China, and two others from the Philippines and Italy, respectively. It is not uncommon to find a frequent mix of nationalities, especially Americans, on the stage at the JZ Club in Shanghai.

The Beijing jazz scene since the mid-1990s reflected a similar pattern. David Moser recounts:

any foreign musician in Beijing tends to be accorded an inordinate amount of respect and attention simply because many Chinese feel they are somehow closer to the mystical source of all this Western music that is so admired . . . It is thus quite natural and inevitable that foreigners would get involved in the jazz scene here. Liu Yuan's band has a Japanese drummer, the groups I'm in usually have a mix of Americans and Chinese, and several foreigners with high-powered day jobs in Beijing take off their ties at night and jam with the three or four jazz groups playing around the city. For example, Christopher Bramsen, by day the Danish ambassador in Beijing, at night often sits in with our group, blowing a very funky and spirited bebop tenor saxophone. (We once joked that the jazz hierarchy has a Count, a Duke, a Prez(ident), a King—and now an Ambassador.)[14]

To this list you can add the likes of American trombonist Matt Roberts and German diplomat/bassist Martin Fleischer in Beijing, and guitarist Dennis Rea in Chengdu.

The clear picture is that the double influence of electronic media—such as tapes and CDs—and the rise of plane travel to China since the early 1990s, growing unabated since then with the only exception of the aftermath of 9/11—jazz musicians from all over the world have traveled to China to perform in growing numbers. Moreover, as time has passed, and especially in the twenty-first century, the number of Chinese cities visited by these musicians has expanded significantly beyond Beijing and Shanghai. They include Beishan, Changzhou, Chengdu, Dongguan, Guangzhou, Hangzhou, Kunming, Macau, Nanjing, Qingdao, Shenzhen, Suzhou, Xiamen, Xian, and Xinghai.

MORE AMERICAN JAZZ MUSICIANS POST-MAO

Appendix I provides a list of the jazz musicians who traveled to China to perform between 1981 and 2016. There are ninety-plus soloists and ensembles reported. It is certainly not complete. In both Beijing and Shanghai there were American expat jazz musicians performing in those cities who have been there for some time but have never received any press for their presence. What Appendix I reflects is the "reported" performances of American jazz musicians in China as researched from print and online articles.

After 1990, however, the chart shows an acceleration of jazz musicians from the United States performing in China, an acceleration that coincides almost exactly with the rise of air transportation between the two countries.

Many of the performers' names are unfamiliar, but several are of high marquee value: Judy Carmichael, Maria Schneider, Wynton Marsalis, Dianne Reeves, David Amram, Norah Jones, Antonio Hart, and Judy Niemack.

Several high school or college-level ensembles are also to be found on the list, such as the Purdue University Jazz Band, the California State University Northridge Jazz Band, the New Trier High School Jazz Ensemble, the Bellevue Community College Jazz Band, and the Southeastern Oklahoma State University Jazz Combo.

After Mao's passing in September 1976, the opening up of China to the West in the late 1970s not only served to rejuvenate jazz in Shanghai, as evidenced by the creation of the Peace Hotel Jazz Band in 1980, it also, therefore, provided the impetus for the trickle, then flood of jazz musicians from the United States (starting with Willie Ruff, 1981) and other parts of the world (reportedly in the early 1990s).

Among the arrivals were jazz/rock guitarist Dennis Rea (to Chengdu), stride pianist specialist Judy Carmichael (to several Chinese cities), and jazz singer/arranger Mary Ann Hurst (to Beijing and elsewhere in China). Their observations of Chinese culture and jazz in early post-Mao China are informative.

JAZZ SINGER/ARRANGER MARY ANN HURST[15]

The first time Ms. Hurst was in China was as a student in 1981–82, just five years after the death of Mao and the beginning of the opening of China. She arrived in Shanxi Province in Taiyuan in the mid-central part of China, twelve to sixteen hours by train south of Beijing. An exchange program had started between the University of South Carolina and the University of Shanxi in China. She had studied the Chinese language and culture.

Her impression of the country at that time?

Shanxi was extremely polluted. It's the coal mining capital of China. The topsoil that comes in from Mongolia on the wind creates a lot of pollution. But the people were very curious about us. We were the first foreigners to be in the province on an exchange program.

The second time Hurst went to China was in 1985 as a commercial tour guide for Pacific Delight Tours. She took American tourists over in the summer, twice. And then from 1986 to 1989, she went over every summer with the University of Minnesota. She administered an arts program in Hangzhou. It was the only program in the world at the time that had a study abroad program for credit. You could study Chinese art for credit. She administered that program for four summers. She elaborated: "It was incredible. It was at the top landscape painting school in China, and we took people to study traditional Chinese landscape painting and calligraphy and bird-flower painting. It was the only program of its kind you could get credit for at that time."

In 1992 she was in the Brauhaus, a German bar in Beijing, one of the favorite watering holes of all foreigners who come through Beijing.

> One night I was there with some friends, and I heard some strains of piano that sounded a little bit like Oscar Peterson playing. And I thought, "Who is playing the piano?" I looked over and lo and behold there was a chubby, short Chinese guy playing, and I thought, "My gosh, he's playing pretty well." It was Kong Hong Wei (see chapter 14) playing piano. Zhang Hui was the bass player. There was also a drummer who was not Chinese. He was very suave and sophisticated. His mother lived in New York, and he traveled back and forth to New York. And he would tell the band how good the musicians were in the subways in the United States. And he had a Japanese guitar player.
>
> I talked to them during a break and told them I had sung with a jazz group in the United States and I wanted to know if they'd be interested in having a singer. Kong Hong Wei said "Come over to where our conservatory is." It was called the Minority Conservatory of Music. It wasn't the Beijing Conservatory. I went over there one day and we played through a few tunes and he said, "Yeah, you can sing. Maybe we could have a group." So we started a group.
>
> And when I came back, I brought some real books. People were interested to get real books as quickly as they could. I also brought a Fender electric bass back. I spent a lot of time in New York picking out a bass. That was a huge thing, bringing a bass into China at that point because you had to claim everything, and anything you brought in, you were supposed to take out.

Between 1992 and 1996 they played at the Correspondents Club. According to Ms. Hurst: "It was way ahead of its time. It was on top of the New World Trade Center. It was like an old British men's club, with a Tiffany lamp over a huge pool table and an incredible brass bar with red furniture.

It was just the most beautiful club. It was on the top floor, the 37th floor, overlooking Beijing."

They played there for about five or six months. The food and beverage people wanted to have players who were from Austria or Germany, depending on who the food and beverage person was—and they wanted to have live music. They had another jazz piano player from the States who came through there and played. She recounted: "We were pretty terrible when we started out. But we got better. There were Fortune 500 people that would come up there all the time. People from Ericsson, from Scandinavia, and AT&T. We were playing for this incredible global clientele. We just didn't have the global chops yet. It was really fun. And every once in a while, later on, a couple of years down the road Bo Bramsen, who was the Ambassador to Denmark, would sit in with us. He played the tenor saxophone. His name was Christopher, but we called him Bo. Christopher Bo Bramsen."

The first time Ms. Hurst travelled to China there was no jazz at all. However, "When I left in 1997 Cui Jian, who was the rock and roll star, was playing jazz trumpet and his musicians were playing jazz, such as Liu Yuan on saxophone. And there were quite a few groups popping up around town that played in different Westernized bars. There was more of an interest in it by the mid-nineties."

Ms. Hurst observed that:

Jazz is in the big cities. I haven't been there since 1997, but in Shanghai and Beijing, the hipper crowd and the intelligentsia, the more educated who have more access to Western things are curious about it and are listening to it more. In fact, I think what you'll find in the Berklee School of Music, what's happening now is what happened ten, twenty years ago with Japanese students coming to the States to study jazz. Now you've got Chinese students coming to study. I think China's going to take jazz on to the next new big step. My dream was to have the Chinese instruments being played. But at that point, in the mid-nineties, it was still too early and there really weren't any musicians in China who were playing jazz on Chinese instruments. Now there are. There are musicians in China who are playing jazz on their indigenous instruments.

She added:

When I was in China, the Chinese were getting their jazz influence from Europe and from Japan, more than they were from the United States. And the Beijing Jazz Festival went on for several years. And for many years they didn't even have people from the United States as part of the Jazz Festival, which is phenomenal considering it's a unique art form born in the United States. There was a European who was having it, Udo Hoffman, who was a German businessman. He had amazing contacts within the business world—Scandinavian Airlines and the European companies would fund this Jazz Festival. And if it weren't for him there probably wouldn't have been anything like that.

ROCK/JAZZ GUITARIST DENNIS REA: OUR MAN IN CHENGDU

Seattle-based pop/rock/jazz guitarist Dennis Rea took up the guitar at age nine. Over the years he has developed a background, as he puts it, "in way-out jazz, oddball instrumental rock, free improvisation, and electronic space...."[16] Rea has also agglomerated musical credits as a producer, sideman, leader, and author. His musical activities span film, theatre, radio, and modern dance, and he has appeared on more than two dozen recordings. He has been awarded grants by the Arts International Fund for U.S. Artists Abroad, the Seattle Arts Commission, the Malcolm S. Morse Foundation, the Jack Straw Foundation, the Washington State China Relations Council, the European Foundation for Chinese Music Research, and New York's China Institute.

He came to be in Chengdu, China, in early 1989 as a result of accepting a position at Chengdu University of Science and Technology where his then fiancée (they subsequently married), Anne Joiner, was participating in an academic exchange program. According to Rea: "For Anne, a China scholar with a degree in East Asian Studies, the teaching assignment in Chengdu was a dream come true. For me, an idiosyncratic guitarist with a modest niche in the tiny Seattle experimental music scene, it was little more than a working vacation in an exotic locale." His teaching position would pay him the equivalent of US$25 a week.[17]

Rea landed in Chengdu, a booming metropolis of more than three million people in 1989. The university's Foreign Languages Department assigned Rea classes in conversation, reading, and composition, based, however, on decades-old textbooks that had cleared "the gauntlet of government censors." His students had never met a foreigner before walking into his classroom. He notes: "They stared at me in wide-eyed wonder as though I were a Sasquatch." He writes further, "My charges were graduate students in such fields as plastics, chemistry, structural engineering, and—fittingly for a province famed for its extensive waterworks—hydrology, many of whom would go to work on the controversial Three Gorges Dam that would soon inundate that magnificent and historical stretch of the Yangtze [River]. Males outnumbered females by about three to one. In most cases, the students were studying English not by choice but by university directive; command of the language was now considered essential to China's technological advancement. Their only previous foreign-language experience had been with Russian, a legacy of the erstwhile alliance of the now-estranged communist giants."[18]

Rea's initial teaching experiences reflect the consequences of a culture previously locked into a rigid and domineering political system. His insistence on active student participation paralyzed his students. Several students turned in writing assignments that had obviously been copied from a standard textbook. He rejected the papers. The students did not understand the response. He protested to the administration who, in turn, explained "the Chinese do not prize originality for its own sake but are encouraged to borrow freely from their betters. After all, who would presume to think that they could improve on the works of the masters?" Rea then draws a parallel between this attitude to learning and music: "It's often impossible to identify the composers of classic Chinese musical works, for compositions were commonly based on anonymous folk melodies of indeterminate origin that were subsequently refined by later generations of musicians."[19]

Not long after his arrival in Chengdu, he developed a relationship with the Chengdu Guitar Association. As he puts it: "audiences were titillated to hear a real, live foreign guitar player, I found a welcome outlet for performing my music, and the Association gained major face in the bargain."[20] Not surprisingly, Rea began to immerse himself in the local musical culture by adapting Chinese songs to his guitar repertoire. In the process, he discovered the parallels between Chinese music and his own background: "The scooped, sliding tones characteristic of the erhu [a two-stringed fiddle] and guzheng (horizontal zither) find parallels in the string-bending and bottleneck techniques employed by blues guitarists; for that matter, a large part of the Chinese traditional repertoire, built on pentatonic scales and suffused with a profound melancholia rooted in centuries of suffering, is strikingly similar in spirit, if not in structure, to rural American blues." He adds: "Another aspect of Chinese music that appealed to me was its rhythmic flexibility; rather than being shackled to a rigid pulse like most Western fare, Chinese music is often marked by subtle fluctuations of tempo, allowing the player greater freedom of expression."[21]

Encouraged by the warm audience response, Rea began to take more risks, cautiously introducing more dissonance and unorthodox playing into his sets. To his surprise, demonstrations of feedback and weird sound effects proved to be perennial crowd-pleasers. He observes: "the audiences that I did reach were unfailingly curious, attentive, and engaged, if somewhat baffled."[22]

Sometimes a trip out of your own backyard gives you a fresh perspective on that backyard. Rea comments: "I was also struck by the remarkable diversity of attendees, ranging from small children to factory workers to Party officials, a refreshing contrast to the hipper-than-thou exclusivity of audiences back in Seattle."[23] He adds later:

> It wasn't unusual for a single concert to include Western classical, Chinese traditional, folk, and pop music on the same bill—imagine a gig shared by Iron Maiden, Karen Carpenter, Yo-Yo Ma, and Chet Atkins and you'll get the picture. The same was true of Chinese television, where variety shows consistently scored the highest ratings. Unlike audiences in the U.S., the Chinese were unusually receptive to the full cornucopia of musical offerings, while American listeners seemed to define themselves more by what they don't like than by what they do.[24]

Rea's commentary on musical improvisation in China is further evidence of the impact of the rigidity and dominance of the political system in China at least during the twentieth century: "Musical improvisation was an especially challenging concept to get across to my listeners. Many people were surprised to hear that much of my playing was completely off the cuff and wondered why any musician would choose to jump without a parachute. Once common in Chinese music, improvisation had long since fallen out of practice, except in out-of-the-way areas where rural folk music traditions had survived intact. The devaluation of improvisation was nowhere more evident than in the state music academies, which focused almost exclusively on the rote reproduction of a handful of approved Chinese and European classical compositions. I'll venture that one reason why China's state-enforced musical orthodoxy allows little leeway for personal interpretation is that improvisation is tantamount to independent thinking, precisely what any totalitarian government fears most."[25]

STRIDE PIANIST JUDY CARMICHAEL: THE US STATE DEPARTMENT SENDS A JAZZ TRIO TO CHINA[26]

In late spring 1992, the United States Information Service (USIS)[27] sent a jazz trio for a month to perform a couple of dozen jazz concerts in China. This was the first time the United States government had sponsored a jazz ensemble to perform in the PRC. They performed in Beijing, Harbin, Tianjin, Guangzhou, Chongqing, and Shanghai. The trio consisted of soprano and alto saxophonist Michael Hashim, electric guitarist Chris Flory, and virtuoso stride pianist Judy Carmichael. The repertoire for the tour consisted of standards from the 1920s and 1930s, such as "Them There Eyes" and "Up a Lazy River," as well as ballads and swing numbers associated with Gershwin, Ellington, Basie, Fats Waller, Benny Goodman, and Louis Armstrong. There was no bass player. As saxophonist Hashim pointed out, "We didn't need a bass player because Judy's monster left hand would render one redundant."[28] The venues the trio played in were big concert venues that could accommodate a thousand to two thousand people.

As Ms. Carmichael understood it, this was the first tour of any kind—artistic or policy-spreading—that the United States government had done since the Tiananmen Square incident in 1989. It was felt it was time to do something, and that bringing music might be the thing to do. The State Department hired the trio for a month. Given the perceptions at the time, Ms. Carmichael recalled: "They were going to say to the Chinese I was a folk singer because jazz was still considered too controversial—and it didn't matter I didn't play folk music and don't sing. And if it went well, and if we got a Chinese sponsor, not a financial sponsor, but one of the Communists to say 'Yes, I think she's great, I will put my backing on this,' we would get to stay; otherwise they would send us home."

The first concert was in Xiamen. It was successful. Carmichael commented on the performances:

This is very engaging music. This isn't avant-garde music. It's very inclusive. And I'm very inclusive in the way I present the music, wherever I present it in the world. I always talk about the music. I reach out for the audience, and I learned some Chinese. I would nod at the audience at the appropriate times for them to applaud after choruses. And they got it very fast. We had a lot of press conferences and handlers. And I kept saying, "I can do it. I'm learning Chinese. Let me say my few words." I wouldn't say a lot. I would say "I'm thrilled to be here. This is a great honor for us." And then I would turn to my musicians and then turn back to the audience and say, "Isn't this fun. They have no idea what I'm saying, that is, the other musicians." And the audience would all laugh because it would all be in Chinese. Most of the people had never heard jazz. The whole concept was unusual to them.

At the beginning of each concert we had a tall, beautiful woman in every city who would wear a tight dress, a very Las Vegas kind of presentation. Long, tight sequins, low-cut. And she would walk out on stage and say, "Now the concert is about to begin. Please sit down." And she'd introduce us. Then she would narrate the concert—sort of. It wouldn't just be a translation. She would say, "Now is the time to applaud. Now is the time to stop applauding." She was really dictating the audience's response, which ruined what we were doing because I would build the audience up, and I'd point to my musicians. The audience got it. They almost immediately understood the concept of applauding for choruses, which is not always the case, as you know, around the world. Some get it; some don't. But, you know, I'd point to my guitar player and I'd start applauding, and that was it. Then they just knew that was the beginning and end of a solo chorus.

One time, when I finally was able to get rid of her, we had a couple of thousand people in the audience. Everybody's yelling and screaming. They're all applauding. And we came back for our encore and she says, "Now you can leave." Everyone gets up and leaves. It was not something that enhanced what we were doing. I eventually proved I could do it without her.

The most emotional incident was we went to a music school. I think it was Shanghai, I can't remember for sure. And they had some Chinese musicians play for us. And it's hard for me to even talk about it without crying because they were playing instruments none of us were familiar with that were some sort of violin kind of string instrument. Perhaps an erhu and a pipa. And they played "Swanee River" and we all started crying. It still chokes me up. It was so beautiful. And if somebody played "Swanee River" to us here, we'd all think it was hokey as three Americans. But somehow these people, choosing a tune they thought would make us happy and then playing it on these instruments, completely killed us. Both my musicians broke down. All of us did. We didn't have enough of those moments where we got to interact with their musicians.

When we were in Beijing, I learned a Cultural Revolution tune that was very simple, called "The Sun Is Red and Now It's Not as Clear." So

I thought it would be interesting for us to take a tune and improvise on it—it only had five notes because, as you know, there was a period of time when I think there were only five tunes that were legal to sing, play, and perform. We were told there was a period of time during the Cultural Revolution when only certain tunes were approved. I thought it would be interesting to take one of those tunes and improvise with it, something that everybody would know—like us taking "Mary Had a Little Lamb" or something—so that they could really understand the concept of improvisation. So we would play this tune and Chris would do it in a semi-rock guitar way, then I would do it in a stride version, and then all of us would play. When we went to Beijing, our handlers said, "It's best if you don't play your little Cultural Revolution tune." And I thought, "Well, I knew that." That it wasn't the thing to do. But when we were in other places, we felt a real different political feeling. And they would tell us this, or we would notice and we'd ask the State Department people, and they'd say, "Well, it's very pro-American here."

In 1992 we stayed in nice hotels and we would get that kind of feeling, but in general we didn't have that constant feeling of that I'm inferring people feel now, from other friends of mine who have been there—this real feeling of modernizing and buildings going up. That was just starting. The main thing for us was a feeling of it was extremely difficult, the whole tour. They told me it would be difficult. We had a lot of conversations about this tour that it would be difficult to get around. The way the plane travel was insane to us because people ran to the planes and ran to get their things on. They would knock you out of the way in a kind of anarchistic way that would never happen anywhere else I've ever been in the world, I've never been in that kind of a situation. Then as soon as the plane took off, everybody sat down and was civilized. And then as soon as it landed, they all knocked you down and ran out again—to a comical effect.

I never felt any anti-American feeling. I felt a huge embrace and, of course, there were lots of dinners that were thrown for us. Everywhere we went, we were honored, but I never felt like anybody was faking that, if you know what I mean. There was just a good, good feeling, and it was more about the personal connection than "Here we are in China. We have this great country. We want you to love our country." It was more about the people.

One story epitomizes this. I have no idea what his real job was with us, he was one of our handlers because generally we had an American who was the liaison from the State Department. We would have our American liaison and we'd have our Chinese liaison. And then sometimes some peripheral characters would come with us. I would never know exactly who these people were; they were always lovely, but did not speak English, so I wasn't necessarily communicating.

We were shopping somewhere and I pointed out to Mike, the saxophonist, that there were some mints with the Kool logo from the cigarettes. They'd obviously stolen this logo and used it. I just pointed it out to Mike. I didn't say anything, and we both smiled at each other. There was something because we'd all been reading about copyright stuff and all those kinds of things. We finished our shopping, got on the bus, and one of these guys, who was one of our little group, came up to me and he'd bought three packs of these mints, thinking I'd pointed at them because I liked them, for me and Mike and Chris. And then my American liaison leaned over to me and said, "He's just spent a third of his yearly disposable income on those candies for you. Just so you know." This was a huge gesture of unfathomable generosity, and that was the most extraordinary example, but things like that happened.

This was not a place we were all dying to go. China wasn't China like it is now. In 1992 people weren't going, "Oh, I have to get to China because China's the future." Only really forward-thinking people were going. We all thought, "Okay, a great adventure. This will be interesting, but it will be difficult." We were surprised by this kind of feeling that we got. One of the things I always say to Mike and Chris, in terms of certain details, I'm really glad they were there because it's hard to describe how hard this was. As the leader of this group, this is the hardest thing I've ever done.

INTERNATIONAL JAZZ MUSICIANS (OTHER THAN AMERICANS)

Appendix II reports on jazz musicians from other parts of the globe who performed in China between 1992 and 2016. Similar to Appendix I, this list is certainly not complete. Again, this chart reflects the stories of those international jazz musicians who received press in either print or online media.

Based on the available reported evidence, the chart shows that air transportation's influence on the reintroduction of jazz into China was formidable. The first year that an international jazz ensemble shows up on the chart is 1992: the George Gruntz Jazz Band from Switzerland. This chronology very much coincides with the expansion of air travel between the two countries described in an earlier chapter.

The several dozen ensembles on this chart reflect performances by jazz musicians from the following additional countries: Australia, Austria, Denmark, England, Finland, Germany, Hong Kong, Iceland, India, Israel, Japan, Lebanon, Lithuania, the Netherlands, Norway, Russia, Singapore, and Sweden.

This list of countries is not only a reflection of the broad spread of jazz musicians who have performed in China between 1992–2016, it is also an indication of the spread of jazz globally—a trend first reported in 1922 by Burnet Hershey in the *New York Times* (see chapter 4).

Martin Fleischer, Godfather of Jazz, and Liu Yuan, So-Called Father of Jazz in Early Post-Mao Beijing

The influence of the Germans on the evolution of jazz in China is an historical thread that begins with the involvement of German military during the Opium Wars of the nineteenth century. And as previous chapters on the "influence of technology" have indicated, Germans are prominent—with the evolution of the phonograph and audiotape and the jet plane.

Clearly, with a significant German population resident in China for one reason or another it was almost inevitable that a German would intersect with China's nascent cadre of indigenous musicians interested in jazz. In Beijing that person was Martin Fleischer.[1]

MARTIN FLEISCHER, GODFATHER OF JAZZ (IN BEIJING)

Martin Fleischer, former Cultural Attaché to the German Embassy, Beijing, is a diplomat by trade. And while he has had different kinds of jobs in the academic field, he ended up in the German Foreign Service. He received postgraduate training at the German diplomatic academy and was sent to China as his first posting.

Fleischer majored in electrical engineering, English, and educational science. He has worked as an engineer in Saudi Arabia and in South Korea, and as a junior researcher at Hannover University and on a research vessel in the North Atlantic. After a two years' postgraduate at the Academy of the German Foreign Service, he assumed his first diplomatic posting with the German Embassy in Beijing in 1987. He subsequently served in Bonn as desk officer for nuclear nonproliferation, in Abuja as head of the Embassy Office, in Brussels as political counsellor with the permanent mission of Germany to NATO, in Berlin as head of division for peacekeeping and conflict prevention, in New York as economic counsellor with the permanent mission of Germany to the UN and, until summer 2011, again in Beijing as minister-counsellor with the German Embassy. He then returned to Berlin to assume the newly established position of International Cyber Policy Co-ordinator at the Federal Foreign Office.

Since August 2014, Fleischer has been with the EastWest Institute as its Vice President for Regional Security and director of its Brussels office.

Primarily self-taught on the bass, he started with the recorder, then the guitar, and then the bass guitar. He discovered jazz in his twenties and realized the electric bass guitar is just a substitute for the real thing, which is the double bass. In his mid-twenties he switched to the double bass. However, as he points out, ever since he was fourteen or so, he had always played in bands and performed on stages and produced albums. He refers to himself as a serious or ambitious amateur musician.

SEARCHING FOR KINDRED JAZZ MUSICIANS

Fleischer arrived in Beijing the first time in May 1987, and like on any other of his subsequent postings, he brought his double bass with him. In addition to serving as a member of the German Foreign Service, he was also a jazz musician looking for people to make music with. That turned out to be much more difficult in 1987 Beijing than he thought: "There seemed to be almost no jazz musicians, there were no jazz clubs at that time, there were not even clubs in the modern sense, like you have now in Beijing where Chinese and foreigners can mix. They did not exist at that time, it was almost unthinkable." It was a "cultural desert," as Fleischer puts it.

With a lack of clubs and jazz bands came a thought. "My idea was to privately organize something like a jazz workshop where musicians who had a certain musical base but were interested in learning this new style could join me," Fleischer says. And join him they did. Among the many were Leo Tsao Sung, a classically trained percussionist who's now a famous rock 'n' roll drummer in China, and Jung Biao, a pianist and son of a famous classical pianist.

After bringing together some of the best, the Joint Venture Jazz Band was born. "That was a very low level amateur workshop band," Fleischer says modestly. No matter how experienced the band, they did encounter their fair share of dilemmas. "It happened twice that a place was closed down because we had been given a concert gig that had not been formerly licensed by both the public order bureau and the cultural affairs bureau." This was in 1987 Beijing.

THE SWINGING MANDARINS

In 1988 Fleischer organized the Swinging Mandarins (piaoyao togzhi), composed of himself as bassist and bandleader, drummer Liu Xiaosong (China), guitarist Paul Shupack (USA), saxophonist Frederic Cho (half French–half Korean), and pianist Liang Heping whose first wife held a PhD in English and helped translate not only sheet music and arrangements, but also the name of the band. This proved difficult as there was no perfect Chinese rendition for the Western concept "swing" nor for "Mandarin"; the Chinese name "piaoyao togzhi" literally means "swaying comrades."

At the time, Fleischer lived in a one-bedroom apartment. Friend Jung Yao helped him acquire a piano through tickets for rationed goods. "When you rationed goods, whether food or other things, people reserve the tickets so they can buy one item in a social planned economy." The two bought a piano (through this system), set it up in Fleischer's apartment in the diplomatic compound, and hosted a rehearsal-turned-party almost every week.

Not long after, the band set out on their first public performance. "The first place where we performed publicly was Maxine's Restaurant, owned by Pierre Cardin as a European partner." Although not the first jazz band, the Swinging Mandarins did hold the title of the first Chinese/foreign jazz band after the Shanghai-based Peace Hotel Jazz Band in China. "There have been foreigners, expats in Beijing before . . . but they were mostly doing rock 'n' roll or other music styles."

Fleischer, who considers himself an amateur, notes that he's better as a bandleader than as a musician. "I know exactly what I want these guys to play to produce a certain sound, a certain rhythm, or a certain swing." He promises that he's not a composer, yet he makes simple arrangements, rearranging standards to give them a "special unmistakable label."

THE BEIJING JAZZ COMMUNITY

The jazz community in Beijing has faced the same fate as in many other countries; at least that's what Fleischer perceives: "Jazz is more a niche music than a broad popular music." For the musician, it is this music community that allows him to bond with people and make connections in other countries. "When I arrive in a new place I try to make contact with musicians." But what Fleischer found was that there weren't any musicians to come into contact with. "So I said to myself, I've got to do something." Many people were interested and wanted to participate. For the audience, it was as he describes it, the cultural desert. "If you provide a drop of water, everybody will run to it."

Years later, times are different. State-sponsored commercial agencies bring in foreign orchestras (especially from Eastern Europe and Asian countries) who try to make their living in Beijing's booming economy. "Booming economies always attract artists. A similar phenomenon occurred in Berlin after the reunification in 1990 where musicians came from all over Germany." The same holds true for the arts scene in Beijing.

HOTELS VS. CLUBS FOR JAZZ

As far as venues for jazz in Beijing go, there's a very distinct difference between hotels now and hotels in the time when Fleischer once occupied the area. At that time, there were no jazz clubs. "The only places to hear jazz at that time were indeed the lobby bars of hotels, and they would have foreign, mostly Filipino musicians." Fleischer remembers some of the first performances he gave in Beijing. "[It] was with a Filipino duo at the Shangri-La Hotel. . . . At that time there were simply no Chinese bands that hotels could hire except for classical music. But that was then, and this is now. Nowadays, there's a younger generation, of course, of jazz musicians. However, the quality of the music depends on where you go. One hotel . . . it still exists, and they had a very good band, a Latin jazz band."

Like music has changed since 1987, so has the economic environment. "You have musicians from all over the world who want to live and survive in China by making music here. That was unthinkable in 1987." Fleischer does note that there was an exception he can think of: the guitarist son of the Madagascar diplomat who decided to stay when his father was posted home again. "Today he's the only foreigner who has for a long time made music, I mean pop-jazz wise, in China."

OLD CHINA VS. NEW CHINA

In Beijing, you can see the old China and the new China side by side within blocks of each other. According to Fleischer, "this very rapid development has a number of side effects." The environmental side effects may be some of the more serious. "If you travel east . . . [to the] beach resorts, you can go for hundreds of kilometers through landscape which is not just environmentally affected, I would call it destroyed." The area, which Fleischer notes, is a quarry for cement (and tire) factories to aid in the tremendous construction boom happening in Beijing. But the common feature the Chinese share? If Fleischer has any say, it's their ability to adapt: "The Chinese have a tremendous ability to adapt, to reorient . . . to preserve some of their values."

LIU YUAN: CIU JIAN'S COLLEAGUE, SO-CALLED FATHER OF JAZZ IN CHINA

During his late 1980s initial search for kindred jazz musicians in Beijing, Fleischer found tenor saxophonist Liu Yuan, who in the last twenty-plus years has become a well-known jazz saxophonist in China, considered by some the father of jazz in China. Fleischer observes that Liu Yuan was almost the only Chinese he met who dealt more intensively with jazz music than all the other musicians he encountered. Fleischer also points out the connection between jazz, rock 'n' roll, and Liu Yuan when I asked him if there was rock 'n' roll in China in the mid-1980s: "Yes, rock 'n' roll was coming up. The recognized pioneer of rock 'n' roll was Cui Jian.[2] He mixed rock 'n' roll with some Chinese folk elements." Cui Jian was backed by a guitarist from Madagascar, and Liu Yuan, his saxophonist. Although Liu Yuan joined the workshop, Fleischer notes he didn't really need the training. "I think he was the only developed jazz musician I had met at that stage."

Liu Yuan was a member of Cui Jian's rock 'n' roll band[3] at the time, playing saxophone but sometimes taking on the suona, a Chinese double-reed horn. "It's an instrument that looks remotely like a clarinet, so it's a woodwind, straight wood wind instrument. Liu Yuan would play that instrument, but he was very, very keen on jazz. He had bought himself an old Selmer saxophone and he would seek every opportunity to play." While Fleischer's approach was to record music for fun, Liu Yuan took a more serious approach. "As a band leader and even more as a workshop leader, I would keep on telling people what they were supposed to play and what they were not supposed to play . . . he didn't like to be told what he had to do, especially in the presence of others." Although Liu Yuan may have been just as experienced, Fleischer's knowledge of arrangements, style, and how to make a band swing was an area he greatly excelled at.

As for Liu Yuan being the "father of jazz music in China": "Success has many fathers," Fleischer recites, "and failure is an orphan, as you know."

Fleischer agrees that, to his knowledge, Liu Yuan was the first Chinese jazz musician [in Beijing] to perform on a professional level, and who had a serious interest in modern jazz. "I wouldn't know of anybody else who seriously did that." Aside from being the father of jazz in China, Liu Yuan had an entrepreneurial spirit. "[He] also opened . . . what is probably the first real, real jazz club in Beijing, the CD Jazz Café, a place uniquely designed for the purpose of light jazz."

As a child, Liu Yuan studied only traditional folkloric Chinese music and, taking after his father, played the suona, a Chinese wind instrument. He began his formal studies at the Beijing Art School in 1975, and after graduation worked for twelve years as a professional suona soloist with the Beijing Song and Dance Troupe. In 1977 the troupe travelled to Europe to perform, and it was then that Yuan was exposed to live jazz performances for the first time. "It felt really close to me," he said. And while he admittedly did not understand jazz music—"I didn't really get it . . . why were they playing like this?"—in the 1980s he attempted to start making it.[4]

Using mostly tapes and CDs from friends and foreigners who would visit, he aimed to create similar music. "[Grover] Washington was a bit easier to understand. I tried to go closer to him, and do something similar. And then, so, at the beginning, it was just random, and just listening more and more. And then I started understanding the difference between different styles, and I got to better understand it."

In 1984, Yuan borrowed 465 yuan (approximately $75) from his brother and sister in order to purchase his first saxophone: "The tone of saxophone was very attractive to me, but when I was 20, I didn't have a clear sense of what jazz was. I just knew I liked the saxophone." Although Yuan's decision to play the instrument was not in line with traditional Chinese rules, time was on his side. "When China opened in the 80s, it became more normal for young people to choose their own ideal. And so, it was not easy, but I really chose sax because it was something that really talked to me."

"People asked me why I gave up playing the suona. My answer was that I loved it (the saxophone) so much, I didn't care. My parents were worried at first, but what my father cared most about was my attitude," Yuan told *China Daily* in 2010. "Once he found out how serious I was about the saxophone, he accepted my decision."

Yuan left the Beijing Song and Dance Troupe and in 1984, formed a popular rock 'n' roll band, Seven Ply Wood, with China's first rock 'n' roll icon, Cui Jian. In 1999 Yuan became the manager of the Beijing jazz club CD Jazz Café, and performed regularly with his quartet, the Liu Yuan Jazz Quartet.

In 2006 Yuan opened the East Shore Jazz Café in Beijing's Houhai district with his childhood friend, jazz drummer Li Yongxian.[5]

The East Shore Jazz Café has been described by *Time* magazine as "the most promising venue in Beijing's budding jazz scene,"[6] and listed in Moon Spotlight Beijing, a travel guide, as "one of the only Houhai bars that's truly worth a look."[7] However, Yuan told *China Daily* that the opening of East Shore Jazz Café came with frustration: "Back then I was pissed off because I was not respected. I don't want to offend Kenny G, but there were times when I would be interrupted by the audience asking me to play Kenny G. A lot of people at that time had a misconception about jazz. They thought Kenny G was jazz."[8]

In an interview, Yuan juxtaposed traditional music in China with the freeform of jazz: "Music, or folkloric music, or whatever it is today in China, it's music that is very clear for the people. They can understand. They can sing it along. It sounds clear. It's very easy to understand. Jazz is very different to all these kinds of music, because it goes through another path. It's something that you have to feel, and to experience with your own feelings, and your own understanding." Yuan believes that jazz will be important for the future development of music—any kind of music—in China: "Jazz is not something new for the Westerners, for the Americans. But in China, it was something totally new. And well, it has its identity, and it can bring a lot to society."

Yuan discussed the future of jazz in China, comparing its music to a kind of precious stone—"something that you don't dare touch," and something that is "close and far from you" at the same time. He believes, though, if people do get to the stone—to understand jazz correctly—it would be very interesting for society. "The future can be gorgeous, and it can be nothing. It all depends; we need that everybody brings in his own efforts. If today nobody does anything, or if there isn't any work going on. Then there's going to be nothing tomorrow. So you can't say tomorrow's going to be good or bad. We have to see the efforts that are done today. It all depends of today."

He is optimistic, though, and predicts that more Chinese musicians and more Chinese audiences will dare to touch the stone, but time is a decisive element. "We have to wait for the development of society, and of education of the society, and for them, time to discover things that are more interesting, and things that can bring meaning to their life," he said.

While time is essential for jazz to realize its true potential in China, according to Yuan, education is also crucial: "In China, you have education for classical music, folk music, opera music, there are so many, many styles.

But jazz doesn't have much education to it. And also, in Chinese education, music is not an important topic." He adds, "It requires both work from education, from the musicians themselves, from the audience, and it's all those coordinating into the development of society today. So it's a lot of things coming together, and with time, that will make it happen."

Does Yuan believe that a "Chinese jazz"—a jazz opposed to American jazz and unique to China—could ever be developed? "It could come in the future, but today, the Chinese musicians who study or perform jazz, they still have to understand well American music and American jazz. And then, once they really understand it, then they can create their own thing." Today, however, he believes that it would be "stupid" to use Chinese folkloric instruments, and play jazz with it. "If you perform jazz music with Chinese instruments, it will give nothing, because we still haven't understood really, I mean, we still have to totally integrate, and totally understand what is jazz music. Otherwise, what we're going to do is not real jazz. It's just a copy, or something. You know? So we need to integrate it, first. And next step, in the future, will be to do our real jazz. But today, we haven't reached this step, this level," he concluded.

Yuan still performs live with his quartet, which includes Si Feng on piano, Huang Yong on bass, and Izumi on drums[9] at his East Shore Jazz Café on Saturday nights at 10:00 p.m. And as for his reputation as the father of jazz in China, Yuan insists the epithet is exaggerated: "I've done a lot, it's true, but a lot of other people are doing a lot of jazz here, and I'm not the only one."

CHAPTER 12

Liu Sola: China's Musically Eclectic Composer

Gunther Schuller, the recognized progenitor of the term "Third Stream"—a fusion of classical music and jazz—would have appreciated the music of Liu Sola. The musical traditions of China have been blended with jazz, blues, and improvisation by composer, author, and vocalist Liu Sola. Her background is testimony to her eclectic musical approach:

> After graduating from the Central Conservatory of Music with a degree in composition, she published an award-winning novella *You Have No Choice*. Since the 1980's, Liu Sola has scored many Chinese and international film sound tracks, as well as TV and drama productions. She has composed music for orchestra, ensemble, opera, modern theater, modern dance, and art exhibitions. Her range of musical styles includes classical music, jazz, early music, rock, traditional and contemporary music. During the 90's, she recorded with Pól Brennan, Bill Laswell, James Blood Ulmer, Jerome Brailey, Henry Threadgill, Umar Bin Hassan, Amina Claudine Myers, Fernando Saunders, and Pheeroan akLaff. In 2003, she founded the Liu Sola & Friends Ensemble, teaming up with several Chinese instrumental virtuosos. In 2012, Chinese guitar virtuoso Liu Yijun (lao wu) joined the ensemble.
>
> She is the founder of Liu Sola Music Studio, located in the Songzhuang art colony, a Beijing artist district. Liu Sola designed and built a music space for her ensemble to rehearse and record. She has composed and produced film soundtracks for directors such as Zhang Nuanxin, Michael Apted, Li Shaohong, Lü Yue, Ning Ying and others. In 2013, she established the Liu Sola & Friends Ensemble Independent Film Music Work Shop.
>
> Her music works include the chamber opera *Fantasy of the Red Queen* (2006), performed by Ensemble Modern and the Liu Sola & Friends Ensemble. Liu Sola is the librettist and music composer, artistic director, costume designer and leading vocalist. The chamber opera *The Afterlife of Li Jiantong* (2009) is a work dedicated to her mother, a Chinese political-historical writer. Liu Sola wrote both the libretto and the music. It was performed by Theatre of Voices, conducted by Paul Hillier.[1]

THE CHINESE MUSIC TRADITION VS. JAZZ

Sitting in her apartment living room in an industrial cum gentrified section of Beijing, following a sumptuous dinner of traditional Mongolian dishes, Ms. Sola commented on a range of subjects dealing with traditional Chinese music and jazz. For example, she perceives indigenous jazz musicians do not know enough about jazz to form a legitimate jazz festival.

LS: I have a lot of difficulty outside of China about how they categorize my music. So I don't want to categorize other musicians in China if they are jazz musicians or not jazz musicians. And if I start to curate a music festival and I call it jazz music, I would refuse many Chinese musicians.

This is not the country that produced jazz music. We love to listen to jazz music and there's a little information about jazz, but most of the musicians or artists are not very familiar with jazz. So if you started a jazz music festival in China, it means you're actually open to foreigners. There's a very small group of Chinese people who know a little bit of jazz. Chinese musicians wouldn't be qualified to come to the festival.

Q: Why is there such a small jazz community here in Beijing?
LS: Jazz is not a Chinese thing. It is not our tradition. Jazz is so foreign to Chinese musicians and the audience. China's been closed for so long. You heard the old-fashioned jazz musicians in Shanghai's Peace Hotel that came from the 1930s and '40s. And then after that, after 1949, after the communists, most music was very limited and controlled by the government. So actually, since 1949 and before the 1980s music information was very limited to revolutionary romanticism, classical music. That's all we could play, our traditional music. Only after the eighties when China started to open the door that some information came out.

But with jazz music, you need to pick up not only the sound of the technique and how to play, you also have to feel it. It's not only what you can read on a score. The musician doesn't have a chance to have this kind of music. This music is very foreign for China.

Introduction to the Blues

Q: How come you feel it?
LS: I went to stay in the United States in 1987, I was invited by the American government. I heard Junior Wells play to me, face-to-face. That's why I feel

this blues so strong. From the blues I started to have this very close contact with blues musicians. I'd really been studying with them. For one month, every day, staying with them, to play with them, learning the rhythm, the feeling. Then after that, I came back to New York again to hang out, recording with jazz and blues musicians. So being around the great jazz musicians, they taught me so much.

But the first time, when I started to play the blues I couldn't do it. It was more of a shock. I think I was the only one, maybe the first one from mainland China who heard the blues. It was such great music. I graduated from a conservatory. I had already composed a rock opera in China. I had already composed mainly music for a film soundtrack, but I still had never heard of blues. Then I said, "okay, for this I have to leave the country; I have to follow this music." So I started to learn.

Q: Do you think there's ever going to be such a thing as Chinese jazz? When I've heard your CDs, I hear the beginning of the blending of certain elements.

LS: After I'd been staying with the blues musicians for a month, and how every day they'd teach me how to sing blues, I slowly figured out I can't be a real blues musician. It's their tradition and the way they sing. What I suddenly heard is our own tradition, there's some familiarity. We have to understand how the blues come, why the blues comes out, and how it was formed and how they use emotions. I suddenly heard my own background, my Chinese background.

Why is it similar to the blues and jazz? I went back to my own tradition to understand my own tradition, then create something from my own background. When I start to hear my own blues tone, my own jazz tone, then I start to create it as a so-called Chinese blues, blues storytelling in China. It's kind of similar to blues. It's like you talk and then you sing, you talk and sing, at the same time.

Also the melody goes dramatically up and down because of the language and the emotions. And in the traditional theater, also you can hear that kind of wave of performance because it's actually based on folk music, like blues. In Chinese folk music they do their own structure. In China, actually, every traditional instrumental piece originally comes from improvisation.

Scoring Traditional Chinese Music vs. Improvisation

LS: Just after about 1949, our education system started to categorize our music at school, into the conservatory system. So after the conservatory system had made all kinds of traditional music become scored, then all the traditional young musician trained from the conservatory. The traditional music became scored music, became classical, became something you had to learn from the score.

But before that, everything was improvisation, just like jazz. They may have a form that may be 31 bars, a very free form, but that form is from the language, from a poem, from the traditional form. A certain form that has a title, and then it's like a sonata.

But with this form, you improvised inside the form. That's how a traditional instrumental piece comes. The teacher tells you how to play the form, then you improvise with the form, a little bit like jazz. So, if you understand the tradition, it's not difficult to combine these two forms, the jazz form and traditional music form. You create something because when you understand that there's two sides, then the music is no longer tradition or jazz, it's become your own new music.

Rehearsing Her Traditional Musicians to Perform Jazz

LS: With some of my traditional musicians, when they rehearse here with me, the first thing I teach them is swing and improvisation. Those are two things they have to get. If they don't get these two things, you'll always be a traditional musician.

Q: A lot of this music is very much like Indian music. Like a lot of Indian music, there is a form, but it's also highly improvised and it takes a lot of ingenuity. Do you really feel the same way about evolving Chinese jazz music?
LS: The thing about it is China is very different. We are a socialist country since 1949. This socialism country music system is everything—all the traditional art is being organized. Not like Indian artists. Indian musicians stay the traditional way. They play like generations played the same. If we find a good musician, they will tie the good musician to a conservatory, train them to read, and everything they play becomes a Marxist score. Then they teach the other students.

That's how the word is spreading in China. How a classical score, Chinese music, how it continues is mostly by scores. It's very different. That's why the traditional musician in China is very different from Indian musicians or Korean musicians. They actually can't improvise. They are good at playing master scores. They read like a Western classical musician.

My pipa player can read Western notation, so can the pianist. You write it, then they read. But they can't improvise. That's why when I organize them together to play music, I write it down. I score jazz music. Actually, it's against the jazz music attitude. I have to write it down in notes for them to make it sound like an improvised solo.

Q: Most of the musicians, maybe all of the jazz musicians I have met here so far, they're very good some of them. But I don't hear any Chinese jazz music. I hear them playing what they've heard from the CDs or the movies or television programs. It's not just imitation, it's also their own individual personality. But I still don't hear any Chinese elements. Why is that?

LS: That's the reason I don't want to organize a jazz festival. If I organize a jazz festival most of the Chinese musicians would think, "Oh, that's trendy. That's the way I get into a festival." They think that's a chance to get into a festival. That's why I don't want to support any traditional musicians in this country. I think you have to understand what we had originally. That's also the reason I write a score for my musicians. I want them to get some sounds first. My notation is based on a traditional Chinese sound, or wave, a kind of a jazz, or swing, or different chords, but not exactly like the jazz. I mix them. I very carefully listen to traditional notes. It's just that what place you put them or what space you create. That's what I learned from [musician and composer] Ornette Coleman, about space, especially free jazz.

Free jazz is about creating your own space. I don't force a pipa player to play a piano. I don't like to make Western songs for the pipa songs. Pipa has to play what is good for pipa. So I carefully reserve pipa sounds, and then just to create a space, I write a notation that's a space for the pipa.

After they play for me I say, "you like that?" They say "yes." It's also easier to play and it feels good after they read the score once. "So from here, now you can be free. You pipa, anything you want to, just feel free." So that's how they start. They say, "okay, here you go out of my score." I let them train their ears first. I train them actually from their own sounds. It's just spaced differently. It feels like a different sound, but actually it's from their own technique. I don't give them a kind of weird sound, like they feel, oh, it's modern music. No. It's their own sound.

That's how I create this Chinese jazz. The player has to feel familiar with the sound. That's also jazz. The jazz musician feels good about their instrument. That's how they play. That's why I want them to feel good about their own instrument, and not to feel difficult about it.

A Woman in a Man's World

Q: It occurs to me as I'm listening to you that all of the musicians I've interviewed so far are all men. You're the only woman in Beijing who's doing anything in the jazz area that I'm aware of. Why is that?

LS: I've grown up as a musician. I graduated from a conservatory as a classical composer. That's why. First I was a classical composer, then I became a novelist. I feel some struggle inside me. I couldn't do music because what I learned was not what I felt at the beginning. So I gave up the training as a classical composer, because what I heard, what I learned, it didn't feel close to me. I didn't know why.

That's why I started to write and use words. Actually most of my early writing is about music. My novels were also about classical music, modern music, pop music, and stories around musicians. And then I heard the blues in Chicago, Junior Wells, the Old Chicago Blues. He sang and played the harmonica. He performed for me in a Chicago bar. He was the master who represents the Chicago blues.

Actualization

Q: What instrument do you play?

LS: I played piano when I was little. It didn't feel close to me. That's why I gave up piano and became a singer. I felt "Okay, let's start with the voice. The words can go as far as I want to." But with the piano, I can't. I just feel like it doesn't connect, so I gave up the piano.

Q: In the United States we would say you're a person who is self-actualizing. You're constantly expressing yourself and it doesn't seem to make any difference, the obstacles, the challenges. Where does that come from? Were your parents like this?

LS: My mom's like that. My mom is a writer. All her life she had trouble with her writing. Her writing was forbidden by the communists. Mao Tse Dong criticized her writing. She was the only writer who criticized by Mao.

Q: Is that an honor?

LS: It's a big disaster for her life as a writer. Her writing was forbidden for many years, until now.

Q: Is she still alive?
LS: No. She isn't, since last year [2005].

Q: What about your father? What did he do?
LS: My father is a high official in the Party. My father is a politician all his life, and a warrior, communist, fighting all his life for what he believed. He's way, way faithful to what he believed. That's why he also had trouble all his life. He was in jail for eight years. He completely protected my mom. He just fights for what he believes. A very honest, beautiful man.

Q: You're the same way. You've got a very quiet way. You fight for what you believe in the music. Do you agree with that?
LS: I feel I fight too much. Because when I fight with everything, I feel not right.

Challenges

Q: What would you say has been your biggest challenge in terms of your music?
LS: Everything for me is challenging. The biggest challenge last year was this opera. It's like I switched back to what I learned and then also brought everything together that I learned this last twenty years with blues and jazz, but in the Chinese way. I went back to my own revolutionary background, because the opera is about our time and it's about the revolution. So I have to put all this together and created an opera that the orchestra can play, my musicians can play, with my own libretto. That's difficult.

Q: You're probably one of the few people, at least in Beijing, who could write an opera, could write the music and the libretto. Is that so?
LS: Yeah.

Q: But you performed this opera in Germany, not here.
LS: In Germany.

Q: Is it because of the nature of the story?

LS: I think, yes. The story. We still hope one day we can perform it in China. We're still trying. You never know.

Growing Jazz in China

Q: What do you think needs to happen for the acceptance of jazz for it to grow jazz in China? Is it more education in the schools, or what?
LS: I think knowledge, information, and education certainly are very useful. I feel like I'd like to make musicians believe that music cannot be categorized. This is one thing I'm really against, why the Chinese have to play world music. This is the way people think. If you're Chinese, you shouldn't play rock and roll. It's what the Western people think, how can Chinese play rock, you know. Why does Russia play rock? It's so old fashioned.

So, America can play jazz, but other people cannot play jazz. Every nation, every kind of people can blend their own songs into a jazz form. Our field is freedom in music. I think that's the whole thing of the spirit. And that's also in New York, many organizations fighting against the cataloging. Everybody's asking, "you play what? Jazz, or funk, or what?"

Q: As opposed to playing music?
LS: Yeah. You just play music. Good music is good music. It doesn't matter what is good music. That's something I hope one day everybody can agree with and open the door for non-mainstream music, or non-European centered music. Even Chinese musicians are sometimes not aware of this. They feel so cool imitating Jimi Hendrix or Miles Davis so well. That doesn't mean anything. I keep telling them it doesn't mean anything about your own spirit. How could they know that there's a world there outside China? They don't know. Musicians are being categorized all the time. That's the big difficulty for good music.

A Trend toward More Individualistic Music in China?

Q: Do you agree that there will be more individualistic music in China as China continues its economic development, which seems to emphasize individual entrepreneurship? Do you think the two will go hand in hand?
LS: I think so. They will go abroad and then come back, and then more foreign musicians will come into China. The international face of music is starting. Lots of musicians who come from different countries will come

here to play. Then the musicians here will think what they should do. This is only the starting point, now, in China.

What you see is not such advanced jazz music going on here, because for the last few years, when there's a jazz music festival here it's always the bad musicians who come from every other country, and they don't feel that Chinese bands play great. They just go ahead and join the festival and then after the experience, maybe the Chinese musicians will try very hard to imitate. That's a problem. The festival is always organized by non-Chinese, so they don't need to care about what the Chinese really think.

Q: Are you referring to Udo Hoffmann and the Beijing International Jazz Festival?
LS: Oh, he's a great guy. He organized the jazz festival. He is a very experienced jazz festival organizer.

Q: What would you like to say about jazz in China, in response to a question I haven't asked you?
LS: I wouldn't call myself a jazz musician. I do feel jazz music really inspired me. I would just say all the jazz musicians, they're all great teachers for me, to inspire my music. So I wouldn't call my music just Chinese jazz music. This is just music, the music I do is inspired by jazz music, by African music, by rock music, by modern music, inspired by all kinds of music, blues, and Chinese traditional music. That's what I feel like I would like to call my own music.

I wouldn't go on the stage to establish American-Peking opera music. That wouldn't make sense. Because jazz for a long time belonged to certain musicians, that's tradition. But I wouldn't think that standard jazz belonged to Chinese people. We had standard jazz music then, because that's something imported, something that's part of the colonial system. I don't think that's the model for Chinese musician to go to. I think that would be wrong.

I think what we should learn is the spirit. All kinds of music, the spirit, and to understand the music background. Why does music come from such a simple standard music, then immediately becomes this jazz influence for the whole world? We should learn and understand that. Just like how we learn modern music. The music of composer Schoenberg influences our whole country, also rock. The way to go is the way to develop our own thing that's been started by all kinds of different music.

Q: You're saying that because of China's current development for the next couple of generations at least, that maybe a new kind of music is going to emerge from China to the rest of the world. It's going to combine classical, with rock, with jazz, with blues, with twentieth century, with world music, and all of these various elements coming together.

LS: Yes. That's what I hope I can hear. I don't hope that the whole China is going to play jazz or the whole of China is going to play 1970s rock. That would be so wrong. We've become like that, we've really become a colonial country culturally.

I always mention to my musicians, I always keep telling them, this is not a colonial country. You have to be aware of that. You have to be aware of how many cultural backgrounds we have, how rich a traditional culture we have, because we have so many different kinds of instruments and a long history about music. We have a lot of time to learn that first, and then, you know, a lot of time to learn everything. I believe something will come out with the younger generation. Maybe this is really a transition time for China because the older generation, or my generation, is too confused. Change is coming too fast, and we are sometimes not ready for the change. Lots of people are not ready because of the trend. But for the younger generation maybe there's a hope. They will be more free.

In Japan they have a great Japanese music tradition. But most of the young people are not aware. They think they do something modern and a good imitation, they think that's a strong point. But sometimes I just feel pity. I feel like you should pick up what you have first, and then do the new thing, combine the new thing together. That's something Asian. That's what I feel.

CHAPTER 13

The Beijing Jazz Scene

While Shanghai has been the main focus of the evolution of jazz in China, since the late 1980s the jazz scene in Beijing (China's capital, once known as Peking) has also evolved. As in Shanghai, you can find jazz in some large venues, in hotel bars and food courts, and especially in a few small clubs dedicated to jazz performance.

The Beijing jazz scene over the last several decades has clearly evolved. As diplomat Martin Fleischer reports (chapter 11), when he arrived in Beijing in the late 1980s there were no jazz clubs in China's capital. Hotel bars and lobbies certainly had groups playing popular music and some jazz, but no clubs dedicated to jazz. While the Peace Hotel Jazz Band rejuvenated jazz in Shanghai in 1980, followed by Willie Ruff's concert at the Shanghai Conservatory of Music in 1981 (see chapter 10), it is not until the early 1990s that jazz becomes a public presence in Beijing with the emergence of the Beijing International Jazz Festival created and curated by German entrepreneur Udo Hoffman.

THE BEIJING INTERNATIONAL JAZZ FESTIVAL 1993–2000

It is perhaps no coincidence that the Beijing International Jazz Festival found a home in Beijing. First, Beijing is China's capital. This makes Beijing a prime candidate for a festival, let alone a jazz festival, because of its population density, and its business and diplomatic activities. Second, Beijing is home to saxophonist Liu Yuan and formerly to German diplomat Martin Fleischer. The latter "trained" Liu Yuan in the mid-1980s in some of the fundamental elements of jazz. In effect, Beijing was ripe for a jazz festival post-Mao (who died in September 1976) and post–Tiananmen Square (1989). By the early 1990s China was on an upswing economically that was drawing more and more foreigners, particularly Westerners, to the city.

In this context, guitarist Dennis Rea reported that

The Beijing International Jazz Festival was founded in 1993 by German entrepreneur Udo Hoffmann, a longtime member of the city's expatriate business community with a passion for modern jazz. Hoffmann's involvement with the Chinese music scene dates from the formative days of Beijing rock in the late 1980s, when he was instrumental in organizing the now legendary "parties" where budding Chinese rockers were given a chance to perform away from official scrutiny. In the early 1990s Hoffmann, recognizing a growing interest in jazz among Chinese musicians and listeners, drew on his musical expertise and contacts among the international jazz community to launch China's first jazz festival. From the start, festival organizers made a point of covering the entire continuum of jazz styles, from Dixieland to free improvisation. Such musical catholicity would be unusual in any major jazz festival, much less a festival in communist China.[1]

Former expatriate Rea described the inaugural event:

> The inaugural Beijing International Jazz Festival took place in 1993 at the 700-seat Beijing Children's Theatre. Co-sponsored by the Goethe Institute, the China International Cultural Exchange Centre, and others, the festival proved so successful that organizers decided to make it an annual event. Performers from 1994 and 1995 editions of the festival included the madcap Willem Breuker Kollektief, the Clusone Trio, turntable terrorist Otomo Yoshihide, trumpeter Palle Mikkelborg, and fusion violinist Didier Lockwood, as well as a number of Chinese jazz bands.

By 1996 the administrative burden of organizing such a large and diverse festival—compounded . . . by the ever-shifting vagaries of Chinese politics—led Hoffmann to take on as his partner Robert Van Kan, the assistant cultural attaché at the Netherlands Embassy. Van Kan brought to the festival a comprehensive knowledge of modern music and years of experience in negotiating cultural exchange activities. The festival venue was shifted to the 1,400-seat 21st Century Theatre, and numerous corporate and foreign government sponsors were recruited to help defray operational costs.

Although a sizable number of foreign expatriates attended, the majority of the audience was Chinese.[2]

Over the course of 1993–2000 Beijing Jazz Festivals, a cornucopia of foreign and indigenous jazz musicians performed:

Andreas Schreiber, violinist
Antonio Martinez "Candela" (Spain)
Banda Sonora & PLA Orchestra (Italy, China)
Beijing Jazz Unit (China)
Betty Carter and Her Trio (USA)
BJ (Beijing) Funky Octet (China, USA)
Cercle Trio (Austria, UK)
Chano Dominguez Group (Spain)
Chen Dili (China)
Clusone Trio (Netherlands)
Cristof Lauer Trio (Germany/USA)
Danish Radio Jazz Orchestra (Denmark)
Danius Pulauskas Sextet (Lithuania)
Dave Holland Group (USA)
Denis Colin Trio (France)
Dieter Glauwischnig, pianist/Andreas Schreiber Duo (Austria)
Ding Wei and Wide Angle (China)
Django Bates Human Chain (UK)
Doctor 3 (Italy)
Doky Brothers (Denmark)
E.M.T. (Lithuania and Germany)
Enrico Rava, trumpeter (Italy)
Enrico Rava's "Carmen Project" (Italy, China)
Ensemble for New Improvised Music (Germany/USA/Russia/New Zealand)
Eugene Pao Group (Hong Kong)
Fred van Hove (Belgium)
Gaoshan Luishui (China and Germany)
George Lewis (United States)
Gianluigi Trovesi Octet (Italy)
Golden Angle Jazz Band (China)
Guys (China)
Guus Janssen Quintet (Netherlands)
Han Bennink Trio
Hiroshi Minami Quartet (Japan)
Howard "Hojo" Johnson (USA)
Illouz (France)
In-Sound-Out (China)
Irene Schweizer/Pierre Favre (Switzerland)
Jazz Crusaders (USA)

John Taylor/John Surman (UK)
Jon Jang Sextet (USA/China)
Jon Rose-Otomo Yoshihide (Australia and Japan)
Karin Krog Group (Netherlands)
Keiko Lee (Japan)
Kiichiro Hayashi (Japan)
LAND (USA)
Lenni Kalle Taipale (Finland)
Liu Yuan (tenor saxophonist) with pianist Kong Hongwei (China)
Liu Yuan Group (China)
Liu Sola and Friends (China/USA)
Lluis-Vidal Trio (Spain)
Lost Chart Ensemble (Canada)
Maria Joao/Mario Laghino Duo (Portugal)
Martin Speake Group (UK)
Michiel Borstlap Sextet (Netherlands)
Misha Mengelberg, solo piano (Netherlands)
Misha Mengelberg/Han Bennink/George Lewis Trio (Netherlands, USA)
Mynta (Sweden/India)
NDR Bigband with Palle Mikkelborg (Germany)
Neighbors (Austria)
New Jungle Orchestra (Denmark)
Nils Landgren Funk Unit (Sweden)
Nordic Sounds (Denmark/Finland/Norway/Sweden)
P.L.A. Orchestra-Golden Angle Jazz Band (China)
Palle Mikkelborg Duo (Denmark)
Paolo Frescu Quartet (Italy)
Papadimitriou-Sylleou Duo (Greece)
Pascal v. Wroblewsky Trio (Germany)
Paul Motian's Electric Bebop Band (USA)
Pierre Doerge's New Jungle Orchestra (Denmark)
Rhythm Dogs Big Band (China)
Richard Galliano Trio (France)
Rios (USA)
Scandinavian Jazz Quartet (Denmark and Finland)
Sixun, multicultural fusion (France)
Steffen Schom/Claudio Puntin Duo (Germany)
Stephane Kochoyan Trio (France)
Stephane Planchon's Rendez-vous (France)

Steve Blailock's Swingthing (USA)
Ten Part Invention (Australia)
The Far East Side Band (USA/China/China/Korea)
The Jorge Pardo/Carles Benavent Group (Spain)
Tien Square (China)
Tony Oxley, drummer
Trevor Watts Moire Music Drum Orchestra (UK)
Ugetsu (Germany)
Uli Lenz/Johannes Barthelmes Duo (Germany)
Vienna Art Orchestra (Austria)
Wide Angle Jazz Band (China)
Willem Breuker Kollektief (Netherlands)
Wonderlust (Australia)[3]

These were clearly "international" jazz festivals with ninety-one ensembles from twenty-five countries represented, many from China, of course, the Pacific Rim (e.g., Japan, Australia, New Zealand), Europe, and the United States. What is of greater import is the large number of ensembles combining musicians from two or more countries:

15 International Combos
11 China
6 Netherlands
6 France
5 Germany
5 Denmark
4 United States
4 United Kingdom
4 Italy
3 Spain
3 Japan
3 Austria
2 Australia
1 Switzerland
1 Sweden
1 Lithuania
1 Hong Kong
1 Greece
1 Finland

1   Belgium
1   New Zealand
1   Russia
1   India
1   Korea

The annual iteration of the Beijing Jazz Festival under Hoffmann's leadership ended in 2000. The 2001 festival was cancelled due to the September 11, 2001, attack on New York City's World Trade Center.[4] The second annual iteration of the festival began in 2007. This time around, however, Hoffmann joined forces with the Beijing-located Midi School (described in chapter 17). The festival morphed into more of a large-scale pop/rock festival than a jazz event.

THE NINE GATES JAZZ FESTIVAL 2007–PRESENT

The jazz festival torch did not lie fallow for long, however. As the interview with jazz electric bass virtuoso Huang Yong, or "Adam," as he prefers to be called, attests to, the "Nine Gates Jazz Festival" picks up in 2007 where Hoffmann's jazz festival left off. In mid-May 2007, Adam mounted an international jazz festival with bands from Europe, Japan, Korea, and South America. American saxophonist Antonio M. Hart and veteran jazz pianist Meddy Gerville from France's Réunion Island were the headliners at the 2013 Nine Gates Jazz Festival in Beijing, plus a string of young performers and local ensembles.

Named after the nine ancient city gates in Beijing, the festival marked its sixth year [2013] by opening at the Cultural Center of Xicheng District with two young jazz bands. The festival comprised performances at three venues in Xicheng district, with two-hour jazz performances nightly.

Twenty-one Chinese jazz bands joined six others from the United States, Austria, France, Poland and Czech Republic by playing improvised music with styles ranging from century-old New Orleans jazz to big band swing and bebop. The opening show was performed by the Abu Jazz Trio, featuring thirteen-year-old pianist prodigy Dai Liang, and the Li Gaoyang Jazz Quartet, led by its namesake eighteen-year-old saxophonist.

According to Huang's estimation, the number of people in Beijing who regularly attend jazz performances stands at fewer than 10,000. The biggest hurdle in holding the festival, Huang conceded, was securing financial support from the government. Each night of the festival is estimated to cost $50,000. "We have been in talks with the Xicheng district government for six months. It pulled out from offering financial support, but fortunately has provided venues for us," Huang said.[5]

THE JAZZ CLUBS

Several clubs in the 1980–present period are—and were—dedicated to presenting jazz. Some still exist, others do not:

1. Moon Shanghai (4 Gongti Beilu)
2. San Wie Bookstore (60 Fuxingmennei Dajie)
3. Le Café Igosso (Dong San Huan Nanlu; south of the Guomao Bridge on the east side of the street)
4. Salsa Caribe (4 Gongtibei Lu)
5. The Guys-Shadow Café (31 Kexueyuan Nanlu, Haidian District)
6. Chenonceau (1F East Gate Plaza, Dongcheng District behind Poly Plaza)
7. CD Café Jazzbar (East Third Ring Road, south of the Agriculture Exhibition Center)
8. Dongan Club (a.k.a. East Shore Club) located in Houhai; owner Liu Yuan
9. The Stone Boat Café (in Ritan Park, West Gate entrance)

THE SURVIVING JAZZ VENUES[6]

Just like any business in any city, some establishments survive, some do not. The jazz venue business in Beijing is no exception.

SAN WEI BOOKSTORE

One of the long-standing jazz venues—just down the road, it seems, from the Forbidden Palace where Mao's picture still hangs—is the San Wei Bookstore. The venue has a long history and from my own visit to the establishment to interview saxophonist Wu Yun Nan (whose day gig at the time was as a member of the Chinese Navy), it has not changed much since the

1990s. American expatriate David Moser recounts his own experience there as a jazz musician:

> I began another gig at the San Wei Bookstore, an unassuming little two-story structure just off the Avenue of Eternal Peace, a stone's throw from Tiananmen Square. The owners had converted the second floor into a traditional Chinese teahouse, with calligraphy scrolls on the wall and Qing Dynasty-style wooden tables and chairs. With its well-stocked bookstore downstairs, the place became fairly popular with some of Beijing's intelligentsia, and it also became a magnet for foreigners who wanted to experience some of the traditional Chinese atmosphere that had disappeared after Liberation. Even [American Vice President] Dan Quayle had sipped tea there one evening during a visit to China. The owners, a spunky middle-aged woman named Liu Yuansheng and her husband Li Shiqiang, had contacted me with the idea of having regular jazz concerts in the teahouse to give Beijingers a chance to become familiar with the music.
>
> "I don't know much about jazz," Liu Yuansheng told me, "But I know it's a great American art form. We want to create an atmosphere where people come week after week and slowly get to really understand the music, rather than just hearing snippets now and then in American movies." Though having jazz concerts was certainly not illegal, I knew she and her husband might possibly arouse the attention of the authorities by publicizing weekly jazz concerts. But from what I knew of their background, they were no strangers to controversy. Li Shiqiang had been attacked politically and spent almost a decade in jail during the Cultural Revolution. During the Tiananmen Square demonstrations in 1989, the bookstore had provided the student leaders with a quiet meeting place to plan their activities. The political situation had cooled down considerably in the years following the massacre, but there was still an air of oppression that hung over the bookstore like a sour aftertaste.[7]

THE CD CAFÉ

Another long-standing jazz venue in Beijing is the CD Café. Both the CD Café and the East Shore Café have one thing in common: pioneer saxophonist Liu Yuan. A visitor of Chinese heritage to the CD Café—Weihua Zhang—in July 1999, described the venue. What is of interest are the familiar names of many of the players, a testament to the permanence of jazz in Beijing and the longevity of the Chinese and non-Chinese players who have embraced the music. Zhang recounts:

> The CD Café has the longest history. It is well known because the pioneer Chinese jazz musician Liu Yuan performs there. He is also part owner of the club.[8] . . . Liu Yuan's regular drummer is from Japan. He studied once at the Berklee College of Music in Boston. He had been playing at the CD Café for years. The remaining members of the quartet were bassist Liu Yue and pianist Yang Dehui (a third year flute major at the Central Conservatory of Music). There were also joint players from the Touchstone band, including drummer Huan Haitao, who is self-taught, and pianist Xia Jia, former student conductor at the Central Conservatory of Music. Other jazz musicians performing there during our visits included Matthew Roberts (Chinese name Rao Menzhi), a businessman from the United States who plays the trombone; pianist Moreno Donadel from Italy; conga player Liu Xiaosong, and another percussionist named Sar. We had the impression that many of the jazz musicians in Beijing frequent the CD Café when they do not have any other engagement, waiting to sit in and listening to each other.[9]

Unfortunately—as reported by longtime Beijing resident, scholar, and jazz musician David Moser—"The historic CD Cafe is already a thing of the past. It was unexpectedly and quickly demolished a year ago [in 2012]. The manager, Zhang Ling (one of the early bassists in Cui Jian's band) was only given two weeks' notice that the club was going to be torn down to make room for a shopping complex, and he had to clear out the club and the equipment in just a couple weeks before the water and electricity was shut off. Very typical of China. The CD Café moved to a new location near Ritan Park, but of course, it's not the old club, and not the historic space."[10]

THE EAST SHORE CAFÉ

The so-called father of jazz in China, saxophonist Liu Yuan (profiled in chapter 12), left the CD Café and opened his own jazz club (as owner) in July 2006. It's a few steps up from the street to get into the club that holds probably up to 100 people. There are two sections to the club. Other than the well-stocked bar that also serves bar food, there is a raised section toward the back of the club where people can have a little more privacy, and a lower level right in front of the stage that can easily accommodate small ensembles. The stage is not big enough for a big band. This is ideally a club for small ensembles—trios, quartets, perhaps octets. It is intimate. It is designed for up close and personal jazz.

The first night we were there, jazz pianist virtuoso Kong Hong Wei was performing with his trio. Apart from his Oscar Peterson–like style, a lit cigarette constantly adorned the right edge of the piano. Smoking is permitted in public places in China. Only recently has the Chinese Communist Party strongly suggested that party officials refrain from public smoking as a way of demonstrating to the populace at large to quit the habit, at least in public. The bathroom facilities were similarly of non-Western style values: Ming Dynasty as opposed to what one wag has dubbed Western-style "Nixon era"–style toilets.

For Liu Yuan, it is apparent that opening the East Shore Café is more personal than about business. When we interviewed him after hours at the club he made the comparison between talking and making jazz music:

> In jazz, you need to study this language, the melody, classical music, the rhythms, a bunch of things. And it's really long and tough work you have to do before you can go up on stage, and for a few minutes, or a few hours, just create something and actually perform it. It's the same thing for language. You have to study many books, and go into literature. And then you are ready, just improvising and talking, and having a discussion around a theme. I think it's the same thing, but I would say that jazz might be the most difficult form of music, the toughest.[11]

Liu Yuan performs at his own club with his quartet several nights during the week. The club is open from 3 p.m. to 2 a.m.

THE JAZZ VENUES THAT DIDN'T MAKE IT

Establishing and managing a jazz venue is the same in any city, large or small. Some make it, some don't. In New York City, there are numerous examples of the shifting sands of making a jazz venue work, the Cookery and Bradley's, for example. In Beijing the jazz venues that remain well established and survive are Liu Yuan's East Shore Café and the CD Café, for example. And as chapter 18 will attest to, other jazz clubs established by non-Chinese entities—such as Jazz at Lincoln Center and Blue Note International—have now come on the scene. This is quite apart from the bountiful hotel food courts and lobbies where indigenous and foreign jazz musicians also perform.

Several clubs, however, have not survived for one reason or another. In one instance, at least, eminent domain was the issue. In two others, management and supply and demand were the root causes.

THE BIG EASY

For many years one of the major jazz joints in Beijing was the Big Easy, located in the Eastern part of Beijing. *China Daily* reported in 2005,

> "When you step through the door of The Big Easy, you are leaving China and entering New Orleans," said Mary Monitto, owner of Beijing's biggest jazz joint. The veranda-rimmed nightspot is authentic down to the smallest details of Louisiana architecture . . . The club is also a portal that transports enthusiasts to different jazz eras, ranging from ragtime influenced first days of jazz a century ago and the Dixieland hybrid that appeared in the 1920s to the freewheeling jazz jams that are now being orchestrated from New York to Tokyo and Beijing, according to Monitto.[12]

The next year, in July 2006 the Big Easy was summarily demolished by the Chinese government to make way for a building that was rumored to become part of the 2008 Olympics. A newspaper article describing the situation had the following opening: "A renowned symbol of American architecture and jazz in Beijing faces demolition on Sunday, adding concern that too much of the city's past culture and diversity is being erased in the quest for modernity." So begins a brief article by journalist Wang Shanshan in the August 5, 2006 issue of *China Daily*. The "symbol of American architecture and jazz in Beijing" is a reference to the Big Easy, as Shanshan writes, "not only a unique example of antebellum American architecture, but also a symbol of Beijing's globalized jazz scene." She further writes: "The elegant, veranda-rimmed architecture, along with its jazz frescoes that were painted by U.S. artists and its once freewheeling stage for improvised music, is now surrounded by demolition squads."[13]

"The Big Easy affair" is not only representative of the Chinese government's willfulness to obtain what it needs and wants, regardless of the consequences to law-abiding citizens, the background to the story also underscores the growing relevance of China's apparent disregard for intellectual property rights, corporate espionage, and cyber warfare.

It was total serendipity that we arrived at the Big Easy the very night before the demolition was scheduled to take place. I spoke with Mary Monitto, widow of Douglas Monitto, who built the Big Easy, opened it in 1999, and unfortunately died in early January 2001 at age fifty-seven.

The scene was surreal. We arrived at the club around eleven in the evening. The air was heavy and hot. A party was taking place in the club, but it was not a celebration, it was a wake-before-the-fact. Ms. Monitto was clearly distraught from the eventuality the club she and her late husband had built was about to be torn down. As Shanshan reported, "American Douglas Monitto spent the last years of his life importing the materials to build a replica of a 19th-century Louisiana mansion on the outskirts of Chaoyang Park in eastern Beijing. Monitto's widow, Mary, said they spent more than US$1 million to fly everything from a New Orleans jazz club, The Big Easy, into China, after being encouraged to open the music outpost by local authorities and signing a 13-year contract that runs until 2011."[14]

Mary Monitto was offered 1.4 million yuan (US$175,000) in compensation. The *China Daily* article reported that Tian Jixian, general manager of Chaoyang Park, told the newspaper the authorities had followed the contract under which the lease rights can be voided for an important government need—essentially the Chinese version of eminent domain. In this situation, the authorities were required to notify the club three months in advance. They were given six months' notice. Jixian added that a Peace Plaza would be built on the site of the club.[15] It was August 2006. The Beijing Olympics were two years away.

This is not the only time the Monittos had encountered frustrations with Chinese authorities. Douglas Monitto's name shows up numerous times in "The Cox Report on Chinese Espionage," a document prepared by the United States House of Representatives Select Committee on the above subject, issued January 3, 1999 during the Clinton administration.[16] There is nothing in the report that implies Monitto was in any way involved in illegal activities in concert with the Chinese. On the contrary, the report quotes telephone interviews with Monitto in 1998 and various correspondence from 1994 between Monitto's company, Monitor Aerospace Corporation, and Chinese representatives that together with a much larger volume of research indicates how the Chinese military had obtained various military secrets, had been doing so for decades, and was in the process of obtaining these secrets.

What is Douglas Monitto's involvement in this instance? His father, Joseph Monitto, started a small aircraft parts company on Cropsey Avenue in Brooklyn, New York, after World War II. The father died in 1975. Douglas, thereupon, took over the business. As the airline industry grew, so did the company, Monitor Aircraft Corporation, ultimately moving to Amityville, Long Island.[17]

The Cox report early on states: "The PRC's appetite for information technology appears to be insatiable, and the energy devoted to the task enormous. While only a portion of the PRC's overall technology collection activities targeted at the United States is of national security concern, the impact on our national security could be huge." Further, "In light of the number of interactions taking place between PRC and U.S. citizens and organizations over the last decade as trade and other forms of cooperation have bloomed, the opportunities for the PRC to attempt to acquire information and technology, including sensitive national security secrets, are immense."[18]

Chapter 10 of this report then states: "Machine tool and jet engine technologies are priority acquisition targets for the PRC [People's Republic of China]." Further, "The People's Republic of China's long-term goal is to become a leading power in East Asia and, eventually, one of the world's great powers. To achieve these aims, the PRC will probably enhance its military capabilities to ensure that it will prevail in regional wars and deter any global strategic threat to its security."[19] While this chapter deals with case studies of McDonnell Douglas Machine Tools and Allied Signal's Garrett Engine Division, a significant portion of the chapter recalls the interaction between Douglas Monitto, president of Monitor Aerospace Corporation, and representatives of the China National Aero-Technology Import and Export Corporation (CATIC). To quote the report, "During those discussions, CATIC expressed an interest in subcontracting with Monitor Aerospace for the production of aircraft parts. Specifically, Monitor would assist the PRC in the production of certain aircraft parts that CATIC was to manufacture for Boeing as part of an offset contract. . . . Representatives of CATIC, Aviation Industries of China, and Monitto signed a Memorandum of Understanding (MOU) regarding [a] machining center joint venture on January 24, 1994. CATIC officials took Monitto to an industrial park in Beijing where the machining center was to be built."[20]

In the summer of 1994 CATIC informed Monitto it had purchased machine tools from McDonnell Douglas. He was asked for his assistance in reassembling the machine tools and placing them in a machining center. The agreement ultimately fell through after CATIC informed Monitto that "it intended to place the McDonnell Douglas machine tools at a facility located in the city of Shijiazhuang," a location too far from his base of operations in Beijing to be viable, according to Monitto.

Douglas Monitto, then chairman of the private company, sold Monitor Aerospace in June 1998 to Stellex Industries, Inc., for total consideration of $95 million. Monitor, which had sales of $86.3 million, is described in the news release announcement as "a leading aerospace subcontractor engaged in the manufacture and assembly of precision-machined structural aircraft components and assemblies." Stellex is described as a privately owned company that is "a leading provider of highly engineered subsystems and components for the aerospace, defense and space industries." Stellex, in turn, is controlled by affiliates of Mentmore Holdings Corporation, a privately owned investment company that had total revenues of over $1.3 billion in 1997.[21]

Following the sale of the company in 1998, with the encouragement of the Beijing authorities, Douglas Sebastian Monitto built and opened the Big Easy in Beijing in 1999. To reiterate, he died about a year and a half later on January 5, 2001, at age fifty-seven. He left a wife, Mary, two sons, Joey and Vincent, and a sister, Pamela.[22]

In August 2006 the Beijing authorities tore the Big Easy down.

Standing in front of the soon-to-be-demolished club on the eve of its demise, I spoke with Ms. Monitto about the club's history and the future of jazz in China. It was around midnight. The air was polluted with the dust from another demolition taking place virtually next door.[23]

I asked her "Why did your husband start this club?" She responded: "He wanted to show the Chinese people what American culture is. In the beginning, we hired all the expat musicians here. One and a half years later, my husband passed away, so I had to take care of the business. So I started contacting local musicians. Then we worked it out quite nice, a mix actually, local musicians with expat musicians. But the singer was always American."

The very first jazz band Douglas Monitto hired for the Big Easy was Venice, California–born Danny California's jazz band. California was a drummer in addition to a vintage motorcycle sidecar aficionado.[24] Another regular at the club was blues harmonicist Mike Hall, also known as "Humble Mike." According to Hall's website, a plethora of American and local musicians appeared at the club. In addition to Danny California, there were the Rhythm Dogs, the Big Easy Band, saxophonist Ray Blue, Louis Hall, and Barbara Gogin. Hall mentions that the Big Easy hosted a 2004 Mardi Gras party on Tuesday, February 24. He says "They're arranging prizes, drinks, promotions, exotic dancers, and, of course, some great music." A Halloween Party is referenced for October 2003.[25] Other musicians who performed at the Big Easy include chromatic jazz hamonicists Tom Stryker & Michael T., the Moreno Trio, Silk, and Beijing Blues Collective guitarist and bluesman Paul Clementson. Apparently, the Big Easy held an annual Blues Memorial gig in honor of the late owner and founder Douglas Monitto. Hall writes: "Doug was a greater lover of live music and by opening The Big Easy gave Jazz & Blues a home in Beijing." Also mentioned by Hall are Angela Fabian who "continues to rock the house with her modern bluesy soul singing, and American Ray Blue colleague Lionel Haas (Germany)." Ray Blue is also mentioned as one of the performers who participated in the Midi School Jazz Festival in 2002.

Mary Monitto herself mentions another American singer who has performed at the Big Easy for some time: "We've had a singer here, for a long time. Her name is Jacqui 'Sugar Mama' Staten. She used to sing backup for Tina Turner. She is my favorite. She's part of my family, Jacqui. Right now, she's in Shanghai at the Cotton Club."

Q: Why did you call this place the Big Easy, because that's very much like New Orleans in America?
MM: The Big Easy is the second name for New Orleans, and the Big Easy, we translate it in Chinese, kwi lo jen, it's a happy place.

Q: What do you think of the audiences for jazz music here in China? What do you think of the receptivity of jazz by Chinese audiences here in China?
MM: When we started in 1999, 95 percent of our customers were expats. Today, we get almost half and half. I think the Chinese customers started to love jazz.

Q: Do you think the audience for jazz in China, specifically in Beijing, is going to grow?
MM: A big future. I don't know how to say it, but I just feel something, if it's good, it doesn't mean for how long, or where. It's always going to be good, and people are going to love it. It's like life.

Q: Do you think there are going to be more Chinese jazz musicians? More Chinese people playing jazz?

MM: Sure. I'm sure about that. Because it gets so popular here in China, a lot of musicians get involved in studying how to play jazz. Every Monday we have a jazz jam session. A lot of new musicians play with our band, even some expat musicians, they play together. And they can learn more from them.

The location of the Big Easy when initially built was both timely and astute. According to an early April 2000 article in *Beijing Scene*, the writer, George Vaughton, reports: "Chaoyang Park is undergoing a US$73 million refurbishment to become a recreational hub for all your dining and entertainment needs. . . . Originally opened in 1984 and covering an area of some 320 hectares outside the East Third Ring Road (larger than all of the Summer Palace), Chaoyang Park, officially known as Sun Park, has been earmarked for extensive development by the Beijing municipal and Chaoyang district governments." Further, "The new concentration of nightspots in Chaoyang Park seems the most obvious alternative for those looking for food and entertainment, especially as the emphasis is on superior choice and quality in a unique green-space environment."[26]

In retrospect, when surveying the various clubs in Beijing where jazz can be found, whether performed by expats or indigenous musicians, or a combination of both, the Big Easy was clearly an American icon of Western jazz. The architecture, the internal décor, the music—all reminiscent of early jazz and especially blues in New Orleans, the so-called birthplace of jazz in the early twentieth century—was clearly American. With its demise, though, the jazz clubs left standing (at the time), literally, in Beijing do not have an American stamp of ownership. The remaining clubs—the major hotel lobbies and bars notwithstanding—have strong Western influences, but the ownership is clearly Chinese, or at least Asian. The Big Easy, physically, was a highly visible American presence in a prominent part of eastern Beijing near Chaoyang Park's south gate.

THE ICE HOUSE

Canadian-born Phoebe Wong, whose parents are from Macau, was the general manager of the Ice House. She got tired of doing auditing work in

Toronto and decided to come to China not only to learn the language but also to seek opportunities. She commented: "I think there's a lot of things going on in the city and for China. I think people don't put you in a box right away. I grew up in Canada and went to school there and then studied accounting. When I went to get work, they just wanted to get me accounting jobs, and I couldn't get out of that. But here, I manage RBL, the restaurant, and Ice House, this jazz bar."[27]

The club she managed used to be the old ice house for the Ch'in Dynasty which ruled from 221 to 206 BCE. The word China is derived from Ch'in, the first dynasty to unify the country by conquering the warring feudal states of the late Chou period. They would cut up big blocks of ice from the river, ship it over, then store it. The walls are about 1.5 meters thick, all around, both sides and up top.

Wong explained how the Ice House became a jazz bar and who performs there: "The owner is Chinese-American and he's very interested in the Chicago Blues. The Ice House as a jazz bar opened in 2005. Right now we have a local group. The Rhythm Dogs. They used to play at the Big Easy, which has just closed down. We've had a lot of people from Chicago: Melvin Taylor, Kenny Coleman, Felton Cruz. The Peaches Staten Blues Band out of Chicago was here. They did about one month of gigs each."

Asked about the audiences, Ms. Wong responded: "When I first started there were more expats and I think as time went on we were getting younger Chinese and less expats. So the mix is not fixed. I don't know what the mix is going to be tonight. Sometimes it's all Chinese, sometimes it looks all foreign, and sometimes it's half-half. Unpredictable. Age-wise it's probably between twenty and thirty, the younger crowd. I think they have the spending money now and they're interested in Western culture, whereas I think, for the Chinese, a lot of the older ones are kind of set in their ways. So if they're not interested in it, or not willing to try—where people in their twenties, they have all this extra disposable income and so they want to try new things. And this is something that they want to explore."

Wong commented on the longer-term interest in jazz: "Definitely, there will be more interest. It's a good type of music, it's fun entertainment. I don't even know how to word it in English now. I'm thinking in Chinese. There's interest in it and it's interesting for people who are not exposed to it. Just seeing how it's grown in the US, definitely it'll grow the same way here."

The Icehouse has since closed for several reasons: poor location and price.

BROWN'S

Brown's was the first venue we visited several hours after arriving in Beijing. There we interviewed expat trombonist Matt Roberts and members of his Ah Q Band. Following the group's second set we interviewed Mr. Philip Cheung, Brown's owner and manager. He was born in Hong Kong but brought up in England. I asked him what his philosophy was with respect to jazz. He responded: "Jazz is a powerful changing culture. There will be new developments as well. At the moment, we have a European style bar. Later on, we will have a Russian bar and then a Mexican bar. The grand idea is having the best drinking culture in the world in one place."[28]

When we were there Brown's was still under renovation. It had opened earlier in 2006. I asked Cheung, "When will you finish all of this? When will it get done?" His answer: "Hopefully within a year's time. The Russian bar is doing it now. We will take two months to do it. And then we will do the Mexican bar in another two months."

I also asked him if there was going to be more jazz in China than there is now: "Yes. There will be. There's not enough bars and jazz in, in Beijing or in China. There is a very strong Chinese classical music tradition here. But with classical you cannot move. You just listen. With jazz you can move a bit, dance a bit."

How do you think jazz is going to grow in China? "Personally, I'm not so much a music lover, I'm a businessman, part owner, but my opinion is China will grow and China's children will grow and I think jazz will grow with it. Brown's will only present jazz and pop music, unlike other local bars where they play much more house music and hip hop. There is a large, growing community of expats who like to hear jazz or hip hop music now that they used to listen to back home. I hope this place will be world famous because it's quite unique. I'm bringing the drinking culture, the fun of drinking, together with jazz in Beijing."

Traffic from the 2008 Olympics in Beijing notwithstanding, Brown's also closed a couple of years later. Reasons unknown.

THE HOTELS

By the mid-2000s one could find live music of various stripes—including jazz—in several hotels:

1. Swissotel Landmark Lounge (2 Chao Yang Men, Bei Da Jie, Hong Kong Macau Center)
2. The Centro Bar and Lounge (The Kerry Centre Hotel, 1 Guanghua Road, Chaoyang District)
3. The Press Club @ the St. Regis Hotel (21 Jianguo Men Wai Da Jie, Chao Yang District)
4. The Aria Jazz & Wine Bar (1 Jianguomenwai, 2nd Floor, China World Hotel, Central Chao Yang District)
5. The Great Wall Sheridan Atrium (10 East Third Ring Road North)

You can also find what purports to be jazz in various food courts in Beijing. The groups that appear in these venues—from expats to local musicians—perform highly commercial repertoire to appeal to foreign travelers or the relatively unsophisticated musical tastes of middle-class Beijing residents or businessmen. I sat in with one of these all-Chinese ensembles at a food court at the invitation of an indigenous tenor saxophonist who had befriended me. We performed "All the Things You Are" and "Satin Doll." It was not a collegial experience. The group didn't swing. They were happy when I stepped off the bandstand.

The real "jazz" action is in the small clubs, described above.

CHAPTER 14

Beijing's Leading Indigenous and Expat Jazz Musicians

While Shanghai certainly owned China's jazz history spotlight in the first half of the twentieth century, Beijing is not without its own indigenous leading lights, musically speaking. Some have been trained in classical music in China and in the United States and have returned to Beijing to perform; others are self-taught. Many are young; some have been around before and after Mao. All are devoted to the music. In Beijing, saxophonist Fan Shengqi is by all accounts the most enduring jazz musician who performed before, during and after Mao.

LEADING INDIGENOUS JAZZ MUSICIANS

FAN SHENGQI: "King of the Saxophone" before, during, and after Mao

According to *Los Angeles Times* reporter Josef Woodard:

> Born in 1933, Fan Shengqi picked up the saxophone at age 11 but had to shelve it in 1949 as the Communist agenda swept out Western cultural influences. By age 18, Fan Shengqi had become the chief saxophone player of the Chinese Railroad Art Troupe. Ironically, he was only allowed to play the saxophone at Chairman Mao's private dance parties, otherwise focusing on Chinese reed instruments, such as the reed pipe, suona, and bamboo flute. Things changed in 1990 when he visited New York and returned to his homeland determined to delve deeper into jazz and a personal approach to it. By then, jazz had been allowed to return to the public sphere.[1]

American singer Mary Ann Hurst knew Fan Shengqi (now eighty-five-plus years old as of this writing) during her sojourn to China and in the United States:

Fan Shengqi started listening to Benny Goodman years ago in China. He had a rough childhood on the Russian-Chinese border, but he was enamored by jazz. He's one of the people often talked about when people talk about jazz in China.

In 1998 Professor Shirley Kennedy, part of the Black Studies Department of the University of California, Santa Barbara (UCSB), brought him to UCSB, and had a symposium built around him. She also brought the late Gene Lees in and flew a woman in from Harvard University to talk about China. She had me on the panel. We talked about "Jazz in the World Diaspora." He played saxophone with the UCSB Band at the college's Multicultural Center Theatre. She made a video of the event and of her filming jazz musicians in Beijing.[2]

Just as Shanghai has its Peace Hotel Jazz Band, Beijing has its own band of senior musicians: The Old Bark, led, of course, by Fan Shengqi. According to CCTV.com: "One of the more unique features of modern China's music scene is a jazz renaissance. Chief among the champions of this movement is a band of eight seniors who call themselves 'The Old Bark.' . . . The group's leader Fan Shengqi is known as 'King of the Saxophone.'" During the 1980s, he encountered various types of foreign music [including a visit to New York City]. This exposure helped further shape his own taste and performance style. He gradually began incorporating elements of Western pop music into some of his own works. He now delights audiences as he seamlessly shifts from the jazz characteristic of the '30s and '40s to more modern pieces, and back again.[3]

On the heels of their performance in the 1996 movie *The Temptress Moon*,[4] the Old Bark achieved sudden and widespread fame. With his braided hair, striking outfits, and characteristic beret, Fan Shengqi quickly became the icon of the group. Now officially retired, he is actually busier than many people half his age. Between playing tightly scheduled world tours and recording his own CDs, he somehow finds time to edit some Chinese classics, such as "Sea Love, Little River Flows," and "Two Springs Reflect the Moon," into his own jazz-saxophone style. Some Western media have classified his works as "Eastern Jazz."[5]

Fan Shengqi's involvement in the contemporary Chinese music scene is also reflected in his participation in China's first guitar festival, held in August 2005 on what is described as "scenic Hainan Island" located in the South China Sea. The event was sponsored by the China Guitar Society and the China Musicians Association. More than 400 guitar players and fans from all over China gathered at the festival. Fan Shengqi was billed as one of several "world famous musicians" invited to the event.[6]

Fan Shengqi's wife was the former dancer Wang Jiaqi. They met in Harbin in 1952. He was twenty, she was eighteen. His wife died in 2011 of melamine poisoning, evidently a victim of the Chinese poison milk scandal.[7]

"ADAM": Virtuoso Bass Player, Jazz Festival Progenitor[8]

Huang Yong, or "Adam," as he prefers to be called, is the virtuoso electric bass player of the Golden Buddha Trio, led by piano virtuoso Kong Hong Wei. His longish solos without benefit of drum backup demonstrates not just extraordinary technique, but also a development of improvisational ideas that is jaw-dropping. In addition to his performing abilities, he also has an entrepreneurial streak: a reference to his involvement in the development of an annual jazz festival in Beijing, now known as the Nine Gates Jazz Festival.

He started playing jazz while attending the Beijing Normal University where he was studying music. His teacher gave him a jazz tape to listen to in 1989. His response: "The first time I heard it, I thought it was quite strange. But later, I thought, 'Oh, it's very good music.' That's why I started to learn jazz." Adam is essentially self-taught on the electric bass. He started by learning walking bass by listening to Ray Brown. Later, a friend gave him a Jaco Pastorius tape. He continued his learning by listening to different kinds of jazz musicians and copying their playing.

When asked for his view on the Beijing jazz scene in particular and the jazz scene in China generally, he responded:

Last year [2005] I organized a jazz festival. We had ten to fifteen bands. I found the jazz bands in China right now are at a very good level. Last year, we had a big band, trios, quartets, quintets, funky bands, some electric jazz bands, many local musicians.

Eight years or ten years ago, I heard somebody playing the guitar and we were asking "Is that jazz?" or "Does this sound like swing, stand up jazz?" I don't think it sounds like jazz. But now, the situation has changed. We grew up musically in China. Many local musicians write down their own music: our blood. We think about music, but not like American jazz, not close to European jazz. We think about local music. We write it down, we play it. Last year, I did the jazz festival. Many, many television stations and newspapers talked with me. I think I can say now we have our own jazz music. It comes from the [Chinese] heart.

I am a bass player. I play with many musicians, saxophone players, piano players, guitar players, many drummers. There are a lot of very good local musicians in China. This year [2006] in August we will have a new jazz festival at the Jon Shan Music Hall, August 23rd to 25th August. The hall has 1,200-something seats. So in three days almost 4,000 people can come to see the performances. And we did more promotion. I printed a little card, and put our jazz festival's information on it. We printed 50,000 pieces and sent it out to music shops around the whole country. This year we will videotape the concerts. This might be the first time a live jazz concert has been recorded in China. It will result in a CD and a DVD.

Last year we had ten local bands, not from Shanghai or Guangzhou, only from Beijing. They all have their own music, their own Chinese jazz songs. Every year in the future I will do this festival. More and more people will come to know jazz music. It's different than pop. But now, many people in China, when we talk about jazz, they think, "Oh, it's long hair. It's different, the music."

In China people think that jazz music is kind of the high-level, or high-life music. And so I think that in a big city, like in Beijing, people are willing to pay money to come to try this kind of music. In China there are not so many chances for jazz musicians to play in a big hall, or a big festival. So once I called the musicians, inviting them to come to our festival, they were very happy.

Many people in China, they know jazz, from radio, sometimes from a magazine, from a newspaper, they know jazz. But they cannot listen to jazz from the radio. They know jazz, this word they know. They know that it's American. They know blues, but they know it's not like rock and roll, punk music, or heavy metal. They know that. So when I do a jazz festival in a big theatre, it's good. They'll pay money to watch and listen.

XIA JIA: Beijing's "Cool" Jazz Pianist of the "Minimalist School"[9]

Beijing-based contemporary jazz pianist Xia Jia (pronounced Shia Jia) is something of a rarity in the Chinese jazz world. He is one of the few indigenous jazz musicians who found his way to the United States to study jazz. He studied at the Eastman School of Music (Rochester, New York) from 1999 to 2004 under the tutelage of Harold Danko, a highly accomplished jazz pianist and composer in his own right who ultimately became director of the Jazz Studies program at Eastman. Danko recalled Xia Jia's sojourn at Eastman:

> Xia Jia was an outstanding student and I understand he is doing well in Beijing. He was a wonderful classical pianist and developed quickly in his jazz playing and composing. He was a member of a small ensemble that won some recognition from *DownBeat* magazine and played in the JVC festival in Bryant Park several years ago. As for other Chinese students at Eastman, I'm just about positive he is the only one, and certainly the only graduate in jazz studies.[10]

In the summer of 2006 he was playing with the Ah Q Band at Brown's in the eastern part of Beijing. The Ah Q Band was organized by American expat and outstanding trombonist Matt Roberts. Xia Jia's playing was restrained, but nonetheless sophisticated. There clearly was thoughtfulness in his playing and the way he built his improvisations.

He said he could not remember the first time he heard jazz music but he believed it was probably from a classical teacher. "He played a record for me. I don't know who is on that record, but that probably was the first jazz recording I heard," he said.[11] When it came time for Jia to study professionally, he had trouble finding a teacher to teach him locally, so he travelled to the United States: "I think that's American music, so I should go there. It's like Americans come here to study Chinese music." Jia's influences include Kenny Kirkland, Keith Jarrett, and Michael Petrucciani, among others.

I mentioned to Jia that he has a very thoughtful way of playing—he seems to be thinking about it instead of just playing all over the place. I asked him if it is a style he particularly likes or if it is just a reflection of who he is. He responded:

> Recently I like a lot of minimalism music that's very simple, just a few elements in the music. I like that kind of style. I remember my teacher Harold Danko told me about that once. Another friend who is a pop musician, he said, "Jazz players always throw in too many ideas. That means you don't stand for one idea and its development. You just have an idea and play a little bit and then there's another new idea, so you go from that. You guys always throw a lot of ideas." I just try to extend an idea and develop that gradually, not just play a lot of ideas.

When questioned on the status of jazz in China now, Jia thinks that China is still trying to find its own thing: "We study all kinds of tunes, we learn from recordings and other artists, but also when we write something," Jia said. He believes jazz in China will eventually evolve into its own kind of jazz, and now "it's really better because I think more people are getting to know about jazz, so more people would like to listen to jazz." He elaborated: "It's like a circle. If you have jazz record company, you have more jazz, and then you have more jazz audiences. All should work together, should work like a circle. You can find some private school or some small school, they teach jazz. For me, in addition to my studies at Eastman, I had a teacher from one school, small school."

Jia hopes that more Chinese people will hear more jazz played by Chinese musicians. "If they feel about jazz the same thing they feel about Chinese culture, that would be good," he said.

If you listen to Xia Jia's music, you can hear not only the American influence, but also the multidimensionality and multiculturalism characteristic of today's Western jazz, as well as some forms of pop music.[12]

KONG HONG WEI: Beijing's "Hot" Pianist

Whether it's Liu Yuan's East Shore Café (still open) or the Ice House (now closed), listening to Kong Hong Wei is like listening to Canadian-born piano virtuoso Oscar Peterson. Forever performing with a cigarette in his mouth, Kong Hong Wei is a master of the keyboard.

Also known as Jin Fo and the Golden Buddha, Kong Hong Wei was born in 1966 in Kaifeng City, Henan Province.[13] He grew up playing traditional Chinese instruments, the sheng and the suona, before learning to play the piano. He was admitted to the Central Conservatory of Music in 1983 and later graduated with honors with a degree in composition. After graduation, he stayed on at the Central Conservatory of Music as a teacher.[14] He didn't begin playing jazz until 1990.

In 1991 Kong Hong Wei founded the ALAS Jazz Band and became China's very first jazz pianist.[15] He joined the Cui Jian band in 1993 as a keyboard player. Other members of the band included Liu Yuan on saxophone, Eddie Luc Lalasoa on guitar, Quan You on drums, Zhang Ling on bass, and Zhang Shu and Bateerfu on percussion.[16]

Kong Hong Wei went on to form two more bands of his own: Tian Square Band (also known as Tian Chang Jazz Band), which was the first jazz band to feature Chinese folk music;[17] and the Rhythm Dogs, a blues band. During this time he also released his first jazz album, *Made in China*, and worked as a music producer at Sony Records in China.[18] In 2004 Kong Hong Wei released his second album, *Summer Palace*, which combined elements of "pop, rock, blues, classical and jazz."[19]

Kong Hong Wei formed the Golden Buddha Jazz Unit (also known as the Golden Buddha Jazz Quartet and the Jin Fo Jazz Group) in 2005. The group includes Kong Hong Wei on piano, Huang Yong from the Liu Yuan Jazz Group on bass, Izumi Kago on drums, and Wan Chun on vocals. The band originated in Beijing's CD Jazz Café and is considered to be one of the most successful bands performing jazz in China today.[20] Kong Hong Wei "has been active at a national level in trying to bring jazz back to the forefront of China's modern music scene," according to a concert leaflet featuring the band. It continued: "Over the past ten years, Golden Buddha's works have been brought together in two albums notable for the inclusion of specifically Chinese elements. The songs from the album *Summer Palace* are often played on Chinese television and radio, representing the highest standard of domestic jazz music, marrying Chinese and Western elements, also combining jazz with elements of pop, rock, blues and classical."[21] The Golden Buddha Jazz Quartet released an album in 2010.[22]

In 2007 the Central Music School Publishing released Kong Hong Wei's first book, *Modern Jazz Improvisation for Piano*,[23] and in January 2012, his Golden Buddha Jazz Band performed four concerts in Romania, Bulgaria, and Ukraine under the auspices of China's Ministry of Culture.[24]

Kong Hong Wei mentored teenage piano prodigy Dai Liang, and is credited with introducing the teenage boy not only to jazz, but to other music genres including rock and roll and Peking Opera.[25] Most recently, Kong Hong Wei was the image spokesman for China's keyboard brand, Rocket.[26]

LIU "KENNY" XIAOGUANG: Virtuoso Alto Saxophonist from Inner Mongolia[27]

Liu "Kenny" Xiaoguang, alto saxophonist with Matt Roberts's Ah Q Band, has been into jazz since he was little. "I listened to a lot of music and I listened to a lot of rock and roll, including American and Chinese rock-and-roll and I started to understand the relationship between rock-and-roll and blues and from there, I started to get interested in jazz," he explained. He studied formally from the age of fifteen in his town in Inner Mongolia and has been playing in Beijing for four years. Along with playing jazz saxophone with the Ah Q Jazz Orchestra, he plays keyboard in a rock band with the famous Mongolian singer, Tongalar. He also plays the flute.

Although Liu Xiaoguang had not put much thought into the future of jazz in China, he thinks that "jazz is a very powerful force in the world and I think as a global force, it is something that will take root in China. China will have its own jazz. I think it's going to get better and better."

In order to get there, he believes there needs to be more people playing jazz: "There's just too few jazz musicians these days. We need to get more people involved in playing the music," he said. He was happy to announce that there is some jazz education in China now. "There are some schools that teach jazz. There have been jazz festivals that they've held themselves within the community for two or three years now. So, it's starting," he concluded.

XIAO DOU: Drummer with the Ah Q Band[28]

Drummer Xiao Dou first learned about jazz in 1991 when he saw Beijing's jazz musicians performing live in a bar. According to Dou, there wasn't much jazz on the radio, so he could only listen to jazz when he got hold of a jazz CD. "But there wasn't much," he said. He has only had one year of formal training from a music school. He listed Mexican jazz drummer Antonio Sanchez as an influence. Regarding the future of jazz in China, Dou believes, similar to Liu Xiaoguang, that "it's better and better." He explained: "It's much better than it was say ten years ago, but it's difficult to develop this type of music in Chinese culture. Those of us who love jazz, give our all in making the music better and better. We do our job. We devote ourselves to jazz year in and year out. And as long as we're doing that, the music is going to get better and better and hopefully the environment will get better and better."

Not only does Dou believe that jazz musicians need to be performing in clubs and bars, they also need to be performing at schools in order to inform young people about jazz because jazz education currently is not comprehensive enough: "In all of China, there are probably twenty really good jazz musicians and of those twenty, maybe ten of them are involved in jazz education and they are all of different backgrounds and different levels. So I believe that the jazz education here is not complete. There are some holes. We need to bring in more people who are really experienced jazz musicians and jazz educators to kind of fill those holes and have a more robust education system for jazz."

YAO YI XIN, Singer: Grandma and the Internet[29]

The inexorable influence of technology on the development of jazz in China is evidenced by the comments of those plying the trade. One example is Beijing jazz singer Yao Yi Xin. I asked her how she got interested in jazz.

> Since I was a little girl, maybe at that time, I didn't know that kind of music is jazz, but I like it very much. I liked very standard songs, such as "When Time Goes By" from the famous movie. I was a little girl, four or five years old. My grandma, who now lives in Shanghai, when she was young, before the new China, saw a lot of movies from America. She remembered a lot of songs from those movies. So when we did housework at home, she would sing, without lyrics, just the melody. When I listened, I think, "oh, very beautiful melody. What kind of music is this?" When I grow up, when China opened up, we could see a lot of movies from America or other Western countries. I know these songs from these movies. I liked them. After several years, I knew many of these songs.

Why do you like the music? She responded: "It gives me a special feeling. This kind of music is very, very different." Do you think the jazz scene in Beijing is going to grow? Yao Yi Xin: "Even in China, jazz music is growing now. More and more musicians are growing up and doing better and better jazz, and a lot of other kinds of music, alternative or punk. I also think more and more Chinese people start to know jazz, what is jazz music's feel. So maybe at first, they feel it's a little difficult to know. But now, more and more people in China start to like jazz."

Do you think the Internet will have a hand in growing jazz in China? "A lot of young people can listen to lots of kinds of music, including jazz, on the Internet. So if we want to know more, we can, on the Internet. It's easier to help us know more and more, and know a lot of kinds of jazz music, and jazz groups, jazz musicians. It's helpful, our Internet."

ZOU TONG, Bassist: Aria Jazz and Wine Bar[30]

Zou Tong became interested in jazz in 1991 after hearing a tune he really loved on the radio. At that time there was no formal jazz education in Beijing so jazz musicians, according to Tong, would learn on their own by listening to tapes and/or CDs, or by taking lessons when musicians came from abroad. "It was really tough. I had no formal jazz education," he said.

Tong believes that the current state of jazz in China, particularly in Beijing, is much better than before. "More and more people listen to jazz and more and more people are attracted by jazz, even students. In Beijing there are a lot of people like me who play for grand hotels because they also need it for their clients. Generally speaking, it is much better than it was before."

And he thinks the future is bright, as he believes that jazz is a "very important element for mankind," although he realizes that jazz is not a very popular genre of music. "It doesn't cater to everyone. The audience is more for classical music in terms of share of the population. It's a very small share of the society, but in China if it's only a little part of the society, it's still a large number of people," he said.

Tong listens to pianist Herbie Hancock, trumpeter Miles Davis, and British bassist Dave Holland.

Concerning Chinese jazz education, Tong lists the Midi School of Music and the Modern School of Music among the jazz schools in China. "You also have these musicians from Beijing and from abroad, especially from countries where jazz is already really developed who come here and teach jazz. There have already been some students who are not bad and who graduated from these departments. For the moment it's still small, but it's going to be better and better. We just need time," he added.

The amount of time is hard to tell. "From nonexistent to now, there has been about fifteen to twenty years, so I think we still have to wait fifteen to twenty years and then there will be a very good level," he said.

ZHANG LING, Bass Player: The Ice House[31]

Zhang Ling was born in Beijing but travelled to Sydney, Australia, from 1989 to 1994 to study jazz. Ling explained: "I like the sound of it and I couldn't figure it out, you know. It sounded nice but I couldn't understand the methods and everything. How to make the strange sound, the scale. I tried to play that but I couldn't figure it out. So I got this chance to go to Australia and I took some lessons and bought a lot of books. I'm self-taught and took lessons from jazz musicians and tried to learn. So that's how I picked it up."

His first experience listening to jazz was in 1986–87: "I wasn't sure who was playing on the record, but I can remember the Weather Report. I have a copy of the tape of a live version of [the American jazz fusion group] Weather Report called "8:30" from 1979. It's a beautiful double CD, double tape."

Now, however, he doesn't listen to anything. He just plays: "I don't really listen. I play, I'm a session player. I play all kind of things, but mainly I focus on blues, nowadays, 'cause I do the singing. So that's my style now. But I also play pop music. I do a lot of recordings for the sessions and everything, pop singers, and I do concerts. So that's how I make my living here. I deal with many, many styles of music."

Ling explained his decision to play the bass:

> I bought a camera because I liked filming and taking pictures. I also bought a bass made by the Taiwanese. That was the first decent bass on the market. Anything before that was local made, a piece of wood, just unusable. And this was the first bass we seen on the market, a Fender copy kind of thing. So I bought a bass and another guy bought a guitar. So we had three or four guys trying to make some music, make some noise; without knowing anything to play, but we just liked to try.
>
> And then one night we got together to play something, just messing around with the guitar, bass. Suddenly it just clicked. So we thought "wow, we can do that." So after that we took things seriously, we started to learn songs from records. We made progress pretty quick.

Ling is not certain about the future of the Chinese jazz scene. "Before I left the country I just knew one band playing jazz. I saw them play and I said, 'wow. A few Chinese guys can do that.' That was the only bunch of people I've seen playing jazz," Ling said. And while there are now many more bands playing jazz, it is still a small group. Ling "no doubt" thinks it is going to grow: "I mean, why not? It's an interesting form of music. I was interested, why not other people? It must be a lot of people are interested in this kind of music."

I asked Ling what he thinks it is about jazz that would be of interest, and is of interest, to Chinese audiences. He credits the fact that there exists a very strong classical music tradition in China. "I know a lot of kids from the Conservatory of Music here, they start picking up jazz, you know, pretty quick, 'cause they have the theories. They're pretty deep on the techniques and everything so they just pick up things real quick. So why not?" he said. "This jazz thing has so much stuff in it. You start with playing the one, four, five, three chords in every song. There's so much in there. I guess serious musicians, maybe guys who want to be serious, they have to learn it. It's a certain routine."

On the improvisation aspect of jazz, Ling believes that it takes time. "Some guys have a feeling for improvisation; they got it real quick, because somehow they can relate to it. I think it's a matter of if you can feel the music and you're somehow related to the music I think makes it easy. Just like how I started playing bass, I don't know how to play the bass, but I just started and I just play. So it's somehow related that makes it easy. I never found playing bass hard, it's just an instrument. I can pick up any instrument and just play a little bit. I'm not good, but I can play many of them."

WU YUN NAN: Former Chinese Navy Band Saxophonist, Jazzer by Night[32]

Beijing native Wu Yun Nan first learned to play jazz from American-born musician Lawrence Ku, who is a leading jazz figure in the Shanghai jazz scene. When he started playing in 1998, access to jazz was minimal. "[It] was very difficult. No school. No CDs. No music," Yun Nan said.

While at that time gaining access to jazz in Beijing was difficult, the future is bright for this genre of music. "I think more and more people listen to jazz music," Yun Nan says. The musician, who is now teaching the art, says that more and more people, specifically in their young twenties, are coming to learn to play jazz, possibly due to the freedom to improvise. Yun Nan believes there are interesting melodies in Chinese that could be influenced by jazz. The harmonies of jazz, according to Yun Nan, are flexible in that there is a lot that can be done with them. As for access to jazz CDs, Yun Nan notes that there are some available, but not many.

Yun Nan speaks about the first time he encountered this genre of music. "I bought these imported CDs that were supposed to be [destroyed]. I didn't know the artist, but I loved the style. I thought the technique was great and I thought I would study him." It wasn't just this skilled musician who attracted him to the genre. "What I love about it is the improvisation because it's not as rigid or boring as playing while reading a sheet." But it's not all about the technique. "Through jazz you can express not only your feelings [but] also your thoughts—everything that's inside you."

Not many feel the same, he explains. "A lot of people are used to the way the teachers are teaching . . . traditional ways of playing music or traditional forms of music." He goes on to say that while there may be some people who feel the same, the majority are conservative and would not understand.

While learning jazz in China was no small task, Yun Nan says the benefits outweigh the struggles. "It was a lot of effort and hard work, but today it feels good to be able to play it and to express feelings through this music."

While in the navy, Yun Nan remembers visiting the United States and Canada, hearing great jazz throughout his journey. "I really liked it, and when I got back I thought I could learn it." Learning from sheet music he acquired in the United States, and through teachings by American musicians performing in China, he was able to explore jazz music more thoroughly. Eventually, he joined a Chinese Navy band as the lead saxophonist.

Because not many people are skilled in jazz, the players range in age from young to old. The musicians will play at CD cafés and at hotels, usually for "jam sessions." He says the future of jazz music in China is bright. "Today there are schools that teach modern music and jazz. Some jazz musicians should come out of the schools."

As for the audience, it first requires an understanding and acceptance of the genre. "There's a process to go through," Yun Nan says. When foreigners come to China, he notes, and perform jazz music, the Chinese audience begins to accept, understand, and appreciate jazz more quickly, in turn investing in the future of jazz music in China."

YINJIAO DU: Saxophonist with the Military Band of the Chinese People's Liberation Army (PLA)

The Military Band of the Chinese People's Liberation Army (PLA) is mentioned in this chapter because it includes brass and saxophones as part of its instrumentation—not typical of the traditional Chinese orchestra, but in keeping with the instrumentation of the traditional military band.

Founded in July 1952, the band is directly managed by the General Political Department of the PLA. Clearly, this band is meant to serve as a political statement in support of the Chinese Communist Party. A cursory read of its repertoire is clearly traditional Chinese with a strong streak of political statement, such as: "Good Message Arrives in Remote Village from Beijing," "Long Live the Great Country," and "Shoulder to Shoulder with the Civilians." It is also well-travelled, with visits to Japan, Thailand, France, Finland, Singapore, Italy, Holland, Hong Kong, and Macao.[33] It has also visited the United States: on May 17, 2011, the band performed a joint concert with the US Army Band "Pershing's Own" on the stage of the John F. Kennedy Center for the Performing Arts in Washington, DC.[34]

The more important reason why this military band is mentioned here is that its repertoire includes jazz and Latin-jazz style arrangements.[35]

The chief saxophonist of this military band is Yinjiao Du. Born in March 1956, Du grew up in Wuhan in Hubei Province, a major transportation thoroughfare and the political, cultural, and economic hub of Central China. His résumé indicates a prolific musical career. He is the conductor and artistic director of the jazz band of the Chinese People's Armed Police Military Band, concertmaster and artistic director of the Beijing Chimaera Band, artistic director of the Golden Horn Jazz Band, and professor of saxophone at the Military Music Department of the Chinese People's Liberation Army Academy of Arts. He has also written texts on Chinese and Western musical compositions for saxophone, introductory and advanced courses for the saxophone, and a collection of jazz-style pieces for saxophone. He has endorsed and performs on Aizen saxophones (Japan).[36]

Du has been on the Beijing jazz scene for some time, collaborating with well-known educator/jazz musician expatriate David Moser in Beijing. Veteran jazz journalist Dan Ouellette reporting on Udo Hoffman's 1997 Beijing Jazz Festival commented on Yinjiao Du's participation in the event:

> In 1982 in Beijing, China, a 17-year-old saxophonist in the People's Liberation Army Band surreptitiously listened to his shortwave radio in his barracks dormitory room. He was tuning in the night-time Voice of America broadcasts of this strange music called jazz. He sat in the dark and softly tried to figure out the fingerings of the melodies. Little did Du Yinjiao realize then that 15 years later he and several of his P.L.A. cohorts would form a jazz ensemble and open a week-long festival celebrating this music—still branded by Communist officials in the People's Republic of China as decadent, bourgeois and spiritually polluting.
>
> In fall of 1997, after months of bureaucratic red tape, Du and the Wide Angle Jazz Group finally received permission to perform from military authorities only two weeks before this year's Beijing International Jazz Festival (November 18–23). The big band did an admirable job launching the fest to a swinging start with standard Billy Strayhorn, Duke Ellington, Herbie Hancock and Glenn Miller tunes.[37]

Du's persistence and passion for jazz music is emblematic of the "individual freedom of expression" theme referenced earlier in this volume. It is even more telling with respect not only to Chinese jazz musicians specifically, but also Chinese citizens generally because of Du's connection to the Chinese military—a 2.2 million-person force that plays a large role in China's "central authority" politics. Ouellette further reports:

> With his pal and bandmate David Moser acting as translator, Du, who admires the playing of Trane, Michael Brecker and Miles Davis, says, "You can't expect fantastic Chinese jazz overnight because we are only now being exposed to the music through the festival. It's not like America where you have tasted jazz all your lives. We're only now beginning to absorb it. But the door is open and no one's going to close it."
>
> Moser adds that growing up in a culture where creativity and originality are constantly squashed down makes it difficult for Chinese musicians to loosen up to express themselves improvisationally. "A lot of Chinese people have said that before a great soloist can emerge there must be a stronger feel of individualism." Will that happen in China where the collective spirit is deemed more important than individual expression? Can the jazz dichotomy—where ensemble uniformity meshes with improvisational free speech—thrive in Beijing? Du thinks so. "Individualism is good for the collective. It gets us all dialoging, communicating with each other. Before, everybody kept their heads down and were afraid to take chances."
>
> Moser, who secured the charts for the P.L.A. performance as well as wrote an arrangement of the famous Chinese folk song "Evening Song" for the big band, points out that Du has been a courageous risk-taker. It's telling that we're sitting in the P.L.A. rehearsal room in the army compound—this is the first time a foreign reporter has ever set foot in the barracks. "The time is right in China. [Chinese president] Jiang Zemin just returned from the United States and the 15th Party Congress just reaffirmed its commitment to modernization. So people aren't as afraid of getting in deep shit anymore.
>
> "Still someone had to take the first step and Du's doing it," Moser says. "He's representing jazz to the younger musicians in the army band. He's encouraging his superiors to come hear the music, to discover that jazz is a legitimate art form and not decadent. He even has plans to take the big band to universities. A foreign group wouldn't be able to do that in a million years. But because it's the P.L.A., Du's promotion of jazz will probably get approved.[38]

THE LEADING EXPATS

IZUMI KOGA: Japanese Drummer[39]

The jazz tradition in Japan has roots that are almost ninety years deep. Apart from the voluminous content of William Minor's 2004 book *Jazz Journeys to Japan*, there is other evidence to show that even prior to the Japanese military attack on Shanghai, China, in 1937 many Japanese musicians had adopted jazz as their repertoire of choice, not only for the many Westerners living in Shanghai, but also for the large Japanese population in that city. Further, it is no cultural accident that jazz found its way into the Japanese mainland in the first quarter of the twentieth century: many steamships in the 1920s–30s made stops in Japan, especially Kobe, on their way to and from the rest of the Orient, such as China. We should not be surprised, then, to find Japanese jazz musicians performing in China in the current century. One such person is drummer Izumi Koga.

Tokyo-born Izumi Koga listened to his father's Art Blakey and Benny Goodman jazz LP records when he was a kid. He did not like pop music, but he did like rock, and especially jazz. His online résumé states that he studied at the Berklee College of Music between 1990–93 under the tutelage of Osamu Minagawa.

Following graduation from Berklee, Koga arrived in Beijing in 1993. He liked it sufficiently enough that he decided to stay. Koga commented on the jazz Beijing jazz scene since he arrived almost thirteen years prior: "It's better than before. The musicians are improving. There are a couple schools teaching jazz music, so a lot of the younger generation are starting to playing jazz music." He was referring to the Midi School and Contemporary Music Institute, where he teaches. The Contemporary Music Institute, as of a few years ago, had 3,000 students; the Jazz Department, approximately 280. There are a total of fifty drum/percussion students. Other students study piano, bass, or guitar.

Koga commented on why students are gravitating toward jazz: "Students like this kind of music. They are studying very hard, and playing in hotels, clubs, and rehearsing and practicing now that they have a chance to study and play. They love it because of the improvisation. They get freedom. They can express themselves."

Koga also commented on the relationship between the Chinese classical music world and the evolving jazz scene in Beijing: "The Chinese classical music world and the jazz world, it's kind of separated. They are not cooperating. Some classical musicians studying from the States are trying to study jazz music. And they want to collaborate with jazz musicians. I did last winter, but it's kind of a jazz form, you know. Some young students want to do these kinds of things, I believe."

When asked what one factor will make jazz grow in China, he said: "The economy, of course. Nobody wants to pay for it. If a lot of clubs, or some hotels, or companies give students or working jazz musicians a chance to play, it's going to grow much faster.

"Jazz is an American artform of music. But it's also global music. Music is like language, and I think that playing a more Chinese way of jazz, it's a little different. It's like talking, sharing, like Chinese speaking. It's kind of like intonations, and there are phrases like this. That's what I feel. Phrasing, it's not like the American way, or the European way. It's Chinese. That's what I feel."

Koga performs with some of the leading jazz ensembles in Beijing, among them pianist virtuoso Kong Hong Wei's Golden Buddha Trio, the Xia Jia Trio, and saxophonist Liu Yuan Jazz Group at the East Shore Café—the latter musician considered the father of jazz in China. All three ensembles perform with regularity at the East Shore Café in Beijing.

Koga's prestige among jazz drummers in China was exemplified when he served as a panel judge for Sabian's first drumming contest in Beijing in 2007. Sabian, headquartered in Meductic, Canada, is renowned as the world's leading designer and manufacturer of cymbals. Koga has since become dean of the jazz department at the Beijing Contemporary Music Institute.

MATT ROBERTS, Trombonist: He Came, He Saw, He Stayed[40]

Matt Roberts, like several other key and influential non-Chinese jazz musicians described in this volume, is an American expatriate. At the time we met in Beijing on July 26, 2006, Roberts was already a fifteen-year veteran of the Beijing jazz scene.

Roberts—whose Mandarin Chinese is as fluent as his trombone technique—initially came to China in 1987 to teach English at Beijing Normal University (BNU). At the time he was studying Chinese at Dartmouth College in New Hampshire. BNU sent teachers to Dartmouth to teach Chinese and Dartmouth sent young graduates back to BNU to teach English. Right after he graduated, he became an English teacher at BNU in 1990 teaching writing classes and conversational English. He has been living in Beijing pretty much nonstop since 1994. While his major at Dartmouth was Chinese, he also studied the trombone. Roberts is an expert trombonist with a clarity of intonation with melodies or improvisation that is rare even among professional gigging players in the United States.

It was not until 1990 when he started one of the first bands in China, a jazz band called ALAS. According to Roberts, the Chinese men who joined ALAS are some of the key musicians playing around town today. They included pianist Kong Hong Wei ("At the time, he was teaching listening skills at the Chinese Music Conservatory [. . .] His instrument of choice was the shum, which is kind of like a mouth organ. It's a big organ-thing that you hold in your mouth and play like a harmonica with a bunch of keys. He had just kind of learned piano on the side. He got hooked up with us learning jazz. Just a true beginner and he's now one of the most interesting composers and players on the Beijing jazz scene today"), saxophonist Jon Mi Ying, bassists Harmowau and later John Weigh, drummer Darrell A. Jenks, and finally Roberts on trombone. Roberts said ALAS was gigging about five or six nights a week: "A lot of gigs and not a lot of competition. And I've pretty much been playing ever since."

Roberts believes the jazz scene has evolved since ALAS was formed in 1990. He explained that when ALAS started, the band members were all beginners: "Amateurs who loved music and were intrigued by jazz." Roberts said he and the band used to listen to a lot of tapes and pick out songs they liked and try to find them in his real book.[41] If they weren't in his real book, they would try and write them out. And then they performed them. "Didn't really have too much of a Chinese following at the beginning and there were not a lot of clubs back in 1990 that we could play at. It was mostly hotel lobbies, hotel bars," he said.

But the expat population grew, and more and more venues began to support live music. He explained: "The CD Jazz Club opened, I'm not sure if it was '93 or '94 with saxophonist Liu Yuan's help and another individual named Dashaung and that was really the home for jazz music in Beijing for many, many years. That was the only place in town where you could really go hear good, live jazz. And then of course the hotel lobbies supported jazz music, but very much in a commercial sense. You know, you show up, and play a forty-five-minute set. As long as you got the double bass and a couple horns and there's sound coming out, that was sufficient. The CD Jazz Club brought a little bit of innovation and musicians playing for themselves."

According to Roberts, the audience has grown past the expats, but only to a certain extent. "It's still very limited. I think the CD Jazz Club has probably been one of the most successful jazz clubs in Beijing in building a local audience over the years. And Liu Yuan just two months ago [in 2006] started his own club called the East Shore Jazz Café and I think they do a fairly good job with building a local audience because they're consistent about the atmosphere in a place just to come and listen to music. So, they are certainly getting more than just the expat crowd."

Roberts said that while the jazz scene in Beijing is larger now than it was in 1990, it is still fairly limited. He believes there is still much work to be done by jazz musicians in Beijing to develop an audience, including jazz education. "It's a difficult music for the average Chinese person to understand. And consider that most Chinese people have not had as much music exposure growing up. Basically Western culture is a recent phenomenon. And they don't teach jazz in any of the schools or they haven't until very, very recently," Roberts said.

The only exception is the Midi School, which opened in 1993 and taught modern music and jazz instruction, though Roberts believed it to be very rudimentary. "A lot of the students who were learning jazz, if they were really good, could come into the industry and they could play the gigs. But the rest kind of went off into more commercial-types of music. And if you look at the scene today, it's probably the same twenty to thirty top jazz musicians in Beijing. It's not a big pool. If my piano player can't make it, I can think of four people to call. If my guitarist can't make it, I can think of three. Bass, I can think of two. It's still a pretty limited pool of really top musicians," he explained.

In order for jazz to really take off in China, according to Roberts, there has to be "active effort" on the part of jazz musicians in China to reach out and develop educational programs: "I think if we get to the point where the music schools start recognizing that there's value in jazz and the musicians find an interest in expanding the jazz audience in China, reaching out to students, reaching out to young people and not only exposing them, but explaining to them 'This is why jazz is interesting,' I think only then can you have a growth in the jazz audience. If it's all predicated on foreigners in China, yes, we'll have a big surge during the Olympics, and then it will drop back again afterwards."

He recalled an outreach program that he and drummer Darrell Jenks worked with:

The idea was to promote US values and for a certain period of time; he arranged a number of jazz lectures open to college students and we would do a lot of promotion to, you know, get 500 college students in a room. We talked about the history of jazz. We talked about how jazz is really an

American phenomenon at its roots. Now it's a global phenomenon. But when it got started, it was about mixing styles and getting people together on one stage, but working together as one unit and kind of the ideas of cooperation. And if you want to extract a democracy from that kind of the idea that everybody is creating one whole and, yeah, you solo for a while and then I'm going to solo for a while, and then everybody's got an important piece in this mix and if we've got anybody who is standing out too much in front, the music suffers. It's all about a group effort. So, we did a bunch of those lectures which was a lot of fun.

While Roberts realizes that jazz education is important, he doesn't blame China's jazz musicians. He explained that his situation differs from other jazz musicians because he has a day job as a consultant. "I do this out of passion. But, if you're Liu Yuan or you're pianist Xia Jia or pianist Xiao-guang—you eat what you kill. You get a gig and that's what you live on. And if you're not getting paid enough, you've got to find something that pays the bills and whether that's teaching students or writing your own music or do-ing commercial music scores or doing karaoke tapes, whatever it is, you got to find a way that pays the bills. And doing jazz recordings in China is not going to make a lot of money."

But he explained that there are not a lot of musicians putting out their own CDs because it is not a lucrative move. "Pretty much you put it out as an effort of love and you put your own money into it and hope that maybe someday you'll recoup your investment. You're not going to make any money off of it."

I asked Roberts if one could make a living off playing jazz in Beijing. His response:

Yes. Can an expat? Maybe. Indigenous jazz musicians? No problem. Here we make $500–600 a night, $100 per person. I'd say most Chinese aren't going to be able to get six gigs a week, but to get three or four, maybe two of them hold out well. You get a couple corporate gigs a month. They pay maybe one, two, three thousand renminbi per person. So, yeah, you can make a living off of it. The corporate gigs, they're nice although they are painful music-wise.

The jazz musicians in China listen to many different styles of music, ac-cording to Roberts. "The guys in my Ah Q Orchestra like modern jazz. We really like odd times signatures which is partly my influence, partly Darrell

Jenks's influence from the original band. He was a drummer and he just loved anything Dave Holland could throw at us. So, we do some of that. We do a lot of original compositions in our group that I think are very much coming from a Wayne Shorter influence. I guess Miles Davis and certainly Dave Holland, and William Parker out of New York. We listen to a lot of modern jazz and I think that influences our sound. When you talk to our sax player, Xiaoguang, he is certainly influenced by a lot of modern jazz saxophonists. Kenny Garrett visited us in December. He listened to a lot of Kenny Garrett."

How does he define jazz in China? "Developing." He elaborated:

There are a lot of musicians who are simply copying. Listening to a lot of Kenny Garrett or listening to a lot of Joshua Redman and just trying to get that sound. [. . .] But then there are some other individuals, and certainly pianist Xia Jia is one of them, who are reaching beyond. Kong Hong Wei is very commercial, but if you listen to some of the recordings he has done, even his early recording from I guess '96 or '97, he incorporates a lot of Chinese elements into his music. Some of the original compositions we do at Ah Q have elements I would identify as having Chinese origins, but still very much in a more tradition, modern jazz tradition. You've still got to have a couple sections, soloing. Maybe we're using some pentatonic chords, pentatonic scales, and maybe some chord structures that are less Western and more Chinese, but it's still very much in a modern jazz tradition.

I mentioned to Roberts that when I talk to people about this project, the first comment is, "There's jazz in China?" The second comment is, "Well, how good is it?" To a degree there seems to be a bias against jazz musicians from other countries other than the United States on the part of American musicians, even journalists. Roberts can relate. He thinks Chinese musicians will probably always be behind US musicians in terms of ultimate jazz skills but he is not sure that that makes Chinese musicians any less listenable or valuable. "I think they've got something to offer. What they really need to develop their skills is an environment where they can play for themselves, where they can interact with other musicians and pursue their ideas. This is really every musician's dream, where you don't have to worry about playing the wedding gig, so you can play the music you're hearing in your soul. I think Beijing has the start of that, but it's going to take a lot more for Chinese jazz musicians to be able to find themselves in that world."

Does he find that being an American in China creates obstacles or presents advantages to trying to get the music played in China? Roberts said that there are certainly some venues that are all about getting the expat musician on stage: "It doesn't matter what they're doing. As long as it's a white guy up there, they pay extra for it." But Roberts wanted to be clear that that's not what he's about, along with most of the other really good expat jazz musicians in China. He does not necessarily think being an American in China even helps getting into the community, because it is more about melding with the group. "I think for the jazz community here to accept you, you really have to have something that they like. They listen to the music, they like what you're playing, you can communicate, you're a team player. But if you show up here and you've got an arrogant attitude, it doesn't matter how well you play, you're not going to be called back for another gig."

Roberts concludes:

> One thing you will find as you meet with the musicians and you listen to the musicians is that there's a lot of talent here as far as I can see and I'm no expert, but there are some very talented musicians I would love to see continue to develop. And it is my hope as I continue to live and work in China that I can find a way working with Peter Zanello and others, to get them plugged into an international community where they can continue to develop their ideas and develop uniquely Chinese jazz, whatever it means to them as Chinese musicians to be jazz musicians, to continue to pursue that. I find it fascinating. I've worked with Chinese musicians for fifteen years now and I've had a blast. There are some very, very good people, very dedicated musicians, very hard-working, and I think they are producing some very beautiful music.

Roberts's choice for naming his jazz group the Ah Q Orchestra is fitting. The name Ah Q is derived from a famous 1921 Chinese short story, "The True Story of Ah Q" by Lu Xun, a pen name for Zhou Shuren (1881–1936). Lu Xun was an "open dissident" who by the latter part of his life had become a household name in China.[42] According to David Pollard of the Research Center for Translation, Chinese University of Hong Kong: "He was a pioneer in China of the modern short story. Modernity was in fact a key concept in all his thinking; not modernity as fashion, but as a basis for China first to survive, then prosper. Lu Xun's own life story is that of the evolution of China's modern man."[43]

Exemplary of his fame, at his funeral cortege, joined by thousands, a banner draped over his coffin read "The Soul of the Nation." He was singled out for extravagant praise by Chairman Mao in 1940. Pollard adds: "Consequently he became an icon in China, for some good and some ill. After the Chinese Communist Party assumed power in 1949 it was a crime even to hint that Lu Xun had any shortcomings. . . . Lu Xun still stands, on his own merits, as the most eminent literary figure [in China] in the first half of the twentieth century."[44]

In this context, the choice of Ah Q for Roberts's jazz group is apt. It parallels Lu Xun's "modernity" philosophy with that of jazz's demand for individual freedom of expression in the context of cooperation among members of the group. Xun's modernity approach was in opposition to the prevailing Confucianist philosophy of the Qing Dynasty "to which the notion of progress was alien: the ideal society was set in the past." The Qing Dynasty was overthrown nationwide in 1911. It was then that China became a republic.

A confusion, though, arises from the short story's central character Ah Q himself. Ah Q is a pathetic, illiterate, delusional, insensitive, and brainless clown who makes his living as an odd-job man. At the end of the story we learn he has been shot, i.e., executed, for a crime he did not commit. Just prior to this end-game, he had been rejected by revolutionaries, a group he had passionately wanted to join. In the story there are references to "the successful county candidate," "the boatman Sevenpounder," "the Bogus Foreign Devil," the "Persimmon Oil Party," and the "Tutelary God's Temple." Clearly, this short story is more than a tale to entertain, it is a story with a point.

In effect, Ah Q (with the Q a metaphor for the old Chinese culture of the pigtail) stands for the Chinese Everyman. He becomes a foil in Lu Xun's hands to comment, albeit harshly, on Chinese values at the time. Of Xun's purpose, Pollard writes, "Instead of thinking and feeling for themselves, people reach for the nearest maxim to direct their response to situations. . . . As Lu Xun said in his 1925 preface to a Russian translation of 'Ah Q,' the Chinese are a silent people, unaware of each other as individuals, and unaware of themselves. What [Lu Xun] attempted to bring about was recognition of this lack of sympathy, not sympathy itself."[45]

Matt Roberts's Ah Q Orchestra is certainly not silent, and it passionately pursues a desire not only for individual performance, but also effective, empathetic group dynamics. In this sense, Roberts's group is well-named. Just as "The True Story of Ah Q" is full of purposeful irony, so, too, is the Ah Q

Orchestra: it performs in the context of the political center of China—Beijing—where thousands of years of conservative Confucianism values still exist side by side with evolving "modernist" values brought on by China's "revolutionary" push to become a world economic power.

CHAPTER 15

Shanghai's Jazz Venues

The historical presence of jazz in Shanghai as the music of the city, from the late 1910s and even throughout the Japanese invasion, continues to this day. Even though Mao suppressed anything Western within a few years of his defeat of the Nationalists in 1949, his passing in 1976 and the subsequent opening up of China to the world in the late 1970s spurred the rejuvenation of jazz in the city.

By the mid-2000s, you could find numerous venues presenting jazz in Shanghai. Some of the venues are housed in the hotels, such as the Shanghai Hilton (250 Hua Shan Road), the George V (1 Wu Lu Qi Nan Road), and the Portman Ritz-Carlton Bar (1376 Nanjing Xi Road). The most historic of the hotel jazz venues is the Peace Hotel Jazz Bar (20 Nanjing East Road) on the Bund.

THE PEACE HOTEL JAZZ BAR ON THE BUND

Mao's demise in 1976—resulting a few years later in the reemergence of China as part of the world community in the last quarter of the twentieth century—together with the influence of electronic and transportation technologies in the second half of the twentieth century (described in chapter 9) had a direct impact on the rejuvenation of jazz in China. On the one hand, it reignited the need for jazz on the part of hotel owners in response to the initial trickle then torrent of Westerners coming to China visiting as tourists and on business. On the other hand, it also provided opportunities for jazz musicians from all over the world to perform in China. Again, the locus of this activity, at least in the second beginning, was Shanghai. The prime example of the former is the Peace Hotel Jazz Bar.

The Peace Hotel location has history written all over it. According to *Shanghai's Dancing World: Carbaret Culture and Urban Politics 1919–1954*, Andrew David Field's excellent book on the dancing scene in pre-Mao Shanghai:

Between the late 1920s and early 1930s, despite the world depression and a local recession, the city continued its building spree. During this period, a number of new hotels arose to outdo those of earlier times in splendor, grandeur and height. Probably the most famous of the 1930s Shanghai, the Cathay Hotel and the Sassoon House, known today as the Peace Hotel, stood as its premier hostelry. It was located on the prime spot of real estate at the corner of Nanjing Road and the Bund—perhaps the most expensive piece of land in the city. Financed by the real estate mogul Victor Sassoon and designed by the British architectural firm of Palmer & Turner, which also built many of the other landmarks on Shanghai's most famous stretch of riverbank, the hotel featured Deco exterior and interior design elements, including highly stylized pairs of greyhounds in the grillwork above the ground floor windows (Sassoon loved both the horse and dog racing and actively participated in both), and the green pyramid-shaped tower overlooking the Huangpu River where Sassoon held wild and lavish parties. Built in 1929 and designed according to American-style Deco principles, the Cathay Hotel soon acquired a reputation as the most elegant in the city, if not in all of China.[1]

The Peace Hotel itself did not have that name until 1956. The original was actually two buildings: one called the Palace, built in 1906; the other, the Cathay Hotel. The Cathay was built at a cost of one million pounds in 1929. Both structures belonged to the complex on the Bund called Sassoon House. This structure was built by Sir Victor Elice Sassoon, descendent of a family of Iraqi Jews whose antecedents had once served in the capacity of bankers to Baghdad's caliphs.[2] At the time it was the last word in luxury: "the Cathay had air-conditioning, water piped in from Bubbling Well Springs outside the city, bright red-flocked wallpaper, and built-in mahogany wardrobes in every room."[3]

The legendary Sassoon family itself is steeped in China's history, let alone Shanghai. The Jewish clan can be traced to David Sassoon (1792–1864). Born into a Sephardic Jewish family in Baghdad, Iraq, David Sassoon set up the Sassoon Company in Bombay, India, in 1833. In 1844, he set up a branch in Hong Kong, and a year later a Shanghai branch on the Bund to cash in on the opium trade. At that time, about one-fifth of all opium brought into China was shipped on the Sassoon fleet. They brought China opium and British textiles and took away silk, tea, and silver.

Victor Sassoon (1881–1961), the fourth generation of the Sassoon family, inherited the new Sassoon Company in 1881. He came to Shanghai in 1923, and in the years to come, expanded his family business mainly in Shanghai and turned it into an empire. Part of that empire was the Cathay Hotel, later renamed the Peace Hotel.[4] The Peace Hotel is now named the Fairmont Peace Hotel Shanghai following a three-year renovation of the entire hotel completed in 2009.[5]

The famed Peace Hotel Jazz Band performs there every night. Their history, personnel, and repertoire are described in the next chapter.

THE JAZZ CLUBS

Other venues can be defined as jazz clubs, such as the JZ Club. Some, like Number Five (20 Guang Dong Road near Zhong Shan Road #5 the Bund), did not last. It was in business for seven months. There are several other smaller clubs, but the ones that are mentioned the most frequently—and that are still in business—are the following.

THE JZ CLUB: SHANGHAI'S CURRENT JAZZ CENTER

> I personally felt I could do more than just play bass, and I wanted to make a home for musicians.[6]
> —REN YUQING, OWNER OF THE JZ CLUB

The JZ Club is considered one of the premier jazz venues and center of the jazz world in Shanghai. Founded in 2004 by Ren Yuqing, former bassist for China's first rock 'n' roll icon, Cui Jian,[7] the JZ Club has become one of the most popular jazz clubs in China—and is frequently mentioned in various travel and Shanghai nightlife guides as "*the* jazz club in China."

In 2016 it moved from its original location on 46 Fuxing Road to Found 158, 158 Julu Lu, near Chengdu Nan Lu, Huangpu district.

Yuqing said: "When I came to Shanghai to play jazz in 2000, the music was performed only in hotels and the Cotton Club. But Shanghai has a history with jazz from the 1930s. Ask some old people, 'do you know jazz?' and they will tell you about how they used to dance to that music in The Paramount every night." He added: "Even though jazz started in the US, it's now an international language—perfect for a cosmopolitan city like Shanghai."[8]

Hosting live performances 365 days a year, the JZ Club offers clients with a wide variety of music including swing, modern jazz-rock, and even Latino. The club also hosts bands of different genres of music, including the Afro-Sonic Orchestra, led by Theo Coker; the JZ All-Star Big Band, the premier jazz ensemble in China formerly directed by Mats Holmquist; the Latino Project, a ten-musician band that plays funk, swing, Afro-Caribbean, and reggaeton; Five Below, JQ Whitcomb's jazz quintet with Hammond organ, drums, guitar, trumpet, and tenor saxophone; and the Red Groove Project, a ten-piece band founded by guitarist Lawrence Ku.

"I want jazz to become the signature music of Shanghai, the music of Shanghai's soul,"[9] said Yuqing of his desire to open the club. He always knew, however, that education must be involved in order for jazz to gain awareness and grow. Yuqing subsequently opened the JZ School,[10] a music education facility committed to developing the creative and productive potential of its students, in 2006 with Ku, Brit Ben Denton, JQ Whitcomb, and Amy Wu.[11]

Soon after, Yuqing created the JZ Shanghai Music Festival that takes place annually in October.[12] "After I opened JZ Club in 2003, people kept coming up to me, asking to see more live jazz. The warm reception and excitement that it generated inspired me to organize a jazz festival to showcase the best of jazz and get it better exposure. In 2005 we had our first festival,"[13] Yuqing said. The JZ Music Festival is the "largest and longest-running music festival in Shanghai."

"Jazz incorporates everything," says Ren. "The heart of the festival is to make people party, make people dance,"[14] Yuqing said. "My aim is for the JZ International Music Festival to become the main jazz festival in China and for it to be internationally recognized on the jazz circuit and by jazz lovers from all over the world,"[15] Yuqing added.

According to Rolf Becker—the German saxophonist who originated the big band at the JZ Club, Ren Yuqing opened another JZ Club in Hangzhou (China) in 2008 and in Shanghai started the Wooden Box and the JZ Lounge. The JZ Jazz Festival has become an internationally recognized major event, with such guest artists as bassist Ron Carter, pianist Chick Corea, the Manhattan Transfer, Dee Dee Bridgewater, Chris Potter, and Tower of Power.[16]

CJW (CIGAR, JAZZ, WINE)

CJW started as a franchise in Taiwan in 1998. Today, there are three locations: Shenzhen, Beijing, and Shanghai. The Shanghai location was established in 2002. According to its website:

> Shanghai Xin Tian Di [Cigar, Jazz, Wine]—Where yesterday and tomorrow meet in Shanghai today. Located in the center of Shanghai City south of Huaihai Zhong Lu, Shanghai Xin Tian Di has become an urban tourist attraction that holds the historical and cultural legacies of the city. Shanghai Xin Tian Di is a fashionable pedestrian street composed of Shikumen and modern architecture style. Shanghai Xin Tian Di is unique because of its concept of construction. It retains the antique walls, tiles and exterior of the Shikumen housing of old Shanghai. On the other hand, its interior embodies a totally different world of international gallery, bars and cafes, boutiques or theme restaurants. When you walk into Xin Tian Di, you will get the taste both of Shanghai in the 1920's and the sonic modern lifestyle of urbanites of the 21st century.[17]

In keeping with Shanghai's cosmopolitan and eclectic history, CJW presents a mix of Chinese-based musicians and non-Chinese. For example, as of this writing the headliner is Emerald Jade, originally from Gary, Indiana, a Best Female Jazz Vocalist nominee at the 2007 American Black Music Awards in Las Vegas. Other musicians include bassist Fred Granade from Mauritius, drummer Chu Wei Ming from Shanghai, saxophonist Alvaro Rafael Cardenas Jr. from Colombia, and saxophonist Saharo Leonardo Sorba from Italy.[18]

THE COTTON CLUB

The Cotton Club was one of the jazz bars to return to Shanghai following Mao's passing in 1976. According to its website, it presents mostly non-Chinese singers and instrumentalists, such as Australian singer/songwriter/guitarist Dave Stone, Uzbekistan singer Raina Skar, Arlene Estrella, Matt "Cadillac" Cooper, American saxophonist/composer Tia Fuller, Shanghai jazz violinist Peng Fei, singer Ginger Zheng, Guitarist Greg Smith, and the David Redic Ensemble.[19]

This club that predates the JZ Club is geographically located just down the road from the latter's original location. Its reputation as one of Shanghai's premiere jazz clubs is well established. Our visit to the Cotton Club in August 2006 was not unlike another visitor's experience—Weihua Zhang—from July 1999:

> In a bar of dark, paneled wood, the music started from 9:30 p.m. and lasted till midnight. The music performed was primarily blues with a jazz influence. We heard a trio consisting of electric guitar, drum-set, and electric bass. A black Canadian singer occasionally joined in. The drummer, Greg Smith, was from San Francisco and Santa Cruz, California.[20] He explained that the performance usually included a trumpet player, who was a young student from the Shanghai Conservatory of Music, and another vocalist, a French singer who was studying at the same school. Greg came to Shanghai a year ago [in 1998] and was a business partner at the club. He did not have a day job. The club initially catered to international diplomats because of its close proximity to the diplomatic neighborhood in Shanghai. According to Greg Smith, there was a mixed audience of non-Chinese and Chinese among the 250 regular core customers. The Chinese audience was growing and on weekends there were always new faces coming.[21]

HOUSE OF BLUES AND JAZZ

From their website:

> Since 1995 the House of Blues and Jazz has been a second living room for those who are hungry for quality live music and a home for blues and jazz musicians from all over the world. In fact, the first blues and jazz bar in new Shanghai. The present Bund location of House of Blues and Jazz is the fourth incarnation of this mainstay of the Shanghai live music scene, however with an increased capacity and an added Dining room is the best yet. It still remains a place to relax with a drink, perhaps a fine cigar, chat with Mr. Lin Dongfu while listening to some of the best blues and jazz Shanghai offers.[22]

One recent reviewer had this to say: "If you thought this is a music place you would be right! It is possibly the best place for this genre of music in

Shanghai. What is interesting is it is also a good place to have dinner amidst the smoky looking (no cigarettes inside) 1920s decor. The bathrooms are period pieces and every fitting reflects the bygone era. The food is good as well and then around 9:30 p.m. the band rolls in and sets the place on fire. The bands keep changing—ours played a reworked Memphis Soul Stew that was appropriately re-named Shanghai Soul Stew."[23]

The usually reliable Frommer's comments: "Relocated from the French Concession to just off the Bund across from the Captain hostel, this is thankfully still an excellent spot to sing the blues. The space is larger here, with two floors, but the vibe is still fairly intimate, relaxed, and unpretentious, with the music (international bands are the norm) usually taking center stage."[24]

THE PARAMOUNT BALLROOM

A description of the contemporary jazz venue scene in Shanghai would not be complete without reference to the Paramount Ballroom—the preeminent dance hall in Shanghai in pre-Mao times, and still the leading dance hall in twenty-first-century Shanghai. The front entrance to the Paramount is pictured on the front cover of this volume.

While the Paramount is neither strictly a jazz club (as in the JZ Club) or a jazz bar (as in the Peace Hotel Jazz Bar), this historic dance hall could be considered the epitome of Shanghai's nightlife at least pre-Mao, when jazz was the music of the age for the elite and burgeoning middle class.[25] Andrew Field in *Shanghai's Dancing World* refers to the Paramount almost immediately on page 1, it had that much prominence: "With its Deco fixtures, its large spring dance floor, and its small upper floor of glass plating with colored lights underneath, people familiar with the Paramount considered it as up-to-date and modern as the ballrooms of New York or Paris."[26] The Paramount (Chinese: 百樂門; pinyin: Bâilèmén; literally "gate of 100 pleasures") is located at 218 Yuyuan Road in Jing'an, Shanghai. A group of Chinese bankers built the ballroom and completed it in December 1933 at a purported cost of nearly one million dollars. Nearly 1,000 invited guests celebrated its opening on Friday night, December 19, 1933.[27]

Field also reports: "[Even] by the advent of the Japanese invasion in 1937, top nightspots in the city included the Paramount ballroom, [as well as] Ciro's nightclub, the Cathay Hotel ballroom and Tower Club, and the Metropole Gardens ballroom."[28] It was the largest and most notorious ballroom in Shanghai during the so-called decadent era before the People's Liberation Army established control over the city in 1949.

It was my good fortune to visit the Paramount in 2006 at the suggestion of our Shanghai guides Scarlett Shao and her father. The lure of the Paramount was compelling. We got there on a muggy evening around 10 p.m. As we walked inside we were met by a statuesque young woman who wanted to know what we wanted. We presented our purpose. We were immediately escorted to the elevator and proceeded to the third floor. No sooner had the doors opened than we heard music coming from around the corner. We asked to see a manager. Within several minutes, a thin, young man appeared. Scarlett explained our mission. I handed him my academic card. I think he understood the implied promotional opportunities. I asked if there were any photos of the dance hall from the 1930s. There were none, but he showed us a staircase that had posters of singers who had appeared there in years past. My more urgent goal was to videotape the goings on in the dance hall itself. Once we had shot the posters, I asked the assistant manager if we could videorecord the dancing in the hall for about ten minutes. I explained, through Scarlett, that I would not get in anyone's way and would limit my shooting to ten minutes. We turned the corner to peer inside the cavernous hall.

I was floored. The musicians on the stage were contemporary, playing contemporary Chinese pop and some jazz standards all for the purpose of dancing. The hall itself had been renovated to its original décor. What was more astounding than anything else was the social scene. It could easily have been the late 1920s or 1930s. There were old and young, Chinese and non-Chinese, male and female—all there to dance and, of course, socialize. It was as if we had been transported back seventy years. The social scene had not changed one iota in all this time. It was like being in a time machine. The Paramount is the only remaining dance hall of the hundreds that existed in Shanghai in the 1930s and 1940s.

Our visit to the historic Shanghai Paramount Ballroom was accidentally well timed. Chao Shichong, president of Shanghai Paramount Entertainment & Restaurant Co. Ltd., had just completed a renovation of the space after it had been used as a cinema for half a century. About US$3 million were invested in restoring the Paramount after Shichong took over in 2001. The hall was again opened to the public as a nightclub in 2002.[29]

CHAPTER 16

Shanghai's Leading Indigenous and Expat Jazz Musicians

Once called the "Paris of the East," today Shanghai represents the economic and entrepreneurial center of China; Beijing is the political heart of China. Both cities have their own vibe: Beijing—spread out like Los Angeles, is clogged by an increasing number of cars and life-threatening smog; Shanghai—compact like Manhattan, New York City, is cosmopolitan and eclectic. Both cities boast their own jazz scene. Beijing is full of expats and the jazz bands tend to be more uniformly Asian. Shanghai, on the other hand, reflects a much greater international mix of musicians.

THE LEADING INDIGENOUS JAZZ MUSICIANS

THE BOYS ON THE BUND

In 2000, during my initial visit to Shanghai, I had a short meeting with Zhou Wanrong, former principal trumpeter with the Shanghai Symphony Orchestra, then leader of the Peace Hotel Jazz Band. This "interview" was my disappointing introduction to "jazz in China" (This is covered in more detail in the preface).

By 2006 Zhou Wanrong was no longer the leader of the Peace Hotel Jazz Bar sextet. That honor had passed to reed player Sun Ji Bing (Mr. Sun).[1] I asked him "When was your first encounter with jazz? When did you first hear jazz?"[2] His reply:

Around 1949 (when China declared its independence) when I was in high school. I first heard and started liking jazz music from American movies that had jazz music as part of the soundtrack. I realized that my love for music was a reflection of my exposure while in French Catholic primary school and was part of a church choir. Later on, the church created a small symphony orchestra which I would perform with on Sundays and holidays (Christmas, Easter, etc.). My school schedule consisted of core curriculum for half the day and two hours of music practice during the afternoon. I did not do well in school; barely passing my basic classes, so I decided to concentrate on music.

He continued:

Around 1949 when China started gaining its independence, Shanghai became a bustling city. They had American, Russian, and Korean bands. During this time, I would study and work. Every neighborhood had their own ethnic band (French, German, American, etc.). At night I would learn music from these bands. This is how I gained exposure to music. At the beginning it was very stressful, but I like music. I did not find it tiring. Once China reached full independence [under Mao's rule], these ethnic bands were no longer allowed in the country. Because I have a music background, I was able to join the Shanghai Orchestra. In my 50's (during the 1979 reform and opening up in China), I opted for early retirement. I organized a group of old friends that all played jazz music (different orchestras). During this time, foreign businessmen started coming to China. At night they had nowhere to go. China's Foreign Affairs Office would invite these businessmen to watch China's local opera shows and acrobatic shows. But they did not understand these shows. Music is a universal concept. In 1980 during Christmas, China's Foreign Affairs Dept. proposed that we set up a music band at the Peace Hotel. That is how our jazz band began. The tourists enjoyed our music very much and would come to watch us every Saturday. People from various consulates, especially from the American consulate, loved our music. This is how we came to fame. From 1980 until now, it's been a wonderful experience to play almost every night at the Peace Hotel. Generally, jazz bands in Shanghai only last one, two years.

I asked Mr. Sun why he chose to play the saxophone: "I started learning the saxophone in school. The school gave me the saxophone to play. Later on I bought my own."

Q: What was your very first experience listening to jazz? The radio, in the movies, where did you hear it?
Mr. Sun: Do you know VOA: Voice of America—a radio station that broadcasts American news and music in China?[3] Every night, they would

broadcast American jazz music for one-half hour. The music would feature well-known American bands from different states of the US. During that era of American jazz music, I would often hear trumpeter Harry James on VOA radio. Also a well-known clarinetist, Benny Goodman. I was mesmerized by their music. At that time, it was frowned upon to listen to American news or music. We had to sneak around to listen to it. But I knew I had to follow that path. Later, Shanghai started importing sheet music and records. I would study the records and sheet music.

Q: What did you do between 1952 when the Communist Party forbade Western music and 1980 when China started opening up to the west after Mao died in 1976?

Mr. Sun: First I was in the Shanghai Orchestra then the Shanghai Opera. I would play clarinet in the orchestra that would accompany operas.

Q: Who wrote the charts for the Peace Hotel Jazz Band?

Mr. Sun: The charts were passed on. They were American charts. We simplified the charts to accommodate a six-piece band from a typical sixteen-piece American band.

Q: Do you think you will ever retire?

Mr. Sun: The musician profession is accepted in America, but in China it's not a highly sought-after and well-respected profession. I love to play music so retirement is not something I think about. There is no retirement. If the place you are playing for no longer needs you, they will dismiss you. There is no sympathy either when they kick you out.

When that time comes, I will deal with it. I'm not worried. There used to be some great jazz bands in Shanghai. Now they're slowly phasing out. The reason they're phasing out is because of the hotel owners. Chinese hotel owners are not experienced and professional in operating this sort of business. That's why they have American or European owners. But Europeans don't like "us" older men playing jazz. They like young Chinese women. Especially sad, there was a fantastic jazz group (some of my old friends) from the New Jia Jiang Hotel. They were replaced by young women. Another hotel called Hua Yang also had a well-respected jazz group but they are no longer respected. Like us, older men are no longer respected in the industry. Now, I'm not relying on my jazz gigs to survive. I have a retirement plan and my kids do well abroad.

Other members of the Peace Hotel Jazz Band have commented else-where on their multi-decade experience. Zhou Wanrong, the eighty-eight-year-old former bandleader of the Peace Hotel's Old Jazz band, and pianist Cao Ziping, eighty-six, first played together in 1947, when local jazz legend Jimmy King formed one of Shanghai's all-Chinese jazz band to play at the Paramount Theatre, a definitive Shanghai Art Deco building that was then the center of a thriving jazz scene. Though Shanghai was a renowned jazz city, it was dominated by foreign audiences and acts, especially Filipino ones.

But, as Zhou remembered in a video interview: "As the Japanese got clos-er all the foreigners started to leave town, so bars had to start using Chinese performers." Cao continues: "We helped Jimmy form his band and perform the Hawaiian-style music he loved. Jimmy became famous and we became quite famous too playing at the Paramount." This was a big deal for Zhou, who learned Western songs while at an orphanage in Wuhan, and Cao, who learned piano and accordion at sixteen from a white Russian after being inspired by 1930s American films.[4]

The band's initial fame was short-lived, as the Communist takeover in 1949 saw the end of the jazz scene. But fast-forward to 1980, when Zhou was asked to form a jazz band once more and brought together seven old jazz hands. Having played their first show on Christmas Day 1980, Zhou says, "We've been playing every day since. Christmas, Western New Year, Spring Festival—every day."[5]

The revived band is now made up of six veteran musicians whose careers span more than half a century and with an average age of seventy-six. Their repertoire consists mainly of jazz standards of the 1930s and 1940s as well as some golden oldies in pops. They purport to play up to 300 pieces to cater to audiences of different tastes.

Over the years, the group has paid dozens of visits to the United States, Holland, Japan, Singapore and Taiwan. They have performed for many ce-lebrities and heads of states, including former US presidents Jimmy Carter and Ronald Reagan, and King Harold V of Norway. Of this group, *Time* wrote: "Listening and dancing to the rejuvenated band is not just a mu-sical diversion. It is a rendezvous with Shanghai history." *China Tourism Magazine* observed: "It is not every day that you hear the sounds of a band that boasts a history of [25] years. Though advanced in years, these vener-able jazzmen are still going strong. Many would head straight to the Peace Hotel Bar as soon as they land in Shanghai just to hear them play. They are a famous tourist attraction in themselves, probably more so than the so-called scenic spots." The members of this group (as of 2006) were:

Zhou Wanrong (leader/trumpet): Born in Hubei in 1920, he is formerly the principal trumpet with the Shanghai Symphony Orchestra.

Cheng Yueqiang (drums): Born in Guangdong in 1918, formerly a drummer with the Shanghai Opera Band.

Zhang Jingyu (piano): Born in Shanghai in 1940, formerly a pianist and percussionist with the Shanghai Symphony Orchestra.

Sun Jibin (saxophone): Born in Hebei in 1933, formerly a saxophonist with the Shanghai Orchestra.

Gu Jinlong (saxophone): Born in Shanghai in 1926, formerly a saxophonist with the Shanghai Acrobatics Troupe.

Li Mingkang (double bass): Born in Shanghai in 1936, formerly a double bass player with the Beijing Film Orchestra.[6]

The jazz band performs in the Jazz Bar nightly at 7:30 p.m. The ensemble has been immortalized on film in *As Time Goes By in Shanghai* (90 minutes; 2013) by German director Uli Gaulke.[7]

THE YOUNGER GENERATION OF INDIGENOUS JAZZ MUSICIANS

In contrast to the octogenarian musicians at the Peace Hotel Jazz Bar are a host of much younger jazz musicians. The indigenous jazz musicians described in this section are certainly not the only leading lights in the Shanghai jazz community. Quite apart from these four, there are many others mentioned elsewhere in this volume.

For example, Ren Yuqing, owner of the JZ Club, is also a virtuoso electric bassist who started out in Cui Jian's rock band in the 1980s alongside saxophonist Liu Yuan (both described in chapter 11). He is now more entrepreneur than musician. In addition to Ren, there's Yang Dehui (piano), Hu Danfeng (trumpet), Zhang Le (vocalist), Huang Jianyi (piano), Zhou Xia (piano), Pen Fei (jazz violin), Hu Qingwen (trombone), Zhu Haiming (electric bass), Jing Yongjun (upright bass), Pan Jianglei (drums), Tang Ying (tenor saxophone), Zhangbo (piano), Li Xiaochuan (trumpet), Ying Di (guitar), and Zhu Donghuan (bass).[8] All these musicians have a range of formal and semi-formal training and have been performing in Shanghai's jazz scene for several years.

The musicians' backgrounds that follow are a representative sampling of the younger generation of indigenous jazz musicians performing in Shanghai.

GUITARIST LAWRENCE KU: Chinese-American-born, Shanghai-based[9]

Guitarist/composer Lawrence Ku is one of a handful of jazz musicians performing in China (primarily Shanghai and Beijing) who has had direct experience in the United States. In Ku's case, he was born and raised in Los Angeles, California. He lives in Shanghai, China where he is among the central figures in the growing jazz scene there.

He plays regularly at the JZ Club in Shanghai (www.jzclub.cn) and is the music director at the JZ school (www.jz-school.cn). He leads his own bands, such as the Lawrence Ku Septet (a group focusing on his original compositions). His Red Groove Project (a funk/groove band) is part of the Far East Quartet (a collaborative quartet involving musicians from Shanghai and Hong Kong), the Toby Mak Quintet, the Ale Haavik All-stars, and the Shanghai Jazz Orchestra. The Lawrence Ku Septet was featured at the Helsinki Jazz Festival in June 2005.

Previously Ku resided in Beijing—where he taught at the Contemporary Music Institute and the Midi School of Music—and Boston, where he received his music training at the Longy School of Music (MA in composition) and the New England Conservatory of Music. He has studied with such jazz greats as Ben Monder, Charlie Banacos, Jerry Bergonzi, George Garzone, George Lewis, and Carol Kaye.

How was he attracted to playing jazz?

> I played rock and blues stuff in high school, and then probably at the end of high school, beginning of college I got into jazz. I started listening to Miles, Wes Montgomery, Charlie Christian, and a lot of classical music. This all happened in the early '90's, '92 or '93, about the first year of college.
>
> I went to UC San Diego, and right after I graduated I went to Beijing. I spent two years there, and then went back to a small school called Longy (Cambridge/Boston) to do a master's in composition there. Then went

back to China and then back to the New England Conservatory for the jazz program.

Ku described the jazz scene here in Shanghai:

It's pretty good. It is obviously smaller than a big city in the US, but there are some good local musicians, and a lot of good foreign musicians. They come here on a contract gig somewhere, and then end up staying. So, the level of musicianship is pretty good, and there are a couple of clubs, especially the JZ Club. It's probably the place where the best local musicians play. There are a couple of other clubs that hire foreign musicians for about three months at a time, but it's six nights a week. But here every night is different and every band is local. Some bands will blow in from Europe and the States and play a night or two. But, mainly it is just local musicians.

Why didn't Ku stay in rock or get into salsa or classical or something else?

I did get into classical and stuff, but jazz is improvisation, you get to communicate with anybody if you know the same tune. I think that the improvisation part of jazz music is probably the most appealing thing and the thing that makes jazz the common denominator in all different types of jazz music. I think every sort of music you can express yourself, but yes, I think with jazz you have more leeway to express yourself in whatever way you want.

What does he think it is going to take to grow the jazz scene in Shanghai?

Definitely more good musicians and more good local musicians from China. There are few really exceptional Chinese musicians, I think. I am going to be directing the JZ music program. Right now it is sort of a small-scale school with a jazz program. But hopefully it might build into a more like legitimate school with a degree and everything. That is more of a long-term goal. I think to start out 100 to 150 students would be nice.

What did he think of the jazz audience in Shanghai? Sophisticated, middle class, upper class, mostly Chinese?

I'd say maybe 50/50. I think the Chinese audience is becoming more and more sophisticated. I think it is just a matter of time and listening to it and becoming accustomed to it, knowing the context. If you ask anybody in the States, even if they don't listen to jazz, they know who Miles Davis is, but they wouldn't here. I think it's just a matter of getting accustomed to it. I think part of it is the performing, part of it is the education, and then part of it is getting recordings out into the market. Right now there really aren't any recordings. There may be a couple of records of jazz bands here. I think there is one.

Five to ten years from now I think it is going to get bigger, because there are a lot of gigs here and a lot of people are coming over and staying over because it is kind of a unique place. It is unusual to have a lot of work as a jazz musician. The ratio of gigs to musicians is pretty good.

What does he think is going to drive it?

A combination of everything. As more people are educated and listening to it, the interest is going to grow and there will be a jazz audience. The more it's in the schools, there will be students listening to it. A new Chinese middle class is definitely an audience or potential audience.

Lawrence Ku's album *Process* was released on the JZ label in 2007.

KE COCO ZHAO, Jazz Singer: Blends East and West, Old Shanghai with the New[10]

It is not too often that you see a performer—in this case a jazz singer—walk onto a stage dressed in contemporary cut yet traditional Chinese garb . . . barefoot! But this is exactly how Ke Coco Zhao—who goes by the single name of Coco, just like Cher, Barbra, Celine, and Sting (but you know who they are)—appeared on stage of Shanghai's JZ Club a few years ago. It did not matter. Coco was home. Not only is Shanghai his home city, the JZ Club—the center of the jazz world in Shanghai—is also his home, or so it seems. Many in the audience were his friends and longtime supporters. And even though Coco had just returned from an overseas concert tour literally the day before, his performance—a mixture of jazz standards and arranged traditional Shanghaiese melodies—was engaging and entertaining, with a touch of flamboyance.

Born in 1977 in a small town in Hunan province in central China, Coco grew up in a musical household the son of two traditional Chinese-opera musicians: his mother a singer, his father a composer. Now in his mid-thirties, Coco has become one of the most sought-after singers in China. His music provides the link between the Shanghai jazz era and the modern American jazz scene. Once a composition student at the Shanghai Conservatory of Music (he also studied oboe), Coco has since been immersed in the study of Chinese traditional music, Western classical music, and jazz. His music blends Chinese, particularly Shanghaiese, and Western elements. He says he learned singing "in the shower."

In 1997 Coco performed with the late jazz vocalist Betty Carter at the International Jazz Festival in Shanghai. Since then, he has performed at jazz festivals in France, Holland, Canada, Spain, England, Switzerland, Thailand, and Hong Kong. His band Possicobilities was featured at the prestigious Montreux Jazz Festival in 2006, where he received much acclaim from the world media, including the Europe One radio program *La Boite de Jazz*. In 1997 he was invited by Parisian radio station Europe One to appear on that jazz music program. During the trip to Paris, Coco performed at renowned jazz clubs Bois D'Arcy and Petit Journal Montparnasse with local Parisian jazz bands. These were his first performances abroad, and the local French media gave him the name "The Boy Billie Holiday from China." At this time he was only nineteen years old. Coco Zhao appeared again in 2007 at the Montreal Jazz Festival and at the Kennedy Center with pianist, composer, and educator Burnett Thompson.

He was a recipient of a 2009 Rockefeller Foundation grant through the Asian Cultural Council (New York City) to observe over five months contemporary jazz activities in New York City and New Orleans in spring 2010. In 2011 Coco premiered an original work (with Mandarin lyrics) by Burnett Thompson, the "Shakespeare Sonnet Song Cycle," in Shanghai.

How did he start singing jazz?

It was maybe about eleven years ago. I was playing in a band playing pop music, some rock and roll as well. We were playing in the Cotton Club and one night this American guy came over. He brought this guitar and he said, "Can I come on and play a song?" I said "Yes, sure." He came on the stage, took his guitar out, plugged it in and started to play "Misty" by Erroll Garner. It was really beautiful. I didn't know what it was yet. I asked him, "What did you play?" and he said "It's called 'Misty.' It's a jazz song."

That was my first time putting jazz music and this jazz concept together. I really liked it, so I asked him for his charts. He gave me "Misty," also "Summertime" and "Autumn Leaves." That's how I started, with those three songs.

Coco also said he was performing a lot of songs from old Shanghai. "We're also doing this new project, which is rearranging all the old Shanghai songs into jazz. Also we're doing more original stuff. That's why more and more we're playing my originals or the band's original stuff more than standards."

Coco studied classical music: oboe and symphony orchestra composition at the Shanghai Music Conservatory. He learned singing in the shower. How did he develop his style? "I think it's by listening to a lot of different vocalists and CDs, also to instrumental CDs. I also listen to a lot of Chinese folk songs. I think every period of time you dig into there's something that would help you to develop some parts of your musical life."

Coco's band is an international mix with himself as singer, Pam Phay on violin, and pianist Wong Chang Lee, and two Americans on bass and drums—EJ Parker (a longtime expat in Shanghai) and Chris Tranzinski, respectively.

Is this typical of a jazz band in Shanghai?

I don't know if it's typical or not, but I think it's kind of destiny, kind of fate that we got together. They are very good players. I think we're lucky to have each other because I think in Shanghai there are a lot of good musicians, but there are not really quite a lot of musicians that can really play together.

The night we observed Coco's performance the audience was about half expatriates and half Shanghaiese people. Is that a typical audience? "Mostly it's like this. Of course, sometimes you have more foreigners, sometimes you have more Chinese, but mostly it's all mixed. I think in Shanghai it's better than Beijing audience-wise. I think here has more than Beijing, but of course it's not enough compared with the whole city size."

What did Coco think it's going to take to grow the jazz audience in China?

I think it's first going to take the musicians to believe in themselves, that no matter if you have an audience or not, you still want to play. Also, we need more people to be here to make the community bigger and stronger, but that comes with time I think. I think it is already so much better than before, but it will take some time to get more people who can enjoy jazz in China or in Shanghai.

And jazz education?

Yes, there is none [in 2006]. I think that's a bit of a pity, but I think actually in the Shanghai Music Conservatory they do have a jazz department right now. I don't really know how everything works there, but I heard it's not really that professional. I think we have to have people here go to study outside first, get education from somewhere else, and then you can have your own things to put with it and come back, so you have a better education. I think it's going to take some time to get people to study outside first.

I've watched the process of how everything became now. I can't really just put one word to describe the character, but for now I think more and more it becomes stronger, this jazz community here, and have more varieties than before. You have more original compositions and different kind of genres of jazz because it was only standards, old-school jazz, and now you have funk, you have Latin, you have post-contemporary style jazz. You have all kinds of groups doing all kinds of music here. It's getting more colorful.

I think since the '20s and '30s Shanghai has always been a place like in New York—well, maybe not as many people as New York—but so many people from all different places are in Shanghai as well. When you get exposed to something, you always can have more information. Also, jazz music is not really a kind of music Chinese people listen to all the time. I think not only about being exposed, I think also it's how you can take them into this. You have to find a way to let them know, how to kind of lead them into this music. I don't think they really know how to find a way to enjoy it, unless if you help them to get a way to help them how to enjoy the music.

For example, we do these Shanghainese songs. I think for them, they probably would be more familiar to start to listening with because they don't know the English songs. They don't know John Coltrane. They don't know Miles Davis. Of course, some people know, but not many. I think, how are we going to make them to get into jazz more? More probably I think we can use, for example, Shanghainese songs.

ZHANG XIAOLU: Saxophonist and Teacher[11]

Zhang Xiaolu heard jazz for the first time around the age of five from his grandfather, also a saxophonist. In fact, all his uncles play the saxophone. According to Xiaolu, his grandfather, who passed away in 1986, played a kind of pop music, very old Shanghai pop music, probably the kind of music heard in the dance halls popular in Shanghai in the 1920s and 1930s. When he was ten years old, Xiaolu's father traveled to the United States and brought back "something like Dixieland" and 33 rpm records. Although his father played the saxophone (and clarinet), he was not a professional musician. He was an acrobat/contortionist in a circus. Xiaolu studied at Boston University and took master classes in 2004 at Stanford, where he worked with Dave Liebman. He went there with a pianist from Shanghai University.

I asked Xiaolu about the attraction of jazz: "Actually, I play classical and jazz. I play all kinds of music. I like all kinds of jazz, from swing to funk. It's the freedom in the jazz music. It's not like orchestral music where you have to play exactly as the composer wished. But with jazz, it's your music. You can play any way you like."

In my conversation with Xiaolu at the JZ Club in Shanghai, I also asked him about the potential growth of jazz in China.

Q: Are there any jazz clubs in those cities?
ZX: Yes, also in Congzhou and I think in Nánjīng there are one or two, not much. Also in Dàlián. They have some five-star hotels that offer jazz music.

Q: Is the jazz scene going to grow in Beijing and Shanghai and then into other parts of China? Is it going to grow in the next five to ten years?
ZX: Yes, I think so. There is a market here. The people like it.

Q: When you say people like it are you talking about foreigners or are you talking about Chinese?
ZX: Chinese. Actually, I heard some students of mine say they go through the Internet making friends. Lots of people ask what do you like, what kinds of music do you like and they will say, "Oh, I like jazz." There is something about jazz that is an intercultural exchange. With jazz anything can happen. You can have fusion. They can put all kinds of music together. Lots of them like Michael Brecker, John Coltrane, Charlie Parker, Eric Alexander, George Garzone, all those people, Jerry Bergonzi.

Q: What is it you like about their music?

ZX: I like the way they play, and Michael Brecker is simply the best. George Garzone, Eric Alexander. George Garzone is from Boston, I think. He is a really good saxophone teacher and a really good player. Eric Alexander is a young saxophone player I met at Stanford.

Q: We are getting a growing sense from all the people we have talked to that there are more young people getting interested in jazz, as opposed to pop music. Is that so, or is pop music still very strong here in China?

ZX: Pop music is strong in China. It is a different kind of music, but jazz is a certain kind of music people are interested in. Right now jazz is really fashionable. The audience for jazz in Shanghai is about half and half, foreigners and locals.

Q: Is jazz becoming more popular with more educated, sophisticated people here in Shanghai?

ZX: Yes, I think so. Right now it is just the more educated people in China. They have more opportunity to listen to jazz. For example, in the club the drink fee is pretty expensive. If you don't have much money, you cannot afford it. Also, it is hard to get CDs in China. If you want to listen to jazz, you better go to the clubs. But, right now you can hear jazz everywhere. For example, Starbucks and Häagen-Dazs ice cream shops are everywhere and they play jazz music. And lots of tea houses play jazz music. Sometimes on TV on some fashion program or something they will have jazz. But it is hard to get a jazz CD.

In addition to performing in Shanghai, particularly at the JZ Club, Zhang Xiaolu is also a professor in the jazz program housed at the Shanghai Conservatory of Music. It was Zhang Xiaolu who moderated the Shanghai side of the video teleconference with the Manhattan School of Music referenced in chapter 17.

WILSON CHEN: Saxophonist/EWI

Wilson Chen is another regular performer at Shanghai's JZ Club. According to the club's website:

Wilson Chen started to play saxophone at the age of 13. At 18, he began to study jazz saxophone with famous Shanghainese teacher, Zhang

Xiaolu (see above). In 2001 and 2002, he twice won the Yamaha Saxophone championship in China and started performing in well-known jazz establishments such as the JZ Club.

In 2006, Wilson started to play with the JZ all-star Big band and subsequently performed with them three times in 2006, 2007 and 2008 at the Shanghai International Jazz Festival. Since 2007, Wilson has been lead saxophone in the Shanghai conservatory of music Jazz Big Band. During Wilson's short career so far, jazz masters such as Bob Mintzer, Kenny Garrett, George Benson, Gene Aitken, and Rusty Higgins have all given him high praise.[12]

He is also a Legere Reeds artist. According to its website:

Chen has performed as a professional musician since the age of 19, and plays at the hottest jazz clubs in Shanghai and the music festivals all around China, such as JZ music festival, Spring Wave music festival, the Beijing Nine Gates Jazz Festival, and the Midi Music Festival.

Wilson plays in various music groups such as the pianist-singer Luxuanchen Quintet, the J3 trio with Huangjianyi and Jhonny Zozef, as lead alto in the JZ All-Star big band, and the Brazilian Group with Tinho Perrera.

He has also performed in Shanghai with Dee Dee Bridgewater and the JZ All-Star big band, the Helen Sung New York Quintet. And the Laura Fygi band.

In October 2012 he was invited to perform at the Shanghai Conservatory of Music's "Jazz it up" Music Festival, and shared the stage with world renowned saxophonist Eric Marienthal, a Grammy Award-winning Los Angeles-based contemporary saxophonist best known for his work in the jazz, jazz fusion, smooth jazz, and pop genres. Chen is also the first Chinese jazz virtuoso to be written up in *DownBeat* magazine.[13]

MS. JOEY LU: Jazz Singer/Pianist[14]

Chinese-born, Shanghai-located singer/pianist Ms. Joey Lu is among a handful of female jazz musicians in China. For the most part, women in the Chinese jazz world perform the usual role of "singer" in front of the band. Ms. Lu is somewhat unique. She also plays the piano while she sings, and she has ventured out, albeit gingerly, into the world of composing.

Ms. Lu started studying classical piano at the age of seven. She's a graduate (with a bachelor's) of the Shanghai Conservatory of Music. Her passion for music drives her own style as a budding composer. Her influences are a reflection of her personal diversity, including jazz, pop, funk, and contemporary music. She has been featured on the Shanghai jazz scene for several years and has performed in many Shanghai venues, including the center of the Shanghai jazz scene, the JZ Club.

The jazz scene in Shanghai, as in Beijing and any major city in the world, consists of three kinds of venues: the large mega-venues, the hotels, and the jazz clubs. I interviewed Ms. Lu at least 100 stories up in the newly built Marriott hotel in Shanghai. The view of Shanghai's geography from this height was breathtaking.

Ms. Lu performed that evening (as she does six nights a week—except Sunday—from 7 p.m. to midnight) with a trio with her on piano, a bass player, and a trumpeter. Apparently, according to Ms. Lu, the six nights a week gig provides a decent living in Shanghai.

In this "interview" instance, because her English is not as good as her Mandarin, the interview was conducted with Ms. Scarlett Chao as translator. Ms. Chao not only speaks Mandarin, but (fortunately) she also knows Shanghaiese, a form of Mandarin specific to Shanghai.

Q: How did you get into playing jazz in Shanghai?
JL: It's just a coincidence. I've played piano and learned classical music from the age of seven. I went to the Shanghai Conservatory of Music. When I graduated I had the opportunity of learning some jazz basics and found I liked jazz more than classical music. So every opportunity I get to gig in any kind of bar in Shanghai to perform jazz music, I take the chance.

Q: What do you like about jazz music that appealed to you more than classical music?
JL: Classical music is more restricted. It's very strict. You have to follow certain rules. In jazz there is more improvisation. There's more freedom. You can put your feelings and emotions into your music, which makes it your own, as opposed to classical music which is someone else's music. It's very contained. There's no freedom. With jazz you can do whatever you want with it.

Q: Who were the first jazz musicians you listened to, the composers?
JL: Herbie Hancock, Bill Evans. I first heard it on the radio. It was a Chinese radio station, a Shanghai music station. I wasn't sure what it was the

first time I heard it, but later on, when I realized what it was, it was totally different from classical music because I was still learning classical music. That opened me up to jazz music. I felt it was so different. I heard I guess the freedom in jazz music. Something that was very different from classical music. I didn't feel restricted.

Q: Do they play a lot of jazz now or is it just some jazz?
JL: Every week they have certain programs where they play jazz, so it's not every day, it's just those certain programs that play jazz to introduce people to jazz music.

Q: How would you characterize the jazz scene in Shanghai? Is it big, booming, small, growing?
JL: Shanghai, as opposed to many other regions and cities in China, has the best opportunity to grow the jazz scene because with all the jazz and all the clubs jazz has been in Shanghai for the past twenty to thirty years, so it's not brand new. It's going to take a while to expand, but every Saturday night most clubs, most bars, they introduce brand new music to the scene to many of the locals.

Q: How important is jazz education to growing the jazz scene here in Shanghai?
JL: It is very important. Jazz education in Shanghai and Shanghai Conservatory of Music has already started giving courses—jazz guitar, jazz piano, jazz bass, so it's very important for the progress of jazz in Shanghai.

Q: You're the first woman pianist we've met between Beijing and Shanghai. You're more of a composer. All of the other women are singers, but none of them play piano. All of the other musicians are men. Is this unusual? Are you one of the first female jazz pianists and singers in China?
JL: Yes, I am the first and men do dominate the jazz scene in Shanghai. However, there are many women who are learning jazz and you will be seeing them very soon, but for now it's me.

Q: How would you describe the audience for jazz? This audience tonight here in the hotel, is it mostly expatriates or is it Chinese, or a combination of the two?

JL: The majority of our foreigners are American because this is a hotel, however, those Chinese who love jazz, they come and go, even pick a song every now and then.

Q: Do you think the Chinese audience for jazz is going to grow in the next five to ten years or is it going to stay the same kind of audience?

JL: I find this question to be very good one because I feel that it will grow and since jazz music is not foreign to Shanghai as of right now, many people will start to grow to like it. Every Saturday night many of the bars and clubs play a lot of jazz music. I feel a lot of people will grow to like jazz music and within the next five to ten years there will be a lot of marketing companies that are advertising, exposing everyone to jazz music very well. A lot of people will have the opportunity to listen to this kind of music and I think it will grow a lot further.

THE LEADING EXPATS

One of the more observable characteristics of the jazz scene in Shanghai is the prevalent international composition of the bands. While the musicians at the Peace Hotel Jazz Bar push away any attempt for anyone other than themselves to perform on the bandstand, in the Shanghai jazz clubs it is not unusual to find European, American, and Asian jazz musicians jamming side by side. Below are descriptions of a few of the leading expats performing in Shanghai.

SEAN HIGGINS: American Jazz Pianist and Composer

According to Higgins's personal website:

> Sean Higgins completed a B.M. in Jazz performance at UNC-Wilmington, and an M.M. at Northern Illinois University. He has opened for Dave Holland, Joe Lovano, Talib Kweli, and Ryan Cohen. Higgins performs worldwide and has completed an 8-week US Jazz Ambassador tours of the Middle East and Russia. He also has played in many NYC clubs such as the Jazz Standard, Smoke, and The Allen Room at Jazz at Lincoln Center. He has released two albums: one in 2008 entitled "The New Thought," which features Iajhi Hampden (drums) and Josh Ramos (bass); and the

other in 2005 entitled "Three Years' Stories," featuring Motoki Mihara (bass) and again featuring Iajhi Hampden (drums).[15]

THEO COKER: American Trumpeter and Composer

According to the JZ Club website:

> Theo Coker is the grandson of jazz trumpet legend Don Cheatham, part of the Louis Armstrong Jazz Oral History Project. He graduated in 2007 from Oberlin College Conservatory of Music with a B.A. in jazz performance and performed professionally with Louis Hayes and his Cannonball Adderley Tribute Quintet at Dizzy's Club Coca Cola at Lincoln Center. He has also shared the stage with jazz legends Clark Terry, Jimmy Heath, Benny Powell, and Frank Wess.[16]

ALEC HAAVIK: American Saxophonist

Haavik's website describes his musical background as follows:

> Raised in the New York City area, Alec has performed internationally in a broad array of jazz and performance groups. During his eight years on the scene in New York City, he performed or recorded with such artists as Jane Monheit, Ronnie Burrage, Daniel Carter, Taro Koyama, Gregory Hutchinson, Shoko Nagai, and Eric Harland, among others. Alec's CD from this period, entitled "Rocks," features a quintet with not one, but two electric guitars. The video of his charged-yet-classic tune, "Instant Death, Part 2," (as recorded by a quartet) appears on this website.
>
> Prior to Shanghai, Alec lived in Taipei, Taiwan, where he performed at top jazz and Latin music venues including The Blue Note, Brown Sugar, and The Stage. He also appeared regularly at Club 75, with local legends Roberto Zayas and Xiao Bai. In 2003, Alec performed in Seoul, Korea, as saxophonist and flautist for Musical: The Play, an original theatrical production.
>
> He has performed or recorded with Jane Monheit, Ronnie Burrage, Daniel Carter, Taro Koyama, Gregory Hutchinson, Shoko Nagai, and Eric Harland, among others in the USA. During his Master's Program at the Manhattan School of Music (New York City), Alec studied with

Dick Oatts and Mark Turner. More recently, Alec has studied with Ralph Bowen, Dave Tofani and George Garzone.[17]

ROLF BECKER: German Expat, Shanghai Big Band Leader[18]

Rolf Becker—composer, arranger, and music producer—plays alto saxophone, flute, and clarinet. He studied in Cologne, Germany, with Jiggs Whigham, world-renowned trombonist. He was formerly a member of the radio big band in Germany and has worked as a saxophonist and bandleader for Sammy Davis Jr., Al Martino, Gloria Gaynor, and Shirley Bassey, among others. As an author, Becker has published seven books on a teaching method that he developed for playing the saxophone.

Becker currently has a forty-piece orchestra that plays concerts in the Shanghai Concert Hall, a radio show, and a television show. Although Becker has created the first big band of its kind in Shanghai, he will not accept the title of the Godfather of jazz in Shanghai—not even the title of uncle. "I think one thing is true. I created the first big band after 16 years, 16 years here in Shanghai. And that was quite exciting," he said.

Starting in Shanghai in 1999, Becker explained how his first big band came to fruition:

> We were doing a concert here. I met some really interesting musicians: Chinese jazz musicians, but also international musicians. And I found it very interesting to think about creating a studio orchestra, a recording orchestra. I am a writer and the problem in Europe, especially for TV shows, especially for movie music and for some record companies, they don't have enough money anymore to record with a big orchestra. It's very expensive. These orchestras asked me to reduce their big band charts to an eight-piece band or a seven-piece band, even with a synthesizer. I've done this a long time. I didn't like it.

Becker described a few of the band's initial problems:

> The first big band was really only Chinese music. It took a long time but finally with some auditions I found really good musicians. And I started with the basics of a big band, like Count Basie charts, basics. And the concerts went really well. Then the television companies here and radio companies, they wanted to do some more concerts. But they don't have

any experience in how to set up audio for a big band. They only put two mics behind me as a conductor. So the audio is terrible for the first television show. [. . .] But we had to start, and, yes, I'm very happy and now everybody wants to join the big band.

Shanghai seems to be known as the commercial center of China, while Beijing the political center. Becker believes this is because Shanghai is "more open for jazz, for the different music styles." There also exists an assumption that there are more jazz musicians in Shanghai than in Beijing, but that jazz musicians in Beijing are more artistic, while Shanghai musicians are more commercial. Becker disagrees:

> There are always different opinions. Some of the musicians moved actually from Beijing to Shanghai because they realized here is more the jazz scene, and Beijing is more the rock and pop scene. For example, guitarist Lawrence Ku moved from Beijing after several years to Shanghai and he's now playing nearly every night in the JZ Club, the Cotton Club, or the Blues and Jazz Club. So, I think there are better opportunities for these musicians to play here.

Becker named Ku from Los Angeles as one of the leading jazz musicians in Shanghai, along with trumpeter Hu Dong Fung: "Hu Dong Fung is, if you're only thinking of Chinese musicians is a Chinese trumpet player, fantastic trumpet player. He is quite young, about 30, 28, 29 years, but he's fantastic." Also in Becker's good graces are singer Coco ("Coco is a star here already"), trumpeter Ho Yu Tong, pianist Tu Mong, violinist/composer/arranger Pung Fei, and Ren Yuqing, owner of the JZ Club. "He's also a pretty good bass player. But he's doing a lot to promote jazz with clubs and starting a school, and he's going to start doing records."

He added: "There are a lot of professional-level foreign musicians here. And a lot of the local musicians are really good. There are a few really exceptional local musicians in Beijing too, but I would say there are more professional-level musicians here right now."

Time and time again we heard that part of the problem with the jazz scene in Beijing is that not enough people have been exposed to jazz, which is why there is not a huge jazz audience. To this observation, Becker replied: "It's getting better and better. The people are listening now. One year ago or two years ago, they only enjoyed drinking, and having fun. If you want to have it fancy, you have to go in a jazz bar and then you can drink your whiskey and smoke your cigar. But to listen to the jazz was secondary. I think that now they are coming especially to this club, the JZ Club, to listen to this music," Becker said. "It's not lounge music anymore. It's more interesting for the musicians now. A lot of small groups do their own compositions now as they've realized people are listening to it," he added.

To Becker, the biggest driver—radio, CD, internet, film, television, etc.—in bringing jazz to China is a mix: "I think it might be [pirated] CDs. You can find everything here and quite cheap, about seven yuan, a little bit more than one dollar for a CD. Some people are not happy to hear it. I told you about the fellow who always wanted to be a trumpet player. He taught himself by listening to CDs. He didn't have any jazz teacher. And he's fabulous."

Becker does believe that introducing more jazz education in schools would help expand the jazz audience, as there are currently [in 2006] only two places to study jazz music in China—the Midi School and the Modern Conservatory of Music, both in Beijing. "It would be one of the important points of the next years, I think. And also to educate the audiences, I think," he said. The Shanghai Conservatory of Music, Becker added, "has a modern music program, which sort of has like jazz stuff in it. But not like a jazz curriculum or anything. I mean, they have like a couple of teachers there, you know, that are jazz musicians."

The growing economy in China may also make a difference in terms of growing the jazz audience. It is not cheap, for example, to listen to jazz in New York or anywhere else in the United States. One has to have some money to be able to go listen to good musicians. It used to be in New York that one could go sit, buy one drink, and listen to great musicians for two or three hours. But now, there's a $25 cover charge per person, one sits for maybe an hour or an hour and a half and then they kick you out. "I think it's a pity to do this. The jazz scene would die in the long term in my opinion," Becker said, but added that in China it's actually quite reasonable to listen to jazz. "In the JZ Club here, it's not very expensive. It's free entrance mostly. [...] No cover charge. For some concerts, yes, for the big band nights people go to, they have to charge something. But usually it's free of charge and yeah, you can enjoy some drinks, they are reasonable too."

Becker's wife, Egyptian-born Amira, shared her opinion as to why big bands and the jazz scene are not flourishing in China, other than in Shanghai: the club owners not wanting to pay the musicians. "In Shanghai there are plenty of bars and places to play, but usually they [club owners] don't want to pay them. So nobody commits hundred percent to the project."

According to Becker's wife, while Shanghai clubs don't charge a cover fee, the club owner still has to pay the band. "So, of course, having a band, a 16-piece or a 17-piece band is quite expensive. This is one of the other problems facing the musicians here," she adds.

She believes that jazz is more popular in Shanghai than in Beijing because Shanghai is considered to be the "most trendy city in China" and "anything coming out of Shanghai is so cool around China. Basically there is a huge foreign community here in Shanghai and they interact very closely with the Chinese communities, as, for example, an expatriate having a Chinese girlfriend. So it's getting more and more popular. Whereas in Beijing, the city is very spread out, so you never get the scene together really. The economics are very key," she concludes.

Within the next five years, Becker hoped to not only establish a big band, but to "have some really good work for them too. To set up a studio that earns some money for the musicians."

The abovementioned comments by Maestro Becker were made in August 2006. Since then Becker's involvement with the big band has been an up-and-down affair. He writes:

> Until December 2008 I did a weekly late Saturday night show at the JZ Club, starting at 11:30pm, for two years. The JZ club was packed and Ren, the owner, started to charge an entrance fee, first 30 RMB, then 50 RMB. Upstairs he charged 1,000 RMB for booking a table. The audience started with about 70% foreigners / 30% locals. Within one year it switched to 60% locals and 40% foreigners. It was great to see that the average age of the crowd was in their 30s.
>
> The band became better and better, but Ren and I started to argue more and more about how to proceed and take care of the band. By the end of 2008 Ren stopped the performance of the Big Band and decided behind my back, that Nicholas, an American pianist and member of the big band, would be the new leader of "his" Big Band. You can imagine how I felt. I started a 12-piece Big Band of my own and continued to do major events in Shanghai.
>
> In April 2009 I got a stroke while in Germany visiting my parents. Luckily Amira, my wife, took the right steps and I survived. I recovered very well, staying in Berlin for about two years. About three months after my stroke I accepted an invitation to play with my 12-piece Big Band at the topping out ceremony of the German Pavilion for the upcoming

EXPO. (I had the pleasure of meeting Quincy Jones.) So I kept traveling back and forth to do various events.

In the summer of 2011 we moved back to Shanghai and was part of the TAG HEUER JAZZ WEEK and continued working. I did nice shows, including one with 87-year-old French singer Charles Aznavour.

Meanwhile the JZ Big Band almost "died." The pianist, who took over my band, was fired and a Swedish conductor was hired by the time I moved back in 2011. Apparently, he did not do better and most of the good players left the Big Band in early 2012.

I met Marc Vincent, President of Sennheiser Greater China, a passionate man who supports significant musicians & bands. We did a lot of great projects, not only in Shanghai. We discovered 13-year-old super talent Abu [profiled in chapter 18], a pianist from Beijing. Marc financed his first Album.

Just two weeks ago [April 2013] I did a special Big Band show with music of the '30s and '40s and invited Mike Herriott, a great lead trumpet player from Canada and wonderful trombonist and professor Tom Smith [profiled in chapter 17]—who started a jazz class in Ningbo—to play. I did a show with my Big Band and my special guests at the JZ club on Monday, April 15. It was a big success and the best Big Band performance during my time being in China. I played the clarinet solos of Benny Goodman and Artie Shaw. Ren was very impressed; since then we are talking about future shows and projects. That's China![19]

CHAPTER 17

Jazz Education in China

GENERAL MUSIC EDUCATION IN CHINA

Gordon Cox—former senior lecturer in Music Education, University of Reading, UK—in his review of Wai-Chung Ho's book *School music education and social change in Mainland China, Hong Kong, and Taiwan*,[1] observes, "Mainland China, [Wai-Chung] Ho reminds us, is the oldest civilisation in the world, and music education has largely adhered to the discipline of moral education, derived from the thinking of Confucius so that music is seen more as ethics than aesthetics." Further, "Increasingly under communism in the twentieth century, music was seen as a necessary tool that promoted moral ideas to serve workers and peasants, and to convey political ideology. However, under Chairman Mao, school music education was destroyed during the Cultural Revolution (1966–76), as part of his anti-culture, anti-intellectual and anti-scientific philosophy."[2]

However, the late Bennett Reimer, writing in 1989, observed: "Now there are beginning to be major trends toward the recognition and valuing of music for artistic-aesthetic reasons."[3] Reimer, formerly a Professor of Music and Chairman of Music Education at Northwestern University (retired; died November 2013), also provides a rare glimpse into China's music education almost fifteen years after Mao's passing and just before the escalation of jazz musicians coming to China starting in the early 1990s.[4] He writes: "My impressions of music teaching in China, at all levels, include the observation that students are generally more compliant and therefore easier to deal with in group situations than we are used to in the United States." With respect to teachers he observes: "In some schools, because of extra training or interest or desire, a teacher is designated as a music specialist and offers all the music classes for that school. The best estimates are that there are some 400,000 such teachers in China, but that is a small number given the size of the population of school-age children, and it includes a great many who are not in any real sense prepared to teach music."[5]

Dr. Reimer also points out the opportunities for music study beyond junior or senior middle school: "At the pinnacle of China's music education system are nine conservatories of music. These train practically all of the country's professional musicians, including soloists and Western and Chinese ensemble performers. Composers, theorists, musicologists, conductors, all are educated in these conservatories. All except the dominant ones—the Shanghai Conservatory and the Central Conservatory (Beijing)—offer a music education degree program so that the two best schools offer nothing to school music education."[6]

Reimer's commentary on music education in China from the mid-1980s stands up to more recent observations. The Shanghai Conservatory (Shanghai) and the Central Conservatory (Beijing) are still the two dominant music conservatories in China. To this short list can be added the China Conservatory of Music. Not only is it considered one of the best colleges of music in China, but also one of the top music colleges in the world, according to the Yale School of Music.[7]

If there has been change, it takes three forms: (1) more Western-style music education, (2) a much greater connection, culturally and musically, to the outside world, and (3) the emergence of music education in jazz at the college level. Gordon Cox, writing of Wai-Chung Ho's study (above), echoes the observation: "Although funding is going into preserving traditional culture, and traditional Chinese music is represented in the school curriculum, students were found to favour listening to a mix of Western, Mandarin and Cantonese pop music."[8]

CLASSICAL MUSIC EDUCATION IN CHINA

The thirst for Western-style classical music education and "arts" in general has been on the increase in China at least since the turn of the twenty-first century. And it is a two-way street: Chinese musicians come to the United States to study and play, and Western musicians make the trek to China looking for new audiences.

A series of earlier articles in the *New York Times* also attest to the growing interest in Western music. For example,

"Classical Music Looks toward China with Hope," *New York Times*, April 3, 2007.

"Increasingly in the West, the Players Are from the East," *New York Times*, April 4, 2007.

"[Chinese] Pilgrim with an Oboe, Citizen of the World," *New York Times*, April 8, 2007.

"For All the Rock in China: With the Western Market in a Downturn, More Performers Look East," *New York Times*, November 25, 2007.

One of the above articles points out that the number of young people studying classical music in the leading conservatories in Beijing and Shanghai, China, numbered in low seven figures, i.e., in the millions! In a way, though, this is a statistical distortion. With a population of 1.3 billion-plus and a strong push from the government for education in general, a proportional million-plus classical music student population should not be surprising.

Even further evidence of China's strong interest in Western classical music is reflected in the November 2013 announcement that IMG Artists, a major representative of classical musicians in the West, had formed a partnership with China Arts and Entertainment Group, an arts and entertainment company in China. The new venture, Sino American Global Entertainment, aims to create new paths for performances and marketing in both countries. The venture, according to the article, also aims to identify new talent in China, in part by developing standardized grading at China's burgeoning music schools.[9]

Another source indicates "[In China] there are between 30 million and 100 million children studying piano, violin or both, either at school or with tutors. In many cases, on a given afternoon in a particular neighborhood, more kids are likely to be practicing piano than playing outside." Further, "The Sichuan Conservatory in Chengdu has more than 10,000 students. By contrast Julliard only has 800."[10]

The pivot to Western-style classical music is no cultural accident. As Dr. Hao Huang, Director of Scripps Humanities Institute, Scripps College (Claremont, California), points out in his comprehensive article "Why Chinese people play Western classical music: Transcultural roots of music philosophy": "Western classical music is still perceived as a tool for personal or business advancement for many ambitious Chinese."[11] Further, he writes: "One of the great ironies of modern Chinese politics is that the Confucian identification of music as a traditional mean of training citizens has endured, with the revolutionary Communist Party as its chief proponent. Despite Maoist condemnations of Confucian pre-feudal thought, the CCP has always shared the Confucian belief that music is inherently political."[12]

In this context, it can be said that jazz education in China is not necessarily political, but it has, from the Chinese government's perspective, an economic motivation, as the next chapter will attest to.

JAZZ EDUCATION IN CHINA

China is not only thirsty for classical music education. It has also reached out to the West for jazz education in several ways. China has established its own schools, notably in Beijing, Shanghai, and Ningbo. It has invited non-Chinese jazz musicians to perform in China. They have used technology, such as teleconferencing, for example, with the Manhattan School of Music, to learn. And several Chinese musicians have traveled to the United States to learn directly from American jazz educators, such as Beijing-based pianist Xia Jia, who studied with Harold Danko at the Eastman School of Music, and Shanghai-based vocalist/composer Coco, who was a recipient of a 2009 Rockefeller Foundation grant through the Asian Cultural Council (New York City) for five months of contemporary jazz activities in New York City and New Orleans in spring 2010.

Jazz education in China has evolved through various phases since its first appearance in Shanghai in the 1920s. But just like the rest of the world, jazz education in China ranges from the highly informal (listening, experimentation, self-teaching) to the highly formal, e.g., studying at the University of Beijing or the Midi School in Beijing, or the Shanghai Conservatory of Music, or the JZ Club School in Shanghai, or the jazz program established at Ningbo University.

SELF-LISTENING, SELF-TEACHING

As chapter 9 points out, the explosion of electronic media—in this context, initially tapes and CDs, and now the Internet—has provided an informal means of education for budding jazz musicians in China. David Moser writes about the scarce availability of these media since China's opening up and the content they carried:

> When Western music began to be permitted and available again in the 1980's under the warmer Deng Xiaoping era, the first forms that made it into the music stores were Western classical music, Hong Kong pop, and a smattering of American soft rock. (The Carpenters are still one of the most popular American groups in China.) John Denver was perhaps the first major American pop star to make a personal appearance in China about ten years ago, and it was such a big deal that he was actually granted an audience with Deng Xiaoping himself. (Denver would later refer

to Deng as his "good friend," which surely stretches the term somewhat.) Since then things have opened up to an astonishing extent, and CDs of everything from Madonna to Megadeth are beginning to spring up like poisonous weeds in the music stores. But so far virtually the only jazz readily available is that of schlock saxophonist Kenny G, whose licorice tones can be heard on the elevator music in foreign hotels and as background music on the radio.[13]

By the early to mid-1990s, however, Moser observed (in 1996) that whatever tapes and CDs were available were held in high regard:

Jazz tapes and CDs are indeed scarce in China, and musicians tend to hoard them like sacred relics. In fact, one of the most common complaints I heard was that certain other musicians wouldn't share their precious stash of tapes with anyone else for fear that others would somehow get the edge on them. The CD stores have no marketing arrangements with overseas companies, and a large percentage of the foreign CDs that exist are pirated versions produced in Chinese factories in violation of international copyright agreements. Jazz tapes pop up every now and then in music stores, but they're clearly the random detritus of discontinued clearing house sales, shipped off by the shovelful to whatever foreign outlets are willing to market them. The result is an absolutely random hodge-podge of a few obscure items. In the summer of 1994 I scoured every single music store in Beijing that sold foreign CDs and tapes, and the sum total of jazz tapes I found were fairly forgettable recordings by Miroslav Vitous, Artie Shaw, Paul Motian, Andrew Hill, Eddie Gomez, and Benny Goodman. That's it. And, of course, Kenny G's total oeuvre.[14]

In addition to CDs and tapes as a means of "learning" Western music, the clear attraction of Western music to Chinese people—and in this context, this means jazz *and* rock—also resulted in the formation in the early 1990s of at least one school. Ironically, while Shanghai was historically the focal point of jazz in the first half of the twentieth century, China's first school to specialize in rock 'n' roll and jazz sprouted just outside Beijing, China's political center.

THE MIDI SCHOOL, CHINA'S FIRST SCHOOL OF ROCK 'N' ROLL AND JAZZ (BEIJING)[15]

In the northwestern section of Beijing, about forty five minutes from the crowded, car-packed, smog-laden center of Beijing, is the Midi School, China's first privately run school of rock 'n' roll and jazz (www.midischool .com.cn).

Founded in 1993, the school is one of the apparent cultural ripple effects of the opening up of China to the West in the 1980s. In the words of Zahn Fan, Midi's founding president: "More and more young people, after they heard foreign music, jazz and rock 'n' roll, they love it, so they wanted to play it. So we decided we would have a modern music school in China. It's the first modern music school in China."

According to its website, its mission is "To promote an artistic and humanistic theory of modern music while offering students classes in advanced musical techniques." In the context of the Midi School, modern music means: blues, jazz, rock, pop, Latin, country, funk, and fusion.

The Midi School moved to its current location in 2001. The campus covers an area of almost five acres with space for an office and teaching building, a dormitory building, a recording studio with ProTools capability, over three acres of teaching and rehearsal space, a large performance hall, and fully equipped professional classrooms. Students have twenty-four-hour access to more than 100 rehearsal rooms. The current campus is located next to Xiangshan (Fragrant Hills) Park and the Beijing Arboretum, and is surrounded by almost 100 acres of orchards and fields.

There are approximately 300 students and twenty-five teachers. The average student age is eighteen to twenty years old, although on occasion a forty- or fifty-year-old student enrolls. The male to female ratio is nine to one, essentially 10 percent female. Some students come to the school who already have a good basic knowledge of music. Others start from scratch. It is a two-year program of study. If the student knows nothing, there is a one-year preparatory program. Basically, the Midi School teaches music theory, ear training, rhythmic training, and non-Chinese music history, primarily American popular music, including rock 'n' roll and jazz.

According to Fan, "Most of the Chinese students know nothing about jazz. They only want to play rock 'n' roll. But we know that jazz is very important. We teach rock 'n' roll and maybe after one year the students can teach themselves. In the second year, the students begin to learn about jazz.

For example, our first-year guitar students learn blues guitar. Blues is the roots of rock or jazz. They also learn chord progressions and improvisation. In the first year, students also work on simple compositions. Each student has to find partners to rehearse and practice with on a daily basis."

The school has identified over 100 books (some of which have been translated into Chinese) for use by the students. These include texts on saxophone, piano, Buddy Rich's Snare Drum Rudiments, guitar, the contemporary singer, charts and scales, slap bass lines, bebop, blues chords, Latin jazz, bossa nova, modern percussion grooves, and funk bass.

Midi School teachers are both homegrown and foreign-born. For example, Beijing-based saxophonist Liu Yuan and pianist Xia Jia, both of whom have their own established groups and gigs, have taught at the school. The Midi School has also established relationships with instructors from Germany, Denmark, Australia, and the United States. These instructors not only teach individual courses, but also supervise the students when they rehearse in small groups. Music publishers, producers, agents, recording engineers, editors, promoters, and distributors all visit the school, giving students a chance to learn firsthand from professionals in the music industry.

The school year is divided into two semesters. Students begin classes on September 1 and begin their winter vacation on January 1. The second semester runs from March 1 to July 1.

The Midi School offers a two-year, 1,200-hour program. Courses include Copyright Issues, Music Industry Overview, Simple Musical Accompaniment, Onstage Skills, Improvisation, Ensemble Work, Critical Listening, Computerized Music, Sound Mixing, Performance Rehearsal, Simple Composition, Ensemble and Soloing, Music Theory, Arranging, Performance Technique and Repertoire Expansion, Harmony Analysis, Musical Analysis, Creating a Performance Program, Leading a Rehearsal, and Sound Recording Production.

When students finish at the Midi School, some go to conservatory to finish getting a four-year college degree. According to Fan,

> Actually in China, we don't have a bachelor degree for modern music. But we have students studying in Cuba, Germany, and in Austria. They can go to Havana, Cuba and study. And they can go to America. But most of the students stay in China and they find a job that relates to music. Maybe they can become musicians, or maybe they work in a music store, or music company, or they'll do recordings.

Fan's own background is part musician, part business. He plays some guitar, but by his own admission not very well. He graduated in 1990 from a Beijing college with a bachelor's degree in business. His enjoyment of music, especially rock 'n' roll and jazz, led him to establish the Midi School.

What is it about jazz music that makes it interesting? What is it about the music that attracts you, the students? Fan stated:

> Jazz is more credible. More freedom, more improvisation, more communication, and requires more technique. Students want to become good musicians. It's very interesting that after graduating, 30 percent of the Midi School students change careers, develop a way they want to become a jazz musician. Jazz is more colorful and has a good history, and it's more complicated, and they can combine traditional Chinese music instruments with jazz.
>
> With jazz you can perform commercial music, you can play in a bar, in a lobby, and can get money. They can make a living playing some jazz. With rock 'n' roll in China, you can jump on the stage, and you can show yourself, you can show the energy. But if you go to some hotel, they don't need rock 'n' roll. If you can play "Autumn Leaves" or other jazz standards, you can make money. But the first thing is the students love jazz because jazz is beautiful music. It's good music.

Why aren't jazz musicians recording in China? Fan replied:

> Although China has a big population, not many people listen to jazz. Or maybe they can download tracks from the Internet, and maybe they can buy some fake CDs. There's some parts of Beijing where you can do that. Yes, people like to listen to foreign jazz bands, but Chinese music companies don't want to produce a jazz CD, because if they pay 100,000 renminbi to produce one jazz CD, they can't get back their cost, their investment.

In a continuing effort to expand the audience for its courses and jazz in particular, the Midi School has hosted several festivals (midifestival.com. cn). But Fan noted that in May 2005 it hosted a jazz festival in Haidian Park, the biggest grassland park in Beijing, and lost money, even though musicians played free of charge. The school, however, has continued its efforts in this regard. It hosted festivals in Beijing and other Chinese cities through 2010. Both local and foreign bands, for example, from Brazil, Japan, the United States, and Finland perform.

THE JZ CLUB SCHOOL (SHANGHAI)

"I want jazz to become the signature music of Shanghai, the music of Shanghai's soul,"[16] said Ren Yuqing of his desire to open the club. He always knew, however, that education must be involved in order for jazz to gain awareness and grow. Yuqing subsequently opened the JZ School,[17] a music education facility committed to developing the creative and productive potential of its students, in 2006 with guitarist Lawrence Ku, Brit Ben Denton, JQ Whitcomb and Amy Wu. The school's website proclaims:

> Music studies start with foundation classes. A junior music syllabus is offered with a choice of instrument, musicianship and junior ensemble classes. Older students, including adult learners, can choose from the Modern Music Program where instrumental instruction, ensemble and modern music theory options can be taken individually or in integrated study packages.

The school faculty consists of foreign and local instructors who are acclaimed professional musicians with extensive performing and/or academic experience both at national and international level. The JZ School's faculty have experience instructing the technical, performance, and theoretical aspects of music study. Many faculty members are alumni from prestigious institutions such as Berklee College, Eastman School of Music, Manhattan School of Music, Longy Institute, Oberlin, Rutgers, University of Music (Rome), and the Shanghai Conservatory.

Associated with the highly respected JZ Club, JZ School is committed to becoming the leading source of music education in China. The school is dedicated to preparing students to become creative and well-rounded musicians. In addition to learning in a classroom setting, students can obtain live stage experience by performing in front of audiences at student concerts, special performances at the JZ Club, or at community events.[18]

The school has practice rooms, piano rooms, and a percussion room. Teachers include Lawrence Ku, guitarist/composer; Rolf Becker, composer/arranger/saxophonist; Huang Jian Yi, pianist/composer; and Alec Haavik, expat saxophonist.[19]

THE SHANGHAI CONSERVATORY OF MUSIC

Zhang Xiaolu is a performing saxophonist who also teaches jazz history, basic theory, and saxophone at the Shanghai Conservatory of Music. He uses Mark Levine books (Sher Music) for theory work. He also plays clarinet. He has twenty saxophone students and eighty students who just study introduction to jazz. Virtually all of the saxophone students are male. The jazz history class breaks down 50/50 between male and female students. The average age is twenty. Some are composers, some are vocalists, and some are instrumentalists.

When asked if he thought jazz education in China would grow in the next few years:

> I think so. Right now I think there are some jazz courses in Shanghai and Beijing, but I know lots of cities in China where the schools are interested in offering something like a jazz course, such as Hángzhōu and Nánjīng. I have some students from those kinds of cities. I travel and introduce jazz to cities like Hángzhōu, Nánjīng, and Kunming, just to name a few. I think jazz is popular in China. It was popular eighty years ago, and then it stopped because of Mao. But now it continues. Like in Beijing, jazz is popular now. Some cities in North China like Shěnyáng are also very interested in jazz.[20]

An extended interview with Zhang Xiaolu can be found in chapter 16.

USING TELECONFERENCING TECHNOLOGY[21]

In the summer of 2006, the Shanghai Conservatory of Music delved into twenty-first-century technology via the use of teleconferencing between its location in Shanghai and the Upper West Side location of the Manhattan School of Music (MSM) (New York City). Organized by Christianne Orto, MSM's Dean for Distance Learning and Recording Arts, the multi-hour session with about fifty jazz students and faculty on the Shanghai side was "taught" by Justin DiCioccio, then head of MSM's jazz program.

The collaboration between MSM and the Shanghai Conservatory began a couple of years prior to the event. A former Manhattan School of Music graduate, classical pianist Ming Fong, was coming through with a delegation of Chinese faculty from various conservatories in mainland China. As he was taking them around the school, Ms. Orto fortuitously was passing them in the hallway and she saw they were looking at various facilities and she said, "Why don't you come in and look at our distance learning facility?" And so they did. She brought them into the distance learning studio and this former student, who was fluent in Mandarin, was able to translate what she was saying. She made a quick connection up to Canada's National Art Center so they could experience the real-time interactivity which is really the hallmark of the teleconferencing technology, the real-time interaction. That was the genesis of the connection.

Ming called her back later and said, "Listen, this delegation was absolutely fascinated with the technology in your program. I'd like to offer to help you. Let's see how we might get Chinese conservatories involved in this technology." That summer of 2005, Orto worked with her videoconferencing vendor, Polycom.

In June 2005 faculty from the Shanghai Conservatory went to a Polycom office in Beijing and then to the Polycom office in Shanghai so that they could demonstrate this technology. Ms. Orto related: "I was so pleased because we had a wonderful turnout on the Chinese side. We had quite a wide variety of faculty members, obviously, including jazz faculty. The first one we did was with the Shanghai Conservatory and it was so clear that they immediately got the potential of the technology. And it's at that point that the jazz faculty in Shanghai made it quite clear this would be an avenue they would like to follow."

Ms. Orto pointed out working with China takes a long time, and so there were a lot of calls after those initial demos. Everyone agreed they wanted to move forward and so they negotiated back and forth. They did an inaugural session with Shanghai with the equipment installed in their own conservatory campus.

A year from the original June '05 presentation, MSM did an inaugural session with Shanghai Conservatory. It was launched by Pinchas Zukerman, the world-famous, Israeli-born violinist. He was in the Far East concertizing, so he stopped in Shanghai and gave a master class from Shanghai back to New York so he could show them how it works. He uses this technology all the time. This is how he connects with his students when he is on the road. MSM wanted to show them what an educational exchange looks like in the virtual teaching environment. MSM gave them a menu of programs that they wanted to pursue with the Conservatory. MSM did a teleconference on composition, and one on orchestral performance, and then Justin DiCioccio taught one on jazz that lasted two and a half hours.

Orto pointed out the need for professional development: "They've got to train the faculty first. So what we're going to start with is a monthly series of professional development with their faculty: big band rehearsal techniques, how to improvise, and one area they're very interested in is creating a jazz program. Justin is perfect for that; you know, what are the elements you need in a curriculum?" Orto also pointed out the challenges of the differences between the Shanghai Conservatory academic calendar and MSM's and the twelve-hour time difference.

NINGBO UNIVERSITY

Hui Yu, Dean of the Ningbo College of Arts since 2011, is the person behind initiating the jazz program there. He recruited Tom Smith and several other short-term teachers to teach in the program.[22] More on Tom Smith below.

Yu offered Tom Smith a three-year full-time working contract that ended in 2014. He taught there full-time and organized several jazz bands. He taught private instrumental lessons, jazz ensembles, jazz chorus, and jazz theory and history. Yu also wrote an article about this jazz program that appeared in *DownBeat* in 2012, ostensibly the first article on jazz published in *DownBeat* written from China by a Chinese scholar.[23]

The Ningbo jazz program also had several visiting teachers from the United States from time to time, including Salim Washington (a Fulbright Scholar), Neil Leonard (from Berklee College of Music), Burnett Thompson (a pianist from Washington, DC, who taught twice a year), and Tia Fuller (saxophonist, composer, and educator who also teaches at Berklee).

Together with Tony Whyton of Salford University (UK), Ningbo organized an international conference on "Jazz Cosmopolitanism from East to West," a three-day symposium in January 2015 attended by over thirty scholars from thirteen countries. Yu is preparing a book of the conference proceedings. He is also writing a paper about trumpeter Buck Clayton's life in China, a short article analyzing the narratives in his autobiography *Buck Clayton's Jazz World*.

Dean Yu pointed out that Ningbo's jazz program is not a degree program but an educational program to broaden the student horizon for World Music. He stated: "I am a Wesleyan trained Ethnomusicologist, and I was trying to model the Wesleyan's program of World Music in China. We also have the first Gamelan which was the first in China's higher education system, including music schools. The jazz program here was supported by the

US consulate in Shanghai who provided substantial support for us during those years."

The courses offered at Ningbo include jazz band ensemble (1–2 years), jazz chorus (1–2 years), jazz piano improvisation (4 weeks), jazz theory and music theory (4 weeks), and jazz instrumental tutorials (1–2 years).

Without a doubt the prime mover in establishing the jazz program at Ningbo (other than Dean Yu) is trombonist Tom Smith. According to his website:

> A longtime American educator, trombonist, wind symphony conductor, studio brass teacher, big band leader, jazz choir director, researcher, concert impresario, and program creator, Smith is a six time Senior Fulbright Professor at the Romanian National University of Music in Bucharest, and Tibiscus University in Timisoara. He was also a Senior Fulbright Professional Specialist at the University of KwaZulu-Natal in Durban, South Africa and at the Serbian Academy of Music in Belgrade, where he additionally initiated their jazz program. In 2003 Tom was the first foreigner to be awarded the Romanian National Radio Prize (for unifying their jazz and popular music community), co-founded/coordinated Romania's first summer music camp, and their first school of jazz and popular music, alongside having performed on three of that country's officially designated 100 Most Essential Recordings.
>
> In 2010, Tom and his wife Sarah relocated to Northeast China where he developed a jazz music strategy for teaching English to native Mandarin speakers. In 2011 he was appointed a professor of music at Ningbo University (Zhejiang Province, China) assigned to establish the first entirely functional jazz program on the Chinese mainland that led to the formation of numerous instrumental groups and a 40-member jazz choir. In 2013, Tom was awarded the Camellia Award, for noteworthy artistic contributions towards social betterment for the Greater Ningbo Region.[24]

FUTURE OF JAZZ EDUCATION IN CHINA

Clearly, jazz education in China is gaining more of a foothold as the twenty-first century progresses. With continuing course offerings by the likes of the Midi School, the JZ Club School, the Shanghai Conservatory of Music, and Ningbo University, it is apparent that jazz has an opportunity to become

more of a cultural presence in China, particularly in the larger and medium-sized cities. What, then, might the future of jazz in China look like?
And what might motivate its growth?

CHAPTER 18

Jazz in China in the Twenty-First Century

The answer to the question "Is there jazz in China?"—or as it is usually posited with incredulity, "There's jazz in China?"—is yes, both literally and metaphorically. As the previous chapters attest to, the history of jazz in China is long, dating back to at least the early 1920s, interrupted by the Chinese leadership under Mao in 1949, and rejuvenated in the early 1980s with the beginning of China's opening up to the world under then Premier Deng Xioaping.

The remaining question is "Will there be more jazz in China as the twenty-first century progresses?" Put another way, will more and more Chinese gravitate to this musical genre not only in terms of study and performance, but also as an audience? The question is not completely answerable. There are many variables. But we can make some speculative stabs.

ECONOMICS: THE STRONG FORCE

Chen Xihe, the warm and highly competent translator during my first trip to Shanghai in May 2000, made a telling comment to me as we were walking one night on the Bund in downtown Shanghai. In answer to a question about the role of the Chinese Communist Party in China, he said: "The attitude is this: make as much money as you want, but leave the politics alone."

His statement was apt. In recent years the Chinese economy has grown by leaps and bounds, compared to Japan's, which languished at near zero percent until 2016, the Eurozone's economy, that grew faster than the US's, and the United States', which has recovered nicely from the banking crisis of 2008–2009. China's economic growth has put it past Japan's to become the world's second largest economy. During the Cold War the saying was "When somebody sneezes in Moscow, someone in Washington says 'Gesundheit.'" Today, substitute Beijing politically or Shanghai financially for Moscow. While China's GDP growth rate has been 10 percent, the new normal for China is projected to be around 6 percent. China's economic growth has pulled tens of millions of Chinese out of poverty. However, economic growth, no matter how impressive, is not without unintended consequences. The International Monetary Fund has warned "of the chilling effect on the global economy that is a result of China's transition to a new economic model focused on domestic consumption and services as well as the fear that slower growth cannot support the large debt buildup that has soared to 237 percent of GDP."[1]

Labor unrest is present in China, and has been for some time. To reference the 1919 song lyrics, "How ya gonna keep 'em down on the farm, After they've seen Paree," China's consumer population has become used to the cash culture and consumer goods and it is only human nature for it to continue. The inherent tension is between a culture driven by consumerism and a culture driven by political ideology. For the Chinese government it is a challenging balancing act.

JAZZ, ECONOMICS, POLITICS, AND TECHNOLOGY

Clearly, the strong force in this scenario is economics, of which demographics is an element, followed by the inexorable press of technology. Strobe Talbott, former president of the Brookings Institution in Washington, DC, posits the following caution in his book *The Great Experiment*:

> What happens in global politics will hinge largely on trends in the global economy. Managing that dimension of the international system will meet basic standards of equity and efficiency only if advanced industrial nations open their markets, share their technology, and invest in the eradication of poverty. Moving in that direction is more than a humanitarian imperative—it is a security requirement. Ensuring a peaceful twenty-first century will depend in large measure on narrowing the divide between those who feel like winners and those who feel like losers in the process of globalization, and on shifting the ratio in favor of those who feel like winners. Otherwise globalization itself will become a loser for us all.[2]

China is a prime example of a nation in the rapid process of evolving into one of the most powerful economies in the world. While in the recent past its per capita income ranked it around 100th in the world, its growing economy will change that. By 2009 China's manufacturing segment surpassed the United States. Its strong showing at the 2008 Summer Olympics, not just in terms of medal count, but opening and closing ceremonies, also points to a country on its way up. Some believe the growing entrepreneurial tone of the economy will ultimately lead to a weakening of the one-party Communist rule. Others, such as Associate Justice Anthony Kennedy of the US Supreme Court, perceive China will become an economic powerhouse and remain a one-party political system.[3]

Either way, China's emergence, along with India, and more collectively the Asian continent, as an economic force, and potentially a military force, to be reckoned with in the twenty-first century is no longer mere speculation. Already a permanent member of the Security Council of the United Nations, as time progresses China will have more say and sway on the world stage in terms of international relations. It also owns a sizable portion of the United States' debt. This is pivotal. In slightly more than a quarter century, since the Reagan Administration, the United States has gone from the world's creditor nation, to the world's largest debtor nation, with China holding a significant portion of this country's IOUs. Its growing role will necessitate a delicate balancing act.

More and more countries are doing more and more business with China. In turn, China's middle class will burgeon further, although China still has at least 200 million people living below the poverty line. Regardless, the growing upper and middle class in China will open its ears, as it already has, to a more sophisticated cultural aesthetic: not only popular music, but jazz as well.

Will jazz become a widely adopted musical genre in China and as popular as pop/rock has among China's youth? Probably not. As we have seen in the twentieth century, jazz went from the popular music of the world in the first half of the century to a niche music in the second half, and if jazz's current status in the United States is any example, its appreciation as a musical art form will not grow by leaps and bounds in China. If anything, jazz in China will incrementally increase in popularity in the large and medium-sized cities if for no other reason than population and demographics: a growing Chinese middle class in the medium and large cities, and a growing population of expatriates and foreigners as a result of increased global business relationships.

Communications media carry a message of their own individual characteristics, as Marshall McLuhan explicated in his famous phrase "the medium is the message." They also transmit cultural values. Each communications medium has inherent characteristics that are quite separate from the content each carries. For example, print is a very individual medium with characteristics that encourage abstract thinking. Television and radio, on the other hand, are visceral media; they appeal to emotional values. Despite the obvious, long-term success of educational programs like *Sesame Street*, television, in particular, is about feelings, not abstract concepts. Abstract concepts are much better suited to print media. Try, for example, to explain the quality of a Bach, Mozart, or Beethoven composition in print, as opposed to letting people hear the music directly for themselves and then analyzing it in oral communication or print. Jacques Attali argues, in his book *Noise: The Political Economy of Music*,[4] music both reflects and predicts. It reflects, as in a mirror, the values of the culture; it also predicts things to come.

Jazz and, more prominently, popular music have staked a claim in China in terms of the Western cultural value of "individual freedom of expression." Rock, acid rock, urban, hip-hop, etc., are not as delicate as a Mozart symphony, or as harmonically complex as a Bach fugue, or as well developed as a Beethoven symphony, certainly. These are loud, raucous, in-your-face musical expressions, sometimes about love and relationships, more often about anger.[5] Jazz, on the other hand, requires a higher level of individual musical skill and conceptualization to perform, let alone listen to, but it is nonetheless also about individual freedom of expression. The level of this musical expression is clearly individualistic.

All human expression is automatically and inherently autobiographical—there is no escaping one's self. How we express ourselves in all our human aspects—speech, dress, hairstyles, friends, lovers, food choices, teachers, and so on—are giveaways to our inner, individual selves. Those who have the talent and work at their aesthetic expressions become the great artists of a time. Individual expression of human thoughts and feelings is inexorable. Just as you cannot legislate morality, you likewise cannot legislate a limited and narrow artistic expression on an entire population for very long. Even the Jews in concentration camps during World War II found ways to express themselves in writing and music in the midst of the most horrific of circumstances. The so-called human spirit and deep need for expression is inherent in human beings. Just think of the icon of the human hand in the caves at Lescaux in southern France. Where did the impulse to make that icon come from? Surely, it came from the inner need of the person who made it.

Repressive governments and empires—the ancient Romans, the Spanish, the French under Napoleon, the colonial-obsessive British, the Nazis, the imperial Japanese, the Russian and Chinese Communists, and now the North Koreans, Iranians, and extremist radical Muslims—all failed or will fail, in part, because of a lack of openness, a lack of adjustment to new circumstances, and improvisation. The second half of the twentieth century and the early twenty-first century, certainly, has witnessed a remarkable trend. When the United Nations was formed in 1945 there were fifty-one charter members of which a few were democracies, such as the United States, Great Britain, and France. Today, there are over 192 member states[6] and over 60 percent of them are democracies. Put another way, in 1975 thirty nations of the world had popularly elected governments; by 2005 that number had rocketed to 119.[7] There is a correlation between popularly elected governments and economic growth.

In the first half of the twentieth century Japan was an imperialist nation. Since its defeat at the end of World War II, in the second half of the twentieth century it became one of the world's largest economies, behind only the United States and China. It is also now a democracy, although until the 1990s it retained vestiges of over-hierarchical institutions reminiscent of its feudal and imperialist past.

The universe is an ever-changing, ever-expanding entity. Everything is always in motion. Attempts to define cultural values that are immobile, fixed, lacking in flexibility, and constraining of individual freedom of expression ultimately lead to failure. To go against the forces of the universe, to go against the inexorable trends of nature, to stubbornly and arbitrarily force a society into fixed ways of being by either fiat or physical means may work in the short term, but it is doomed to failure in the long run. Closed systems do not grow; they ultimately implode or wither. Open, diverse systems thrive. Adjustment and improvisation with support for individual freedom of expression against the backdrop of an extant culture are the hallmarks of a society that will evolve and thrive. The Constitution of the United States is both a fixed and flexible document that for over two centuries has served the United States well by allowing changes that reflect the times.

JAZZ AND DEMOCRACY

There is a strong and meaningful relationship between jazz and democracy. In *Jazzocracy: Jazz, Democracy, and the Creation of a New American Mythology*, author Kabir Sehgal writes: "It is illuminating that those who were the most oppressed in America [blacks] have created the most democratic of arts." This simple statement is fraught with layers of meaning in a book that delves comprehensively into the metaphor of jazz-as-democracy. He says: "When jazz was the music of popular entertainment [in the first half of the twentieth century], it reflected the jam session character of America, as millions immigrated to America in search of opportunity."[8]

Another perspective on jazz and democracy comes from David Moser writing in the mid-1990s. He compares the relationship of jazz—as an expression of individual freedom of expression—between intellectuals of the Soviet Union and East Bloc countries and the Chinese intelligentsia:

> for intellectuals of the Soviet Union and East Bloc countries in decades past, jazz tended to be a kind of spiritual background music for their underground movements. Jazz was associated with a certain freedom of spirit that was powerful enough to have a liberating effect, but subtle enough to escape any kind of official censure. The Chinese intelligentsia, by contrast, are not as organized as that of formerly communist states of Eastern Europe, and the Chinese government has much more control over the media and lives of the people, so that artistic forms of protest tend to be less visible. In addition, the standard of living is low enough that there is relatively little access to Western art forms like jazz. Yet a few Chinese intellectuals are beginning to perceive it as an artistic tool worth exploring, and they, like the authorities, see rock and jazz as tapping into a similar force of creative revolt.[9]

A third perspective on the relationship between jazz and democracy comes from Dr. Martin Luther King Jr., at the opening address to the 1964 Berlin Jazz Festival. His remarks speak directly to the issue of "individual freedom of expression":

> And now, jazz is exported to the world. For in the particular struggle of the Negro in America there is something akin to the universal struggle of modern man. Everybody has the Blues. Everybody longs for meaning. Everybody needs to love and be loved. Everybody needs to clap hands and be happy. Everybody longs for faith. . . . In music, especially this broad category called Jazz, there is a stepping stone towards all of these.[10]

JAZZ AND CHINA'S FUTURE

Virtually all the indigenous jazz musicians in Beijing and Shanghai interviewed specifically for this book said or implied that for them jazz meant "individual freedom of expression"—very much an echo Dr. King's perspective. Does the current Chinese government have it right then? If Sehgal is correct that popular music, in particular rap and hip-hop, is a highly non-individualistic, repetitive, and predictable music, that by allowing China pop/rock concerts they are actually purveying a form of population control?

This seems counterintuitive. Every older generation looks at the younger generation and says, to quote a song from the Broadway show *Bye Bye Birdie*, "What's the matter with kids today?" Every older generation looks at the younger generation and bemoans the music created. Every new generation creates its own "revolution." In its early days, jazz was a revolution, as were all the art forms of the early twentieth century. Today, however, jazz functions as music for those who can tolerate improvisation, conversation, negotiation, exchange. It takes a certain level of emotional and intellectual sophistication to appreciate jazz. Rap and hip-hop do not engender these characteristics of human interaction. Jazz explores individuality against the backdrop of certain constants. Rap and hip-hop songs and performers are interchangeable, much like the interchangeable part that characterized the formative underbelly of the Industrial Age.

While it is a matter of conjecture if the Chinese will evolve their political system as its economic system grows and matures, there is little doubt that within a generation or two China, economically speaking, will surpass the United States as the world's largest. China has apparently learned to balance its deep cultural and social heritage with an openness to the world, at least with respect to economic and capitalist methodologies. It has learned to improvise economically against the backdrop of the larger world institutions with great skill. It has learned to "jazz it up" economically speaking, on the world stage.

There is a striking link between jazz as a "concept," never mind a musical style, and China. And that link is mostly economic. According to a June 2005 conference on "Global Transmission: Demystifying China's New Path," sponsored by the Wharton School China Business Forum of the University of Pennsylvania's Wharton School, there is jazz all over China. Professor Marshall Meyer pointed out "China eliminated firms in 1950 [shortly after the Communist takeover] and didn't reconstitute them until 1988 . . . Therefore, it only has 17 years of experience with Western-style businesses." Professor Meyer then states "The U.S. economy operates like a big city symphony, with companies playing their parts with well-schooled precision. China, in contrast, is like a jazz combo, improvising furiously. Just as jazz's swirl of sound and rhythm can be disorienting, so can the business environment in

China's fast-growing, quasi-capitalist economy."[11] Professor Meyer's defini-
tion of jazz notwithstanding—there are, of course, many other definitions,
and his seems a tad obtuse—it is interesting to hear this kind of metaphor
to describe China of recent times. Of course, this is an American description of the Chinese economy, not a Chinese description.

Another example: the Honda Corporation, a Japanese automaker, began
exporting its newest compact to Europe. The name of the car? Jazz. And
where is it being manufactured? In China, of course. The first 150 cars left
the southern port of Guangzhou toward the end of June 2005 as part of
Honda's joint venture with China's Guangzhou Auto and Dongfeng Motor.
About 10,000 cars will be exported to Germany and other European mar-
kets, but not the United States.[12]

In 2003 Jazz Semiconductor of Austin, Texas, took another step toward
ensuring its customers of second-source capabilities, signing up Shanghai-
based Hua Hong NEC in a process technology licensing agreement for .25-
and .18-micron processes. Hua Hong NEC is one of China's largest semiconductor manufacturers formed as part of China's so-called 909 Project
several years ago.[13]

Further, the Global Education Corporation offered hip-hop/rap and
jazz internships in, where else, Shanghai, China. The description reads "The
Music Internship Project recognizes the growth of American music genres
across the globe. This internship exposes participants to music trends and
acceptance in Shanghai. Participants will work at a local radio station, coor-
dinate functions at a local nightclub, and advise university professors on the
most current music trends in the United States."[14]

Is there jazz in China? Yes, but according to Bruce Iglauer, president of
Chicago-based Alligator Records, testifying before the Committee on Small
Business in Washington, DC, to a group of representatives, "When it comes
to ripping off American sound recordings, China is one of the worst. The
magnitude of record piracy there eclipses any other country. China is potentially the biggest market in the world for American music . . . maybe
even bigger than the USA. With the growth of the Chinese economy and
the huge population, the potential for massive sales of American music in
China in the next few years is great. . . . [However], it is not a matter of 'if'
our music will be pirated in China, but rather 'when.'"[15]

MORE JAZZ WILL COME TO CHINA

It is telling to look back to 2005 (one year before this author's second visit to China) for a perspective on the state of jazz in that country. What follows is commentary from entrepreneur Peter Zanello, my initial and prime contact in China in anticipation of my 2006 monthlong research trip. This is how he described the state of jazz at the time:

> As far as the jazz scene is for today, since there is very little jazz education in China, the number of good jazz musicians is not large. The gigs that I go to often have a difficult time finding a bass player who can truly perform jazz. There are two well respected bass players in Beijing. (This is the capital and home to the National Conservatory of Music and the Central Conservatory of Music, China's finest music institutions.) Certainly, the numbers of jazz musicians are gradually growing. Relatively speaking, to see ten to twenty jazz musicians in a city like Shanghai or Beijing, in a country as large as China, this is not a cultural breakthrough. It would be very interesting to find out more about jazz in the smaller cities, which have less exposure to the international community.

Further,

> The entire entertainment industry is still government controlled. Although changes in the laws have opened up the industry, what can and cannot be performed is the result of political as much as economic considerations. All public performances within a theater, arena, stadium or similar gathering places must obtain a performance license from the Cultural Ministry. The economic side of the performance industry is also quite interesting. Most of the foreign performances in China over the last fifty years have been either government exchanges or sponsored by commercial interests. Without getting into a great amount of detail, the performances have depended upon the generosity of the foreign governments and sponsors. There have been very few foreign "commercial performances." For instance, the Beijing International Jazz Festival was the result of many foreign embassies providing a jazz musician for the festival, foreign artists agreeing to be paid very little and commercial sponsorship.
>
> It is still a growing market. In the early days, most jazz in China has come from foreign students and teachers, embassy personnel, and business folks. It is my estimate that most of the jazz musicians of the late

1980's & 1990's had to have been first exposed to jazz by expats or friends of expats. There was no jazz available elsewhere. Today, if you were to ask the average Chinese about jazz, most will define jazz as "gao ya" which translates as "high (upper class) and refined." Jazz is now a symbol of worldliness and refined tastes. People who can afford it and who want to demonstrate their fine tastes go to the jazz clubs. Of course there are also diehard fans who understand improvisation and the artistry of jazz, but they are the minority.[16]

Several of the non-Chinese jazz musicians interviewed for this volume also reflected on the future of jazz in China:

Jazz Singer/Arranger Mary Ann Hurst:

I think they're going to take it a next step. And it's going to happen with the indigenous pentatonic scale. Somebody once said that Oscar Peterson only played pentatonic scales. I don't know who said that, but he played pentatonic scales all the time. I just think that between their instruments, what they'll do with their instruments, they'll learn it so well. They'll learn it like the Japanese learned it, but they'll take it farther. I think they have a little more creative spirit in the culture.

Rock/Jazz Guitarist Dennis Rea:

Jazz gained a small but enthusiastic following in the 1980s fueled by the increasing availability of jazz recordings from abroad and renewed public exposure to expatriate jazz musicians. The first noteworthy statement from China's new jazz generation was the 1988 China Record Company CD release *Jazz in China* by pianist and composer Gao Ping, who passed through Anne's [Rea's fiancée] intensive English program the same year. Although only marginally jazz by most standards, this early effort was nevertheless significant for its spirit of openness and emphasis on improvisation. Remarkably, within just ten years, China would produce a number of truly impressive jazz soloists [such as Liu Yuan] and boast an acclaimed international jazz festival [the Beijing International Jazz Festival], raising the possibility that jazz, with its accommodating open structures, might hold the key to a truly democratic union of Chinese and other world musical traditions.

Former German Diplomat (and Bass Player) Martin Fleischer:

I foresee that a similar process that has taken place in Beijing is taking place or is going to take place in more and more big . . . cities all over China. As for the future of jazz, or more specifically, a jazz that has a very specific Chinese flavor? It's definitely possible; I'm not aware of any such developments. In the cultural and social sense, China is currently undergoing development that other countries have done over centuries—they're doing it in a few decades.

As previous chapters have mentioned, the Chinese government's attitude toward Western music—such as rock and jazz—has moved from lumping rock and jazz together to perceiving the two genres separately. Chinese rock-god Cui Jian's activities notwithstanding, rock—because it tends to draw large crowds and has the patina of a music that is anti-authoritarian—is viewed more suspiciously by government officials than jazz. Perhaps because jazz held such cultural sway in Shanghai, in particular, in the first half of the twentieth century, and as a musical genre appeals more to a cultural and educated class, jazz appears to be untouched by Chinese authorities. In fact, several events seem to underscore the Chinese government's tacit endorsement of jazz.

JAZZ AT LINCOLN CENTER/BLUE NOTE

On April 12, 2013, Jazz at Lincoln Center announced a joint venture with several Chinese-based firms to establish a jazz presence in Shanghai. The news release headline reads as follows:

BIG and Global Institutions, Shanghai Bund Investment Group & Jazz at Lincoln Center Announce Joint Expansion in China

Jazz at Lincoln Center Shanghai at the Central in the Bund To Revitalize the Jazz Capital of the Far East

The release continued:

Shanghai Bund Investment (Group) Co., Ltd. (BIG) and Jazz at Lincoln Center announce today their joint development of Jazz at Lincoln Center Shanghai in the historic Bund district. The announcement was made at the groundbreaking ceremony of The Central, a high-end, mixed-use development by BIG, scheduled for completion and operation in 2016. Jazz at Lincoln Center (JALC), led by Managing and Artistic Director Wynton Marsalis, will program jazz concerts at The Central, and through this development, residents and visitors of Shanghai alike will enjoy a night of great Jazz music in one of Shanghai's premier retail properties against the backdrop of a revitalized Bund. Also, people of all ages will learn about Jazz—the music, and its contemporary relevance—through JALC's many Jazz education programs.

Further, "the Jazz club will be similar in character to JALC's Dizzy's Club Co-ca-Cola at its home in New York City, where excellent acoustics and an intimate club setting, with great food and drink, are framed visually by a classic backdrop of a great world city—for Dizzy's, it's Central Park and for Jazz at Lincoln Center Shanghai, it will be the Bund waterfront. The development of The Central and the opening of Jazz at Lincoln Center Shanghai add to the Bund and Nanjing Road as the epicenter of commerce, leisure, and culture in Shanghai." The club opened in 2017, not 2016 as originally announced.[17]

Jazz at Lincoln Center will have some competition. In mid-2015 Blue Note International, whose renowned flagship jazz club is located in Greenwich Village, New York City, announced plans to open several jazz clubs in China: a Blue Note Beijing in the Chinese capital and within three years spread to Shanghai. "I believe we can help develop the music and the market," said Steven Bensusan, president of the Blue Note Entertainment Group. Bensusan said the 250-patron club could distinguish itself in China by offering an intimate concert accompanied by food, which will be adapted to local tastes.

The clubs, like JZ Club in Shanghai, will also feature local jazz bands as well as international performers. "In some senses, it's not like buying a concert ticket and just relying on the artist to draw people. . . . It's more about a venue. It's a lifestyle place, it's a place for people to experience the music, even not knowing who the musicians are," Bensusan said. Blue Note Beijing will set up in the renovated site of the former US embassy near Tiananmen Square. The complex—a group of elegant stone buildings around a grassy courtyard—dates from 1903 and briefly served as the Beijing base of the Dalai Lama before the Tibetan leader's flight into exile. Blue Note has opened clubs in Tokyo and Nagoya and succeeded in building Blue Note's brand, with Japanese visitors now making up a significant portion of the clientele at the original New York venue.[18]

Stephen Li—whose company Winbright is the exclusive licensee and developer of the Blue Note Jazz Club in the Greater China Area—confirmed

Blue Note's Beijing club is located next to Tiananmen Square in the former Legions Quarters of Beijing. He said: "Our current plan is focused on developing the club here in Beijing, and a club in Taipei [Taiwan] (still in the development phrase). A Shanghai club is also in the plans, but it will probably open after Taipei."[19] The Beijing club opened in spring 2016.

JAZZ RADIO IN CHINA

While Voice of America's jazz programming to China has waned, jazz radio programming in China has emerged. Evidence of this is the emergence of Beijing jazz radio host Youdai. According to his online bio:

> Zhang Youdai studied Dramaturgy at the Central Academy of Drama in Beijing and graduated in 1991. Since 1993 he became a radio host and DJ on "Beijing Music Radio" until today. There he introduced all the facets about western music that had been almost unknown to Chinese music fans. He had a huge influence and impact on a whole generation of music listeners and musicians. He was the first DJ who played rock, jazz and electronica on the radio in China since 1989, introducing new music and a new lifestyle to hundreds of millions young people in China. Now he also hosts shows on other radio stations such as China Radio International (CRI.cn) and does DJ performances in local dance clubs such as Suzie Wong. In 2006 and 2007 he went to Germany to participate on Loveparade and the music festival of Popkomm. Since 2008 he also works in collaboration with Goethe Institut Peking.[20]

He worked with Blue Note International on the jazz club it opened in Beijing.

There are two other Chinese jazz radio DJs of note: Chao Gu, of FM94.7 from Shanghai; and Fangzhou Mu, of EZFM China Radio International (CRI) from Beijing. Both Gu and Mu were invited by WFMT Radio (Chicago) to attend the September 2017 Chicago Jazz Festival.

WFMT RADIO (CHICAGO)

According to Tony Macaluso, WFMT Radio Network Director of Network Syndication, starting in 2016 the international arts radio network based in

Chicago, the WFMT Radio Network (known for classical music, jazz, folk, and literature radio programs and as the longtime home of legendary oral historian Studs Terkel), formed partnerships with several Chinese radio stations that opened the door to jazz radio program syndication from the United States on a regular basis.

The WFMT Network, under the leadership of General Manager Steve Robinson, began to offer twice-weekly jazz broadcasts to China Radio International (CRI) in Beijing featuring hosts Dee Alexander (a celebrated jazz vocalist) and Neil Tesser (jazz writer and veteran radio host). This partnership paved the way for the WFMT Radio Network to offer broadcasts from the Chicago Jazz Festival (produced by the City of Chicago Department of Cultural Affairs in Millennium Park) to CRI and Shanghai 94.7FM in 2017 and to bring jazz radio critics from both stations to Chicago to attend the festival and learn more about the history of jazz in Chicago, meet and interview jazz artists, and visit various historic jazz venues in order to produce original programs for radio audiences in China.[21]

THE CHINESE JAZZ ASSOCIATION

When an activity gains enough critical mass, an "association" usually emerges. And that is exactly what has happened in China. Below is the official "mission statement" of the Chinese Jazz Association:

> Founded in 2013, the Chinese Musicians' Association (CJA) is a nonprofit organization that connects jazz musicians, composers, sound technicians, music educators, producers, critics, and millions of jazz music audiences all over China. CJA's members come from all over China in various fields, sharing the same passion in jazz performance and music education. CJA's mission is to promote the art of jazz music to the general public and support young Chinese jazz artists in exploring and experimenting with new works. CJA also plays a critical role in connecting local audience with artists around the world, opening up new dialogues between the Chinese and foreign musicians and artists, and providing a platform for musicians, music technicians, students, and educators to share and spread the knowledge of the art of jazz.[22]

THE NEXT GENERATION OF CHINESE JAZZERS

And there's more jazz news from China. With the Chinese government's apparent blessing, twenty-year-old saxophonist virtuoso Li Gao Yang attended International Jazz Day, April 30, 2013, in Istanbul, Turkey. Heading up the delegation was saxophonist Liu Yuan, the so-called "father of jazz" profiled in an earlier chapter. Ian Patterson, writing in allaboutjazz, describes Yang as follows:

> With dreadlocks tumbling over his shoulders, Li Gao Yang already cuts a striking figure. When he's on stage blowing his tenor saxophone and leading his quartet with quiet assurance, the impact is all the greater. Chinese jazz stars are few and far between, at home or abroad, but already this unassuming musician from Beijing has appeared on television and made the Chinese press on numerous occasions. He's also had the honor of opening both the Hong Kong International Jazz Festival 2011 and the Nine Gates Jazz Festival in Beijing in September, 2012.[23]

Another example of the next generation of Chinese jazzers: Beijing-born pianist A Bu was a featured player at the April 2015 International Jazz Day in Paris. A Bu is not only young, he is very young. He was fifteen when he performed.

I had the good fortune to interview A Bu in New York City in the summer of 2016 on the stage of Engelman Recital Hall (Baruch Performing Arts Center). At the time he was studying at the Juilliard High School. Aware that he was going to be interviewed on camera, he was professionally prepared with a fresh shirt.

I asked him to play something on the piano, which he did readily. His playing was smooth, intricate, and harmonically rich. I asked him what he was studying musically. He replied that his teachers were encouraging him to study and play early jazz and the blues because "that's where it all comes from." I have also seen video recordings of other "standards" in his repertoire. One of these is his own arrangement and improvisation on Coltrane's "Giant Steps," one of the more complex and challenging jazz pieces ever written. You can find it on YouTube. Mid-point in the video a title indicated that A Bu is playing the piece in real time. In other words, the video is not being sped up.

His eleven-track 2015 album *Butterflies Fly in Pairs* was released by Sennheiser Media. It features American saxophonist Antonio Hart on two tracks.

THE JAZZ FESTIVALS

A further indication of the growth of jazz in China is the number of jazz festivals in several Chinese cities. The first post-Mao Chinese jazz festival—the Beijing International Jazz Festival, which ran from 1993 to 2000—notwithstanding, other Chinese jazz festivals include:

    Guangzhou Jazz Festival (Guangzhou)

    JZ Music Festival (Shanghai)

    Midi Music Festival (Beijing)

    OCT-LOFT Jazz Festival (Shenzhen)

    The Beishan International Jazz Festival (Zhuhai, Southern China)

    The Changsha Jazz Festival (Shenzhen)

    The Ditan Park Music Festival (Beijing)

    The Nine Gates Jazz Festival (Beijing)

As the prior chapter mentioned, the oldest jazz festival is the Midi Music Festival started by the Midi School. Clearly, though, other Chinese cities are picking up the jazz festival baton.

Is there jazz in China? There most certainly is, quite literally. And it seems reasonable to assert that once you open a society to the world at large, even though the motivation to do so is primarily economic, it may be difficult if not impossible to reverse course. In all likelihood, China will continue to emerge as a major economic player on the world stage, and, to re-reference Kabir Sehgal's *Jazzocracy*, perhaps, if we're lucky, what will evolve is more equity, more conversation, more negotiation, and more reconciliation within China itself, and between China and the world community. A jazz metaphor indeed!

Reported American Jazz Musicians Who Performed in China 1981–2016

Date	Musician/Group	Style	Instrumentation	Cities Visited	Reaction to China
1981	Mitchell-Ruff Duo		Piano/Bass/ French Horn	Shanghai/ Beijing	Ruff felt the Chinese knew nothing about jazz.
1986	Howard University Jazz Ensemble			Beijing	
October 1986	Bob Hallahan		Piano (working with singer Lisa Rich)	Beijing	Trip was sponsored by United Airlines; the program also featured the Howard University Jazz Ensemble.
1991	Eau Claire Jazz I Ensemble			Beijing/Tianjin	
1991	The Vagaries	Rock	Keyboards/Bass/ Guitar/Drums	Chengdu	
1992	Judy Carmichael	Swing	Piano		First jazz musician sponsored by U.S. to tour China.
1992	The Black Dogs	New Orleans Traditional	Brass/Piano	Beijing/Hong Kong	Toured China for the U.S. State Department.
1992–95	Carol Stein		Piano	Hong Kong	Said that it was an amazing time to be in Hong Kong.
1993	The Shenandoah Conservatory Jazz Ensemble		Brass/Piano/ Guitar/Bass		

Date	Musician/Group	Style	Instrumentation	Cities Visited	Reaction to China
1993	Charlie Bertini		Trumpet	Hong Kong	Was funded to go by Hong Kong Hilton and British Airways.
1994	Luca Bonvini	Contempo-rary	Slide Trumpet/Trombone	Beijing/Hong Kong	Formed first Chinese orchestra of contemporary jazz, the Beijing Jazz Unit.
1994	Keiko McNamara		Piano/Vocal	Xiamen	Professor of Jazz at Shin-Yu University.
1994	Carol Kidd		Vocal	Beijing	Says her love affair with Asia began in China.
1995	Maria Schneider Jazz Orchestra	Big Band		Macau	Invited to perform in the opening concert of the International Music Festival.
May 1995	Purdue University Jazz Band			Beijing/Shang-hai	
1996	Steve Blailock/Swing Thing	Swing/Zydeco	Guitar/Banjo	Beijing	
1996	LAND	Electronic	Keyboards/Bass/Guitar/Drums	Hong Kong	Said audiences reacted favorably everywhere they played.
1997	Bill Ware	Latin-influenced	Vibraphone		Toured China with the group Jazz Passengers.
1997	Victor Noriega		Piano	Shanghai	Said jazz was new to the Chinese.
1998	Charito	Brazilian/Swing	Vocal	Beijing/Shang-hai/Chengdu	
1998/2002	Scotty Wright	Soul	Vocal/Piano/Drums	Hong Kong/Shanghai	
1999	California State University Northridge Jazz Band			Shanghai	Participated in International Jazz Festival.

Date	Musician/Group	Style	Instrumentation	Cities Visited	Reaction to China
October 1999	Natural Gas Jazz Band	Traditional	Drums/Piano/Brass/Banjo	Beijing/Shanghai/Suzhou/Hangzhou	Said government once saw jazz as a "decadent music" but was now exposing it to the Chinese.
1999–2002	String of Pearls	Swing/Dance/Octet	Brass/Vocal/Piano/Guitar/Drums	Beijing/Toured	Fused jazz with Chinese Opera.
1999–2003	Phil Morrison and Keith Williams		Bass/Piano/Vocal	Shanghai	Performed in Shanghai four times in four years. In 2003 Williams said there was a jazz culture emerging in China.
February 2000	Wynton Marsalis with Lincoln Center Jazz Orchestra			Beijing/Shanghai/Guangzhou	His goal was to share American music with the people of China and learn about their music as well.
June 2000	New Trier High School Jazz Ensemble			Beijing/Henan Province	Said the Chinese had a huge amount of enthusiasm at the concerts.
December 2000	Chris Erway		Trombone	Beijing/Shanghai	
2000	John Eaton		Piano		
2000	Johnnie Eason		Vocal	Shanghai	
January 2001	Dianne Reeves	Pop Jazz	Vocal	Beijing	
March 2002	Bellevue Community College Jazz Band		20-member band	Beijing	Director of the band taught Chinese music teachers how to teach jazz.
2002	Steve Lucas	Modern	Bass		Toured with Canadian Chinese Ensemble.

Date	Musician/Group	Style	Instrumentation	Cities Visited	Reaction to China
2002	Nicholas McBride		Drums	Shanghai	Said the people were open to jazz but the places where he played insisted that he have a vocalist.
2002	Bob Mocarsky		Piano	Shanghai	
2002	Charles Bou-loukos		Piano	Shanghai	Said House of Blues in Shang-hai was one of the best jazz clubs anywhere in the world.
2002	Mariah Ralston		Trombone	Beijing/Shang-hai	Most shows were cancelled due to protests against U.S.
September 2003	Greg Henry Waters	Latin-themed	Clarinet/Flute	Shenzhen/Hong Kong	Said Hong Kong was very conservative and Shenzhen was a place without culture.
2003	Gwen Hughes	Swing	Vocal	Dongguan	
May 2004	Fred Randolph/ Anton Schwartz/ Adam Shulman		Bass/Saxophone/ Piano	Shanghai	
June 2004	David Amram	Blues & Jazz	French Horn	Chengdu	Performed and taught there.
October 2004	Afro-Latin Jazz Orchestra	Afro-Latin	Brass/Bass/ Drums	Shanghai	China was the only out-of-U.S. part of their "Mambo Mad-ness" tour.
October 2004	U.S. Military Academy Band		Three Wind Ensembles	Beijing	Chinese and American musi-cians performed together.
2004	Cal Poly Jazz Band			Beijing/Shang-hai/Hangzhou	The director felt that the Chinese were curious about jazz. They took their first international tour to China.

Date	Musician/Group	Style	Instrumentation	Cities Visited	Reaction to China
March 2005	Southeastern Oklahoma State University Jazz Combo		Brass/Piano/Drums/Vocal	Guangzhou/Hong Kong/Beijing	The director said that the Chinese students were very interested in American jazz.
March 2005	Norah Jones		Vocal/Piano	Shanghai	It was Jones's decision to go to China.
May 2005	Kansas University Wind Ensemble		Winds	Beijing/Chengdu	
June 2005	The West Valley College Jazz Ensemble	Vocal	Vocal	Shanghai/Beijing	Went as part of a cultural exchange.
June 2005	Rex Richardson		Trumpet	Guangzhou	
July 2005	Gregory Smith/Cotton Club House Band	Blues	Guitar	Shanghai	Played in a venue called the Cotton Club in Shanghai.
2005	Calabasas All Star Jazz Band	High School Band		Guangzhou/Shenzhen/Zhuhai/Hong Kong	
May 2006/2007	Jess Meider		Vocal	Beijing	
2006–2008	Vastine Pettis		Saxophone/Vocal	Shanghai/Hong Kong	Frequent performer at Park 97 and Muse 1 & 2 and RedBeat.
2006	Wallace Roney		Trumpet	Shanghai	
2000–2007	Andy Hunter		Trombone	Shanghai	Performed and lived in Shanghai.
2007	Black Cat Bone		Drums/Guitar	Beijing	A band consisting of Americans and Canadians.*
2007	Abigail Washburn		Banjo/Vocal	Beijing	
2007	Donny McCaslin Jazz Quartet		Saxophone	Beijing	
2009/2015	Dee Dee Bridgewater		Vocal	Shanghai	
May 2009/October 2015	Shunza		Vocal	Beijing/Shanghai	

Date	Musician/Group	Style	Instrumentation	Cities Visited	Reaction to China
2010–16	Murray James Morrison		Saxophone	Chengdu	
October 2010/2011	Kenny Garrett		Saxophone	Shanghai/ Beijing	
2010	Bob James		Keyboard	Shanghai	
2010	Roy Hargrove		Trumpet	Shanghai	
2010	Nathan East		Bass/Vocal	Shanghai	
2010	Dianne Reeves		Vocals	Shanghai	
2010	Jeff "Tain" Watts		Drums	Shanghai	
2010	Branford Marsalis		Saxophone	Shanghai	
October 2011	McCoy Tyner		Pianist	Shanghai	Performed at the Shanghai Center Theatre.
August 2011	Peter Buffett		Piano	Beijing	
July 2011/ March 2016	Antonio Hart		Saxophone	Shanghai/ Beijing/Guang- zhou	Found the Chinese to be very interested in jazz.
October 2011	Judy Niemack	Modern	Vocal		Performed at the Hotel Kempinski in Beijing.
September 2012	Moreno Jazz Group + Laurant		Guitarist	Beijing	
December 2012	Jaleel Shaw Quartet		Saxophone	Beijing	
October 2013	Tim Ries		Saxophone	Shanghai	
December 2013	Lawrence Ku Trio		Guitarist/com- poser	Beijing	
October 2014/2015	David Binney with Joshua White, Elvind Opsvik, Dan Weiss		Saxophone	Beijing	
September 2015	Hristo Vitchev Quartet		Guitarist	Beishan	
October 2015	Steve Weingart		Keyboard	Shanghai/Hong Kong	
October 2015	Victor Wooten		Bass	Shanghai	

Date	Musician/Group	Style	Instrumentation	Cities Visited	Reaction to China
October 2015	Al McKay All Stars		Guitar	Shanghai	
December 2015	Nathaniel Gao		Saxophone	Beijing	
December 2015/June 2016	Adam Nussbaum		Drummer	Kunming/ Shenzhen	
May 2016	Eddie Daniels Quartet		Clarinet/Saxo-phone	Shanghai	
May 2016	Petra Haden & Jesse Harris		Vocal/Violin	Shanghai	
May 2016	Mixx Company		10+ member band	Shanghai	
May 2016	Redic & the Storm Riders			Shanghai/	
June 2016	Kurt Rosenwinkel Trio		Guitarist	Shanghai/ Guangzhou	
June 2016	Pat Matheny Group		Guitarist	Shanghai	
July 2016	The Harvard Din & Tonics		A Cappella group	Shanghai	

Reported International Jazz Musicians Who Performed in China 1992–2016

Date	Musician/ Group	Style	Instrumentation	Country of Origin	Cities Visited	Reaction to China
1992	George Gruntz Jazz Band		Brass/Piano/ Drums/Guitar/ Harp	Switzerland	Beijing/ Guangzhou	
1992	Jeremy Monteiro	Swing	Piano	Singapore	Hong Kong	Started playing jazz when he re-alized his friends were making money in Chinese jazz clubs.
1994	Nikolai Panov		Trumpet/ Clarinet	Russia	Beijing	
1994	Vladamir Tarasov		Drums	Russia	Beijing	
1994	Heinz von Hermann		Saxophone/ Clarinet/Flute	Austria	Beijing	
1994	Heinz-Erich Gödecke		Trombone	Germany	Beijing	
1994 /1997 /2004/2005	The Willem Breuker Kollektief	Contempo-rary/ Impro-visational	Reeds/Brass/ Drums	Netherlands	Hong Kong	
1995	Trio Toykeat		Piano/Drums/ Bass	Finland	Hong Kong	
1996	Campbell Burnap		Trombone	England	Beijing	Gave a recital at Beijing University.
1998	Liels Lan Doky		Piano	Denmark	Beijing	Said Chinese had background in classical music.
1998	Myanta	Indian-influenced	Tabla	India	Beijing	
1999	The Dainius Pulauskas Sextet		Piano/Brass/ Drums/Bass	Lithuania	Beijing	Went for International Jazz Festival.

Date	Musician/ Group	Style	Instrumentation	Country of Origin	Cities Visited	Reaction to China
1999	Kazda	Soul	Brass/Guitar/ Drums/Key- board/Bass	Germany	Hong Kong	Recorded an album in China.
2000	Otomo Yoshihide's New Jazz Ensemble	Electronic/ Contempo- rary	Vibraphone/ Brass/Contra- bass/Guitar	Japan	Qingdao	
2001	Rabih Abou-Khalil	Arab- inspired	Oud	Lebanon	Beijing	
2002	Come Shine	Quartet	Drums/Bass/ Piano/Vocals	Norway		Toured China with two Chinese soloists.
2002	Klaus Kugel		Drums	Germany	Nanjing	
2002	Sina	Rock	Vocal	Switzerland	Beijing	Performed with a Chinese rock band.
2002/2007/2009	Sonic Cal- ligraphy		Vocals/Piano	Switzerland	Shanghai/ Hong Kong	
2003	Urban Con- nection		Saxophone/ Drums/Double Bass	Norway	Beijing	Very well received by Chinese audi- ences.
2003	Organism	Blues/Swing	Organ/Guitar/ Drums	Australia	Shenzhen	Performed over 300 gigs in Shenzhen.
2003	Helmut Iberer		Piano	Austria		
2004	Tolvan Big Band	Big Band		Sweden	Beijing/ Shanghai	
2004	The Sound of Vienna	Latin-style	Vibraphone/Pi- ano/Saxophone/ Bass/Drums	Austria	Shanghai	First Austrian jazz band to play in Shanghai.
2004	Jamie Oehlers		Saxophone	Australia	Hong Kong	
2004	African Footprint	Extrava- ganza by Richard Loring		Africa	Chuxiong Beijing	
2005	E.S.T.		Piano/Bass/ Drums	Sweden	Shanghai	
2006/2007	Mordy Ferber		Guitar/Vocal	Israel	Hong Kong/ Beijing	
2008	Björk	Rock/Pop	Vocals	Iceland	Shanghai	

Date	Musician/ Group	Style	Instrumentation	Country of Origin	Cities Visited	Reaction to China
2010/2011	Rusconi Trio	Free Rock/ Groove/Elec-tronica	Piano/Vocal/ Synth	Switzerland	Beishan	
2010	The Swingin' Fireballs	Swing	Piano/Saxo-phone/Bass	Germany	Beijing	
2011	Anthony Miller	Funk jazz/ Rock	Saxophone	Toronto	Hong Kong/ Beijing	
2011/ April 2016	Danilo Rea		Piano	Italy	Hong Kong/ Shanghai	
2008– 11/2015/2016	Mademoi-selle et son Orchestra	Gypsy Jazz		Quebec	Beijing	
September 2012	McGrady Gewei La Jazz			France	Beijing	
September 2012	Yannick Rieu Swiss Trio		Piano/Guitar/ Double Bass	Switzerland	Beijing	
September 2012 (China tour in October 2016)	Grzegorz Karnas Quartet	Polish jazz/ Modern jazz		Poland	Shanghai/ Guangzhou	
September 2012	Artur Dutkiewicz Trio		Piano	Poland	Beijing	
September 2012	Flow Jazz Group		Piano/Drums/ Guitar	Austria	Beijing	
September 2012	Viklicky Trio		Piano/ Contra-bass/Drums	Czech Republic	Beijing	
September 2012	Meddy Gerville Band		Piano/Vocal	France	Beijing	
December 2012/2013/June 2016	Carl Winther		Piano	Denmark	Shenzhen/ Kunming/ Beijing	
February 2013/ May 2015	Stefan Karlsson	Quartet	Piano	Sweden	Beijing/ Shanghai	
2000– 2004/2013–2014	Jean Sebastien Hery a.k.a. Zhang Si'an	Folk/Rock		France	Beijing/ Shanghai	

Date	Musician/ Group	Style	Instrumentation	Country of Origin	Cities Visited	Reaction to China
October 2014	Janne Schra		Vocal	Netherlands	Shanghai/ Shenzhen	
May–July 2015	Rafal Sarnecki	Quartet	Guitar	Poland	Beijing/ Changzhou/ Hangzhou	
September 2015	CMI Quartet	Quartet		Italy/Korea/ China	Beishan	
October 2015	Dock in Absolute		Drums/Double Bass/Piano	Luxembourg	Zhuhai	
October 2015	Ernesto Jodos Trio		Piano	Austria/ Argentina	Hong/Beis-han	
October 2015	Charles Pasi		Harmonica	Paris	Shanghai	
October 2015/ June 2016	Red Groove Project	Jazz funk/ groove band	Saxophone/Key-board/Drums/ Bass	Australia/ Brazil/USA/ China	Shanghai	
April 2016	Kalaha			Denmark/ Sweden	Beishan	
April/May 2016	Fabrizio Bosso Quintet	Quintet	Trumpet/Piano	Italy	Shanghai	
April/May 2016	Funk Off Band	Funk jazz	15-member band	Italy	Shanghai	
April 2016	Gast Waltz-ing		Conductor/ Trumpet	Luxembourg	Shanghai	
April 2016	David Laborier		Guitarist	Luxembourg	Shanghai	
June 2016	Ignore Butman Quartet	Quartet	Saxophone/ Clarinet	Russia	Shanghai	
June 2016	Tina May Quartet	Quartet	Vocal/Accor-dion/Double Bass/Piano	UK	Shanghai	

NOTES

PREFACE

1. John King Faribank and Merle Goldman, *China: A New History* (Cambridge, MA: Belnap Press of Harvard University Press, 2006), 18.

2. Stella Dong, *Shanghai 1842–1949: The Rise and Fall of a Decadent City* (New York: William Morrow, 2000), 152.

3. Ibid., 153.

4. Ibid., 157.

CHAPTER 1: CHINA: EAST IS EAST . . .

1. John King Fairbank and Merle Goldman, "Origins: The Discoveries of Archeology," in *China: A New History*, 2nd ed. (Cambridge, MA: Belknap Press of Harvard University Press, 2006), 31.

2. Rudyard Kipling, "The Ballad of East and West," in *A Victorian Anthology, 1837–1895,* ed. Edmund Clarence Stedman (Boston: Houghton Mifflin, 1895). This is the opening line of Kipling's poem, and it is often interpreted as Kipling's views of race and empire, but the third and fourth lines present a different view: "But there is neither East nor West, Border, nor Breed, nor Birth / When two strong men stand face to face, though they come from the ends of the earth!" This can be interpreted as: geographic location has meaning, but when two equals face each other, the playing field is level. In the early part of the twenty-first century, clearly China (and the rest of Asia, including India) is coming up in the world, at least economically, to eventually equal the economic stature of the west.

3. C. A. S. Williams, *Chinese Symbolism and Art Motifs: A Comprehensive Handbook on Symbolism in Chinese Art Through the Ages*, revised ed. (Tokyo: Tuttle, 2006), 146.

4. "Asian, Oriental Dragons," *Dragons Inn*, accessed May 1, 2017, http://dragonsinn.net/east-2.htm.

5. Williams, *Chinese Symbolism and Art Motifs*, 147.

6. David Bayles and Ted Orland, *Art and Fear* (Santa Cruz, CA: Image Continuum, 1993), 96.

7. Sin-Yan Shen, *Chinese Music and Orchestration: A Primer on Principles and Practice* (Chicago: Chinese Music Society of North America, 2005). This same organization has published other titles dealing with Chinese music, such as *China: A Journey into Its Musical Art*; *What Makes Chinese Music Chinese?*; *Musicians of Chinese Music*; and *Chinese Music of the 20th*

Century, among others. This series of titles is clearly meant to foster appreciation for Chinese classical music, and it is no accident the publisher is supported by an organization located in the United States. You can even join the Chinese Music Society of North America (in 2017 it celebrated its forty-first year) for which you receive the *Chinese Music Quarterly.*

8. Ibid., v.

9. Ibid., 47.

10. Hongwan Liu, "Chinese Orchestra," *Quora,* last modified July 11, 2011, http://www.quora.com/Chinese-Orchestra/best_questions.

11. Ibid.

12. Shen, *Chinese Music and Orchestration,* 10.

13. Ibid., 15.

14. Ibid.

15. Ibid.

16. Ibid., 2.

17. Joseph Kahn and Daniel J. Wakin, "Classical Music Looks Toward China with Hope," *New York Times,* April 3, 2007.

18. Shen, *Chinese Music and Orchestration,* 140–43.

19. Ibid., 16.

20. Ibid., 18.

21. Ibid., 36.

22. Various, *Phases of the Moon: Traditional Chinese Music,* China Record Company, CBS Records, 1981, CD.

23. Xiao Baiyong, *Selected Masterpieces from Chinese Traditional Music,* Shanghai National Music Orchestra, 1998, CD.

24. Gu Guanren and Qu Chunquan, *Selected Masterpieces from Chinese Traditional Music—Pipa solo album,* Shanghai National Music Orchestra, 1998, CD.

25. Various, *Classical Chinese Folk Music,* Arc Music Productions, 1999.

26. Gunther Schuller, *Early Jazz: Its Roots and Musical Development* (New York: Oxford University Press, 1968), 3.

27. Ibid., 62.

28. Billy Taylor, *Jazz Piano: A Jazz History* (Dubuque, IA: Wm. C. Brown, 1982), v–vi.

CHAPTER 2: THE OPIUM WARS

1. Lynn Pan and Xue Liyong, *Shanghai: A Century of Change in Photographs, 1843–1949,* 9th ed. (Hong Kong: Peace Book, 2005), ii.

2. W. Travis Hanes III and Frank Sanello, *Opium Wars: The Addiction of One Empire and the Corruption of Another* (Naperville, IL: Sourcebooks, 2002), xii.

3. Ibid., 14.

4. Ibid., 16.

5. Ibid., 22.

6. Ibid., 24–25.

7. Ibid., 153.

8. Ibid., 154–55.

9. Ibid., 163.

10. Ibid., 296.

11. Fairbank and Goldman, *China: A New History*, 276.

CHAPTER 3: THE INFLUENCE OF EARLY TWENTIETH-CENTURY TECHNOLOGY

1. Malcolm Falkus, *The Blue Funnel Legend: A History of the Ocean Steam Ship Company, 1865–1973* (London: Macmillan Academic and Professional, 1990), 6.

2. Falkus, *The Blue Funnel Legend*, 1.

3. Fairbank and Goldman, "Origins: The Discoveries of Archeology," in *China: A New History*, 220.

4. There is much more to the history of the early recording industry—gramophones and phonographs—than is presented here. For a highly detailed and insightful recounting and analysis of the early sound recording industry, see Peter Tschmuck, *Creativity and Innovation in the Music Industry* (Dordrecht: Springer, 2006), chapters 1 and 2.

5. Ben Bergonzi, *Old Gramophones* (England: Shire, 2000), 7.

6. Frank Dikötter is a Dutch historian and author of *Mao's Great Famine*. The book won the 2011 Samuel Johnson Prize. Dikötter is Chair Professor of Humanities at the University of Hong Kong, where he teaches courses on both Mao Zedong and the Great Chinese Famine, and Professor of the Modern History of China from the School of Oriental and African Studies at the University of London. See Frank Dikötter, *Mao's Great Famine* (London: Bloomsbury Publishing, 2010).

7. Frank Dikötter, "Singing Machines: The Gramophone and the Radio," in *Exotic Commodities: Modern Objects and Everyday Life in China* (New York: Columbia University Press, 2006), 255.

8. Ibid., 256.

9. Ibid., 257.

10. Tschmuck, *Creativity and Innovation in the Music Industry*, 45.

11. www.pbs.org/wgbh/amex/pickford/peopleevents/e_silents.html.

12. Ibid.

13. Wang Chaoguang, "American Films in Chinese Reviews (1895–1949)," *American Studies in China* 2, trans Wang Huaiting (1996): 1–2. http://www.mgyj.com/american_studies/1996e/9607 .txt.

14. Ibid., 2.

15. Ibid., 3.

16. Mark Stone, "China Film Market Set To Take Over Hollywood: The film industry is thriving despite the limitations of censorship, and here are predictions it may overtake Hollywood," *Sky News*, February 16, 2013, http://news.sky.com/story/china-film-market-set -to-take-over-hollywood-10454423.

17. Andrew F. Jones, *Yellow Music: Media Culture and Colonial Modernity in the Chinese Jazz Age* (Durham and London: Duke University Press, 2001), 13.

18. Dikötter, "Singing Machines," 261.

CHAPTER 4: SHANGHAI IN THE 1920s–1930s: THE JOINT WAS JUMPIN'

1. David Moser, "The Book of Changes: Jazz in Beijing," *Jazz Now* 6, no. 1 (1996): 3.

2. Stella Dong, "The Ugly Daughter Rises," *Shanghai 1842–1949: The Rise and Fall of a Decadent City* (New York: William Morrow, 2000), 1.

3. Ibid., 4.

4. Ibid., 2.

5. Ibid., 75.

6. Aaron Copland, *Music and Imagination* (Cambridge: Harvard University Press, 1952), 30–31.

7. R. Reid Badger, *A Life in Ragtime* (New York: Oxford University Press, 1995), 163.

8. Ibid., 180.

9. Ibid., 214.

10. Burnet Hershey, "Jazz Latitude," *New York Times Book Review and Magazine*, June 25, 1922, in *Keeping Time*, Robert Walser, ed. (New York: Oxford University Press, 1999), 31.

11. Ibid., 26–27.

12. Ibid., 28.

13. Ibid.

14. Ibid., 29.

15. Dong, "The Ugly Daughter Rises," 138.

16. Da Ren Zheng's twelve-page account (in Mandarin Chinese) of the evolution of jazz in Shanghai and the formation of all Chinese jazz bands, including the Jimmy King Band, was published in an unnamed Chinese magazine. Unfortunately, when we interviewed him in Shanghai in 2006 (on video) the eighty-three-year-old Zheng could not recall the name of the magazine or when it was published, although he generously offered a copy of the article that was published in four parts and gave permission to quote from it.

17. The entire document was translated by colleague Professor Eva Chou, a professor and now chair of the Department of English, Baruch College, City University of New York. Throughout, I have taken the liberty of smoothing out the literal translation for greater readability.

CHAPTER 5: INTERNATIONAL JAZZ MUSICIANS FLOCK TO SHANGHAI: 1920s–1930s

1. This quote is drawn from Da Ren Zheng's twelve-page account (in Mandarin Chinese) of the evolution of jazz in Shanghai and the formation of all Chinese jazz bands, including the Jimmy King Band, was published in an unnamed Chinese magazine. When we interviewed him in Shanghai in 2006 (on video) the eighty-three-year-old Zheng could not recall the name of the magazine or when it was published, although he generously offered a copy of the article that was published in four parts and gave permission to quote from it.

2. "Filipino Music Trivia," *HIMIG: The Filipino Music Collection of FHL*, accessed May 1, 2017, http://www.himig.com.ph/features/20-filipino-music-trivia.

3. Richie C. Quirino, *Pinoy Jazz Traditions* (Mandaluyong City, Philippines: Anvil Publishing, 2004), 20.

4. Da Ren Zheng article.

5. John Fordham, "Obituaries: Oleg Lundstrem, Russian band leader whose passion for jazz took off in Shanghai and survived Stalin," *The Guardian*, October 28, 2005.

6. "Serge Ermoll," *Australian Jazz Real Book*, accessed May 1, 2017, Australianjazzrealbook .com/artists/serge-ermoll.

7. Shanghaijournal.squarespace.com/journal/2007/5/28/strange-cities-a-multimedia.

8. Material in this section is drawn primarily from Whitey Smith's autobiography. Whitey Smith and C. L. McDermott, *I Didn't Make a Million*, 5th printing (Manila: Philippine Education Company, 1961).

9. Ibid., 51–52.

10. Ibid., 14.

11. Ibid., 16.

12. Ibid., 4.

13. Ibid., 5.

14. Ibid., 21.

15. Ibid., 22.

16. Ibid., 25.

17. Ibid., 27.

18. Ibid., 28.

19. Ibid., 94.

20. Ibid., 97.

21. Ibid., 97–99.

22. Ibid., 129–30.

23. Ibid., 132.

24. Ibid., 132.

25. Ibid., 134–35.

26. Eric Sven and Larry Doran, *Whitey of Shanghai* (Quezon City: JMC Press, 1966).

27. "Sven Eric Schmidt," *Little Beat Records*, accessed on May 1, 2017, https://www.little beatrecords.dk/LittleBeatDK/Biografier_files/Schmidt,%20Sven%20Eric%201897–1972.pdf.

28. Larry Ross, *African American Jazz Musician in the Disapora (Studies in African Diaspora*, vol. 2), (Lewiston, NY: Edwin Mellen Press, 2003), ii–iii.

29. Ibid., 9, 17.

30. Ibid., 176.

31. Unless otherwise noted (such as the description of Weatherford by African American writer and poet Langston Hughes), Weatherford's biography is drawn directly from Howard Rye, "Teddy Weatherford," *American National Biography*, accessed May 1, 2017, http://www.anb .org/articles/18/18-03780-print.html.

32. Langston Hughes, *The Collected Works of Langston Hughes*, ed. Arnold Rampersad, Dolan Hubbard, and Leslie Catherine Sanders (Columbia: University of Missouri Press, 2001), 251–59.

33. Unless otherwise noted (such as the Rosetta Reitz and Brendan I. Koerner material), Valaida Snow's biography is drawn from "Women in History—Valaida Snow," *Women in History*, last modified February 25, 2013, http://www.lkwdpl.org/wihohio/snow-val.htm.

34. Rosetta Reitz, "Hot Snow: Valaida Snow (Queen of the Trumpet Sings & Swings)," *Black American Literature Forum* 16.4 (1982): 158–60, http://www.jstor.org/stable/2904225.

35. Brendan I. Koerner, "Piano Demon, The Imperial Circuit," *Atavist*, January 12, 2011, http://magazine.atavist.com/piano-demon.

36. Ibid.

37. Unless otherwise noted, Buck Clayton material is drawn from Buck Clayton and Nancy Miller Elliott, "Shanghai," in *Buck Clayton's Jazz World* (New York: Oxford University Press, 1986), 66–78.

38. "National Endowment for the Arts Jazz Masters: 1991 NEA Jazz Master Wilbur 'Buck' Clayton," *National Endowment for the Arts*, accessed May 1, 2017, http://www.nea.gov/honors/jazz/jmCMS/master.php?id=1991_02&type=bio.

CHAPTER 6: THE FORMATION OF ALL-CHINESE JAZZ BANDS

1. Jones, *Yellow Music*, 101–2.

2. This material is drawn from the same twelve-page article on jazz and popular music in China penned by Da Ren Zheng and published in a Chinese magazine that appears in chapter 4. Da Ren Zheng was interviewed (on video) while we were in Shanghai in August 2006. The translation is by Professor Eva Chou, now department chair of the Department of English, Baruch College, City University of New York.

3. Joshua Shi, "Jazzin It Up and Down," *Shanghai Star*, March 29, 2001, http://App1.chinadaily.com.cn/star/2001/0329/cu18-2.html.

4. The Paramount (Chinese: 百樂門; pinyin: Bǎilèmén; literally "gate of 100 pleasures") is a historic nightclub and dance hall at 218 Yuyuan Road in Jing'an, Shanghai, China. It was the largest and notorious ballroom in Shanghai during the so-called decadent era before the People's Liberation Army established control over the city in 1949.

5. Louisa Lim, "Survivors of Shanghai's Jazz Age Play Anew," *NPR*, September 24, 2007, http://www.npr.org/templates/story/story.php?storyId=14655091.

6. The renminbi was introduced in China in 1948. Today, it is also called yuan.

7. Several of these musicians formed the nexus of the Peace Hotel Jazz Band reconstituted in 1980.

CHAPTER 7: THE JAPANESE INVASION

1. "List of Japanese-run internment camps during World War II," *Wikipedia*, last modified October 16, 2012, http://en.wikipedia.org/wiki/List_of_Japanese_run_internment_camps_during_World_War_II.

2. Fairbank and Goldman, *China: A New History*, 312.

3. "Japanese War Crimes," *Wikipedia*, last modified July 8, 2017, http://en.wikipedia.org/wiki/Japanese_war_crimes.

4. Clayton and Elliot, *Buck Clayton's Jazz World*, 77–78.

5. "I was born and raised in Tientsin. My father had left poverty-stricken Ireland in 1912 to take a job as a tidewaiter with Chinese Maritime Customs. They posted him to Tientsin. My mother was the daughter of an English Irish French couple who ran their own marionette theatre that toured the world. They settled in Tientsin after selling their marionette show. Their daughter married my father in 1915. In quick succession they produced four sons and a daughter, the latter dying in her infancy. After my father's death in 1924 my mother married an Englishman. His earnings were insufficient to keep the family especially when a boy and a girl were born to them, so my mother continued working at a bank, a job she took when my father died. My three brothers left China when they reached their late teens. I stayed on in Tientsin. My first job after school was an installer of electrical meters. My second was with a stock broker who used me mostly to interpret the needs of his Chinese clients whose language I spoke fluently." Email message from Desmond Power to the author, November 1, 2012.

6. E-mail message from Desmond Power to the author, October 30, 2012.

7. Desmond Power, "The Jazz Scene at Japanese Prison Camps in China" (unpublished manuscript, 2012), 1. For an abridged version of Power's recollection, see "Jazz in Occupied China," *Blackpast.org*, accessed May 1, 2017, http://blackpast.org/perspectives/jazz-occupied-in-china-black-jazz-japanese-prison-camp-weihsien-china-durig-world-war-II/.

8. The use of word "Coloured" was not Power's description. It appears on a promotion poster touting nightly swing music from 9 p.m.

9. Power, "The Jazz Scene," 2.

10. The river's name is also spelled Huangpu.

11. Greg Leck, "The Japanese Internment of Allied Civilians in China and Hong Kong, 1941–1945," *Captives of Empire*, accessed May 1, 2017, http://www.captives-of-empire.com/wst_page5.php.

12. Email message from Desmond Power to the author, October 19, 2012.

13. Power, "The Jazz Scene," 2.

14. Leck, "The Japanese Internment."

15. Ibid.

16. Power, "The Jazz Scene," 4.

17. Email message from Desmond Power to the author, October 30, 2012.

18. Power, "The Jazz Scene," 7.

19. http://www.answers.com/topic/reginald-jones.

20. Ibid.

21. Email message from Desmond Power to the author, October 30, 2012.

22. Power, "The Jazz Scene," 5.

23. Ibid.

24. Ibid.

25. Andrew David Field, *Shanghai's Dancing World: Cabaret Culture and Urban Politics, 1919–1954* (Hong Kong: Chinese University Press, 2010), 130.

26. Power, "The Jazz Scene," 8.

27. Ibid., 9.

28. Ibid., 9–10.

29. Ibid., 10.

30. Taylor E. Atkins, "Jammin' on the Jazz Frontier: The Japanese Jazz Community in Interwar Shanghai," *Japanese Studies*, vol. 19, no. 1 (1999): 6.

31. Ibid., 7.

32. Ibid.

33. William Minor, *Jazz Journeys to Japan: The Heart Within* (Ann Arbor: University of Michigan Press, 2004). The book is also a personal journey for Minor. It is apparent, from the outset, that Minor is deeply passionate about his subject, having previously written *Unzipped Souls: A Journey through the Soviet Union*. In a way, the title of Minor's opus can be interpreted at least two ways. It is at one and the same time about jazz's journey to Japan in the early decades of the twentieth century and Minor's own several journeys to this far eastern isle to discover for himself the jazz scene there.

34. This section is drawn from Eugene Marlow, "William Minor's Jazz Journeys to Japan, University of Michigan Press, 2004," in *JazzNotes: The Journal of the Jazz Journalists Association* (2004): 16–17.

35. Minor, *Jazz Journeys to Japan*, 7.

36. Taylor E. Atkins, *Jazz Planet* (Jackson: University Press of Mississippi, 2003), xix.

CHAPTER 8: JAZZ AND INDIVIDUAL FREEDOM OF EXPRESSION

1. Fairbank and Goldman, *China: A New History*, 345.

2. Ibid., 350.

3. Ibid., 368.

4. Yang Jisheng, *Tombstone: The Great Chinese Famine, 1958–1962*, English translation ed. (New York: Farrar, Straus and Giroux, 2012).

5. Tania Branigan, "China's Great Famine: the true story," *The Guardian*, January 1, 2013, http://www.theguardian.com/world/2013/jan/01/china-great-famine-book-tombstone.

6. Ibid.

7. Fairbank and Goldman, *China: A New History*, 383.

8. Ibid., 383–84.

9. "From Mao to Mozart: Isaac Stern in China," *Wikipedia*, last modified February 8, 2017, https://en.wikipedia.org/wiki/From_Mao_to_Mozart:_Isaac_Stern_in_China.

10. https://www.bso.org/brands/bso/features/2013-14-bso-season/bso-tours-china-and-japan.aspx.

11. Unfortunately, Xia Jia is not commercially recorded, but samples of his playing can be found on the Internet at http://english.cri.cn/4026/2007/05/26/269@231714.htm.

12. Gao Ping, interviewed by the author, August 26, 2008.

13. The place of Gao Ping's birth has later consequence. In the late 1980s he would make the acquaintance of Dennis Rea, primarily a rock/jazz guitarist teaching at Chengdu University.

Rea's wife taught English at the university. Gao Ping was one of her students. Dennis Rea's sojourn in China is covered in chapter 10.

14. "Ping Gao," *Naxos.com*, accessed May 1, 2017, http://www.naxos.com/person/Ping_Gao_18813/18813.htm.

15. Dennis Rea, "The LAND Tour and the Rise of Jazz in China," *Speakeasy.org*, accessed May 1, 2017, www.speakeasy.org/~nunatak/chinatour.html.

CHAPTER 9: THE INFLUENCE OF MID-TWENTIETH-CENTURY TECHNOLOGIES ON THE EXPANSION OF JAZZ IN CHINA

1. Much of this section is drawn from Eugene Marlow, "Perspectives: The Use of Interactive Media in United States Corporations," *Interactive Unternehmenskommunikation, Interactive Corporate Communications*, eds. Dr. Ansgar Zerfass and Dr. Michael Krzeminski (Frankfurt: Frankfurter Allgemeine Zeitung, 1998), 107–18.

2. Marshall McLuhan, *Understanding Media* (New York: McGraw-Hill, 1964), 177.

3. "Sales volume of television sets in China from 2011–2015 (in million units)," *Statista*, accessed May 1, 2017, http://www.statista.com/statistics/468944/china-television-set-sales-volume/.

4. "The Chinese Media: More Autonomous and Diverse—Within Limits," *CIA.gov*, last modified Jun 19, 2013, https://www.cia.gov/library/center-for-the-study-of-intelligence/csi-publications/books-and-monographs/the-chinese-media-more-autonomous-and-diverse-within-limits/copy_of_1.htm.

5. Ibid.

6. "Asia: Asia Marketing Research, Internet Usage, Population Statistics, and Facebook Information," *Internet World Stats*, last modified July 8, 2017, http://www.internetworldstats.com/asia.htm; "Basic Data," *China Internet Network Information Center*, accessed May 1, 2017, http://cnnic.com.cn/IDR/BasicData/.

7. Broadcasting Board of Governors, "VOA Marks 70th Year of US Broadcasts to China," news release, December 27, 2011, http://www.bbg.gov/press-release/voa-marks-70th-year-of-us-broadcasts-to-china/.

8. "Voice of America (VOA)," *Wikipedia*, last modified July 7, 2017, http://en.wikipedia.org/wiki/Voice_of_America.

9. Alan L. Heil Jr., "Music the Universal Language," *Voice of America: A History* (New York: Columbia University Press, 2003), 289.

10. "Voice of America Jazz Hour," *Wikipedia*, last modified February 20, 2017, http://en.wikipedia.org/wiki/Voice_of_America_Jazz_Hour.

11. Heil, "Music the Universal Language," 290.

12. Ibid., 290–91.

13. Ibid., 291.

14. William Baum, VOA, East Asian Pacific Division Director, email message to author, June 9, 2016; Pamela Commerford, VOA Media Asset Management Branch Chief Central Production Services Division, email message to author, June 13, 2016.

15. Soo Hoo Winyan, "Sasha Gong, 1st Asian American VOA Branch Chief," *Asian Fortune News*, accessed May 1, 2017, http://www.asianfortunenews.com/article_0312.php?article_id=26.

16. Roger E. Bilstein, *The Enterprise of Flight: The American Aviation and Aerospace Industry* (Washington and London: Smithsonian Institution Press, 2001), 234.

17. Mary Bellis, "The Evolution of Modern Aircraft," *About.com*, accessed May 1, 2017, http://inventors.about.com/library/inventors/bljetengine.htm.

18. Tim Robinson, "London-Thames Estuary Airport Plans—déjà-vu all over again!" *Royal Aeronautical Society*, last modified September 7, 2012, http://media.aerosociety.com/aerospace-insight/2012/09/07/londons-thames-airport-plans-deja-vu-all-over-again/7288/.

19. Matt Rosenberg, "Current World Population: World Population Growth Since the Year One," *ThoughtCo*, last modified May 28, 2017, http://geography.about.com/od/obtainpopulationdata/a/worldpopulation.htm.

20. "Aircraft Manufacturers," *Aviation Knowledge*, last modified March 23, 2017, http://aviationknowledge.wikidot.com/aviation:manufacturers.

21. "Airlines to China," *skyscanner*, accessed May 1, 2017, http://www.skyscanner.com/flights-to/cn/airlines-that-fly-to-china.html.

22. Ibid.

23. Roger Yu, "Chinese travelers are seeing the USA in record numbers," *USA Today Travel*, February 2, 2012, http://travel.usatoday.com/flights/story/2012-01-31/Chinese-travelers-are-seeing-the-USA-in-record-numbers/52905866/1.

24. "(untitled)," *Sinotrans&CSC Holdings Co., LTD.*, accessed May 1, 2017, http://www.sinotransone.com/Sinotransgroup.html.

25. "DHL in China," *DHL*, accessed May 1, 2017, http://www.cn.dhl.com/en/about_us/dhl_china.html.

26. "Fact Sheet: UPS and China," *UPS*, accessed May 1, 2017, http://www.pressroom.ups.com/Fact+Sheets/UPS+China+Fact+Sheet.

27. "Time Flies: The FedEx Timeline," *FedEx*, accessed May 1, 2017, http://about.van.fedex.com/article/fedex-timeline. Based in McMinnville, Oregon, Evergreen International Aviation is a privately held global aviation services company active through several subsidiary companies.

28. Larry Diamond, "A Report Card on Democracy" (Report, Hoover Institution, Stanford University), http://www.hoover.org/publications/hoover-digest/article/7310.

29. Kabir Sehgal, *Jazzocracy: Jazz, Democracy, and the Creation of a New American Mythology*, 1st ed. (Mishawaka, IN: Better World Books), 2008.

CHAPTER 10: FIRST A TRICKLE, THEN A FLOOD: JAZZ MUSICIANS PERFORM IN CHINA FROM ALL OVER

1. "Willie Ruff," *Yale School of Music: Faculty*, last modified November 25, 2012, http://music.yale.edu/faculty/ruff.html. This summer trip to the Shanghai Conservatory of Music is reaffirmed by a *New Yorker* article; see William Zinsser, "Shanghai Blues," *New Yorker*, September 21, 1981.

2. Willie Ruff, "Improvising in Shanghai," in *A Call to Assembly: The Autobiography of a Musical Storyteller* (New York: Viking, 1991), 387–96. This book received the Deems Taylor Award for excellence in a book on music.

3. Ibid., 387–88.

4. Ibid., 388.

5. www.msmnyc.edu/FacultyBio/FID/1020005002; www.nyiaa.org/html/iframe_govboard sub.html, undated.

6. Ruff, "Improvising in Shanghai," 388.

7. Ibid., 391.

8. Ibid., 392.

9. Ibid., 392–93.

10. Ibid., 393.

11. Ibid., 394.

12. Ibid., 395.

13. Lucille Bruce, "Willie Ruff retires having given 'conservatory without walls' a home at Yale," news release, *Yale School of Music*, May 1, 2017, http://music.yale.edu/2017/05/01/ willie-ruff-retires-given-conservatory-without-walls-home-yale/

14. David Moser, "The Book of Changes," *Jazz Now* (1997): 19.

15. Mary Ann Hurst, singer/recording artist, in discussion with the author, September 2, 2006.

16. Dennis Rea, *Live at the Forbidden City: Musical Encounters in China and Taiwan* (Bloomington, IN: iUniverse, 2006), 20.

17. Ibid., 3.

18. Ibid., 11.

19. Ibid., 13.

20. Ibid., 25.

21. Ibid., 25–26.

22. Ibid., 26.

23. Ibid.

24. Ibid., 29.

25. Ibid., 29–30.

26. Ms. Carmichael, in discussion with the author, July 28, 2006.

27. The United States Information Agency (USIA), which existed from 1953 to 1999, was a United States agency devoted to "public diplomacy." The agency was previously known as the United States Information Service (USIS). Michael Hashim, a member of the abovementioned trio, described the USIS as the cultural branch of the Foreign Service in charge of spreading a positive image of American culture abroad.

28. Michael Hashim, "Michael Hashim's Jazz from New York to China," *Saxophone Journal* (July/August 1994): 34–39. Hashim's description of the tour and his reflections on the Chinese cultural scene is highly detailed and informative.

CHAPTER 11: MARTIN FLEISCHER, GODFATHER OF JAZZ, AND LIU YUAN, SO-CALLED FATHER OF JAZZ IN EARLY POST-MAO BEIJING

1. Martin Fleischer—at the time First Counselor/Cultural Attaché, Embassy of the Federal Republic of Germany—in discussion with the author, August 9, 2006. All of Fleischer's comments in this section are drawn from this interview.

2. Dennis Rea's book *Live at the Forbidden City* goes into great detail about Cui Jian's life, his impact on the Tiananmen freedom movement, and his relationship with Liu Yuan.

3. Cui Jian is considered the father of rock in China and remains the most famous of China indigenous rock musicians. Although he is known primarily for his anti-government rock songs and recordings, he is also a jazz enthusiast who plays the trumpet. It is perhaps no mere coincidence that Jian and Liu Yuan performed together in Beijing in the 1980s.

4. This paragraph and the next few draw from Christine Laskowski, "Pioneering Saxophonist, 50, Still Hitting the Right Note," *China Daily*, March, 29, 2010, http://www.chinadaily.com.cn/life/2010-03/29/content_9655355.htm.

5. "Liu Yuan (musician)," *Wikipedia*, last modified October 1, 2013, http://en.wikipedia.org/wiki/Liu_Yuan_(musician).

6. Lina Tornquist and Poppy Toland, "The Best Jazz Club in Beijing," *Time*, February 29, 2008.

7. Susie Gordon, "Live Music," in *Moon Spotlight Beijing* (Berkeley: Avalon Travel, 2012), 63.

8. Laskowski, "Pioneering Saxophonist, 50, Still Hitting the Right Note."

9. "Liu Yuan Jazz Quartet," *Cityweekend.com.cn*, last modified January 14, 2011, http://www.cityweekend.com.cn/beijing/events/81024/.

CHAPTER 12: LIU SOLA: CHINA'S MUSICALLY ECLECTIC COMPOSER

This chapter includes quotes from Liu Sola in discussion with the author, August 7, 2006.
1. https://en.wikipedia.org/wiki/Liu_Sola.

CHAPTER 13: THE BEIJING JAZZ SCENE

1. As quoted in Rea, *Live at the Forbidden City*.

2. Dennis Rea, "The Land Tour and the Rise of Jazz in China," *Speakeasy.org*, accessed May 1, 2017, http://www.speakeasy.org/~nunatak/chinatour.html.

3. "Waiting for Jazz, das Jazzfestival in Beijing," *AvantArt*, accessed May 1, 2017, www.avantart.com/personal/avantart-cis/peking94.htm; "Beijing Jazzfestival 1995," *AvantArt*, accessed May 1, 2017, www.avantart.com/personal/avantart-cis/peking95.htm; http://home.t-online.de/home/xtend.ww/jzww_ge.htm; "Programme, International Jazz Festival, Beijing, China, November 10–16, 1996," *China Today*, accessed May 1, 2017, http://www.chinatoday.com/art/jazz/a.html.

4. For me personally this was a disappointment. I was on the verge of making all the necessary travel plans to visit Beijing during the 2001 festival: all the jazz musicians I needed to interview would have been there. I had to wait until July-August 2006 to make the trip.

5. Jiang Yuxia, "All the Jazz," *Global Times*, September 13, 2012, http://www.globaltimes.cn/content/733035.shtml, 09/13/2012.

6. This volume is not intended to be a travel guide. Thus, only the major jazz venues—past and present—are described.

7. David Moser, "The Book of Changes," *Jazz Now* (1997): 5.

8. As of Summer 2006, this is no longer true. Whatever the circumstances, Liu Yuan no longer performs there, preferring instead, of course, to play at his own club, the East Shore Café.

9. Weihua Zhang, "Notes on the Current Jazz Scene in China," *Journal of Music in China* vol. 2, no. 2 (2000): 266.

10. Email message from David Moser to author, May 15, 2013.

11. Liu Yuan, saxophonist and owner of Dogan Club (a.k.a. East Shore Club), and often referred to as the father of jazz in China, in discussion with the author, July 30, 2006. This interview would have been impossible without the Mandarin Chinese translation skills of Ms. Hortense Halle.

12. Kevin Holden, "Modern day jazz resurgence draws on bygone eras," *China Daily*, December 5, 2005, http://www.chinadaily.com/cn/english/doc/2005-12/05/content_500283.htm.

13. Wang Shanshan, "US jazz culture symbol faces demolition," *China Daily*, http://www.chinadaily.com.cn/china/2006-08/05/content_657762.htm.

14. Ibid.

15. Ibid.

16. www.time.com/time/daily/special/newschina/cox/overview/pg1.html.

17. Mr. Rich Delarie, Human Resources, Monitor Aerospace Corporation, in discussion with the author, September 17, 2010.

18. Select Comm. of the United States House of Representatives, "Chapter 10: Manufacturing Processes," in US National Security and Military/Commercial Concerns with the People's Republic of China, "Chapter 10." US House of Representatives, accessed May 1, 2017, www.house.gov/coxreport/body/ch10bod.html.

19. Ibid.

20. Ibid.

21. Staff, "Stellex Industries Completes Acquisition of Monitor Aerospace Corporation," news release, June 3, 1998, http://aviationweek.com/awin/stellex-completes-acquisition-monitor-aerospace.

22. "Obituaries: Douglas Sebastian Monitto," *Garden City Life*, February 2, 2001, http://www.antonnews.com/gardencitylife/2001/02/02/obituaries/.

23. Mary Monitto, owner of the Big Easy, in discussion with the author, August 2, 2006.

24. www.vsidecars.com/danny.htm.

25. Mike Hall, "Music Bio," *humblemusic.com*, accessed May 1, 2017, www.humblemusic.com/bio.html.

26. George Vaughton, "Chaoyang Paradiso," *Beijing Scene* vol. 7, issue 11 (March 31–April 6, 2000), http://www.beijingscene.com/v07i11/feature.html.

27. Phoebe Wong, general manager of the Ice House, in discussion with the author, August 3, 2006.

28. Philip Cheung, CEO/Owner of Brown's, in discussion with the author, July 27, 2006.

CHAPTER 14: BEIJING'S LEADING INDIGENOUS AND EXPAT JAZZ MUSICIANS

1. Josef Woodard, "East-West Jazz Link: Chinese reed player, visiting UCSB, will perform with the campus band," *Los Angeles Times*, April 16, 1998, *SOUNDS*: Special to the *Times*, http://articles.latimes.com/1998/apr/16/entertainment/ca-39687.

2. American singer Mary Ann Hurst in discussion with the author, September 2, 2006.

3. Wang Ping, "Sunset Happiness," *cctv.com*, accessed May 1, 2017, http://www.cctv.com/ program/rediscoveringchina/20060714/103515.shtml.

4. "'Temptress Moon,' set in 1920's China, is a sensuous cinematic whoosh of opium smoke, lily pads and seductively lowered eyes. In evoking Shanghai's decadence during the pre-Communist era, the film, Chen Kaige's follow-up to his acclaimed epic, 'Farewell My Concubine,' conjures a world of fabulous dance halls and elegant corruption, all seen through a gauzy, opiate haze. Beautiful women swoon in the arms of icy, white-suited gigolos. Exquisite revenge is exacted by lacing an enemy's opium with arsenic and turning him into an immobilized, ashen ghost of his former self." Steven Holden, review of *Temptress Moon*, by Chen Kaige, *New York Times*, October 5, 1996, http://movies.nytimes.com/movie/review?res=9D02E5D8133FF936A35753C 1A960958260.

5. Ping, "Sunset Happiness."

6. "China Holds First Guitar Festival," *Modern Guitars*, last modified August 23, 2005, http:// www.modernguitars.com/archives/001066.html.

7. Email message from David Moser to author, May 15, 2013.

8. "Adam" (virtuoso bass player, Nine Gates Jazz Festival progenitor) in discussion with author, July 28, 2006.

9. Xia Jia, Beijing's "Cool" jazz pianist of the "Minimalist School," in discussion with the author, July 27, 2006.

10. Email message from Harold Danko to author, August 22, 2011.

11. All material pertaining to Xia Jia is from my interview with him.

12. Unfortunately, Xia is not commercially recorded, but samples of his playing can be found on the Internet at http://english.cri.cn/4026/2007/05/26/269@231714.htm.

13. http://webcache.googleusercontent.com/search?q=cache:http://www.jzclub.cc/node/135.

14. "Kong Hong Wei 孔宏伟 (金佛| JZClub 黄楼)." http://webcache.googleusercontent .com/search?q=cache:http://www.jzclub.cc/node/135.

15. "5 Chinese Pianist Heroes," *JZClub China*, last modified January 1, 2013, http://www .jzclub.cn/en/concert/5-chinese-pianist-heroes.

16. "Cui Jian on AllMusic," *AllMusic*, accessed May 1, 2017, http://www.allmusic.com/artist/ cui-jian-mn0000139728.

17. "5 Chinese Pianist Heroes," *JZClub China*.

18. "Hongwei Kong (Jin Fo)—Summer Palace," *NoNaMe*, accessed May 1, 2017, http://nnm .ru/blogs/myway58/hongwei_kong_jin_fo_summer_palace/.

19. "Fear of a Blank Planet." *Fear of a Blank Planet*, http://www.fearofablankplanet.com/artists/jazz/jazz_fusion/hongwei_kong_jin_fo_sum mer_palace_jin_fo_his_friends.html.

20. "Golden Buddha Jazz Unit," *Music-China Wiki*, accessed May 1, 2017, http://www.rock inchina.com/w/Golden_Buddha_Jazz_Unit.

21. Kong Hongwei Jazz Band, "Kong Hongwei Jazz Band Live @ the Vip Club, Zagreb," *YouTube* video, posted by "CherryPicks," May 26, 2012, http://www.youtube.com/watch?v=bd9ppV8OFuo.

22. "Golden Buddha," *Last.fm*, accessed May 1, 2017, http://www.last.fm/music/Golden Buddha.

23. "Golden Buddha Jazz Unit," *Music-China Wiki*.

24. Ibid.

25. "Not Music for Old Men," *China Daily Entertainment News*, September 3, 2012, http://english.sina.com/entertainment/p/2012/0903/502680.html.

26. "The 4th Beijing Ninegates Jazz Week 2009—Opening Concert," *City Weekend China*, accessed May 1, 2017, http://www.cityweekend.com.cn/beijing/events/44837/.

27. Liu "Kenny" Xiaoguang, saxophonist, in discussion with the author, July 27, 2006.

28. Xiao Dou, drummer, in discussion with the author, July 27, 2006.

29. Yao Yi Xin, singer, in discussion with the author, on the eve of the demolition of the Big Easy, August 2, 2006.

30. Zou Tong, bassist, in discussion with the author, August 1, 2006. The Aria is in the lobby of the China World Hotel in the Central Chao Yang District. While the upstairs restaurant draws kudos for its contemporary continental cuisine, the downstairs bar is also worth exploring. In addition to nightly jazz, Aria features an impressive wine list with prices to match.

31. Zhang Ling, bass player, in discussion with the author, August 3, 2006.

32. Wu Yun Nan, former Chinese Navy Band saxophonist, in discussion with the author, August 3, 2006.

33. "Military Band of the Chinese People's Liberation Army," *China Culture*, accessed May 1, 2017, http://www1.chinaculture.or/library/2008-02/18/content_40379.htm.

34. Sarah M. Rivette, "U.S., Chinese bands perform together in historic concert," news release, *US Army*, accessed May, 2017, http://www.army.mil/article/56625/.

35. This military band primarily performs marches of a nationalistic nature and national anthems of visiting dignitaries at formal occasions. Yet when we arrived in Shanghai from Beijing in 2006 and turned on the television, we discovered quite by chance the PLA band performing on one of the channels. One of the pieces had a distinct Latin-jazz style.

36. "Testimonial from Yinjiao Du," *Aizen*, accessed May 1, 2017, http://www.sax.co.jp/eaizen43.html.

37. Dan Ouellette, "First Views: Beijing International Jazz Festival," *Salon.com*, June 1, 1998, http://www.salon.com/1998/07/01/feature_37/, 1.

38. Ibid., 3–4.

39. Izumi Koga, Japanese drummer, in discussion with the author, July 28, 2006.

40. Matt Roberts, in discussion with the author, July 27, 2006.

41. "Real book" is a euphemistic term for a fake book, a compendium of jazz and pop standards with a melody line and chord symbols.

42. An excellent examination of Lu Xun's early work can be found in Eva Shan Chou, "A Story about Hair: A Curious Mirror of Lu Xun's Pre-Republican Days," *Journal of Asian Studies* vol. 66, no. 2 (2007): 421–59.

43. Lu Xun, *The True Story of Ah Q, with an introduction by David Pollard*, trans. Yang Xianyi and Gladys Yang (Hong Kong: Chinese University Press of Hong Kong, Traditional Chinese-English Bilingual Edition, 2002), viii.

44. Ibid., xxviii.

45. Ibid., xxxii, xxxiv.

CHAPTER 15: SHANGHAI'S JAZZ VENUES

1. Field, *Shanghai's Dancing World*, 90.

2. Dong, *Shanghai 1842–1949*, 198.

3. Ibid., 219.

4. "Legend of the Sassoons," *Shanghai Star*, May 10, 2001, http://www.china.org.cn/english/LI-e/12461.htm.

5. Alison Wellner, "A Shanghai Art Deco Landmark Reopens," *Luxist*, July 29, 2010, http://www.luxist.com/2010/07/29/a-shanghai-art-deco-landmark-reopens/print/.

6. Casey Hall and Peijin Chen, "The Right Notes," *Enterprise China*, June 2011, http://enterprisechina.net/node/28.

7. Ren Yuqing's connection to Cui Jian is noteworthy. As chapter 11 points out, saxophonist Liu Yuan was also a member of Cui Jian's troupe. All three have achieved prominence in China in one way or another.

8. Hall and Chen, "The Right Notes."

9. Coughland, "Best jazz bars in Shanghai."

10. Unless otherwise stated, information regarding JZ School is drawn from an official JZ School bulletin in PDF form.

11. The JZ Club's school is described in more detail in chapter 17, "Jazz Education in China."

12. Unless otherwise noted, all information on the JZ Festival is from Nick Taylor, "JZ Festival: Full Line-up and Details," *SmartShanghai.com*, last modified September 24, 2012, http://www.smartshanghai.com/wire/nightlife/jz-festival-full-line-up-and-details.

13. http://www.expatcn.com/node/9401.

14. Jenn Chan Lyman, "You Ready to Get Jazzed?," *Jenn Chan Lyman*, accessed May 1, 2017, http://www.jennchanlyman.com/mag_jazzedSep09.html.

15. Dan Shapiro, "JZ International Music Festival 2010: Jazz to be 'signature of Shanghai,'" *cnn.com*, October 11, 2010, http://travel.cnn.com/shanghai/play/shanghai-jazz-jz-festival-788923.

16. Email message from Rolf Becker to author, May 2, 2013.

17. http://www.cjwchina.com/ensh/info.aspx?m=20091126165607623665.

18. http://www.cjwchina.com/ensh/info.aspx?m=20091126165919090683.

19. Cotton Club, "Customer Newsletter," *The Cotton Club China*, February 2012, http://www.thecottonclub.cn/newsletter/newsletter.pdf.

20. An echo of drummer Whitey Smith's locale before coming to Shanghai.

21. Weihua Zhang, "Notes on the Current Jazz Scene in China," *Journal of Music in China* vol. 2, no. 2 (October 2000): 265–66.

22. http://www.houseofbluesandjazz.com/.

23. "House of Blues and Jazz," *TripAdvisor*, accessed May 1, 2017, http://www.tripadvisor.com/Restaurant_Review-g308272-d1886283-Reviews-House_of_Blues_Jazz-Shanghai.html.

24. "House of Blues and Jazz," *Frommer's*, accessed May 1, 2017, http://www.frommers.com/destinations/shanghai/N28790.html.

25. Da Ren Zheng's frequent reference in chapter 9 to the Paramount in pre-Mao days and the advent of jazz bands playing mostly American dance music there also underscores the hall's historic importance.

26. Field, *Shanghai's Dancing World*, 1.

27. Ibid., 97.

28. Ibid., 89.

29. Xie Fang and Li Luxia, "Historic dance hall steps lightly into 21st century," *China Daily*, May 11, 2006, 5.

CHAPTER 16: SHANGHAI'S LEADING INDIGENOUS AND EXPAT JAZZ MUSICIANS

1. In 2006 I traveled 8,000 miles to interview at least one member of the current Peace Hotel Jazz Band. It will be of interest that the manager of the Jazz Band Bar demanded $500 to do an interview. I rejected the request. Instead, we managed to "persuade" Mr. Sun to do an audiotaped interview off hours at the bar surreptitiously. We told him if he did not do the interview, he would not be in the book.

2. This conversation held in a corner of the space where the Peace Hotel Jazz Band performs was translated from the original Shanghaiese by Jenny Zhou Shao, mother of Scarlett Shao. Both now live in New York City. The younger Shao was a student of mine at Baruch College. It was our good fortune that Scarlett was in Shanghai visiting family at the same time of our trip. She was present at many of the interviews requiring translation from Shanghaiese Mandarin to English. Her mother reviewed the translation originally recorded on audiotape.

3. See chapter 9 for a description of the VOA's activities directed at China.

4. "Peace Hotel Old Jazz Band," *YouTube* video, posted by "halloletterbox," May 17, 2011, http://www.youtube.com/watch?v=-6zJwDlOTt8.

5. Ibid.

6. "Shanghai Peace Hotel Old Jazz Band," *Leisure and Cultural Services Department, Hong Kong*, last modified June 5, 2005, http://www.lcsd.gov.hk/CE/CulturalService/Programme/en/music/jun05/jazz.mtml.

7. Hannah Lau, review of *As Time Goes By in Shanghai*, Flying Moon Filmproduktion/Berlin, *ChinaSource*, February 10, 2017, http://www.chinasource.org/blog/posts/as-time-goes-by-in-shanghai. I hosted a showing of this film with the director Uli Gaulke at the Margaret Mead Documentary Festival organized by the American Museum of Natural History in 2013.

8. *Music Design brochure*, JZ Club (Shanghai, China, 2006).

9. Guitarist Lawrence Ku in discussion with the author, August 14, 2006.

10. Ke Coco Zhao, jazz singer, in discussion with the author, August 13, 2006.

11. Zhang Xiaolu, saxophonist and teacher, in discussion with the author, August 19, 2006.

12. "Wilson Chen (China)," *JZ School*, accessed May 1, 2017, http://www.jz-school.com/index.php?page=wilson-chen.

13. "Wilson Chen," *Legere Reeds LTD.*, accessed May 1, 2017, http://www.legere.com/artists/wilson-chen-%E9%99%88%E5%98%89%E4%BF%8A.

14. Ms. Joey Lu, jazz singer and pianist, in discussion with the author, August 17, 2006.

15. All information on Higgins from his personal website: http://www.seanhiggins.net/.

16. All information on Croker is from his biography on the JZClub website, found here: http://www.jzclub.cn/en/musician/theo-croker-2.

17. "Jazz Meets Rock," *Alec Haavik*, accessed on May 1, 2017, http://www.alechaavik.com/bio.php?PHPSESSID=4437b92a59165f01c2e61083b4ae3928.

18. Rolf Becker, musician/composer/arranger, in discussion with the author, August 13, 2006.

19. Email message from Rolf Becker to the author, May 2, 2013.

CHAPTER 17: JAZZ EDUCATION IN CHINA

1. Wai-Chung Ho, *School music education and social change in Mainland China, Hong Kong, and Taiwan* (Leiden: Brill, 2011).

2. Gordon Cox, review of *School music education and social change*, by Wai-Chung Ho, *Music Education Research* vol. 14(3) (September 2012): 403–5.

3. Bennett Reimer, "Music Education in China: An Overview and Some Issues," *Journal of Aesthetic Education* vol. 23, no. 1 (Spring 1989): 68.

4. Reimer was Director of a three-year research project on the general music curriculum sponsored by the US Office of Education and was a research exchange scholar studying music education practices from kindergarten through conservatory in China for a three-month period in 1986, sponsored by the Chinese government and Harvard Project Zero. See "Bennett Reimer," *Wikipedia*, last modified April 8, 2017, http://en.wikipedia.org/wiki/Bennett_Reimer.

5. Reimer, "Music Education in China," 67.

6. Ibid., 73.

7. Marcello Viridis, "The Best Music Schools in China," eHow, accessed on May 1, 2017, www.ehow.com/list_6387729_music-schools-china.html.

8. Cox, 403–5.

9. Michael Cooper, "New Musical Partnership in China," *Arts Beat* (blog), November 23, 2013, http://artsbeat.blogs,nytimes.com/2013/11/23/new-musical-partnership-in-china?/_r=0.

10. Jeffrey Hays, "Western Classical Music in China," *Facts and Details*, last modified January 2014, http://factsanddetails.com/china/cat7/sub41/item250.html.

11. Hao Huang, "Why Chinese people play Western classical music: Transcultural roots of music philosophy," *International Journal of Music Education* vol. 30, no. 2 (May 12, 2012): 2.

12. Ibid., 6.

13. David Moser, "The Book of Changes," *Jazz Now* (1996): 3–4.

14. Ibid., 4–5.

15. The description of the Midi School is based primarily on an on-site interview with Zhan Fan, the school's founding president, August 8, 2006, by the author.

16. Dan Shapiro, "JZ International Music Festival 2010," *cnn.com*, October 11, 2010, http://travel.cnn.com/shanghai/play/shanghai-jazz-jz-festival-788923.

17. Unless otherwise stated, information regarding JZ School is drawn from an official JZ School bulletin in PDF form.

18. "About JZ School," *JZ School*, accessed May 1, 2017, http://www.jz-school.com/index.php?page=background.

19. Shapiro, "JZ International."

20. Zhang Xiaolu, saxophonist, JZ Club, in discussion with the author, August 19, 2006.

21. This section is based on an interview with Ms. Christianne Orto, Dean for Distance Learning and Recording Arts, Manhattan School of Music, January 2008.

22. Email message from Dean Yu to the author, May 10, 2016. As of this writing he has departed from Ningbo University to take a deanship at another university in May 2016.

23. Yu Hui, "Chinese Program Breaks Down Walls," *DownBeat*, November 2012, 78.

24. "Tom Smith: Musician. Educator. Cultural Ambassador. Writer Program Builder," accessed September 17, 2017, http://tomsmithjazz.wixsite.com/music.

CHAPTER 18: JAZZ IN CHINA IN THE TWENTY-FIRST CENTURY

1. Nathan Gardels, "These Charts Show How China's Economy Is Changing Amid Labor Unrest," *Huffington Post*, April 27, 2016, http://www.huffingtonpost.com/nathan-gardels/charts -china-economy-labor-unrest_b_9778790.html.

2. Strobe Talbott, *The Great Experiment: The Story of Ancient Empires, Modern States, and The Quest for a Global Nation* (New York: Simon & Schuster, 2008), 395.

3. Anthony Kennedy, US Supreme Court Justice, "Speech at McCloskey Speaker Series, The Aspen Institute" (speech, Aspen, CO, August 4, 2008).

4. Jacques Attali, *Noise: The Political Economy of Music*, 9th printing (Minneapolis: University of Minnesota Press, 2006).

5. The eleven-time Tony-winning Broadway show *Hamilton* is a notable exception for several reasons, not the least of which is its historical perspective.

6. http://www.un.org/members/growth.shtml, as of August 19, 2008.

7. Peter Grier, "Global Spread of Democracy Stalled," *Christian Science Monitor*, November 21, 2007, http://www.csmonitor.com/2007/1121/p01s02-usgn.html?page=1.

8. Sehgal, *Jazzocracy*.

9. David Moser, "The Book of Changes," *Jazz Now* (1996): 8.

10. Martin Luther King Jr., "On The Importance of Jazz" (speech, Berlin 1964), 1964 Berlin Jazz Festival, http://www.hartford-hwp.com/archives/45a/626.html.

11. "Wharton Panel Hears 'Jazz' in China Economy," *Plexus News* (Allentown, NJ), June 9, 2005.

12. "Chinese Jazz exports heads for Europe," last modified June 24, 2005, www.motoring.co.za/index.php?fArticleId=259857&fSectionId=753&fSetId=381.

13. David Lammers, "Jazz signs up second Shanghai partner," *EETimes Online*, October 27, 2003, http://www.eet.com/news/design/silicon/showArticle.jhtml?articleId=17408713&kc=6325.

14. "Teach, Study, Intern and Volunteer Abroad," *Global Education Corporation*, accessed May 1, 2017, http://www.globalcorp.com/music_shanghai.php.

15. "Bruce Iglauer: Effects of international piracy on American independent record labels," *Jazz News*, May 31, 2005, http://home.nestor.minsk.by/jazz/articles/2005/05/0037.html.

16. Email message from Peter Zanello to the author, April 29, 2005.

17. Dwayne Ashley, Vice President of Development for Jazz at Lincoln Center, in discussion with the author, July 5, 2016.

18. Martin Chilton, "Blue Note to Open Jazz Club in China," *Telegraph*, July 4, 2015, http://www.telegraph.co.uk/culture/music/worldfolkandjazz/11716649/Blue-Note-to-open-jazz -club-in-China.html.

19. Email message from Stephen Li, Winbright Corporation Ltd., to the author, June 19, 2016.

20. "Zhang Youdai," *Miro/China*, accessed May 1, 2017, http://miro-china.ch/en/view/article/artists/147/zhang-youdai.

21. Email message from Tony Macaluso (Director of Network Syndication, WFMT Radio Network–Chicago) to the author, July 2, 2017.

22. Email message from Melinda Zhang, Assistant to the Director, Chinese Jazz Association, to the author, July 3, 2016.

23. Ian Patterson, "Li Gao Yang: Locks, Stock, and Smoking Barrel," *allaboutjazz*, accessed September 17, 2017, https://www.allaboutjazz.com/li-gao-yang-locks-stock-and-smoking-barrel-li-gao-yang-by-ian-patterson.php.

BIBLIOGRAPHY

BOOKS

Atkins, Taylor E. *Jazz Planet*. Jackson: University Press of Mississippi, 2003.

Attali, Jacques. *Noise: The Political Economy of Music*. Minneapolis: University of Minnesota Press, 1985.

Badger, R. Reid. *A Life in Ragtime*. New York: Oxford University Press, 1995.

Bales, David, and Ted Orland. *Art and Fear*. Santa Cruz: Image Continuum, 1993.

Bergonzi, Ben. *Old Gramophones*. London: Shire Publications, 2000.

Bilstein, Roger E. *The Enterprise of Flight: The American Aviation and Aerospace Industry*. Washington and London: Smithsonian Institution Press, 2001.

Clayton, Buck, and Nancy M. Elliott. *Buck Clayton's Jazz World*. New York: Oxford University Press, 1986.

Copland, Aaron. *Music and Imagination*. Cambridge: Harvard University Press, 1952.

Dikötter, Frank. "Singing Machines: The Gramophone and the Radio." In *Exotic Commodities: Modern Objects and Everyday Life in China*. New York: Columbia University Press, 2006.

Dong, Stella. *Shanghai 1842–1949: The Rise and Fall of a Decadent City*. New York: William Morrow, 2000.

Fairbank, John K., and Merle Goldman. *China: A New History*. 2nd ed. Cambridge: Belknap Press of Harvard University Press, 2006.

Falkus, Malcolm. *The Blue Funnel Legend: A History of the Ocean Steam Ship Company, 1865–1973*. London: Macmillan Academic and Professional, 1990.

Field, Andrew David. *Shanghai's Dancing World: Cabaret Culture and Urban Politics 1919–1954*. Hong Kong: Chinese University Press, 2010.

Gordon, Susie. *Moon Spotlight Beijing*. Berkeley: Avalon Travel, 2012.

Hanes, William T. III, and Frank Sanello. *The Opium Wars: The Addiction of One Empire and the Corruption of Another*. Naperville: Sourcebooks, 2002.

Heil, Alan L. Jr. *Voice of America: A History*. New York: Columbia University Press, 2003.

Hershey, Burnet. "Jazz Latitude." In *Keeping Time*, edited by Robert Walser. New York: Oxford University Press, 1999.

Ho, Wai-Chung. *School Music education and social change in Mainland China, Hong Kong, and Taiwan*. Leiden: Brill, 2011.

Hughes, Langston. *The Collected Works of Langston Hughes*, edited by Arnold Rampersad, Dolan Hubbard, and Leslie Catherine Sanders. Columbia: University of Missouri Press, 2001.

Jisheng, Yang. *Tombstone: The Great Chinese Famine, 1958–1962.* English Translation Edition. New York: Farrar, Straus and Giroux, 2012.

Jones, Andrew F. *Yellow Music: Media Culture and Colonial Modernity in the Chinese Jazz Age.* Durham and London: Duke University Press, 2001.

Marlow, Eugene. "Perspectives: The Use of Interactive Media in United States Corporations." In *Interactive Unternehmenskommunikation, Interactive Corporate Communications,* edited by Ansgar Zerfass and Michael Krzeminski, 107–18. Frankfurt: Frankfurter Allgemeine Zeitung (F.A.Z.), 1998.

McLuhan, Marshall. *Understanding Media.* New York: McGraw-Hill, 1964.

Minor, William. *Jazz Journeys to Japan: The Heart Within.* Ann Arbor: University of Michigan Press, 2004.

Pan, Lynn, Li Y. Xue, and Zonghao Qian. *Shanghai: A Century of Change in Photographs, 1843–1949.* 9th ed. Hong Kong: Peace Book Co., 2005.

Power, Desmond. "The Jazz Scene at Japanese Prison Camps in China." Unpublished manuscript, 2012.

Quirino, Richie C. *Pinoy Jazz Traditions.* Pasig City, Philippines: Anvil Publishing, 2004.

Rea, Dennis. *Live at The Forbidden City.* Bloomington, IN: iUniverse, 2006.

Ross, Larry. *African American Jazz Musicians in the Diaspora* (Studies in African Diaspora, vol. 2). Lewiston, NY: Edwin Mellen Press, 2003.

Ruff, Willie. *A Call to Assembly: The Autobiography of a Musical Storyteller.* New York: Viking, 1991.

Schuller, Gunther. *Early Jazz: Its Roots and Musical Development.* New York: Oxford University Press, 1968.

Sehgal, Kabir. *Jazzocracy: Jazz, Democracy, and the Creation of a New American Mythology.* Advance reading copy. Mishawaka, IN: Better World Books, 2008.

Shen, Sin Y. *Chinese Music and Orchestration: A Primer on Principles and Practice.* Chicago: Chinese Music Society of North America, 2005.

Smith, Whitey, and C. L. McDermott. *I Didn't Make a Million.* 2nd ed. Manilla, Philippines: McCullough, 1961.

Sven, Eric, and Larry Doran. *Whitey in Shanghai.* Manila, Philippines: JMC Press, 1996.

Talbott, Strobe. *The Great Experiment: The Story of Ancient Empires, Modern States, and the Quest for a Global Nation.* New York: Simon & Schuster, 2008.

Taylor, Billy. *Jazz Piano: A Jazz History.* New York: William C. Brown, 1982.

Tschmuck, Peter. *Creativity and Innovation in the Music Industry.* Dordrecht: Springer, 2006.

Williams, Charles A. S. *Chinese Symbolism and Art Motifs: A Comprehensive Handbook on Symbolism in Chinese Art Through the Ages.* Revised ed. Tokyo: Tuttle Publishing, 2006.

Xun, Lu. *The True Story of Ah Q.* Translated by Yang Xianyi and Gladys Yang. Hong Kong: Chinese Press of Hong Kong, 2002.

ARTICLES

Atkins, Taylor E. "Jammin' on the Jazz Frontier: The Japanese Jazz Community in Interwar Shanghai." *Japanese Studies* 9, no. 1 (1999): 6.

Charles, Mario A. "The Age of a Jazzwoman: Valaida Snow, 1900–1956." *Journal of Negro History* 80, no. 4 (Autumn 1995): 183–91.

Chaoguang, Wang. "American Films in Chinese Reviews." *American Studies in China* 2 (1996).

Chou, Eva Shan. "A Story about Hair: A Curious Mirror of Lu Xun's Pre-Republican Days." *Journal of Asian Studies* 66, no. 2 (2007): 421–59.

Cox, Gordon. Review of *School music education and social change*, by Wai-Chung Ho. *Music Education Research* 14, no. 3 (September 2012): 403–5.

Fang, Xie, and Li Luxia. "Historic dance hall steps lightly into 21st century." *China Daily*, May 11, 2006.

Fordham, John. "Obituaries: Oleg Lundstrem, Russian band leader whose passion for jazz took off in Shanghai and survived Stalin." *The Guardian*, October 28, 2005.

Hashim, Michael. "Michael Hashim's Jazz from New York to China." *Saxophone Journal* (July/August 1994).

Huang, Hao. "Why Chinese people play Western classical music: Transcultural roots of music philosophy." *International Journal of Music Education* 30, no. 2 (May 12, 2012): 2.

Kahn, Joseph, and Daniel J. Wakin. "Classical Music Looks Toward China with Hope." *New York Times*, April 3, 2007.

Marlow, Eugene. Review of *Jazz Journeys to Japan*, by William Minor. *JazzNotes: The Journal of the Jazz Journalists Association* (December 2004): 16–17.

Moser, David. "The Book of Changes." *Jazz Now* (May 1996): 8.

Moser, David. "The Book of Changes." *Jazz Now* (Spring 1997): 19.

Reimer, Bennett. "Music Education in China: An Overview and Some Issues." *Journal of Aesthetic Education* 23, no. 1 (Spring 1989).

Reitz, Rosetta. "Hot Snow: Valaida Snow (Queen of the Trumpet Sings and Swings)." *Black American Literature Forum* 16, no. 4 (Winter 1982): 158–60.

Tornquist, Lina, and Poppy Toland. "The Best Jazz Club in Beijing." *Time,* February 29, 2008.

"Wharton Panel Hears 'Jazz' in China Economy." *Plexus News* (Allentown, NJ), June 9, 2005.

Yu, Hui. "Chinese Program Breaks Down Walls." *DownBeat*, November 2012.

Zhang, Weihua. "Notes on the Current Jazz Scene in China." *Journal of Music in China* 2, no. 2 (October 2000): 265–66.

Zinsser, William. "Shanghai Blues." *New Yorker*, September 21, 1981.

ONLINE

"Airlines to China." *Skyscanner.com*. Accessed May 1, 2017. http://www.skyscanner.com/flightsto/cn/airlines-that-fly-to-china.html.

Alexander, Scott. "The First Jazz Records." *Red Hot Jazz Archives*. Accessed May 1, 2017. http://www.redhotjazz.com/jazz1917.html.

"Amateur Performers." *Embassy of the United States*. http://beijing.usembassy-china.org.cn/amateur_performers.html.

"Band Profile." *Cigar Jazz Wine*. Accessed May 1, 2017. http://www.cjwchina.com/ensh/info.aspx?m=20091126165919090683.

"Basic Data." *China Internet Network Information Center.* Accessed May 1, 2017. http://cnnic .com.cn/IDR/BasicData/.

http://www.bbc.co.uk/london/content/articles/2006/10/09/orchestra_feature.shtml.

"Beijing International JazzFestival '94–'99." Accessed May 1, 2017. http://home.t-online.de/ home/xtend.ww/jzww_ge.htm.

"Beijing Jazzfestival 1995." *AvantArt.* Accessed May 1, 2017. www.avantart.com/personal/ avantart-cis/peking95.htm.

Bellis, Mary. "The Evolution of Modern Aircraft." *About.com.* Accessed May 1, 2017. http:// inventors.about.com/library/inventors/bljetengine.htm.

Branigan, Tania. "China's Great Famine: the true story." *The Guardian,* January 1, 2013. http:// www.theguardian.com/world/2013/jan/01/china-great-famine-book-tombstone.

Broadcasting Board of Governors. "VOA Marks 70th Year of US Broadcasts to China." News release, December 27, 2011. http://www.bbg.gov/press-release/voa-marks-70th -year-of-us-broadcasts-tochina/.

Bruce, Lucille. "Willie Ruff retires having given 'conservatory without walls' a home at Yale." Yale School of Music, May 1, 2017. http://music.yale.edu/2017/05/01/willie-ruff-retires -given-conservatory-without-walls-home-yale/.

http://www.bso.org/brands/bso/features/2013-14-bso-season/bso-tours-china-and-japan.aspx.

Chen, Vivian. "Shanghai Knights." *South China Morning Post,* July 19, 2012. http://www.scmp .com/article/705967/shanghai-knights.

Chilton, Martin. "Blue Note to Open Jazz Club in China." *Telegraph,* July 4, 2015. http://www .telegraph.co.uk/culture/music/worldfolkandjazz/11716649/Blue-Note-to-open-jazz-clubin -China.html.

"China Holds First Guitar Festival." *Modern Guitars Magazine.* Last modified August 23, 2005. http://www.moderngtuitars.com/archives/001066.html.

"China." *ETC NewMedia TrendWatch.* Last modified April 30, 2013. http://www.newmedia trendwatch.com/markets-by-country/11-long-haul/49-china.

"Chinese Jazz exports heads for Europe." Last modified June 24, 2005. www.motoring.co.za/ index.php?fArticleId=259857&fSectionId=753&fSetId=381.

"The Chinese Media: More Autonomous and Diverse—Within Limits." *Central Intelligence Agency.* Last updated July 7, 2008. https://www.cia.gov/library/center-for-the-study-of -intelligence/csi-publications/books-and-monographs/the-chinese-media-more-autono mous-and-diverse-within-limits/copy_of_1.htm.

http://www.cjwchina.com/ensh/info.aspx?m=20091126165607623665.

http://www.cjwchina.com/ensh/info.aspx?m=20091126165919090683.

http://www.cjwchina.com/ensh/info.aspx?m=20091126165607623665.

Cooper, Michael. "New Musical Partnership in China." *Arts Beat* (blog), November 23, 2013. http://artsbeat.blogs.nytimes.com/2013/11/23/new-musical-partnership-in-china?/_r=0

Cotton Club. "Customer Newsletter." *Cotton Club.* February 2012. http://www.thecottonclub .cn/newsletter/newsletter.pdf.

Coughlan, John. "Best jazz bars in Shanghai." *CNN Travel.* October 12, 2011. http://travel.cnn .com/shanghai/drink/city-essentials/best-jazz-bars-shanghai-680850.

"Cui Jian on AllMusic." *AllMusic*. Accessed May 1, 2017. http://www.allmusic.com/artist/cui-jian-mn0000139728.

"DHL China." *DHL*. http://www.cn.dhl.com/en/about_us/dhl_china.html.

Diamond, Larry. "A Report Card on Democracy." (Report, Hoover Institution, Stanford University.) http://www.hoover.org/publications/hoover-digest/article/7310.

"Fear of a Blank Planet." *Fear of a Blank Planet*. Accessed May 1, 2017. http://www.fearofablankplanet.com/artists/jazz/jazz_fusion/hongwei_kong_jin_fo_summer_palace_jin_fo_his_friends.html.

"FedEx Timeline." *FedEx*. http://about.van.fedex.com/article/fedex-timeline.

"Filipino Music Trivia." *HIMIG: The Filipino Music Collection of FHL*. Accessed May 1, 2017. http://www.himig.com.ph/features/20-filipino-music-trivia.

"Film Industry in China." *China.org*. Accessed May 1, 2017. http://www.china.org.cn/english/features/film/84966.htm.

"5 Chinese Pianist Heroes." *JZClub China*. Last modified January 1, 2013. http://www.jzclub.cn/en/concert/5-chinese-pianist-heroes.

"The 4th Beijing Ninegates Jazz Week 2009—Opening Concert." *City Weekend China*. Accessed May 1, 2017. http://www.cityweekend.com.cn/beijing/events/44837/.

Gardels, Nathan. "These Charts Show How China's Economy Is Changing Amid Labor Unrest." *Huffington Post*, April 27, 2016. http://www.huffingtonpost.com/nathangardels/charts-china-economy-labor-unrest_b_9778790.html.

"Golden Buddha Jazz Unit." *Music-China Wiki*. Accessed May 1, 2017. http://www.rockinchina.com/w/Golden_Buddha_Jazz_Unit.

"Golden Buddha." *Last.fm*. Accessed May 1, 2017. http://www.last.fm/music/Golden Buddha.

Grier, Peter. "Global Spread of Democracy Stalled." *Christian Science Monitor*, November 21, 2007. www.csmonitor.com/2007/1121/p01s02-usgn.html?page=1.

"Growth in United Nations membership, 1945-present." *Member States*. www.un.org/members/growth.shtml.

Hall, Case. "The right notes." *Enterprise CHINA*, June 2011. http://enterprisechina.net/node/28.

Hall, Mike. "Music Bio." *humblemusic.com*. Accessed May 1, 2017. http://www.humblemusic.com/bio.html.

Harris, Craig. "Liu Sola—biography." *AllMusic*. Accessed May 1, 2017. http://www.allmusic.com/artist/liu-sola-p126823/biography.

Hays, Jeffrey. "Western Classical Music in China." *Facts and Details*. Last modified January 2014. http://factsanddetails.com/china/cat7/sub41/item250.html.

Holden, Kevin. "Modern day jazz resurgence draws on bygone eras." *China Daily*, December 5, 2005. www.chinadaily.com/cn/english/doc/2005-12/05/content_500283.htm.

Holden, Steven. Review of *Temptress Moon*, by Chen Kaige. *New York Times*, October 5, 1996. http://movies.nytimes.com/movie/review?res=9D02E5D8133FF936A35753C1A96095820.

"Hongwei Kong (Jin Fo)—Summer Palace." *NoNaMe*. Accessed May 1, 2017. http://nnm.ru/blogs/myway58/hongwei_kong_jin_fo_summer_palace/.

Hoo, Winyan S. "Sasha Gong, 1st Asian American VOA Branch Chief." *Asianfortunenews*. Last modified September 13, 2012. http://www.asianfortunenews.com/article_0312.php?article_id=26.

"House of Blues & Jazz." *Tripadvisor*. Accessed May 1, 2017. http://www.tripadvisor.com/Res taurant_Review-g308272-d1886283-Reviews-House_of_Blues_Jazz-Shanghai.html.

Iglauer, Bruce. "Effects of international piracy on American independent record labels." *Jazz News,* May 31, 2005. http://home.nestor.minsk.by/jazz/articles/2005/05/0037.html.

"International Programs." *United States Census Bureau,* August 15, 2008. http://www.census .gov/ipc/www/popclockworld.html.

"Internet World Stats." *Internet World Stats*. Last updated February 17, 2013. http://www.inter-networldstats.com.

King, Martin Luther Jr. "On the Importance of Jazz" (speech, Berlin 1964). 1964 Berlin Jazz Festival. http://www.hartford-hwp.com/archives/45a/626.html.

"Jazz Meets Rock." *Alec Haavik*. Accessed on May 1, 2017. http://www.alechaavik.com/bio.php ?PHPSESSID=4437b92a59165f01c2e61083b4ae3928.

Kennedy, Anthony, US Supreme Court Justice. "Speech at McCloskey Speaker Series, The Aspen Institute." Aspen, CO, August 4, 2008.

Koerner, Brendan I. "Piano Demon, The Imperial Circuit." *Atavist*, January 12, 2011. http:// magazine.atavist.com/piano-demon.

Lammers, David. "Jazz signs up second Shanghai partner." *EETimes*, October 27, 2003. http:// www.eet.com/news/design/silicon/showArticle.jhtml?articleId=17408713&kc=635.

Laskowski, Christine. "Pioneering Saxophonist, 50, Still Hitting the Right Note." *China Daily*, March 29, 2010. http://www.chinadaily.com.cn/life/2010-03/29/content_9655355.htm.

Lau, Hannah. Review of *As Time Goes by in Shanghai*, Flying Moon Filmproduktion/Berlin. *ChinaSource*, February 10, 2017. http://www.chinasource.org/blog/posts/as-time-goes -by-in-shanghai.

Leck, Greg. "The Japanese Internment of Allied Civilians in China and Hong Kong, 1941–1945." *Captives of Empire*. Accessed May 1, 2017. http://www.captives-of-empire.com/wst_page5.php.

"Legend of the Sassoons." *Shanghai Star*, May 10, 2001. http://www.china.org.cn/english/ LIe/12461.htm.

Li, Xiao. "Film Industry in China." *China.org*. Last modified January 17, 2004. http://www.china .org.cn/english/features/film/84966.htm.

Li, Yang, and Xuan Liu. "Texan vows to continue last stand." *Global Times*, September 3, 2009. http://www.globaltimes.cn/china/society/2009-09/463569_2.html.

Lim, Louisa. "Survivors of Shanghai's Jazz Age Play Anew." *NPR Music*, September 24, 2007. http://www.npr.org/templates/story/story.php?storyId=14655091.

"Liu Yuan Jazz Quartet." *Cityweekend: Beijing*. Last modified January 23, 2011. http://www .cityweekend.com.cn/beijing/events/81024/.

Lyman, Jenn Chan. "You Ready to Get Jazzed?" *Jenn Chan Lyman*. Accessed May 1, 2017. http:// www.jennchanlyman.com/mag_jazzedSep09.html.

"Major manufacturers of civil transport aircraft." *AviationKnowledge*. Last modified March 23, 2010. http://aviationknowledge.wikidot.com/aviation:manufacturers.

"Maria Schneider wins four jazz awards in N.Y." *China Post*, June 17, 2005. http://www.china post.com.tw/art/.

McMahon, Eliot. "London's Top 5 Jazz Clubs." *Jazz Club Jury*. Last modified July 7, 2012. http:// jazzclubjury.com/jazz-journal/londons-top-5-jazz-clubs/.

"Military Band of the Chinese People's Liberation Army." *China Culture*. Accessed May 1, 2017. http://www1.chinaculture.or/library/2008-02/18/content_40379.htm.

"National Endowment for the Arts Jazz Masters: 1991 NEA Jazz Master Wilbur 'Buck' Clayton." *National Endowment for the Arts*. Accessed May 1, 2013. http://www.nea.gov/honors/jazz/jmCMS/master.php?id=1991_02&type=bio.

"Not Music for Old Men." *China Daily Entertainment News*, September 3, 2012. http://english.sina.com/entertainment/p/2012/0903/502680.html.

www.nyiaa.org/html/iframe_govboardsub.html.

"Obituaries Garden City Life: Douglas Sebastian Monitto." *Garden City Life*, February 2, 2001. http://www.antonnews.com/gardencitylife/2001/02/02/obituaries/.

Pacey, Philip. "Music and Railways." *Philpacey.co.uk*. Last modified April 18, 2013. http://www.philpacey.co.uk/musrail.html.

Pickford, Mary. "The Early History of Motion Pictures." *PBS.org*. Last updated July 23, 2004. http://www.pbs.org/wgbh/amex/pickford/peopleevents/e_silents.html.

"Ping Gao." *Naxos.com*. Accessed May 1, 2017. http://www.naxos.com/person/Ping_Gao_18813/18813.htm.

Ping, Wang. "Sunset Happiness." *cctv.com*. Accessed May 1, 2017, http://www.cctv.com/program/rediscoveringchina/20060714/103515.shtml

"Programme, International Jazz Festival, Beijing, China, November 10–16, 1996." *China Today*. Accessed May 1, 2017. http://www.chinatoday.com/art/jazz/a.html.

Rea, Dennis, "The Land Tour and the Rise of Jazz in China." *Speakeasy.org*. Accessed May 1, 2017. http://www.speakeasy.org/~nunatak/chinatour.html.

Rivette, Sarah M. "U.S., Chinese bands perform together in historic concert." *US ARMY*, news release. http://www.army.mil/article/56625/.

Robinson, Tim. "London's Thames Estuary airport plans—déjà-vu all over again." *Royal Aeronautical Society*. Last modified July 9, 2012. http://media.aerosociety.com/aerospace-insight/2012/09/07/londons-thames-airport-plans-deja-vu-all-over-again/7288/.

Roozekrans, Joost. "JZ Music Festival, Shanghai." *Behance*, January 20, 2013. http://www.behance.net/gallery/JZ-Music-Festival-Shanghai/6574143.

Rosenberg, Matt. "Current World Population." *About.com*. Last modified July 11, 2012. http://geography.about.com/od/obtainpopulationdata/a/worldpopulation.htm.

Rye, Howard. "Teddy Weatherford." *American National Biography*. Accessed May 1, 2017. http://www.anb.org/articles/18/1803780-print.html.

"Sales volume of television sets in China from 2011–2015 (in million units)." *Statista*. Accessed May 1, 2017. http://www.statista.com/statistics/468944/china-television-set-sales-volume/.

Scott, Jess C. "Asian, Oriental Dragons." *Dragons Inn*. Last modified January 2012. http://dragonsinn.net/east-2.htm.

"Sean Higgins Music." *Sean Higgins Music*. http://www.seanhiggins.net/.

Select Comm. of the United States House of Representatives. "Chapter 10: Manufacturing Processes." In *U.S. National Security and Military/Commercial Concerns with the People's Republic of China*. US House of Representatives. Accessed May 1, 2017. http://www.house.gov/coxreport/body/ch10bod.html.

"Serge Ermoll." *Australian Jazz Real Book*, accessed May 1, 2017, Australianjazzrealbook.com/artists/serge-ermol.

Shanghaijournal.squarespace.com/journal/2007/5/28/strange-cities-a-multimedia.

Shanshan, Wang. "US jazz culture symbol faces demolition." *China Daily*, August 5, 2006. http://www.chinadaily.com.cn/china/2006-08/05/content_657762.htm.

Shapiro, Dan. "JZ International Music Festival 2010: Jazz to be 'signature of Shanghai.'" *CNN Travel*, October 11, 2010. http://travel.cnn.com/shanghai/play/shanghai-jazz-jz-festival-788923.

Shi, Joshua. "Jazzin It Up and Down." *Shanghai Star*, March 29, 2001. http://App1.chinadaily.com.cn/star/2001/0329/cu18-2.html.

"Sinotrans Group." *Sinotrans&CSC Holdings Co., LTD.* Accessed May 1, 2017. http://www.sinotransone.com/Sinotransgroup.html.

Staff. "Stellex Industries Completes Acquisition of Monitor Aerospace Corporation." News release, June 3, 1998. http://aviationweek.com/awin/stellex-completes-acquisition-monitoraerospace.

Stone, Mark. "China Film Market Set to Take Over Hollywood: The film industry is thriving despite the limitations of censorship, and here are predictions it may overtake Hollywood." *SkyNews*, February 15, 2013. http://news.sky.com/story/china-film-market-set-to-take-over-hollywood-10454423.

Taylor, Nick. "JZ Festival: Full Line-up and Details." *Smart Shanghai.com*, September 24, 2012. http://www.smartshanghai.com/wire/nightlife/jz-festival-full-line-up-and-details.

"Teach, Study, Intern and Volunteer Abroad." *Global Education Corporation.* Accessed May 1, 2017. http://www.globalcorp.com/music_shanghai.php.

"Testimonial from Yinjiao Du." *Aizen.* Accessed May 1, 2017. http://www.sax.co.jp/eaizen43.html.

"Theo Croker—Trumpet Player/Composer." *JZ Club CHINA.* Accessed May 1, 2017. http://www.jzclub.cn/en/musician/theo-croker-2.

"UPS China Fact Sheet." *UPS.* Accessed May 1, 2017. http://www.pressroom.ups.com/Fact+Sheets/UPS+China+Fact+Sheet.

"US Performers in China." *Embassy of the United States.* Accessed May 1, 2017. http://beijing.usembassy-china.org.cn/china_performers.html.

Vaughton, George. "Chaoyang Paradiso." *Beijing Scene* 7, issue 11 (March 31–April 6, 2000). http://www.beijingscene.com/v07i11/feature.html.

"Waiting for Jazz, das Jazzfestival in Beijing." *AvantArt.* Accessed May 1, 2017. http://www.avantart.com/personal/avantart-cis/peking94.htm.

Wellner, Alison, "A Shanghai Art Deco Landmark Reopens," Luxist, July 29, 2010, www.luxist.com/2010/07/29/a-shanghai-art-deco-landmark-reopens/print/.

Wilford, John N. "Flutes Offer Clues to Stone-Age Music." *New York Times*, June 24, 2009. http://www.nytimes.com/2009/06/25/science/25flute.html?_r=0.

"Wilson Chen," *Legere Reeds LTD.* Accessed May 1, 2017. http://www.legere.com/artists/wilsonchen-%E9%99%88%E5%98%89%E4%BF%8A.

"Women in History—Valaida Snow." *Women in History.* Last modified February 25, 2013. http://www.lkwdpl.org/wihohio/snow-val.htm.

Woodard, Josef. "East-West Jazz Link: Chinese reed player, visiting UCSB, will perform with the campus band." *Los Angeles Times*, SOUNDS: Special to the *Times*, April 16, 1998. http://articles.latimes.com/1998/apr/16/entertainment/ca-39687.

Yu, Roger. "Chinese travelers are seeing the USA in record numbers." *USA Today Travel*, February 2, 2012. http://travel.usatoday.com/flights/story/2012-01-31/Chinese-travelers -are-seeing-the-USA-in-record-numbers/52905866/1.

CDS

Baiyong, Xiao. *Selected Masterpieces from Chinese Traditional Music*, by the Shanghai National Music Orchestra. 1998.

Guanren, Gu, and Qu Chunquan. *Selected Masterpieces from Chinese Traditional Music—Pipa solo album*, by the Shanghai National Music Orchestra. 1998.

Various. *Classical Chinese Folk Music*. Arc Music Productions, 1999.

Various. *Phases of the Moon: Traditional Chinese Music*. China Record Company, CBS Records, 1981.

INDEX

A Bu, 238

Adam (Huang Yong), 157–58

Adams, Wayne, 69, 73

Africa, 11, 12

African American Jazz Musicians in the Diaspora, 48–49

African Americans, 48–49, 99

Afterlife of Li Jiantong, The, 126

Ah Q Band, 86, 153, 159, 161, 162

ALAS, 160, 172

Americans, 10, 14, 18, 19, 21, 25, 43, 48, 63, 99, 105, 106, 114, 116, 124, 159, 196

"anti-Yellow music," 19

Apollo Theatre, 52

Armstrong, Louis, 19, 36, 49–52, 54, 72, 95, 113, 204

Atkins, E. Taylor, 76, 77

Attali, Jacques, 227

ballrooms, 45, 59, 62, 65, 73, 185–86. *See also* dance halls

Basie, William James "Count," 35, 49, 52, 72, 206

Bauer, R. H., 36

Becker, Rolf, 26, 182, 208–9, 218

Beijing, 3, 4, 12, 18, 25, 26, 32, 77, 78, 82, 83, 85, 88, 89, 90, 92, 97, 98, 102, 105–10, 113–15, 118–24, 126, 127, 132, 136–38, 183, 187, 191, 192, 196, 198, 200–202, 206–9, 211–17, 219, 220, 229, 232–39

Beijing International Jazz Festival, xvii, 136–41, 168, 232, 233, 239

Berliner, Emile, 24, 25

Big Easy, 146–51

Blue Funnel Legend: A History of the Ocean Steam Ship Company, 1865–1973, The, 22

blues, 9, 90, 127–28, 131, 185, 206, 229, 238

Bolden, Buddy, 19

Borromeo, Luis, 40

Boston Symphony Orchestra, 84–85

Britain, 15–18, 22, 28, 33, 75, 96, 228

Brown's, 153, 169

Bruce, James (Earl of Elgin), 18

Buck Clayton's Jazz World, 68, 221

Buck Clayton's Orchestra, 42

Call to Assembly: The Autobiography of a Musical Storyteller, A, 102

Canton, 15, 17, 60

Cantonese jazz bands, 59–61

Cao Ziping, 190

Carmichael, Judy, 107, 113–16

Carter, Jack, 50, 52

CD Café, 86, 142–44, 146, 167

central authority, 3, 30, 82, 87, 169

Central Committee of the Communist Party, 83–85

Central Conservatory of Music, 84, 125, 144, 160, 232

Chen, Wilson, 199–200

Chen Tu-hsui, xiv

Chen Xihe, ix, 224

Chiang Kai-Shek, 18, 30, 43, 52

China: A New History, xii, 3

Chinese Communist Party (CCP), xi, xii, xvi, 20, 81, 84, 145, 167, 177, 224

Chinese culture, xix, 5–9, 101, 107, 160, 167, 177

Chinese Jazz Association (CJA), 237

Chinese language, xiv, 93, 107

Chinese Music and Orchestration: A Primer on Principles and Practice, 6

Cixi, 16

CJW, 183

classical Chinese music, 6–9

classical music education, 211–13

Clayton, Buck, 11, 23, 25, 36, 43, 49, 50, 54–57, 68–72, 75, 221

Coco (Ke Coco Zhao), 194–96, 206, 213

Coker, Theo, 204

Communists, 20, 28, 30, 33, 64, 113, 127, 131, 227

community, xii–xiv, 4, 60, 76, 102, 107

community vs. individualism, xiii

Confucian beliefs, 210

Conover, Willis, 94, 95

Copland, Aaron, 34, 85

Cotton Club (New York), 49, 72

Cotton Club (Shanghai), 86, 105, 150, 181, 183–84, 195, 206

Cox, Gordon, 210, 211

"Cox Report on Chinese Espionage," 147, 148

Creationists, xiii

Cui Jian, 85, 86, 109, 122, 123, 144, 160, 181, 234

cultural dislocation, 29–31

Cultural Revolution, xiii, 8, 24, 83–84, 114, 115, 143, 210

Dai Liang, 141, 161

dance halls, 14, 19, 20, 39–41, 58–62, 64, 65–66, 185–86. See also individual dance halls

Danko, Harold, 158, 159, 213

Davis, Russ, 95

"Daybreak Express," 24

democracy, vii, xi, xiii, 94, 99–101, 134, 228–29

Deng Xiaoping, 83, 84, 87, 213

DiCioccio, Justin, 219–21

Dikötter, Frank, 24, 25, 30

Dila, Apolo, 40, 41, 103

Dong, Stella, xiii, 33, 35, 58

DownBeat, 95, 159, 200, 221

dragons, 5

Du, Yinjiao, 167–69

Dutch, the, 16, 70

Dutch East Indies, 50, 67

Earl Whaley band, 69–75

Early Jazz: Its Roots and Musical Development, 11

East India Company, 16

East Shore Café, 78, 43–46, 160, 171

economics, 12, 13, 85, 96, 208, 224–28

Edison, Thomas Alva, 24, 25, 27

electronic media, 91–93

Ellington, Duke, 42, 49, 95, 168

Ermolaeff, Sergei, 42–43

Europe, 11

Europe, James Reese, 34, 49

Europeans, 10, 14, 17–19, 21, 42, 63, 189

expats, 120, 150–54, 170, 172, 187, 293, 233

"Express Train," 23, 23, 57

Fairbank, John King, xii, 81, 82

Falkus, Malcolm, 22

Falla, Manuel de, 34

family, xii, xiii, xiv, xvii, 3–5, 7, 9–10, 24, 25, 40, 42, 44, 50, 51, 59, 62, 71, 72, 82, 82, 103, 150, 180

Fan Shengqi, 155–57

Fantasy of the Red Queen, 126

farmers, 10, 25, 30, 49

Field, Andrew David, 58, 72, 179, 185

filial piety, xiii

Filipino bands, 40–41, 59, 62

Filipinos, 11, 21, 40, 42, 58, 67, 68

film, xi, xii, xiii, xvii, xxii, 19–21, 26–29, 61, 77, 84, 91, 110, 126, 128, 190

Film in Contemporary China, ix

film industry, xii, 28, 29

Fleischer, Martin, 26, 106, 118–25, 136, 234

Flay, Chris, 113

folk music/folk songs, xiv, 6–10, 25, 37, 57, 101, 111, 112, 122–25, 128, 160, 169, 176, 237. See also traditional Chinese music

freedom of expression, xii, 3, 4, 31, 81–90, 100, 112, 168, 177, 227–29

French, the, 14, 16–19, 27, 50, 53, 55, 227

From Mao to Mozart: Isaac Stern in China, 84

Gao Ping, 88–91, 233
Gentlemen of Harlem, 35
George III (king of England), 15
Germans, xvi, 19, 25, 52, 118
globalism, vii, 11
Golden Horn Jazz Band, 168
Goldman, Merle, xii
Goldsby, John, 73
Gong, Sasha, 95
gramophone, 19–21, 23–26, 29, 91, 96
Great Experiment: The Story of Ancient Em-
    pires, Modern States, and the Quest for a
    Global Nation, The, 225
Gu, Chao, 236

Haavik, Alec, 204–5, 218
Hanes, W. Travis, III, 14, 17
Hardy, William C., 25
Harpsichord Concerto (Falla), 34
Hashim, Michael, 13
He Da, 58
Heil, Alan, 94
Henderson, Fletcher, 36, 48, 52
Hershey, Burnet, 34–37 117
Higgins, Rusty, 200
Higgins, Sean, 203–4
Histoire du Soldat, 34
Hitchcock, Peter, viii, ix
Ho, Wai-Chung, 210, 211
Hoffman, Udo, 26, 85, 110, 134, 136, 137, 168
Holmquist, Mats, 182
Hong Kong, 17, 18, 22, 41, 51, 65, 67, 119, 192,
    195, 213
hotels, 39, 115, 121, 153–54, 164, 167, 170, 171,
    179–81, 198, 201, 204
House of Blues and Jazz, 184–85
Hsu Chimo, xiii
Hua Guofeng, 83
Huang Feiran Band, 64–65
Hu Dong Fung, 206
Hui Yu, 221
Hughes, Langston, 50
Hurst, Mary Ann, 107–10, 155, 233

Ice House, 51–52, 160, 164
I Didn't Make a Million, 25, 43
improvisation, xiv, xv, 3, 6, 11, 31, 89, 103, 110,
    112, 115, 126, 128, 137, 157, 159, 161, 166, 169,
    170, 172, 193, 201, 216, 217, 222, 228, 230,
    233, 238
India, 8, 15, 16, 28, 34, 36, 51, 177, 180, 226
individual, the, xii, xiii, xiv, 3–5, 90
individualism, xii, xiii, xiv, 101, 169
individualistic music, 133–35
International Association for Jazz Education
    (IAJE), xviii
Internet, viii, xii, xiii, 72, 91, 93–95, 101, 163,
    198, 207, 213, 217
Izumi Koga, 78, 170–71

Jack Carter Orchestra, 52
Japan, 8, 23, 30, 34, 47, 59, 64, 109, 117, 135,
    138–41, 218, 224, 228. See also Japanese, the
Japanese, the, 4, 11, 12, 18, 19, 23, 43, 46, 48,
    55, 56, 63, 66–78, 93, 109, 170–71, 179, 188,
    190, 221, 233, 235. See also Japan
Jazz America, 94, 95
Jazz at Lincoln Center (JALC), 146, 204,
    234–35
Jazz Bass Book: Techniques and Traditions, 73
jazz clubs, 83, 86, 119, 121, 136, 142, 146, 151,
    172, 181, 184, 195, 198, 200, 201, 203, 233,
    235, 243, 247. See also individual clubs
jazz education, 162–64, 173, 174, 197, 202, 207,
    210–23, 232, 235
jazz festivals, 129, 140, 162, 195, 239
Jazz Journeys to Japan: The Heart Within,
    76, 77, 170
Jazzocracy: Jazz, Democracy, and the Cre-
    ation of a New American Mythology, 101,
    228, 239
Jazz Planet, 77
jazz radio, 236–37
Jenks, Darrell, 172–74
Jiemei Jin Band, 61, 62, 64, 65
Jimmy King Band, 36, 57, 62, 63, 88
Jin Huaizu, 61, 62. See also King, Jimmy

Jin Jiemei, 61, 62, 64, 65
jixing, xiv. *See also* improvisation
Jones, Andrew F., 23, 58
Jones, Reginald "Jonesy," 53, 68, 69, 71–75
journalism, xi
jueshi yinyue, 32
JZ Club, 86, 105, 184, 185, 191, 192, 194, 198–201, 204, 206–9, 213, 218, 222, 235
JZ Club School, 213, 218, 222
JZ Jazz Festival, 182

Kaixuan Band, 64–65
King, Jimmy, 62, 64, 190. *See also* Jimmy King Band
King, Martin Luther, Jr., 229
Koerner, Brendan I., 52
Kong Hong Wei, 86, 145, 157, 160–61, 171, 172, 175
Ku, Lawrence, 192–94, 206
Kuomintang (KMT), 52

La Création du Monde, 34
Ladow, Louis, 44, 45
Lerner, Murray, 84
Li Gao Yang, 238
Li Jinhui, 23, 24, 51
Li Lanquing, 9
Liu "Kenny" Xiaoguang, 86, 161–62
Liu Sola, 126–35, 139
Liu Yuan, 85, 86, 106, 118, 122–25, 136, 139, 142
Live at the Forbidden City, 89
locomotives, 20, 21, 23–24, 91, 96. *See also* railroads
Lu, Joey, 200–203
Lu Hsun, xiii
Lu Xun, 176, 197
Lundstrem, Oleg, 42

Macartney, Lord George, 15, 16
Made in China, 161
Manchuria, 23, 56, 66, 67
Mao Zedong, 4, 20, 40, 32, 57, 87
McLuhan, Marshall, 27, 92, 226

media, the, xi, 229
Megatrends, 91
Midi School, 41, 150, 169, 170, 173, 192, 207, 213, 215–18, 222, 239
Milhaud, Darius, 34
Ming Fong, 219
Minor, William, 76, 170
Mitchell, Dwike, 102–5
Mitchell-Ruff Duo, 102
Modern Jazz Improvisation for Piano, 161
Modern School of Music, 164
Monitto, Douglas, 147–50
Monitto, Mary, 146, 147, 149, 150
Morrison, Phil, xix
Morse, Samuel Finley Breese, 92
Morton, Jelly Roll, 19
Moser, David, 21, 105, 143, 144, 168, 169, 213, 229
Mu, Fangzhou, 236

Naisbitt, John, 92
nationalism, 19
Nationalists, 28, 30, 82, 179
nature, 9–10
New Orleans, 12, 31, 36, 37, 48, 51, 72, 141, 146, 147, 213, 150, 151, 195
night clubs, xix, 32, 45, 46, 53, 70, 142
"Nighttime in Old Shanghai," 25
Nine Gates Jazz Festival, 141–42, 157, 200, 238, 239
Ningbo, 17, 97, 209, 213
Ningbo University, 213, 221–22
Noise: The Political Economy of Music, 227

Oleg Lundstrem Orchestra, 42
Oliver, King, 19
opium, 15–18, 33, 52, 180
Opium Wars, 10, 13–20, 33, 101, 118
Orto, Christianne, 219
Ory, Kid, 19
Ouellete, Dan, 168, 169

Pace, Harry, 25
Pan, Lynn, 14

Paramount Ballroom, 43, 57, 185–86
Peace Hotel, xv, xvi, xix, 85, 88, 127, 181, 188
Peace Hotel Jazz Bar, xi, 64, 86, 88, 107, 120, 136, 156, 179–81, 187, 189, 190, 191, 195, 203
Peking, xiv, 15, 18, 25, 32, 85, 134, 136. *See also* Beijing
Peking Man, 3
Peña, Angel, 41
People's Republic of China (PRC), 19, 23, 30, 83, 148, 168
Pfleumer, Fritz, 26
Piano Demon, 52
planes, 77, 96–98, 115
Pollard, David, 176, 177
Power, Desmond, 69, 75
Pu Yi, Emperor, 19

Qianlong, Emperor, 15
Qing dynasty, 5, 19, 30, 143, 177
Quirino, Carlos, 40
Quirino, Richie C., 40
Qui Zongliang, 58

racism, 38, 43, 48, 49, 87
radio, xi, xv, 18, 24–37, 36, 40, 41, 47, 48, 77, 90–94, 110, 148, 161–63, 168, 188, 189, 195, 202, 205–7, 214, 228, 231, 236–37
railroads, 23. *See also* locomotives
Rea, Dennis, 87, 89, 91, 106, 107, 110–12, 136, 233
Reimer, Bennett, 210
Reitz, Rosetta, 52
Ren Yuqing, 86, 181, 191, 206, 218
Roberts, Matt, 86, 106, 153, 158, 161, 171–78
Ross, Larry, 48
Ruff, Willie, xviii, 85, 87, 102–5, 107, 136
Russians, 10, 11, 14, 18, 19, 21, 42

Sanello, Frank, 14, 17
San Wei Bookstore, 142–43
Sassoon, Victor, 40, 180
Schenkel, Thalia, viii
Schoenberg, Arnold, 11, 124

School music education and social change in Mainland China, Hong Kong, and Taiwan, 210
Schuller, Gunther, 11, 126
Sehgal, Kabir, 100, 228, 239
Shang dynasty, 5
Shanghai, 1892–1949, 35
Shanghai: A Century of Change in Photographs, 14
Shanghai Conservatory of Music, 63, 84, 85, 136, 184, 195, 199–202, 207, 213, 219–22
Shanghai's Dancing World: Cabaret Culture and Urban Politics 1919–1954, 58, 73, 179, 185
sheet music, 19, 21, 63, 120, 167, 189
Shen, Sin Yan, 6
Shi, Joshua, 62
Shigeya Kikuchi, 76
Shuōwen Jiězi, 5
Smith, Helen, 47, 48
Smith, Tom, 209, 221, 222
Smith, Whitey, 43–45
Snow, Valaida, 11, 35, 43, 49, 51–53
Soviet Union, 12, 42, 95, 102, 229
steamships, 19, 21–22, 25, 29, 170
Stern, Isaac, 84
Stravinsky, Igor, 11, 34
Suez Canal, 22
Summer Palace, 161
Sun Ji Bing, 187–80
Sun Yat-sen, 30

Talbott, Strobe, 225
Tan Shu-chen, 102, 103
tea, 15, 16
technological developments, 29, 219–21. *See also individual technologies*
Tin Pan Alley, 34, 36
Tombstone: The Great Chinese Famine, 1958–1962, 82
traditional Chinese music, 120–31. *See also* folk music/folk songs
Treaty of Kanagawa, 75

Treaty of Nanking, 17, 18
Treaty of Paris, 40
Turkey, 16, 100, 238

Understanding Media: The Extensions of Man, 27
values, vii, xi, xiv, 8, 28–30, 75, 83, 88, 145, 173, 177, 178, 226–28
Van Kan, Robert, 137
veracity, xi
Versailles Treaty, xiv
Victrola, 25
Voice of America, 95, 168, 188, 236
Voice of America: A History, 99
Voice of America Jazz Hour, 94, 95

Wang, Chaoguang, 28
Weatherford, Teddy, 11, 36, 43, 49–53
WFMT Radio, 236–37
Whaley, Earl, 69–75
Whitey of Shanghai, 48
World War II, 40–43, 49, 52, 57, 61, 63, 65, 67, 69, 77, 93, 100, 148, 227, 228
Wu Yun Nan, 142, 166–67

Xia Jia, 86, 158–60
Xianfeng, Emperor, 16
Xiao Dou, 162
Xuan Tong, Emperor, 19

Yang Jisheng, 82
Yang Renshan, 24
Yao Yi Xin, 163
Yellow Music, 23, 29, 57, 58
Yin dynasty, 5
Yui Shoichi, 77
Yu Yuezhang, 59
Yu Yuezhang Band, 59

Zanello, Peter, xviii–xix, 176, 232
Zhang Ling, 144, 160, 164–66
Zhang Xiaolu, 198–200, 219
Zhang Youdai, 236

Zhao, Ke Coco ("Coco"), 194–96, 206, 213
Zheng, Da Ren, 6, 37, 39, 41, 42, 57–59, 61, 62, 64
Zheng Guangwei, 58
Zheng Rongchu, 58, 63, 64
Zhou Xuan, 23, 57, 60
Zhou Wanrong, xv, 64, 187–91
Zhu Baosan Road, 37–39
Zou Tong, 153–64
Zuckerman, Pinchas, 220

CPSIA information can be obtained
at www.ICGtesting.com
Printed in the USA
BVHW03s0234270618
520142BV00001B/1/P